Security and International Rel

CW00401966

This new textbook presents security studies as a branch of international relations theory, providing readers with critical conceptual tools to develop their expertise. The author evaluates the claims of rival theories – realism, neorealism, liberal institutionalism, classical economic liberalism, and Marxism – to explain why international actors choose or eschew force and coercive threats in order to elicit favorable outcomes in their interdependent exchanges. Also discussed are behaviorism and constructivism, contesting approaches to validate prevailing security paradigms. The author argues that only an interdisciplinary approach to security, drawing on the insights of each perspective, can meet the rigorous requirements of testable theory and the practical needs of actors in an increasingly globalizing world. The book will provide students, practitioners and scholars of international relations and security studies with a valuable new survey of the subject, and includes essay questions and guides to further reading.

EDWARD A. KOLODZIEJ is Director of the Center for Global Studies at the University of Illinois, Urbana-Champaign. He is also the first Director of the Program in Arms Control, Disarmament and International Security at Illinois. Professor Kolodziej has written or edited thirteen books on security and foreign policy. His latest publication is an edited volume, *A Force Profonde: The Power, Politics, and Promise of Human Rights* (2003).

Themes in International Relations

This series of textbooks aims to provide students with authoritative surveys of central topics in the study of International Relations. Intended for upper level undergraduates and graduates, the books will be concise, accessible and comprehensive. Each volume will examine the main theoretical and empirical aspects of the subject concerned, and its relation to wider debates in International Relations, and will also include chapter-by-chapter guides to further reading and discussion questions.

Titles in series

David P. Forsythe, *Human Rights in International Relations*
Jack Donnelly, *Realism and International Relations*
John M. Hobson, *The State and International Relations*

Security and International Relations

Edward A. Kolodziej

CAMBRIDGE
UNIVERSITY PRESS

CAMBRIDGE UNIVERSITY PRESS
Cambridge, New York, Melbourne, Madrid, Cape Town, Singapore, São Paulo

Cambridge University Press
The Edinburgh Building, Cambridge CB2 2RU, UK

Published in the United States of America by Cambridge University Press, New York

www.cambridge.org
Information on this title: www.cambridge.org/9780521806437

© Edward A. Kolodziej 2005

This book is in copyright. Subject to statutory exception
and to the provisions of relevant collective licensing agreements,
no reproduction of any part may take place without
the written permission of Cambridge University Press.

First published 2005

Printed in the United Kingdom at the University Press, Cambridge

A catalogue record for this book is available from the British Library

ISBN 0 521 80643 7 hardback
ISBN 0 521 00116 1 paperback

Cambridge University Press has no responsibility for the persistence or accuracy of URLs
for external or third-party internet websites referred to in this book, and does not
guarantee that any content on such websites is, or will remain, accurate or appropriate.

To Zachary, Sander, Colin, Aiden, Charlie and Quinn
— in hope of a peaceful future
And in memory of Peter, 3 March 2005

organizing the footnotes and bibliography and in protecting me from numerous errors.

There is, of course, no way of repaying my wife, Antje, for her patience and support in seeing this project to completion – as she has over two score years. Her careful editing of the volume caught and corrected countless errors of form and substance.

Remaining lapses are my own.

Introduction

"For every complex problem there is a simple solution. And it's always wrong."

– H. L. Mencken

Security is a complex and contested notion – heavily laden with emotion and deeply held values. Most people would agree that a security problem arises when someone – a person, gang or group, or state – threatens another's life, limb, or livelihood; say, a gunman in a dark, dead-end alley demanding your wallet or your life. Consider the dread that the inhabitants of London and Berlin must have felt during World War II when bombed by enemy planes or missiles. Think also about the Japanese survivors of Hiroshima, the first city to be destroyed by an atomic bomb. Put yourself in the place of New Yorkers on September 11, 2001, who witnessed first-hand the destruction of the World Trade Center, not to mention millions more on television around the world in real time. Imagine, too, the terror of the Tutsi and Hutu peoples of Rwanda in 1994 when thousands were killed in three months – estimates run to 800,000 – by a genocide launched by Hutu extremists using primitive machetes and garden hoes.[1]

While few would likely dispute these examples of a security threat, many would extend the meaning of security to other values and interests. They would apply the term to environmental damage caused by global warming; or to the struggle for subsistence of billions of peoples in the developing world; or to human rights protections from capricious incarceration, torture, or genocide. For these observers, their competing images of security are very real, urgent, and threatening; for some even more so than notions of security associated with violence and coercive threats.[2]

---

[1] Kolodziej (2000a).
[2] Croft and Terriff (2000). See also the symposium on the meaning of security in *Arms Control*, 1992: 13.

1

Where do we draw the line in studying security? What should be included or excluded? If a broad and inclusive understanding of security is taken as the starting point, coterminous with whatever is in the mind of the observer, then it would be tantamount to saying that almost every human value and interest, if perceived by the affected party to be threatened, is a security issue. We may be including so much in our definition of security that we have posed the problem in ways that impede or preclude our quest for knowledge about this vitally important human concern. Conversely, if a narrower conception of security were adopted, identified solely with force and coercive threats, we may be excluding actors and factors bearing crucially on security.

Agreeing on a common definition for security will not be easy. Unless we can find common ground, we will be talking about different things designated as security. We will be unwittingly relying on conceptual filters that project widely contrasting and refracted images of what security is and how to address it. This volume will try to help you think about security and to view security as an autonomous domain of human behavior. It will equip you with basic conceptual tools to pursue the study of security as a discipline and to use these tools in making knowledgeable evaluations and informed choices about security policy. I would like to challenge you, the reader, to judge the success of this volume by the degree to which it enables you to explain and understand international security and its entangling connection to international politics and to use this knowledge for your benefit as a citizen of an open society and as a member of an ever more expanding and globalizing world.

Roadmap: organization and rationale of the volume

My task is to convince you that my understanding of security makes sense. More pointedly, I wish to show that it can be a useful tool of analysis by which you can assess the claims of what this volume identifies as the leading schools of thought about security contesting today for our attention and allegiance. Once you get a hang of how to evaluate these rival positions, you will be able to fashion your own theory and approach to security studies.

The volume is divided into three sections. The first, composed of three chapters, lays the foundation for the evaluation of seven schools of security thinking and practice. Chapter 1 presents a broad understanding of security and distinguishes this human concern from international relations. For the purposes of this volume, security as a humanly created phenomenon embraces *both* the use of force and coercive threats by humans and their agents *and* the transformation of these exchanges, charged with real or potential violence, into non-lethal, consensual exchanges. These twin and contesting incentives capture the implicit choice posed by inter-dependent social transactions between humans, their agents, and human societies: viz., whether to use *or* not to use force to ensure their preferred outcomes of these exchanges.

An inclusive and reliable theory of security must include those non-violent means and strategies devised and relied upon by actors to reduce and potentially surmount the incentives to employ force and threats to resolve conflicts and to foster cooperation. In other words, from the per-spective of international politics, students of security studies are obliged, simultaneously, to develop a theory of war *and* peace. Short of this ambi-tious aim, what knowledge we acquire about security will be flawed in one of three ways.

First, there is the serious conceptual (and normative) problem of deter-mining whose notion of security should count. Should it be the actors whose behavior is being described, explained, predicted, and understood or the perspectives of the theorist, policy analyst, or decision-maker in security? This volume privileges actors – humans and their agents, like states, Intergovernmental Organizations (UN), Non-Governmental Organizations (NGOs), etc. – and how and why they address security issues. What do they mean by security? How do they respond and solve these problems? It is their thinking, decisions, and actions that matter most. This priority is often neglected or marginalized in the debates between rival schools of security thought. They tend to have a bias of presenting their selected notion of security as if it were coterminous with what actors think and do about security, as the latter perceive this multi-faceted issue. This volume will try to keep actors at the center and evaluate contending schools of thought by how close they come to capturing the actors themselves.

As this discussion proceeds, it will become clearer that to capture what actors conceive to be a security issue, we need a definition of the phe-nomenon of security that maps as closely as possible with the wide range of conflicting perceptions and perspectives of actors about security. We need a definition of sufficient scope that includes all possible choices and behavior by actors in responding to security imperatives. Such a defini-tion would stipulate that security arises as a human experience and phe-nomenon when interdependent actors decide to use or not to use force to get what they want from each other. This understanding of security is sufficiently capacious to include, in principle, within a set marked "secu-rity" all relevant human choices and actions through time and space. A less inclusive test of security – say limited to using force or searching for peace – would leave out critical observations or, worse, load on the interests and biases of the observer rather than privilege the actor.

Second, if an inclusive definition is not adopted for the study of security, we risk falsifying the historical record where security issues are in play. Certainly history abundantly shows continuing actor reliance on force and threats. This is particularly true of states, since their inception as central international actors of the modern era. No adequate reckoning of the twentieth century's security problems would pass muster if World Wars I and II, the Cold War, and the armed struggles for self-determination of former colonial peoples were excluded. Conversely, we also know that bitter enemies have learned to make peace with each other. Witness France and Germany after World War II or the United States and Britain in the wake of the Revolutionary War and the War of 1812. Actors display impressive wit, imagination, and resourcefulness in creating social incentives and institutions to manage and even surmount their profound differences over fundamental interests and values. As one widely cited observer of state behavior suggests, states have been able to live under conditions of anarchy for a long time; peace, not war, largely characterizes their relations.[3] Another internationally respected historian also suggests that the long peace in Europe between 1815 and 1914 can be explained by the shared view of leading statesmen who, in light of the Napoleonic Wars, were agreed, however much they remained adversaries, that war itself was a threat to the stability of their regimes and the survival of their nations and empires.[4]

Finally, the policy analyst and decision-maker should be mindful of the potential efficacy of soft and hard forms of power to get one's way.[5] In the face of a determined adversary bent on using violence to impose his will on another state or people – say Nazi Germany or imperial Japan – it makes sense for threatened policy-makers to narrow their search to combat these aggressors with countervailing force. Similarly, few would expect terrorists to be credible partners in negotiating peacefully to spare the lives of innocent citizens they kidnapped.

In other instances, a one-sided approach to security as the use of force would be wrong and wrong-headed when there is some basis for optimism that competing high-stake interests can be optimally achieved through non-coercive solutions even under the continuing threat that one or more of the actors might defect and invoke force or war. If states and their populations, for example, mutually understand that armed conflict might preclude sustainable economic growth, an assumption that can be readily predicated of the states comprising the European Union and

[3] Bull (1977).   [4] Schroeder (1989, 1994b, 2004).   [5] Nye (2002).

American–Chinese relations today, they can consensually agree to rules for market operations and competition even while deeply split by other policy concerns. Even seemingly implacable enemies – the United States and the Soviet Union – were able to reach arms control and disarmament agreements to limit their global rivalry and arms race and to restrain their clients and allies to preclude the expansion of local conflicts to a global conflagration.[6] These examples meet a test of cases where powerful incentives are working on all sides to use force, yet actors choose non-violent means to manage or resolve their security differences.

Chapter 1 next identifies four levels of exchanges between human actors and their agents at which the incentives to use force or coercive threats are at work. These levels of exchange are important to distinguish the principal actors and the factors driving actor behavior at each level. The schools of security that will be discussed can be distinguished by the degree of significance and salience attached by each to one or more of these levels of analysis. Chapter 1 closes with a discussion of relevant criteria by which to assess the rival claims of the schools of thought contending for the crown of hegemon in security studies. These rely principally on the methodological tests devised by Imre Lakatos. These are widely used in the natural and social sciences to evaluate the explanatory and predictive power of opposing theories.

Chapter 2 introduces the reader to the three theorists who have had the most profound impact on security studies: Thomas Hobbes, Carl von Clausewitz, and Thucydides. More than any other thinkers, they established security studies as an autonomous sphere of human thinking, decision, and action. They laid the foundations for a science of security of potentially universal applicability over time, space, and social conditions. They are a useful starting (if scarcely stopping) point in learning how to think about security.

If security is a science in the sense of a body of acquired and accumulating knowledge, an implicit point on which these three thinkers agree, then we need to submit the seven contending schools of thought about security to a common test to see which has the greatest explanatory power. Chapter 3 develops a Cold War "laboratory" for testing and evaluating these schools. What is their relative capacity to explain the rise and demise of the Cold War from 1945 to 1991 and the passing of the bipolar system? Parts 2 and 3 apply Lakatosian criteria to each school of thought in responding to this question.

If an approach or theory of security is flawed in explaining the beginning, evolution, and end of the Cold War, we can scarcely be confident

---

[6] Kolodziej and Kanet (1991).

about its reliability to understand and explain the post-Cold War world in which we live today. Several considerations support this claim. First, the Cold War was global. It enveloped all of the peoples and states of the world in some measure, whether they wished to be implicated in this struggle for hegemony or not. Second, it posed the highest stakes for all of the peoples of the world. An all-out superpower nuclear war would have effectively destroyed these states and most of their populations. It would have killed or injured countless hundreds of millions more, as the deadly radioactive clouds created by triggering the nuclear "Doomsday Machines" of the superpowers would have hovered over the globe for decades.[7] Any armed conflict that risks the extinction of human life on earth intuitively meets a test of relevance as a security problem of the first order.

Third, while the Cold War was a deadly contest, it surprisingly did not end that way. Since the dawn of the modern nation-state a half-millennium ago, the competition for dominance between implacable state rivals typically ended in war to decide who was on top. This had pretty much been the pattern of nation-state competition until the end of World War II. Yet despite this long record of big power clashes, which claimed by most estimates over 100 million lives and produced untold misery for hundreds of millions more in the course of the twentieth century, the Cold War ended abruptly and unexpectedly with hardly a shot being fired. What happened? Any security theory worth its salt should be able to explain this unexpected outcome as well as the transition and workings of the post-Cold War.

The second part of the volume is straightforward. Chapter 4 reviews realist, neorealist, and liberal institutionalist thinking and submits them to a Cold War test. Chapter 5 develops a similar critique for neoclassical economic and neo-Marxist theories of conflict and security. The third part of the discussion departs from these paradigms, as *theories* of security and international relations, and presents two broadly defined, rival *approaches* to the development, testing, and validation of prevailing paradigms. However much scholars in these two camps may otherwise clash, they are allies in problematizing the theories of security discussed in part 2. They are especially useful as critical methodological, epistemological, and ontological tools (terms to be defined along the way) to assess the claims of disputing security positions.

Chapter 6 focuses on behaviorism or what some would prefer to call rational or empirically based and driven approaches to theory-building about security. Behaviorism concentrates, by and large, on what can be observed, counted, measured, and replicated by other researchers using

---

[7] Herman Kahn (1960) first used the term Doomsday Machine.

the same methods and data. Scholars working in this tradition rely on methods drawn principally from the physical and biological sciences. Chapter 7 introduces the reader to constructivism. This is a complex and contentious school of thought. Its partisans are as much in fundamental disagreement among themselves over the question of how to study international politics as they are united in their rejection of prevailing paradigms and behavioral approaches as sufficient to explain or understand security. Constructivists of all stripes try to explain how actors construct their identities and the social structures these actors author to enable them to define and pursue their interests, aims, and values. They contend that understanding how this ceaseless process of actor reaffirmation, mutation, and transformation of their identities and social constructions is the key to explaining the creation and surmounting of security concerns.

The volume argues that each of these schools of thought has something to offer. This said, the user of these bodies of thought must still be alert to their strengths and weaknesses to effectively exploit their knowledge about international security for social and personal benefit. These theories, if applied with care and discrimination, can provide some foresight, however dim or slim.[8] Each will be found to explain part of the unfolding, evolutionary process of international security. Each will be found wanting, too. Much like the parable of the blind men and the elephant, partisans of each paradigm or approach explain security (the elephant) by way of selective observation of what they "see." Some seize on the tail and proclaim the beast a snake or rope. Others fall against its shoulders and call it a wall. Still others, feeling the elephant's curling trunk or drenched by water issuing from its end, conclude that the object is a fountain. In evaluating these several paradigms of security we can conceivably rise above them to "see" the whole elephant – an integrated understanding of the relation of security and international relations.

Let's try.

Edward A. Kolodziej
University of Illinois, Urbana-Champaign,
October, 2004

---

[8] While I remain critical of the impoverished state of security theory, my reservations should not be taken as an attack or dismissal of the utility of different approaches to security. The critique of this volume is more a call for better theory and more empirical work to improve our knowledge and practice of security than a rejection of currently competing security theories or approaches. See Kolodziej (1992a, b, c). In this quest, the study of history is absolutely vital for theory-building and practice in security, but history is not self-revealing along these dimensions, as some historians believe. See Gaddis (1992–3) and especially Schroeder (1994b), who is especially sensitive to this point.

Part I

Introduction to international security and security studies

1 International relations and international security: boundaries, levels of analysis, and falsifying theories

Why another book on security?

Security as a Tower of Babel

The shelves of any city or college library are stacked with books about security. A closer look would also reveal that most of the books are out of date – stale reminders of past security issues now overtaken by events rather than compelling volumes speaking to real and urgent security issues. Part of the explanation for these piles of tired texts arises from the rapid changes besetting the world's peoples and states. It's hard for practiced observers and scholars, much more so for an informed, but otherwise preoccupied, public to keep pace with rapidly changing events, notably those impacting security.

Only a decade ago, it seemed a lot easier to make sense of the world. Many believed the globe to be permanently divided between two military blocs led by two superpowers – the United States and the Soviet Union. Few believed that either would be challenged anytime soon.[1] The Soviet Union's unexpected implosion changed all that overnight. With the collapse of the Cold War and bipolar superpower competition, the world today appears much more complex – and decidedly more confusing. The seeming simplicity of the Cold War period, stretching roughly from the end of World War II in 1945 to the sudden demise of the Soviet Union in December 1991, has been replaced by what appears to be a new world that defies easy explanation or understanding. This is a world beset by unprecedented security threats, dramatized by global terrorism and the diffusion of weapons of mass destruction.

The frustration about what to believe or expect is highlighted by the fundamental discord and debate among practiced and accomplished scholars, analysts, commentators, and political leaders about what the future holds for us as members of an emerging global society. The

---

[1] Waltz (1964).

superpower bipolar system, built disquietingly on two nuclear Doomsday Machines, appeared to provide a precarious but seemingly unchallengeable and stable global order. No other state could contest the nuclear capabilities of either superpower. By that token neither superpower had incentive to attack its rival and risk almost certain annihilation, even as both ceaselessly prepared for a nuclear showdown. Both also had reason to cooperate, implicitly and explicitly, to restrain their allies and clients to prevent local conflicts from escalating to an all-out nuclear war. Unlike the volatile balance of power shifts of the interwar era before World War II, the Cold War nuclear bipolar balance of power appeared to offer an uneasy peace, orchestrated under the directing batons of two rational, prudent superpowers.[2] If each prepared for a nuclear Armageddon, each no less strove to cooperate with its rival to prevent accidental, unintended, or unwitting nuclear war.[3]

Some respected scholars and informed observers see things today in a darker light. They predict that we will envy the stability and seemingly predictable safety of the Cold War and the superpower nuclear balance of terror.[4] They project a grim future of an enlarging profusion of power centers – state and non-state – emerging with no one in charge to order the world's affairs. Even empowered individuals, like determined and demented terrorists, can attack a superpower and provoke a global war on terrorism with no clear end in sight. Once close allies within the Atlantic Alliance are increasingly at odds over global security policy – a split already apparent in conflicting European and American reactions to the Balkan Wars of the 1990s and to the Iraq War of 2003. The divisions among the Western democracies are viewed as even more profound and fissiparous than between the American and European components of the Western coalition that emerged victorious in the Cold War, as some suggest.[5] For many American security policy-makers, Europe itself is divided between "new" – the East European states freed from Soviet rule during the Cold War – and the "old" Europe, principally France and Germany, which opposed the Iraq War.[6] This disorder even among the victors provides evidence for those who view not only a *World Out of Order* but also one in which a potentially rogue superpower threatens to deepen and widen disorder through a vain play for global domination.[7]

---

[2] The leading theorist holding this position is Kenneth N. Waltz. See Mearsheimer (1990, 1994) and Waltz (1964, 1979, 1993).
[3] Kolodziej and Kanet (1991).
[4] This portrayal of the Cold War and its aftermath are pursued at length in Mearsheimer (1990, 1994).
[5] Kagan (2002).   [6] United States (September 2002).
[7] Brzezinski (1993, 2004).

Many others project a bleak future of culture clash. Rising, seemingly intractable conflicts between the world's cultures appear to be inflaming already widely rampant interstate, national, ethnic, and racial conflicts. Each culture is depicted as bound together by deeply rooted values and emotional ties. Culture is portrayed as a force working through its adherents and driving global politics. These conflicting religious beliefs, historical memories, traditions, shared customs, and worldviews embodied in contrasting cultures are argued to be unbridgeable. The fault lines between them are invitations to violent clashes. Among the most important of those cited are Western, Muslim, Confucian (China), Hindu (India), Japanese, and Slavic-Orthodox (Russian) cultures.[8] The hope of a peaceful society of states is now replaced by an ominous vision of a world of diverse peoples, divided against themselves with little likelihood of the emergence of some universal form of shared culture and values to surmount their profound differences.[9]

In this view globalization spurs, not stifles, cultural conflicts. Great strides in the efficiency and effectiveness of modes of transportation, communications, and computer technologies have shrunk the world. Previously isolated peoples and cultures, which had infrequent contacts with outsiders, like the Australian Aborigines for over forty millennia,[10] are now cheek by jowl. Increased and sustained contacts are seen to invite mutual animosity, not understanding and tolerance. Conflicts over fundamental values – whose religion is the true word? – appear intractable and irresolvable by compromise when compared to disputes over material resources – oil, water, etc. – or even state boundaries. Most notable is the posited split between the "West and the Rest." This asserted (if not demonstrated) cultural divide, is alleged to have been deepened by the ascendancy of the Western coalition of liberal, democratic states since the collapse of the Cold War. To balance Western power, a coalition of anti-Western cultures is projected, pivoting on an alliance of Confucian and Islamic peoples, adamantly opposed to a dominant Western Christian-secular culture.[11]

Others insist on reducing the world's conflicts to irreconcilable group identities within and across cultures. These are alleged to undermine the cohesion of cultures and to challenge the authority of nation-states. The future of mankind is cast in the imagery of advancing tribalism, anarchy, and group chaos. The ethnic cleansing and genocidal episodes

---

[8] Huntington (1996).
[9] Compare the guarded optimism of Hedley Bull (1977) to the unrelieved pessimism of Ada Bozeman (1984).
[10] Blainey (1988). [11] Huntington (1996, 1991).

in Rwanda and central Africa, Sudan, the Balkans, and Indonesia are cited as harbingers of a grim tomorrow already here.[12]

Others posit a more hopeful future. Some foresee cultural convergence. The rise of global markets and the adoption of the nation-state as the principal units of economic and political organization over the past several centuries are offered as evidence of a coming together of the world's populations. They are viewed as increasingly conscious of their common biological roots and their shared humanity as a species. These new conditions of social life are said to generate an increasingly shared psychological disposition to human unity. Multiplying and reinforcing socio-economic and political exchanges across state boundaries set the stage for the integration of humans into a world system.[13] As William McNeill observes,

> Just as most of the nations of the earth were created by political events, and then, with the help of historians, achieved a common consciousness, so, it seems to me, real human consciousness can only be expected to arise after political and economic processes have created such a tight-knit community that every people and polity is forced to recognize its subordination to and participation in a global system.[14]

If humans have not reached such a common psycho-social state of consciousness and cultural convergence, these integration theorists believe it is only a matter of time before humans will adapt to the unprecedented conditions of globalization. This social environment will select out particular identities and the conflicts they provoke in favor of a human identity more responsive to the needs of a globalizing world. Previously held Darwinian notions of the survival of the fittest and of natural selection are turned on their head. For these observers, survival depends on the cooperation of the human species; those persisting in old habits of conflict and war will eventually become extinct and pass into history. War, like dueling and slavery, is believed to have run its course as a social institution. Lacking purpose, utility, and legitimacy, mass armed conflict between states is expected to atrophy and wither away, much like the smile of the Cheshire cat in *Alice in Wonderland*.[15]

For many this adaptive process leading to cultural convergence will be fashioned on a Western, liberal model. According to partisans of this particular brand of Western liberalism, the age-old problem of conflicting

[12] Brzezinski (1993), Gellner (1983), Kaplan (2000), and Mayall (1992).
[13] Waters (1995). See also Diamond (1992, 1997).
[14] That is McNeill's (1992) message. See also Singer (2002) for the ethical scope of globalization.
[15] Mueller (1989).

interests between rulers and ruled has been conclusively resolved by the Western project as the definitive solution to global governance. Whereas before, ruler and ruled were fundamentally opposed to each other in an endless stream of regimes since the dawn of civilization, liberalism purportedly surmounts these failures by basing the authority and legitimacy of political regimes on the principle of the fundamental equality of all humans and their universal need for mutual respect. Liberalism accords each individual regardless of social status or gender the respect humans seek but are denied by all other forms of governance. Once humans agree to respect each other, following a liberal prescription, the problem of legitimating political authority and rule is fundamentally solved in theory. Everyone is afforded equal access and influence to the process by which the rules and regimes governing them will be decided.

This arresting vision dissolves differences of race, ethnic background, religion, culture, and language. The ageless conflict over who has a right to rule as the central plot of history is declared at an end. The march toward peace and convergence of human values – a utopian endgame – is alleged to be bolstered and accelerated by the rise of global market capitalism and what is predicated as the inevitable spread of consumerism.[16] All humans are therefore standardized on the Western political and economic liberal model. States, nations, and peoples of different social make-up may well oppose globalization, but the force is posited as irresistible. The only choice available to resisting societies and states is how, not whether, to adapt to these political and market-driven imperatives.[17]

The future of globalization as a crucible also has its uncompromising opponents. For these observers the sources of conflict are economic, not cultural, national, or tribal. Humanity is divided between rich and poor, not ruler and ruled, as a consequence of the inexorable workings of global capitalism. Identity differences are viewed as surface and ephemeral. Down deep it's the conflict between the few rich against the many poor that drives international relations. This division of wealth and power is identified as the source of the security dilemma confronting the populations and states of the world. Political pluralism, advanced by liberal proponents, is said to mask and ideologically support this oppressive economic system. For these anti-globalists, the growing economic and digital inequality between rich and poor evidences a critical worldwide capitalist crisis promising new and widespread violence within and across state boundaries. The wealthy capitalist North of one billion people, no less divided by class, is pitted against the impoverished South of five

---

[16] Fukuyama (1992).   [17] Friedman (2000).

billion exploited inhabitants. The axes of global politics are portrayed to turn on this neo-Marxist image of class warfare.[18]

Multinational corporations, in league with complicit Western states, principally the United States, are identified as the leading oppressors of the world's poor. They allegedly rule through international organizations like the International Monetary Fund, the World Bank, and the World Trade Organization. Using the enormous resources at their disposal, this misalliance of state and corporate power shapes public opinion to their liking through media concentration and massive advertising campaigns, and imposes its self-serving rules on powerless populations. The disadvantaged, comprising most of the developing world, are viewed as subservient to international corporate power, whose decisions determine who will be wealthy or winless – decisions taken behind closed doors by anonymous and faceless executives accountable to no one. The result is a race to the bottom among competing corporations and putatively helpless states and peoples. World labor wages are depressed and healthy working conditions are sacrificed to corporate profits. The environment is also held hostage to market competition with allegedly devastating implications for the preservation of the global commons.[19]

According to some observers, the increasing power of multinational corporations, commanding greater human and material resources and exercising more potent political influence than most states of the globe, deepens culture clashes and threatens the rights of peoples everywhere for a fair share of the earth's material wealth. Placed at risk are the nation-state and the world's impoverished masses. Until recently the nation-state, maligned as a threat to international security, is increasingly assigned the responsibility by many security analysts to defend human rights, to protect minorities against ethnic cleansing and genocide, and to promote social welfare by checking the power of multinational corporations.[20]

Seeking a way out of the impasse

What is a person to think about this confusing array of possible but irreconcilable projections of the future? Are humans moving toward more or

---

[18] See chapter 5 for a discussion of Marxism and neo-Marxism. Meanwhile, consult Bergesen and Bata (2002), Firebaugh (1999), Hardt and Negri (2000), and Wallerstein (1995).

[19] This is a vast and growing literature. For a recent overview, see McBride and Wiseman (2001). Illustrative, but scarcely comprehensive, are Gill (1997) and Hurrell and Woods (1995). Even strong advocates of global markets foresee problems or conflict and disorder unless reforms are instituted to compensate for market flaws. See, for example, Gilpin (2000, 2001) and Soros (2000).

[20] Barber (1995).

less armed conflict? Are they more or less secure than ever before? How does one choose among these conceptual maps? Depending on one's preferences, what would have to be done to speed or arrest one or the other of these contesting futures? Each appears to have some basis in fact confirmed by observation and experience. Yet they obviously can't all be right. Or can they, depending on what part of the globe one is observing? Or, conversely, does the increasing connectedness of the world's populations channel what appear to be fundamentally different and rival security systems toward one over-arching political system that remains to be completed, as some visionary theorists contend?[21]

As you read on, it will become clear that each expert's view of what the future holds for international relations and security will depend critically on the assumptions that the writer makes about the key actors who are implicitly or explicitly identified as the major shovers and shapers of global politics and the power they ostensibly exercise. Actors and factors alleged to be driving international politics are variously cited as states,[22] peoples sharing cultural values, political ideologies, or national, ethnic, or tribal identities,[23] systemic structures like global markets or the interstate system,[24] and multinational corporations.[25] Different actors are assumed to be disposed to get what they want from others through conflict or cooperation – or some combination of these two approaches, depending on the conditions of the exchanges between them. Each will be expected to use or threaten force to get its way or to resist or insist on controlling and limiting the use of force by others in resolving conflicts. Security studies, as a branch of international relations, is primarily interested in understanding and explaining why and how actors use force. Security theorists, analysts and decision-makers are also interested in knowing whether force works. By using force or threats, do actors get what they want at acceptable costs and risks?

Of equal importance from the perspective of this volume's approach to security and, in particular, to international security, we also want to know why and how actors reject force and coercive threats and whether that approach works to achieve their purposes. Knowing only what the positive and negative effects of coercion and threats might be is of little value unless they can be compared to opportunity costs of *not* using force and other non-coercive strategies. These might produce better results at less material cost to valued material assets and desired goals than force and violence.

---

[21] Wendt (2003).   [22] See ns. 1 and 2.   [23] See ns. 10–12.   [24] See ns. 1–2, 18–20.
[25] See n. 18.

Assumptions about actors and actor behavior and the factors affecting them arise from many sources, too numerous and complex for this discussion to plumb thoroughly. Suffice it to say for our purposes that to become an expert in international relations and global politics and, specifically, to generalize with authority about security problems, you, the reader, will also have to decide what you believe are the key actors in global politics, to make assumptions about why they behave the way they do, and to posit the conditions that prompt their thinking and actions. Once you have clearly made these decisions (and they do not admit to crisp and concise responses), you are obliged to test them against the behavior of the actors and against conflicting interpretations drawn from rival schools of security theory. This volume is designed to help you make those decisions without dictating your choices. By evaluating how established schools of thought have made these decisions, you will be in a better position to describe and explain how different security systems are organized as human constructions and to discern what incentives dispose actors to cooperate or clash in pursuing their interests and values. The volume will assist you to make defensible choices about such matters.

This volume makes no claim to omniscience. As the sketch above of opposing views about the future suggests, security is a contested notion. That should not be surprising or an excuse to give up trying to make sense of security as a central concern – some would even say *the* central concern – of international relations.[26] Anything as important and as human as security is bound to be controversial. What humans value – presumably their personal safety and the protection of all those things they hold dear – prompts them to do everything they can, even using force or authorizing and legitimating the state and society to which they severally belong to use violence and coercive threats to keep what they have or get more of what they want.

Ironically, to achieve the security humans seek for themselves and for their nation – or for the world – requires that they "get out of themselves" to "see" the world as it is rather than as they might like it to be. They will be obliged to develop criteria that meet an objective test of observation, free of as much bias and self-interest as possible. Otherwise, there is the risk of creating a distorted or misleading understanding and explanation of why and how other actors, given their security interests, act the way they do. There is always the temptation to see the world we would like rather

---

[26] Patrick Morgan presents the case for this focused and constrained conception for security, affirming the position of most realist and classical thinkers in Morgan (2000). For the reasons developed in this chapter, this conception of security and security studies provides a necessary but not sufficient understanding of the scope of security and its relation to international security and contemporary international relations.

than confront the world we actually live in. It would also be desirable, to the degree that it is humanly possible, to develop objective tests of reality that meet a rigorous scientific test. That would presume that observations about the world would also be potentially replicated and affirmed by others, even those at odds with what observers might want to see and what kind of world they might prefer.

Rigorous scientific tests are hard to come by in security studies. Behavioral and rational choice scholars who are discussed in chapter 6 claim that their approach has made significant strides in this direction. By their own admission, however, they have a way to go to achieve the kind of accumulated knowledge associated with the natural and biological sciences.[27] That won't be easy or even feasible, as the discussion will attempt to explain later on, in addressing many – arguably most – security questions and problems, largely because humans have radically opposed notions of security as an interest, aim, or value. This subjective state of mind is not amenable to study by the typical methods associated with scientific inquiry. To the degree that international relations and security studies are scientific disciplines, they are more akin to geology or astronomy than chemistry or physics. These disciplines cannot control the factors and forces they study through rigorous laboratory experiments. Actors pursuing security goals are not easily submitted to controlled experiments. Viewed from the perspective of their social behavior, they cannot be organized in a way easily susceptible to laboratory manipulation.

When, for example, was the last time you had lunch with the United States? Or the Chinese Communist party? Or, with the New York Stock Exchange? Of course not. Yet these humanly constructed institutions and organizations are central to the study of security and international relations. Security studies in international relations will have to generalize about the behavior of most of the actors it examines although they are not, and cannot be, directly experienced, except by their effects or what we perceive to be the impact of actor choices on events. We use shorthands like the United States and China every day. Much that is relevant to security is lost by such conceptual devices. When we look "inside" a state, we discover deep rifts within the society along fault lines defined by race, tribe, ethnic origin, language, religion, culture, class, ideology, and gender. We will have to be careful about what we precisely mean when we use these collective nouns and social constructions.

Actors, like states, and systems of states also change over time. These changes in the form, purpose, capabilities, and identity of these actors

---

[27] That is the conclusion reached essentially by one distinguished behavioral scholar in bringing together some of the leading scholarship in the field. Midlarsky (1989, 2000).

and the implications of these changes for security must also be explained if we are to recognize major shifts in their behavior. This cautionary note is especially relevant today. Recall how rapidly in the course of a century the world system of nation-states has evolved, quite abruptly and unexpectedly for most of the actors engaged, from a complex balance of power system to the bipolar struggle of the Cold War, and now to the emergence of an American hegemon that dominates the system. The United States spends more for defense than any other state and more than all its NATO allies combined and, next to an expanding European Union, supports the largest internal market in the world.

Security studies must rely on history and past events to develop propositions or hypotheses about actor behavior.[28] Security analysts and scholars draw on any body of thought and human experience that helps them get hold of reality. It certainly is too simple to say, like Joe Friday in the TV program *Dragnet*, "Just give me the facts, Ma'am." Facts and historical data, however packaged and presented, are central material from which we weave our conceptions of security and verify them by reference to these empirical "facts." This subjects observers to the test of whether they present all of the facts relevant to a theory of security or whether they have "romped through history," choosing only those incidents bolstering their prejudices and interests. They are also required to justify their interpretation of the facts they present by carefully specifying the criteria relied upon to select historical data to illustrate or support a point or to demonstrate a line of argument or proposition – say that balance of power systems provoke war[29] or that democracies don't fight.[30] The section below on falsifying theories of security has more to say about this issue.

Second, the problem of historical selectivity is particularly acute for security analysts. In seeking to find "truths" that hold across historical periods, they are not concerned with the detailed circumstances affecting actors, their specific choices and their behavior in any particular period of time. The generalizations of security specialists will always fall short of the rich and textured renderings of a period of time portrayed by historians. We also know from experience that circumstances and actors – like you and me and states – change, too. Historians are typically focused on reproducing what occurred at a particular point or era in time. Security

---

[28] Some of the key problems associated with relying on history, principally in distilling what is nomothetic or general from what is contextual and particular to a period are discussed in a symposium published by *International Security*, Elman and Elman (1997).

[29] See chapter 6 and the theory of hegemonic behavior developed by A. F. K. Organski and Jacek Kugler in Organski (1958) and Organski and Kugler (1980).

[30] Russett (1993), Russett and Starr (2000), Russett and Oneal (2001) and Lipson (2003).

analysts are also interested in these reconstructions, but seek rather to find what is similar about the security issues confronting different human societies across time and space and how they resolve them rather than what is different about them. This makes them chronically exposed to criticism that they are leaving out key actors and factors or that their generalizations don't fit the facts as presented by historians. They almost never will – precisely. These hazards should be recognized to caution against bold generalizations that can't be supported by observations and historical analysis rather than to abandon the enterprise of searching for more powerful explanations of human security behavior and a more comprehensive understanding of this crucial dimension of social life.

With this brief sketch of some of the limits facing anyone trying to make sense of the security behavior of actors of all kinds, let's define our terms from the start about what this volume takes to be security and its implications for understanding and explaining international relations and global politics at different levels of analysis. I am also obliged to outline my understanding of theory and how theories can be validated and falsified. These are daunting tasks to accomplish in a few brief pages, since the concepts presented below and the view of social science theory that is sketched are fundamentally contested in social, philosophical, and moral inquiry. Adding to this confusion is the ambiguity of such terms as security and national security, quite apart from genuine differences about their meanings. Theorists, policy-makers, and observers who might otherwise agree on what they mean by security are often hampered in using these concepts as tools of analysis and policy-making because the term 'security' covers a range of goals so wide that highly divergent policies – say combating global poverty or terrorism – can be interpreted as policies of security.[31]

Once I have defined what factors, actors and levels of analysis fall within my understanding of security and how these elements can be theoretically studied, I will retrace my steps in chapter 2 and discuss the contributions of Hobbes, Clausewitz, and Thucydides, proven thinkers who are the starting point of almost every security theorist, including those who reject their understanding of the security dilemma confronting humans and the societies and states they construct. The reader is not obliged to affirm the approach of this discussion of international security and relations. What is of key importance is the process of thinking about security that readers are encouraged to develop on their own by critically evaluating

---

[31] Wolfers (1952). See also Baldwin (1997) who insightfully develops the implications of Wolfer's path-breaking discussion of the concept of security.

the assumptions, definitions, and conceptual processes of analysis that I have adopted.

Defining security and international security

Politics in human affairs arises whenever there is a difference over an outcome sought by two or more interdependent actors – individual humans or their agents – with respect to their disputed interests, aims, and values. If there are no differences or conflict, there is no politics, either. As long as human preferences and assertions of will to realize them clash, there will be politics. In its widest scope, politics invades love relations and the family, class conflicts, and interstate battles over tariffs or boundaries. Viewed from this expansive perspective, politics is embedded in all human relations. It is fashionable to decry "politics" or to insist that "I am against 'politics,'" but these very statements belie one's unwitting engagement in political activity by consciously withdrawing from its perceived disruptive and disturbing conflicts. Claiming a superior or privileged position over others is *ipso facto* a political act.

Security is a special form of politics – a species of the more general genus of politics. All security issues are political problems, but not all political conflicts are security issues in the sense used in this volume if the solution to a dispute is reached by the engaged parties by accord or by agreement on shared rules, principles, or institutions to resolve their differences by non-violent means. At that point of accord the political problem continues but its potential security dimension is marginalized to the point of extinction or elimination. Security arises as a central property of a political dispute whenever actors threaten or use force to get what they want from each other. That is, politics assumes a dual aspect – as dispute and as a security issue – as soon as physical hurt or damage may be possibly, or is actually being, visited on one or more of the engaged actors.

The scope of security problems is co-extensive with the history of human interaction through time and space where force or coercive threats are at play. Like politics, it is a phenomenon that continues to be created by human intent or action. Its future emergence as a problem is potentially coterminous with politics when, as developed in chapter 2, a condition of "pure war" is reached. Most exchanges of conflict between humans and their agents that fall within the ambit of politics do not directly involve violence or its imminent use. Most political exchanges where disputes arise are resolved non-violently; these are not security problems in the sense meant by this volume. These transactions, like economic exchanges in global markets or interstate cooperation to cope with global warming,

like transnational terrorists. Since security studies is concerned with the use by actors of force and violence, it seems reasonable that we know more about the greatest wielder of violence first – the state.

Discrete levels of security: the state and other actors

State-to-state

For purposes of this volume, the use of force and threats by states, or limits on these capabilities, will be seen to arise at four, conceptually distinct but interdependent levels of actor relations. The first is simply between states. All states claim to be the ultimate authority in resolving conflicts between them. No other political unit exercises this right to the extent that the state does in governing the affairs of the world's populations. Since all are equal in making that claim, legally and morally, they are induced to find ways to support this claim by acquiring sufficient material capabilities by their own means or to increase their power by alliance with other states. When all other non-coercive means have been exhausted to resolve their differences, state conflicts are then reduced to a trial by arms. Or, to avoid an armed clash, each has to muster enough credible material power to deter its rival from attacking its vital interests.

Bargaining and negotiating over whatever issues divide them proceeds by way of what Carl von Clausewitz called "politics by other means,"[39] a concept described in more detail in chapter 2. States are implicitly engaged in ceaseless bargaining through the use of their coercive means. The possible exercise of the state's coercive power is implicitly embedded in every exchange with another state. War is but the most extreme form of this bargaining process. When a state imposes a tariff on imports, it uses its coercive power to tax goods and to favor its domestic industries. When a state insists on issuing visas to foreigners before they can enter its territory, it is equally relying on its material power to ensure compliance. These illustrations only scratch the surface of the state's power to use force and threats to get its way.

The system of state relations

The structure or system of power that states create through their interactions also has a significant impact on whether they will be disposed or not to using force. This structure of power is assigned causal power by many security scholars. The state system is alleged to weigh in the thinking,

---

[39] Clausewitz (1976).

decisions, and actions of all states. States, as Kenneth Waltz argues, are not only concerned about their relative power toward rivals and allies, but also about their relative power position within the system of states. It is through this structure of power that states pursue their interests and realize their aims.[40] The absolute gains from these transactions, say trade and investment, are alleged to be less important to the state than the relative gains in power from these outcomes. The pressure of systemic positioning is so strong that those theorists of state behavior stressing this systemic factor insist that states will forgo absolute gains if other states gain more from a transaction and their own relative position is diminished.[41] Theorists of this persuasion argue that in the long run states will prefer relative gains to absolute gains. For example, imagine a case in which each state through trade gains, respectively, $20 billion and $13 billion, but in terms of perceived power, the relative distribution is the reverse. Systemic theorists will expect that the state that stands to gain the most from trade but the most to lose in overall relative power will relinquish trade gains to at least equalize its power position. More will be said of this line of analysis in succeeding chapters.

State systemic structures, defined exclusively by the material power disposed by states, can assume one of three forms.[42] They can be multipolar, bipolar, or unipolar. Within each system, and most notably in multipolar systems, a wide range of possible different configurations and mutations are conceivable among relevant units. Each system generates a distinct set of constraints and opportunities for the states in their ceaseless competition to impose their preferences on other states and actors. These structures of power can also be shown to change over time. The European state system, which became the model for the world system of states today, was a multipolar system for most of its history. The form it assumed before the end of the Napoleonic Wars of 1789–1815 was essentially built around the governing principle of a balance of power. To preserve its independence and the system itself from becoming unipolar, states and their regimes tended to balance against the rising power of one of its members which sought hegemony and dominance. This system disposed the members of the system to be constantly preoccupied with using war or threats to regulate their affairs with other states in desirable ways and to maintain their power position relative to their rivals. War was implicitly embedded in their daily dealings and was central to their

[40] Waltz (1979).
[41] See Grieco (1990) and Powell (1993) for contrasting views.
[42] Chapter 7 develops an alternative, constructivist, categorization of state systems depending on their propensity to use force to resolve differences. This position is elaborated in Wendt (1999: 246–312).

thinking and preparations in negotiating and bargaining with other states. The balance of power was the principal rule of order; war, the key instrument or institution to ensure that order.[43]

States – notably big states of Europe – succeeded in organizing Europe, as they wanted to suit their interests. Possessing more territory, people, and resources, the European states eventually subjugated or eliminated competitor systems, including city-states, feudal enclaves, small principalities, and tiny kingdoms. Those states that failed to adapt to this coercive environment were eliminated from competition. Illustrative was Poland's extinction in being divided among Russia, Prussia, and Austria at the end of the eighteenth century. This predatory behavior, according to some analysts, preserved both the balance of power among these rivals and the peace of Europe.[44] Poland in realist theory was selected out of the system because it could not play by its harsh rules. The European states subsequently extended their struggle for dominion in Europe to the non-European peoples of the globe. Absent the superior war-making capability of the European states, foreign peoples, tribes, and empires became tributaries of the European powers.[45] They lacked Europe's military and civilian technological prowess, economic resources, and loyal citizen-soldiers – power capabilities unmatched in history until then.

This rapacious multipolar system was transformed into a less war-prone system of state relations in Europe (but scarcely so in Europe's expansion around the globe) with the institutionalization of the so-called Congress of Vienna system. This multipolar mutation lasted for almost a century from 1815 to 1914. As scholarly research suggests, an unstable balance of power system, as an institution of governance among the European states, became a threat to the regimes and states of the system.[46] Uncontrolled armed rivalry also threatened Europe's political regimes. At risk were the aristocratic ruling houses, which battled the rising tide of nationalist and liberal ideas unleashed by the French and American Revolutions. With the defeat of the Napoleonic grab for hegemony, the states of Europe developed a system of consultation through conferences and ad hoc congresses to resolve their competing interests short of cataclysmic war. These concerns largely revolved around mutually agreed upon adjustments and compensations in borders, territorial acquisitions, regime changes, and selected protections for minority religious practices. These factors were critical in the pre-Industrial Revolution era of

---

[43] For an opposed explanation of the long peace from 1815 to 1914, see Schroeder (1989, 1992, 1994b).
[44] Bull (1977).
[45] Watson (1984, 1992). Also relevant is Diamond (1997).
[46] Schroeder (1994b).

maintaining equilibrium of power in Europe responsive to the conflicting demands of the states.

The Congress of Vienna system brought relative peace to Europe for a century. It collapsed when the European states and their leaders lost control of their political conflicts and plunged into a Thirty Years War for European and world hegemony from 1914 to 1945.[47] The European states, now joined by the rising power of non-European states, principally Japan and the United States, reverted to the rapacious balance of power system of the pre-Napoleonic period. What had dramatically changed, however, was the material power of these states. Their destructive capacity and that of the system far exceeded the pre-industrial wars of the Napoleonic period. A massive increase in the amount of violence available to states constituted a transformation in the workings and incentives of the system itself.

The Cold War ushered in a brief period of bipolarity. The logic of this system, as chapter 3 traces, introduced an entirely new set of incentives for state behavior. This sharp departure from the traditional European multipolar system sparked a rich, if inconclusive, debate among security analysts about the relative disposition of a bipolar vs. a multipolar system to foster conflict and war or cooperation between rivals.[48] The implosion of the Soviet Union and the end of the Cold War has now shifted that debate to an exchange over whether we are witnessing a return to a multipolar system or to a unipolar system under American leadership and dominion in the post-Cold War era.[49] As these examples suggest, a system of states and the structure of power sustaining that system can be as important as specific bilateral relations in determining the security of a state and its population. Each of the security theories of this volume has a different conception of the impact of the system of states as a security problem. It is a key point of comparison across these security positions which we will address in the next chapter.

The state and transnational civil society

But actors, notably individuals and groups, want more than just a life secure from physical harm. Being safe is not enough if human societies are to survive and thrive. This is not to trivialize the difficulty of achieving this level of confidence. Humans quite understandably wish to know whether their person and property will be protected at home and abroad.

---

[47] Keylor (2001) makes a useful comparison between the religious wars of the seventeenth century and the ideological conflicts of the twentieth.

[48] Compare Deutsch and Singer (1964) and Waltz (1964).

[49] Ikenberry and Kupchan (1990), Keohane (1984), Layne (1993), and Nye (2002, 1990).

rights? Can the Catholic minority or Protestant majority in Northern Ireland, for example, rely on the Irish and British governments and their support of local autonomy to protect the interests of these rival groups? Can Muslims living in India count on the Indian secular state to defend their religious beliefs and practices when attacked by the majority Hindu community?

Constructing a state that meets these two tests – limiting the state's coercive power yet relying on that power to protect civil liberties and human rights – is obviously not easy. It is a ceaseless work in progress. There is a fundamental contradiction between these two functions. Holding the state and its agents accountable to these conflicting objectives is an endless challenge under changing socio-economic and political conditions, not to say differing conceptions of moral practices. How to create a state capable of acting on behalf of the liberties of its citizens, yet not so powerful that it threatens their lives, freedom, and property, are central security issues for all popular governments.[60] No universally accepted formula exists about the best way to strike this balance. Yet the security and rights of individuals and groups hinge critically on striking the right balance.

Third, under conditions of globalization and increasing connectedness, no state or people can remain indifferent to the kind of security regime that is created by the people of another state. This is scarcely a new issue, although it has far greater material repercussions than before because of the existence of weapons of mass destruction and state-supported terrorism. Under traditional balance of power rules of European state politics, rulers were always keen to align through marriages of convenience with neighbors and other states and strove mightily to place their friends on the thrones of these states. In the wake of the French Revolution, which unleashed the twin revolutionary forces of nationalism and liberalism, regimes based more on blood than ballots – notably Russia, Austria, and Prussia – were threatened with overthrow. They had to resort to force repeatedly to quell popular uprisings. Intermarriages and military interventions in each other's affairs were sufficient for a century to keep these autocratic governments in power, only to be swept away by the democratization of war in World War I.[61]

The incentive to define the governing regimes of other states was also clearly one of the driving forces of the Cold War. Both the United States and the Soviet Union expended hundreds of billions of dollars and

---

[60] This is a central challenge to the viability of popular or democratic governments, which James Madison addresses in *Federalist* No. 10 (n.d.: 53–62). See also No. 51 (n.d.: 335–41).

[61] Tuchman (1962).

engaged in local wars around the world through their clients and allies. These wars cost the lives of tens of thousands of their own soldiers to ensure regimes supportive of their security interests. Ideological affinity was systematically subordinated to this security imperative. Now, in the aftermath of the destruction of the World Trade Center and the attack on the Pentagon, the United States and those states joined in the coalition against terrorism assert the same right to define how other states will be ruled to foster their security aims. Afghanistan's post-Taliban regime is precluded from supporting terrorist organizations. Washington also overthrew the regime of Saddam Hussein in Iraq because of its alleged manufacture of weapons of mass destruction and ties to terrorist organizations like Al Qaeda. As these charges were gradually exposed to be without foundation, the coalition cobbled together by the United States shifted its justification for war to ending the tyranny of the Hussein regime in order to create the first democratic Arab state – an outcome claimed to be vital to American national security interests.

Finally, and related to the last point, research and experience are accumulating evidence for the proposition that how a state's coercive powers are arranged and disciplined at home bear directly on international security and peace. There is a large, if not yet universally accepted, body of research that appears to show a statistically significant correlation between peace and the spread of democratic regimes, institutions and values.[62] If it can be conclusively substantiated that a state is less war-prone if it is checked by a rule of law to which it must adhere and is accountable to open and free elections, then there is an incentive for democratic states to expand the zone of such regimes and for populations to revolt against authoritarian governments and to expect assistance from democratic states in this quest. Thus the democratic values held by humans and their strivings for freedom and equality can't be isolated from security studies, as the Iraqi case suggests. Like the imperative of welfare, different conceptions of moral authority and legitimacy – of personal or state behavior – will either expand or contract the play of violence in human affairs at a domestic level. In turn, these security regimes have critical negative and positive effects on the disposition of the international security system to use or not use force between states and within contending factions within a state.

Table 1.1 summarizes the actors, levels of analysis, the scope of the security problem posed at each level, and the tendency of relevant actors at each level to use force. They signal the mutual dependency of state and non-state actors on each other with respect to the crucial question of using or desisting from using force to get their way. In succeeding

---

[62] For contrasting views about the democratic peace, see Layne (1994) and n. 30.

Table 1.1 *The dimensions of security and international security viewed from the state*

Levels of analysis	Principal actors	Scope of actor relations
Interstate	States and intergovernmental organizations (IGOs)	Bilateral and multilateral relations of states: security and welfare functions of the state; United Nations, NATO, etc.; actor exchanges are coercive
Systemic	States	The expectation of violence or coercive threats in resolving interstate differences; actor exchanges are coercive
Transnational actors and their roles in international civil society: economic and socio-political dimensions	1. *Economic*: States; economic actors, including multinational corporations, IGOs and non-governmental organizations (NGOs)	1. Globalizing markets and the diffusion of technology and innovation; actor exchanges are voluntary and non-coercive
	2. *Socio-Political-Cultural*: States, IGOs, NGOs, individuals and groups	2. Humanitarian programs; educational /cultural exchanges; terrorist attacks, etc.
Domestic	States, individuals, groups, associations, corporations, and transnational actors	1. The state as threat to civil liberties and human rights
		2. The state as protector
		3. Regimes and their impact on the security interests of other states
		4. Regimes and international security
		Actor exchanges are a mix of coercion and non-coercion

chapters we will apply this table to compare the seven security paradigms and approaches competing for our validation and adoption and to identify the actors and factors each stresses at each of the levels of actor decision and action.

Theory and falsification

How do you know which security school of thought is the right one? Which theory or approach to theory appears best suited to describe, explain, and predict the thinking and actions of relevant actors? These questions are crucial. How they are answered determines fundamentally whether we will be properly equipped to discriminate between and among these rivals for hegemony in security studies and whether we, as members of an open society, will be able to use their insights and conceptual tools to best advantage as guides to adapt effectively and efficiently to a complex world of 200 nation-states and a global society of over six billion diverse and divided peoples.

It should come as no surprise to learn that, like the substantive study of security, the notion of "theory" is also a contested notion in the social sciences. While many scholars are so convinced of their methods and approaches that they believe there is no problem in understanding what theory is and how to use it, this volume's review of the schools of thought about security provides ample evidence that what constitutes valid and reliable theory is much in dispute among the warring partisans of the competing paradigms and approaches under review. Many constructivists, as chapter 7 discusses, even deny the possibility of an objective, empirically based theory of human behavior and, specifically, of security. Behavioral scholars, as chapter 6 relates, insist that international relations and security studies can be made a science.

Since this volume makes no claim that it can definitively resolve the rivalry over security between contesting schools of thought, it is equally circumspect in addressing the thorny and tangled issue of theory. What I propose to do is to adopt the strategy already applied to security studies. In the interest of full disclosure and transparency, I will stipulate what I believe are key properties of a theory of security, a position on which this volume relies in evaluating and validating the claims of disputing security and international relations theorists. The work of Imre Lakatos will be especially relevant. The discussion below will adopt a set of criteria, based on Lakatos' innovative and widely acknowledged contributions to falsifying theories, to guide the evaluation of security theories. This move is also made to assist readers to make up their own minds about what security theory to vote for.

Molière, a seventeenth-century French dramatist, wrote a play still much produced around the world about a pretentious businessman, *Le Bourgeois Gentilhomme*. In his dotage, the play's protagonist puts on airs, hires poets, musicians, philosophers, and rhetoricians to teach him the graces of high culture that his rude beginnings denied him. After several lessons, he discovers to his amazement that "he is speaking prose," ostensibly for the first time in his life. Absurd? Of course, since to speak is to speak prose. What has this to do with theory? Everything. Whether we know it or not or whether we are prepared to acknowledge this human aptitude or deride it as irrelevant to practical affairs, we all are theorists. Readers must be "doing theory," since it is inconceivable that you here.[66] I will simply assert, with the volume as testimony, that partial and uncertain but still credible and valid knowledge about security is possible, but always under the condition of ceaseless testing and challenge.

If falsifying a theory or proposition about security is the immediate aim and if the security theorist is under the gun to constantly rethink assumptions and findings, it is important to understand the pursuit of knowledge about security is an ongoing process, not a fixed result or end product. From this perspective, however tentative and problematic it may appear, several guidelines can be invoked to sort out the claims of different theories. Most important among these is a clear understanding of the questions that the theory is attempting to answer. Recall that the central concern here is to search for an explanation of why actors use or choose *not* to use force or coercive threats to get the outcomes they prefer in exchanges with other actors. This question is only partially addressed and from different and conflicting perspectives by the paradigms and approaches of this volume. Some do better explaining why actors use force; others, why they eschew this option or temporize in appeals to coercion and threats. This volume insists that prevailing theories and approaches fail to pose the question of security in a sufficiently plausible and convincing way. In a sense, they all take a wrong step (choosing a partial definition of security) in the right direction (an attempt to generalize about security). One of the principal claims of "value added" of this volume is its challenge to theorists and practitioners concerned with security studies either to enlarge the scope of their investigations or, at least, to be candid and clear about the limits of their claims to knowledge about security.

Imre Lakatos provides some useful guidelines about how to falsify a theory, including theories of security and international relations. Lakatos states his falsification guidelines better than I can summarize them. They demand more than simply finding conflicts between facts and theories. Facts are always subject to reinterpretation and qualification. They become significant only when filtered through a theoretical framework. So the task of the wannabe security theorist is less that of assessing a particular theory by citing countervailing data to its descriptions, explanations, and predictions of actor behavior and events than that of evaluating its claims by comparing its findings to other relevant conceptual frameworks or paradigms. As Lakatos explains:

For the naïve falsificationist a theory is falsified by a . . . 'observational' statement which conflicts with it (or which he decides to interpret as conflicting with it).

---

[66] Giddens (1984) develops these theoretical issues in this and in the works cited in the course of this volume.

For the sophisticated falsificationist a scientific theory T is falsified if and only if another theory T' has been proposed with the following characteristics: (1) T' has excess empirical content over T: that is, it predicts novel facts, that is, facts improbable in the light of, or even forbidden, by T; (2) T' explains the previous success of T, that is, all the unrefuted content of T is included (within the limits of observational error) in the content of T'; and (3) some of the excess content of T' is corroborated.[67]

The implications of Lakatos' guidelines for falsification for this volume are twofold. First, chapter 3 will build a "laboratory" – a mind experiment if you will – to test how well the seven schools of thought explain the rise and demise of the Cold War and the implosion of the Soviet Union as the death blow to the post-World War II bipolar system. This line of evaluation will be cast at the level of the naïve falsificationist. The volume will also take up Lakatos' challenge of the sophisticated falsificationist and assess the relative explanatory power of these different theoretical perspectives, using each to contest the other along the three criteria advanced by Lakatos. Readers are invited to join this evaluative process and to reach their own conclusions. Those made in the succeeding chapters should be used, as Lakatos advises, as a target and point of departure rather than as a definitive conclusion and closure about the worth or weakness of a particular theory.

Emphasis is placed on the perfection and development of security theory through sustained falsification. This orientation encourages a constructive approach to theory building since better explanatory and predictive power is what both scholars and interested citizens have a mutual interest in promoting. Theories will be viewed as progressive if they meet Lakatos' criteria. They will be seen as degenerative if they progressively fail to meet countervailing facts and interpretations about security, if they rely increasingly on ad hoc explanations that weaken and dilute the explanatory power of a theory to save it, and if they also fail to generate new insights and address novel and challenging security issues that will have arisen.

Learning to live with partial and uncertain knowledge about so crucial a human concern as security may be somewhat disquieting to many readers. Rejecting imperfect but tested knowledge because it is flawed literally makes "no sense." This unsettling condition is an invitation to narrow uncertainty, not a justification to abandon the quest for knowledge, however tenuous or problematic. However much our theorists may differ, they would appear to agree at least on this point.

---

[67] Lakatos (1978: 32). See also Lakatos (1970).

Conclusions

We have stipulated (a) an inclusive definition of security that covers both the use *and* non-use of violence; (b) relevant actors, notably states, but also individuals, groups, multinational corporations, non-governmental associations (NGOs) and intergovernmental agencies (IGOs) as relevant to a study of international security; (c) four levels of actor interactions, where the problems of security are posed in international relations; and (d) a method for validating security theories through falsification. We have identified these four levels of actor behavior principally from the perspective of the state. We have briefly explained why states are central to security studies whether in discharging their functions of domestic order or national and international security or, and not ironically, in failing to meet these imperatives.

Readers are again cautioned that these stipulations defining the scope of international security and the actors and factors associated with security studies are contested moves. Many constructivist theorists, as chapter 7 delineates, reject any privileged place for the state. For some, to stipulate the centrality of the state as a matter of empirical fact is to implicitly validate and legitimate its political and moral claims. Others who acknowledge the central importance of the state in security studies are also nuanced in challenging the notion of the sovereign equality of states as legal or moral norm when contrasted with the vastly differing power of actual states to discharge their security functions.[68]

Discussion questions

1. What are some of the principal competing perspectives or visions of international relations and security advanced by leading theorists, practitioners, and informed observers? Which do you find most persuasive and why?
2. What are some of the principal obstacles impeding the development of a science of security and security studies equal to the rigor and reliability of the knowledge produced by the physical and biological sciences? Specifically, what is the importance and role of history in security studies?
3. When and under what circumstances does the phenomenon of security arise in human affairs? How is security related to politics and, specifically, to international politics?
4. Critically evaluate the claim of this volume that the scope of the study of security extends to the choices of international actors both to use

---

[68] Krasner (1999).

and not to use force and coercive threats to ensure their preferred outcomes in their interdependent exchanges with other actors.

5. From what four perspectives or levels of analysis can security be approached? Who are some of the principal actors at each level and what in general is the scope of their aims and activities?

6. Why is the state central to international security and what are some of its principal roles at each of the four levels of analysis identified as key viewpoints from which to understand and explain international security?

7. Distinguish between a naïve and a sophisticated falsificationist and explain why falsification is a superior strategy in attempts to validate a security theory rather than simply citing supportive data.

Suggestions for further reading

Overviews of security studies

A useful starting point to gain a bird's eye view of security studies can be drawn from reading several contrasting perspectives. See David A. Baldwin (1995), "Security Studies and the End of the Cold War," *World Politics* 48: 117–41; Stuart Croft and Terriff Terry (eds.) (2000), *Critical Reflections on Security and Change*, London: Frank Cass; Peter J. Katzenstein (1996), *The Culture of National Security: Norms and Identity in World Politics*, New York: Columbia University Press, chapter 1, pp. 1–32; Edward A. Kolodziej (1992a), "Renaissance in Security Studies? Caveat Lector," *International Studies Quarterly* 36: 421–38; (1992b), "What is Security and Security Studies?" *Arms Control* 13: 1–31; and Stephen M. Walt (1991), "The Renaissance of Security Studies," *International Studies Quarterly* 35: 211–39.

Hedley Bull (1977), *The Anarchical Society: A Study of Order in World Politics*, London: Macmillan. This is a must read. It makes the case for privileging the state in security theory and practice and establishes *the* foundation for the English school of security theory.

Barry Buzan (1991), *People, States and Fear: An Agenda for International Security Studies in the Post-Cold War Era*, Boulder: Lynne Rienner Publishers. Buzan is the leading proponent today of the English school of security theory. This volume is a useful introduction to key security concepts and their significance in international relations theory.

William R. Keylor (2001), *The Twentieth-Century World: An International History*, New York: Oxford University Press. This is an excellent overview of the evolution of international relations since the early 1900s to the post-Cold War era. The extensive bibliographic references are particularly useful.

Stephen D. Krasner (1999), *Sovereignty: Organized Hypocrisy*, Princeton: Princeton University Press. This is a well-argued critique of the state and its claims to a monopoly of legitimate violence. The flaws of the state as a solution to security are developed throughout this volume.

Colin S. Gray (1999), *Modern Strategy*, Oxford: Oxford University Press. This volume presents security studies as a strategic problem of using or threatening force in contrast to this volume, which understands security studies as a branch of the social sciences with implications for the use or non-use of force.

2 The foundations of security studies: Hobbes, Clausewitz, and Thucydides

Building a foundation under security and international security

We need a foundation on which we can construct a conceptual framework to understand and explain security. Such a foundation is also needed to justify the choices we've made in chapter 1 about the relevant actors, factors, and levels of actor exchanges associated with security and the central role of the state. One tried and tested way is to examine how thinkers and statesmen have traditionally understood what security means and to draw on this knowledge in forming our own positions. This may well lead to rejecting "old" thinking and striking out on our own. In critically evaluating the thinking of the past, there is no presumption at the start of this intellectual journey that we are necessarily prejudicing where our views about security will eventually take us.

If we examine the thinking of three great theorists – Thomas Hobbes, Carl von Clausewitz, and Thucydides – who devoted much of their genius to explaining and understanding security, we can get a jump start in our quest to develop our own theory of security by trading on their insights. Their contributions provide a point of departure, not a final resting point. Studying the thinking of these theorists won't tell us all we want to know, but it will help us to learn *how* to think about security and quite a bit about *what* to think about security and *why*. These thinkers were able to go well beyond their eras. They were able to standardize the behavior of all actors – humans and their agents – with respect to security without reference to time, space, or social circumstances. That analytic and psychological capacity to stand outside ourselves is among the most important lessons to learn from them.

In succeeding chapters, we will also have to look beyond these thinkers. They were in no position, given their times, to identify other factors and actors, noted in table 1.1, who are crucial today for a fuller comprehension of security. Many of these actors, like the United Nations or the Soviet Union, did not exist when they lived. We need to exploit what we have experienced and learned about security after they wrote. Fundamental changes in human society pose new security challenges for the human species. This relentless process of change is driven by the explosion in scientific knowledge, ceaseless technological innovations and diffusion, global markets, and increasing contacts and clashes between culturally different peoples and their divergent social systems and values. The events of 9/11 and the global war on terrorism, launched by the United States in September 2001, can only be fully grasped against the background of these tectonic shifts in power and human purpose.

These ongoing changes have altered security as a global problem and, accordingly, its systematic study. Weapons of mass destruction (WMD), notably nuclear arms, in the hands of states or groups or individuals pose grave, time-urgent threats to the security of populations around the globe. However serious the threats to security facing peoples and states during the lifetimes of our three theorists, they pale before those of mankind today. Hitherto nations might be annihilated – Melos by Athens or Carthage by Rome – but there was no inkling that the human species itself was in danger of extinction. We have to take into account these fundamental changes in our social environment if we want to be up-to-date in thinking about international security.

This said, Hobbes, Clausewitz, and Thucydides still speak to us across time and space and historical circumstance – Hobbes from seventeenth-century England, Clausewitz from nineteenth-century Prussia, and Thucydides from the much earlier time of fifth-century BC Greece. If our situation and preoccupations about security can hardly be compared to theirs, as globalization works through the world society today, it is no less true that the underlying dilemmas of choice arising from the use of force, which they were among the first to delineate, are as real today as they were when they lived. These dilemmas of choice and action by states – or by individuals and groups – may appear under different guises over time, but the structure or architecture of these dilemmas remain essentially the same, if the insights of these thinkers are given full credit. They exposed to light the continuing and underlying dilemmas of choice, raised by using or threatening force, that confront all human societies and the exchanges between them.

Their insights apply to such diverse conflicts as those between Egypt and the Hittite kingdom millennia ago as well as Athens and Sparta and Rome and Carthage several centuries before the birth of Christ. They are equally useful in trying to understand the wars for European hegemony between France and Hapsburg Austria during the seventeenth and eighteenth centuries, the great power struggles for global rule in World Wars I and II, and the Cold War between the United States and the

Soviet Union for world ascendancy. The dilemmas of choice posed by security challenges are no less present as problems today than before. Take the armed struggle between the Jewish and Palestinian peoples or that between Hutus and Tutsis in Rwanda or the American invasions of Iraq in 1991 and 2003. To be sure, armed conflict and the endless threats exchanged between opponents vary significantly in different regions and over different epochs. Their forms and modalities and the range of destructive capabilities available to rivals will evolve with other elements of human society.[1] Changes in socio-economic organization and practices or new technologies and increased (or decreased) economic resources will expand or contract the opportunities and incentives to appeal to force in determining the preferred outcomes of these human transactions. Knowledge of these historical or time-bound differences is central to human concerns. Tracing this complex evolution, while critical for security studies, falls outside the scope of our immediate interest. For our purposes at the moment, we are interested first in identifying what is the same, not different, about the security dilemmas facing humans as humans. That is why it is useful to invoke our three guides, who have made such lasting contributions to our understanding of security. These are as fresh and alive today as when they were first penned.

A second reason why we may wish to study the work of this triumvirate revolves around their shared assumption, contested by many security theorists today, that a necessary, if not sufficient, solution to the tendency of humans and their agents to use force and violence to get their way is countervailing force. This constraint and the hard choices it generates are attributed to the imperative of order confronting all human societies. This imperative arises from the endemic and continuing conflicts between individuals and groups within societies and those between societies. These theorists assumed that consensual cooperation among actors – individuals, tribes, societies, or states – depended on a preceding condition: that engaged and interdependent actors had already created a regime or order capable of resolving the inevitable disputes and conflicts among them. None could envision a state of "pure peace" in which political clashes would not ultimately be resolved, directly or implicitly, by resort to force or threats – specifically the overwhelming and overweening material power possessed by the modern state. They assumed that what was "real" or true about humans and their societies was the embedded presence of force as the ultimate and final instrument to resolve preference clashes.

---

[1] On the security problems of primitive societies, see Blainey (1976, and, more generally on the causes of war, 1988).

These writers assumed that conflicts would erupt into violence when non-violent means were exhausted to resolve differences. Our triumvirate shared a capacious understanding of the creative capacity of humans to devise non-violent ways to improve their lives and to perfect their social conditions. Restraining appeals to force, paradoxically, became the primary objective of politics if human freedom and creativity were to flourish. The incentive to use force or threats did not preclude cooperation across a wide range of human concerns. Hobbes put the matter squarely and eloquently about the necessity for security or order as a precondition for societies to survive and thrive:

Whatsoever therefore is consequent to a time of Warre, where every man is Enemy to every man; the same is consequent to the time, wherein men live without other security, than that their own strength, and their own invention shall furnish them withall. In such condition, there is no place for Industry; because the fruit thereof is uncertain; and consequently no Culture of the Earth; no Navigation, nor use of the commodities that may be imported by Sea; no commodious Building; no Instruments of moving, and removing such things as require much force; no Knowledge of the face of the Earth; no account of Time; no Arts; No Letters; No Society, and which is worst of all, continuall feare, and danger of violent death . . .[2]

As chapter 4 explains further, the assumptions made by these theorists place them in the realist school of security. Since the possibility and often the high probability of appeals to violence lurked always below the surface of all human cooperation and conflicts, Hobbes stipulated the need for a fearsome and awesome power – what he called a Leviathan – capable of arbitrating differences between individuals and groups within a society.[3] The Leviathan – what moderns call the state today – had to be sufficiently powerful to settle definitively the divisions between members of a society if order were to be established. This problem or condition beset all societies from within.[4]

This was no less true of authoritarian and dictatorial governments than modern democracies or primitive hunter and gatherer societies.[5] This force also had to be sufficiently powerful to protect and defend a society against rivals. It had to be always at work and at the ready to ensure the security and survival of the society to which it was dedicated, while mere mortals rested and replenished their energy through sleep or were preoccupied with other concerns. This formidable power had to continue beyond the life of an individual to ensure the security and replication of

[2] Hobbes (1997: 70).   [3] Hobbes (1997).   [4] Wrong (1994).
[5] Compare two theorists, Mansbridge (1996) and Maine (1909), respectively a partisan and a skeptic of popular government, who converge on this point.

the society itself in which humans were enmeshed and on which the realization of their individual life chances depended. At the very least the state had to be sufficiently materially powerful to balance or offset the opposing force of other societies to neutralize their capacity to impose their demands and rule on others.[6] For a stable order to be created between rivals, all of the participants must also agree, implicitly or explicitly, that the distribution of power and force between them is acceptable and legitimate, however great the disparities between the units. It was precisely this principle of mutual accord among rivals and allies that Athens violated, as Thucydides recounts.

Finally, our triumvirate also understood that the awesome power of the state had to enjoy the support of the people it protected and governed. Allied states also had to be confident that their alliances with other states were sufficiently reliable to respond to their particular security interests. The state alone or in alliance is expected to deliver on security to earn internal and external support. The state's authority and the legitimate exercise of its monopoly over violence depended decisively on discharging its security functions within and outside its territorial boundaries. Why else submit to such an authority and its material power unless it could deliver on personal and societal security? Conversely, in discharging its security functions, the state was also expected, as a matter of right and legitimate order, never to become a threat to the very interests, aims, and values it was created and contracted to protect. This point is especially clear in Hobbes' understanding of security. Otherwise, the state and those in possession of its coercive powers would be pursuing their own interests at the expense of those over whom they ruled and whom the Leviathan or state was obligated to defend.

In briefly summarizing the shared assumptions made by our triumvirate about the behavior of humans and their agents, notably states, we can better understand how they arrived at their conception of security. By that token, we can also learn to model our thinking about security by initially following their example without necessarily affirming definitively either their assumptions about security or the implications of their explanation of actor behavior in appealing to force. What we can principally learn from these authors is how to generalize about security – personal, societal, and interstate – and about how each is related to the broader study of international relations.[7] What we want to be able to do, and it is by no means easy or effortless, is to identify the key properties of

---

[6] Hedley Bull (1977) makes these points eloquently in his widely read and admired *The Anarchical Society*.
[7] Baldwin (1995) makes the same point.

security problems as an enduring feature of the human condition. We are not obliged – or even expected – to agree with these theorists. We are asked only to enter into a dialogue with them as a first step in examining the *why, how,* and *what* of security. We may well find the paradigms or approaches in chapters 4–7 more to our liking – more persuasive and useful in explaining security behavior and more compelling as guides to get the kind of security we are seeking. These thinkers have much to say about *how* we might think about security rather than *what* we are supposed to think about what they have to say that applies to our own times. We can rely on the contributions of our triumvirate then as a conceptual crutch on which to lean as we learn to walk alone in becoming independent and accomplished players in thinking about international security. The principal reason we rely initially on these ancients is to become self-reliant to understand and solve the security problems besetting us today.

Hobbes: the security dilemma and the individual

Let's begin with Thomas Hobbes. Hobbes identified the problem of security in the broadest conceivable terms. He rooted security as a problem in just being human. He stipulated that the material and psychological conditions arising from simply being human generated a continuing social problem – what is today characterized as a security dilemma. That dilemma confronted all humans, whether they were conscious of the problem or not. In using or threatening force to get their way, humans set in motion a vicious and perpetual circle and cycle of violence and counter-violence. On the one hand, to neglect or dismiss the threat that force might be used by others to impose their preferences on competitors ran the clear risk of subjugation and even death; they but not their rival would get their way. On the other hand, to appeal to force set in train a counter-cycle of violence that, theoretically, had no limit, save the imposition of the will of one of the antagonists on the other or the elimination of one or both. The many instances of war between peoples and states are but historical instances of an underlying security dilemma endemic to all human societies and their relations with each other. The security dilemma arose, ironically, from humans themselves as intelligent, creative, rational bipeds seeking to survive and thrive in eliciting the cooperation of others on their own egoistic terms.

Hobbes assumed, reasonably enough, that all humans have preferences and care about what they want. They have preferences of all kinds: for power, wealth, comfort, social status, prestige, social regard, dominance, blissful aesthetic or hedonistic pleasures, or spiritual peace and ascetic solitude. You name it. Under conditions of scarce material and symbolic resources, preference clashes were inevitable and ceaseless. Take social status and prestige. These values obviously cannot be equally divided between competing claimants without robbing them of their value. If everyone is top dog, no one is. Similarly, a society that promotes hedonism and promiscuity cannot at the same time foster ascetic self-denial as ideals or models of virtuous behavior. Choices have to be made and disincentives, including violence and threats, created to discourage alternative practices or norms. If two people fear each other, both can't be secure unless one gets the upper hand or eliminates his rival.

These and countless other examples illustrate the Hobbesian condition of human and social exchanges as permanently "at sixes and sevens," to borrow from Shakespeare. In Hobbes' view, the differing views among humans about lifestyles and state and societal priorities were fundamentally non-congruent and non-convergent. In sum, they were irreconcilable. The prospect of a utopia, defined by the reconciliation of divergent human preferences and wills, was ruled out both by observation of human conduct and by assumptions about the make-up of humans and their capacity to create clashing interests and values for themselves, as individuals, and for the societies of which they were members.

For Hobbes, human preferences naturally diverged, not converged, in the absence of a materially superior awesome force to bring about order, defined as the coercive harmonization of conflicting human wills. This is just another way of saying humans, as humans, cannot expect in their social exchanges that a congruence of human preferences will naturally arise with respect to social practices, rules, and governing principles. Just the opposite should be expected. There is nothing to suggest that in a world of six billion diverse and divided people and 200 nation-states, each claiming sovereignty and ultimate authority to use its violent capabilities to arbitrate conflicts at home and abroad, that the expectation of convergence is any more likely today than in Hobbes' seventeenth-century England split between class and religion. If this is the actual state of affairs in human exchanges, peace and harmony are but temporary respites between hostile clashes and war. So Hobbes thought (and taught): "So the nature of War, consisteth not in actuall fighting; but in the known disposition thereto, during all the time there is no assurance to the contrary. All other time is peace."[8]

Hobbes took humans as he observed or studied them through written accounts of an abundant historical record available to him. He resisted the Greek penchant to pose the problem of political order as an ideal, much the way the issue is framed in Aristotle's *Ethics*,[9] as the creation by humans

---

[8] Hobbes (1997: 70).   [9] Aristotle (1947: 308ff.).

It is a normative moral construct of the prerequisite for political order. History and contemporary experience yields a picture of the state at odds with this Hobbesian "pure" model. States have always been unequal in the material power at their disposal. Notions of sovereign equality do not square with the differential power of states to shape their environments in preferred ways. Nor does Hobbes' or Weber's conceptualization of the state map with the discordant failings of states either to fulfill their security functions (Lebanon), their predatory record (Rwanda, Sudan, Cambodia, or Mao Tse-tung's China), or the violation of norms of civil conduct and human rights and support of terrorists (the defunct Taliban regime in Afghanistan).

Hobbes' aim was not historical description. Nor is the tracing of that complex and controversial history of the rise and spread of the state and the ascendancy of the nation-state system our aim here, however critical that history may be for a theory of the state and its role in addressing security imperatives.[15] Hobbes focused, like this discussion, on describing, explaining, and understanding security as central to the human condition. Solving the security dilemma, however provisionally, and establishing a working political order were prerequisites for the preservation and replication of social life beyond the life of any of its members. Hobbes' solution of a Leviathan or the creation of awesome power and its legitimization by an imagined social contract that might have occurred at some time in history is simply that – purely imaginary as his critics insist.

Their trenchant criticism notwithstanding, the universal and continuing problem of security persists today.[16] If security was a problem for a few million British living on an island in the seventeenth century, how much more so is it an abiding concern for six billion people and 200 nation-states today, which are increasingly interdependent under conditions of an ever-enlarging globalization of preference clashes across state borders. Given Hobbes' underlying assumption that human preferences cannot be realized under conditions of inherently scarce means to satisfy them and given his prescient stipulation of the human capacity to create ever new differences, the temptation to appeal to force is ever present in human thoughts, decisions and actions. The incentive to use force, unless checked, lurks below the surface of all human exchanges in which the actors seek to ensure a favorable outcome in transactions keyed to whatever is at stake: love, domination, wealth, privilege, and prestige. Force and coercion are also no less attractive to the agents of human

---

[15] For extensive discussions of the origin of the modern state and its shortcomings as an institution of rule, see, *inter alia.*, Spruyt (1994), Tilly (1990), and Krasner (1999).
[16] Reinhard Bendix traces this evolution in Bendix (1964a, b, 1978).

striving, notably states, as they seek to shape and shove each other to their liking to reflect their competing notions of what they want.

Hobbes could not foresee that the state would eventually become the basic unit of political organization of the peoples of the world. What order or security the world has attained today rests on a decentralized system of nation-states. The member states provide in greater or lesser measure what order there is in the world for its six billion inhabitants.[17] Hobbes would have been surprised, too, to see that the dominant internal or domestic solution to the security dilemma would not be kings or princes, but popular rule. No regime today, however oppressive or authoritarian, claims to merely represent itself and its particular interests and survival. This is true of the liberal democracies of the West as well as states which claim that an historically privileged party (China or Vietnam) or charismatic leader (Cuba's Fidel Castro) or military junta (Myanmar) or religious leaders (Iran and Saudi Arabia) represent the popular will. However flawed the principle of popular sovereignty underlying the authority and legitimacy of the state, the sovereign state is the provisional solution to the global security dilemma. Repairing and surmounting its flaws, principally its war-making capabilities and inclinations, is one of the great and unresolved problems of the twenty-first century.[18]

Clausewitz: the security dilemma and the state

Each state of the world system of states claims to exercise a monopoly of legitimate violence over the territories and populations over which it is sovereign. Formed then is a decentralized system of states as the shaky and unreliable guaranty of international security and order. This solution is obviously flawed from a Hobbesian perspective. There is no awesome power to resolve or impose solutions on contending states. Indeed, the principal focus of state power is fixed on precluding that outcome. Hence the problem of security or order that nation-states solve at a local or national level is fundamentally unresolved at the level of the nation-state system. A weak and fragile decentralized system of nation-states shifts the focus of the security dilemma from the individual and societal level to the relations of states themselves and the power they dispose in unequal measure.

---

[17] Barry Buzan (1991) makes this point too often overlooked by many who focus on the anarchy of the state system.

[18] This review of security studies would be remiss if it failed to underline the important contributions of Barry Buzan and his colleagues who form the "English school" of security studies. See Buzan (1991), Buzan, Little and Jones (1993) for an introduction to their contributions to security linked closely to the earlier work of Hedley Bull, noted earlier, and Wight (1978, 1966b).

dilemma precisely because the problem of force has to be confronted by taking into account the countervailing use of force by other actors. The security dilemma is neither relaxed nor resolved nor are the political aims driving the use of force achieved solely by reducing the security problem to rapport of force. That is the clear lesson from Thucydides' rendering of this classic struggle.

Much of the continuing interest in Thucydides' account of an ancient war for supremacy between two implacable rivals is the exposition of the dilemmas of choice posed by the ceaseless search for security. If only the Melian dialogue is cited as the text to follow, as many security analysts insist, then material power should be pursued to the utmost. Security would then lie in the weakness of one's rivals and allies. Dominance would bring security. That advice ultimately got the Athenians in trouble. The Melians also lost their city and their lives in the Athenian quest for unconditional security.

On the other hand, if Thucydides' explanation for the war – Athens' growing power and its disposition to use that power to feed its ambition to assume the role of a coercive over a consensual hegemon – is taken as a point of departure, as other security theorists and strategists insist, then reserve and prudence is advised in relying solely on violence and threats to assure security.[30] A state or people may not have enough material power, alone or allied, to impose their will on others. Their ambition to control others, as the Corinthians and other Greek city-states believed, had the unintended effect of inducing Sparta and other Greek city-states to raise arms against Athens, leading to its defeat and also to their unforeseen collective demise. Athens might well have been able to pursue a defensive strategy and also to reach an agreement with their real or potential rivals, but this accommodating political solution to its security dilemma was rejected in favor of all-out war.

No formula has yet been devised that can tell decision-makers, states, or people which interpretation of Thucydides' history of the Peloponnesian war to follow in resolving their conflicts with other states and actors. What we can say, based on Thucydides' accounting of the security dilemma, is that reliance on force to solve or relax the security dilemma has to be cast in politically and morally meaningful ways acceptable to adversaries and allies alike. Absent these shared meanings, force moves to its logical endgame as Hobbes and Clausewitz show. The result is eventually a lose-lose game for all participants as pure war overtakes the capacity of humans to mutually define acceptable and tolerable conditions for security and order. These values are the product of the mutually contingent choices

---

[30] Lebow (2003: 65–167) stresses this point.

interdependent actors are impelled to make in constructing their security relations.

Security theory and studies can help pose these choices more clearly and comprehensively to enhance the possibility that the right choices will be made to ensure or strengthen the security of a state or its people. The study of security cannot be expected to definitively resolve these dilemmas of choice in the same way, say, that physicians can cure rabies, polio or smallpox or that scientists and engineers can build space crafts capable of landing on Mars. Human behavior is too free, protean, variable, creative and unpredictable to provide a solution to the security dilemma that approaches the rigor of the natural sciences. In understanding the complexities of the problems posed by individual, societal and interstate security, we are better positioned to address and cope with these challenges. Knowledge is knowing what problems you have, not just knowing what solutions may be available.

Choosing whether to use force: Thucydides' relevance to contemporary war

Two additional examples, touching on the two great wars of the first half of the twentieth century, illustrate these problems. Examine the contrasting possibilities of choice available to the European states and peoples before World I and before World War II. Taking a page from the Melian dialogue, all of the states of Europe before World War I armed for total war, planned for the rapid mobilization of their military forces once hostilities commenced, and envisioned a short war with the swift and decisive defeat of rivals.[31] The war preparations of the major powers were driven, as one analyst observes, by a "cult of the offensive."[32] These plans reached such levels of organized rigidity that, when political negotiations broke down over Austria's determination to impose its will on Serbia in response to the assassination of the Austrian Archduke, pressures to strike first to win a quick and decisive victory overwhelmed efforts to reach a political settlement.

Such consensual solutions through joint consultations had been reached before under the Vienna system.[33] This system prevented a world war for a century between 1815 and 1914 among the big powers in Europe. A century later, such political solutions through compromise and accommodation were viewed as obstacles to what misguided military planners and political leaders believed would be a political solution dictated by a trial of arms.[34] They viewed alternatives to settling

---

[31] For a popular but accurate portrayal of these expectations, see Tuchman (1994).
[32] Van Evera (1984).   [33] Schroeder (1994b).   [34] Ritter (1979).

accounts by war as ineffectual and dangerous, given the massive arms build up and war preparations of their rivals. All acted like the Athenians at Melos. Compromise was ruled out by the mutually shared perception of the big powers that they were in a struggle for hegemony; whichever power or combination controlled Europe ruled the world since outside of the Western Hemisphere, the European empires dominated most of humanity. The political regimes of Europe, egged on by popular opinion, reverted to the traditional European state habit of an appeal to force to impose their preferred solutions for European and world order on their opponents. Mutual political accommodation might well have prevented the catastrophe of World War I. We'll never know. War certainly did not resolve Europe's security problems as World War II was born of this global conflagration.

Conversely, accommodations and compromise may not always work, either. In the face of a rival bent on expansion and domination at all costs, preparing for war may be the only feasible option to prevent or deter war. In hindsight, we know that the efforts of the liberal democracies, led by Britain and France, to reach an accord with the Nazi regime, proved futile. Efforts to appease Germany's Adolph Hitler were interpreted by Berlin as signs of weakness, much as the Athenians predicted their allies would conclude about their power and determination if they did not attack Melos or force it into alliance. The efforts of the liberal democracies to reach a compromise over Nazi Germany's absorption of the German-speaking parts of Czechoslovakia merely fueled German appetites to attack Poland in September 1939. The Soviet Union also failed to halt German aggression in signing a non-aggression pact with Germany on the eve of the German invasion of Poland. The pact freed Germany of a two-front war and opened the way for its seizure of Western Europe in the spring of 1940. Once its western flank was secure, Germany launched an attack on the Soviet Union.

What kind of world would we now have if the German security threat had not been defeated by what was a flawed alliance of the liberal democratic states and an anti-democratic, totalitarian Soviet Union? Race, as defined by a triumphant Nazi Germany, would determine who ruled Europe and the world. Germanic ethnic identity, not popular elections and human rights, would have been installed as principles of international law, backed by Nazi power. The absence of compromise and the determination of Nazi Germany to impose its rule on Europe and, by that token, on Europe's empires and the world compelled the decision of total war against the German war-machine. The strategic problems facing Nazi Germany, the Western democracies, and the Soviet Union were mirror images of each other, quite apart from the radically clashing value

systems at stake in the struggle. The preferences of the Western democracies, Communist Soviet Union, and Nazi Germany were reduced and
standardized in warfare by their mutual and incompatible security interests as they defined them. The duel or war to the finish made its own
claims on each rival and forced upon them a common set of constraints
in devising coercive means to overwhelm their rival. As George Kennan
observed, the liberal democracies, including the United States, allied with
the Stalinist Soviet state to defeat Germany and then Japan under terms
of unconditional surrender, "pure war" by other means.[35] Total war, cul-
minating in the nuclear bombing of Hiroshima and Nagasaki, was for
total stakes – the governance of the world.

These two contrasting examples of the security dilemma, each advis-
ing a radically different approach to resolving a security problem – one a
political settlement, the other all-out war – suggest the range of choices
available to societies and states in addressing and provisionally addressing their security concerns. World War I might have been avoided if the
proven mechanisms of accommodation and compromise, following the
prescriptions of the Vienna system, had again been invoked and if (as liberal theorists argue) imperial policies had not been aggressively pursued
at the expense of open markets that would have fostered economic interdependence, calculated to entwine the welfare interests of the European
peoples into a social system resistant to war. But against a determined,
ideologically driven adversary armed to the teeth, only countervailing
force is likely to deter war or to defeat the aggressor. These contrasting cases exemplify the security dilemma. They illustrate the problem of
resolving inevitable value conflicts between humans, within and between
societies, in appealing to force. They do not provide clear and unambigu-
ous rules of evidence and guidelines about which course to follow. They
do alert knowledgeable security practitioners of the hazards of using violence and the need to be prudent. Sometimes compromise and accommodation, discreetly backed by force, is the sensible course to assure
security. At other times, force must be met by force with the dire consequence that rivals will be placed on a path leading quite possibly to their
self-destruction.

As the succeeding chapters indicate, security theorists and strategic
and political decision-makers have attempted either to perfect classical
realist theory, represented by the triumvirate whose thinking we have
briefly summarized, or they have tried to surmount the limits of the realist
paradigm to escape the security dilemma or at the very least relax its harsh
consequences of capitulation or all-out war. In explicating the claims of

---

[35] Kennan (1984a).

these rival camps and their implicit or explicit solution to the security dilemma, this volume aims not to convince you that one is right and the others wrong. Much depends on the context within which engaged actors make their mutually contingent choices about security and the composition and aims of these rivals and allies. Change any of these variables and the appropriate security paradigm to apply to a historical case or circumstance will change, too. This volume seeks to help you make up your own mind in a domain of human thought, decision, and action that is fundamentally contested. It purports to aid you to participate in the debate over what course to follow without dictating the path you will choose, presumably aided by considerations and alternative choices advanced by each school of security.

Conclusions

Before we proceed further, let's see what we have learned from classical theorists. Hobbes, Clausewitz and Thucydides are not important because they had definitive answers for our understanding of security. Their importance lies in their ability to define the security dilemma in universal terms. It is not a problem just for the Greeks, British, or Germans, the respective societies in which our triumvirate lived in widely separated eras and in which they sought to create the political and moral conditions to ensure the security of their societies within which their societies could flourish. Security confronts all human societies. No less is this true of our times. Only if the problem of security is understood in its several, key dimensions, as a continuing and inescapable social problem, can apt historically bound solutions be found to provisionally relax if not conclusively resolve it. The breadth and depth of their contributions are starter kits for thinking about the problem.

As we proceed, it will become clearer that these classical writers and their critics are joined by other inventive and influential theorists in their attempts to generalize or universalize their positions about security. It's that quest for broad generalizations – to explain and understand security – that is the driving force behind the systematic study of phenomena endemic to the human condition as we have come to know it. Classical writers have shown that it is possible to generalize across historical time and space. They depict what humans say and do. They take humans as they are. How they behave in one historical era can be replicated in other times. There is an invisible linkage across centuries between Thucydides' Greece (fifth century BC), Hobbes' England (seventeenth century AD), and Clausewitz's Prussia (nineteenth century). However much humans and the societies that existed in each epoch may have differed in language, customs, economic development, socio-political institutions, religious beliefs, or culture, they faced similar problems posed by the security dilemma. That dilemma presents itself at all of the levels of analysis identified in chapter 1.

Hobbes exposed the logic of violence and coercive threats between and among humans. He demonstrated that what was "real" about humans is that they have different, diverse, and conflicting preferences about what they want from each other to suit their wishes. They want different outcomes from these exchanges with their kind. Failing to get what they want – their way – by non-violent means, they resort to force and threats where opportunities arise to compel others to cooperate with them on their terms. The result is an ongoing war of all against all underlying every human exchange. For Hobbes, everyone loses in a world moving from anarchy to chaos. Unless arrested by an awesome force, the Leviathan, which can assure the social conditions needed for physical survival, economic development and the perfection and nurturing of civilization are sacrificed to ceaseless internecine conflict. The security dilemma is rooted, therefore, in individuals and in their conflicting personal and social preferences. We have met the enemy and the enemy is you and me. No matter that we might be Greeks, English, Germans, Americans, Chinese or Indians.

In turn, Clausewitz and Thucydides expose the security dilemma between states and societies. They clarify the security dilemma, posed by the existence of interacting societies and states. Not unlike Hobbes' projection of the endgame of power between individuals, Clausewitz grasped the inexorable tendency of force against force to move toward pure war, unless limited by political aims and clear and calibrated moral purposes. Thucydides likewise recognized these limits in his explanation of Athens' descent from a position of hegemony, consensually acknowledged by the other Greek city-states, to defeat in a generation, as it sought to impose its rule on allies and adversaries alike. Its determination to expand its empire by military conquest beyond its material power to realize its excessive political ambitions unwittingly undermined the security it so desperately sought.

Clausewitz understood, too, that the security dilemma was embedded in a nation-state system. It is co-extensive with a system of sovereign states. Each claims a monopoly of legitimate violence over its populations and the territory over which it asserts its sovereignty. Under these conditions, each state must arm or seek allies with arms to ensure its security and its vital interests. If it arms too much, its adversaries will do likewise. All risk pushing their conflict to its pure form. If one or the other fails to arm enough, they are vulnerable to the intimidation of its rival or even once close allies. Its vulnerability may well tempt others to take advantage of its weakness.

The triumvirate agrees that some form of countervailing force, guided by human reason and calculation, is needed to resolve or relax the security dilemma. Hobbes tried to solve the problem between members of a society through the creation of a Leviathan or state possessing a monopoly of legitimate violence. If the sovereign could deliver personal safety at home and protect the lives and property of citizens from foreign depredations, the sovereign would have met its part of the contract with the citizens of the state. In providing order, the state would have legitimated its possession and use of force and violence.

In the same vein, Clausewitz and Thucydides agree that the problem of violence in relations between states and societies has to be addressed by the construction of countervailing force. All three also agree that this ingredient of force is only a necessary but not a sufficient element for a durable solution to the security dilemma. A human and natural problem – the security dilemma – can only be solved by a human solution. That is, the self-interests of individuals, states and societies must take account of those of others. That generates a political and moral imperative to contain violence to preclude its frustration of human purposes and design.

All this, of course, begs the question of what these restraints should be. They may be so broad, ill defined and uncompromising that they may actually spur movement toward the pure endgame of force. That is the lesson of the Napoleonic wars, World Wars I and II, and implicitly, the superpowers' nuclear arms race of the Cold War. On the one hand, heinous and morally nauseous institutions – slavery – and repulsive social outrages – genocide – have been arrested by the exercise of power and force. That is the story of the American Civil War and the defeat of Nazi Germany. If the South had won the war, slavery would have been institutionalized for many decades to come until its passing, if ever. The Nazi solution to legitimate governance was racism and the Holocaust – scarcely the foundation for a just and peaceful order encompassing the vital interests of all members.

These examples pose the paradox of using force to free people. Human rights, democratic values, national independence, and self-determination depend on the use or threat of force within and outside the state. Yet one plays with fire, as the Athenians learned, in using force. Even when in the service of ennobling purpose, its use still generates the dilemmas of choice in which the exercise of power can quickly become at fundamental odds with claims of justice, right, or religious strictures. The Melians would be among the first to second this proposition. On reflection, the Athenians might also in light of their defeat as a consequence of the overextension of their power. Unless disciplined to human design, force against force spirals out of control to a Hobbesian endgame. In moving toward its pure form, it becomes senseless. Meaning or sense is not carried by force. It emerges from the political and moral values justifying the use of violence.

However difficult or intractable the problem of reconciling violence with moral and political claims, our triumvirate keeps open the timeless debate between the realization of human values and the violence pervading the social exchanges of humans in pursuit of what they want. What is compelling about the understanding of the human condition of classical theorists is that they squarely confront the problem of violence and its control, even as, paradoxically, they envision no final solution to human exchanges and interaction – individual, group, inter-societal or interstate – that does not imply the decision to use *or not* to use force to effect a desired outcome. Humans are free to succumb tragically to the limitless demands of countervailing violence. Or, they can strive to shape the material conditions under which they act to advance their purposes by other means, an option and strategy that the members of our triumvirate nurture and preserve. A theory of security must account both for the potentially limitless expansion of violence and for the limits placed on force. Violence and the security dilemma that it prompts invite human thought and ingenuity to advance human purposes by non-violent means.

If the triumvirate offers a good start on this journey toward a comprehensive security theory, they can hardly be said to have the last word. Critics of these writers also have much to say of value in deepening our knowledge of security, how it relates to the world around us, and how we might cope with this pervasive imperative. Rather than assume that there is one, irrefutable position on security and security studies, it would seem more sensible to recognize that there are contending points of view. The aim of the security analyst or theorist then is less to unreflectively embrace one or the other of these contending views to the exclusion of the others than to be able to weigh the explanatory power each has to offer depending on the security problem at hand. This also implies an ability to discriminate among the solutions advanced by these rival schools to resolve a security problem at hand. No one suit fits all; no one paradigm trumps others. Learning to pick and choose and to establish criteria for these choices is the principal learning tool to devise, develop, and apply. Security studies should draw on any body of thought and human experience that helps to gain a hold on reality. Learning to make these discriminations will preoccupy our attention in the following chapters now that we have some crude tools to work with.

The next chapter will construct a "laboratory test" not only for classical thinkers but modern partisans and critics of their approach. Once this laboratory is up and going, we will use it to test the explanatory power of prevailing theories competing for our attention and approval by applying the criteria for falsification outlined by Imre Lakatos in chapter 1.

Discussion questions

1. Why does Hobbes believe that, absent a Leviathan, humans will devolve into a condition of a war of all against all in which life will be "solitary, poore, nasty, brutish, and short?" Do you believe that this is an accurate and convincing representation of the underlying state of the human condition and that Hobbes' solution makes sense and is justified?
2. In what ways does the modern state play the role of Hobbes' Leviathan and in what ways does it go beyond his conception? Do all states today provide the security and order that Hobbes' Leviathan is expected to provide?
3. Does a decentralized system of nation-states, each claiming to be sovereign and possessing a monopoly of legitimate violence, pose any of the same problems associated with anarchy described by Hobbes in the relations of individuals to each other?
4. Distinguish between Carl von Clausewitz's concepts of "pure" and "real" war. What are the principal checks on a real war from devolving into a pure war?
5. What are the specific objections raised by the Melians to the Athenian demand that Melos abandon its neutrality and become an ally of Athens in its war against Sparta? What are the specific responses of the Athenians to these objections and why do they insist that the power struggle and war with Sparta compels Athens to make Melos an ally?
6. What is the value of thinking through the logic of coercive power in the pure terms relied upon by the triumvirate of Hobbes, Clausewitz, and Thucydides to understand the security dilemmas confronting peoples and states in ordering their affairs today?

Suggestions for further reading

Carl von Clausewitz (1976), *On War*, Princeton: Princeton University Press. This is the most reader friendly of the translations of Clausewitz's work. Michael Howard and Peter Paret, the editors and translators, provide useful historical background and keen analysis of Clausewitz's major contributions to the theory and practice of war. Their informed commentary is free of the polemics associated with some evaluations on Clausewitz's thinking; these accuse him of advocating total warfare and of inspiring the strategic planning of the European states that resulted in the carnage of World War I.

Thomas Hobbes (1997), *Leviathan*, New York: W. W. Norton. Of the several available translations of Hobbes, this volume, edited by Richard E. Flathman and Daniel Johnson, furnishes rich and informed notes to guide the reader as well as commentaries by noted Hobbesian scholars.

For recent interpretations of classical realism and whether it maps with prevailing realist theory, see Daniel Garst(1989), "Thucydides and Neorealism," *International Studies Quarterly* 33: 3–27, and Richard Ned Lebow (2003), *The Tragic Vision of Politics; Ethics, Interests, and Orders*, Cambridge, UK: Cambridge University Press.

Donald Kagan (2003), *The Peloponnesian War*, New York: Viking. This recent volume caps a series of volumes published by one of the foremost scholars on Thucydides and the Peloponnesian War. It provides important historical background to Thucydides' commentary and the war itself.

S. Sara Monoson and Michael Loriaux (1998), "The Illusion of Power and the Disruption of Moral Norms: Thucydides' Critique of Periclean Policy," *American Political Science Review* 92: 285–97. While this volume, following traditional practice, associates Thucydides with realist thought, it sides with a growing body of scholarship that Thucydides' account of the war was not intended as a defense of power politics. Rather, it was to explicate the self-destructive consequences of policies emptied of moral content and contemptuous of prudent norms guiding the conduct of public affairs. This article and its citations open the reader to this body of scholarship.

Thucydides (1998), *The Peloponnesian War*, New York: W. W. Norton. This volume, translated by Walter Blanco with editorial assistance from Jennifer Tolbert Roberts, presents very helpful background notes for the student in reading Thucydides as well as useful charts and historical material to follow the complexities of the war and its many actors.

Dennis H. Wrong (1994), *The Problem of Order: What Unites and Divides Society*, Cambridge, MA: Harvard University Press. This is a thoughtful and probing sociological treatment of the problem of order, which updates and relates Hobbesian thought to contemporary international relations.

3   Testing security theories: explaining the rise and demise of the Cold War

Hobbes, Clausewitz, and Thucydides laid the foundation for security studies. Their work has stood the test of time. They demonstrated that humans could step out of their own time and look beyond their own particular historically defined security problems to generalize about the security behavior of actors across different societies and eras. They compressed space and time in explaining security. If they can do that, there is no reason why we can't, too, and build on the foundations they laid to fit our times and needs. Security can be subject to systematic study. Generalizations can be validated by reference to the thinking, decisions, and actions of humans and their agents, like states and international organizations.

This triumvirate has also shown that force and coercion have a distinctive logic. Whether it can be directed to human purposes depends on the ability of actors to discipline force to their strategic, political and socioeconomic interests and moral aims. Absent meaning, value, and political purpose in directing the use or threat of violence, competing actors are induced to submit to its logic, unmixed and unconstrained by any other humanly created limit. They are led rationally toward Hobbes' endgame or a war of all against all or toward Clausewitz's more narrowly conceived conception of pure war, as a duel between two rivals to the death or the subjugation of one to the other.

These insights are a good start toward the study of security. They are scarcely enough to address the complex problems raised by international security today under conditions of growing globalization. There have been profound changes in warfare and in the many ways that actors, state and non-state, can threaten each other by force since these theorists first posed the possibility of a science of security. These new dimensions of security must inform our security theories. The inability of the seven prevailing security schools of thought to reconcile their rival explanations, understanding, and methods of studying security also evidences the formidable obstacles to progress in this vital field. How do we distinguish and discriminate between the contradictory claims of these schools?

How do we know which school and paradigm to follow? Which merits our support? Is one more apt to be useful than another for some circumstances than others?

Devising a test of security theories: the Cold War

What we need is a test to evaluate the claims of these schools. Devising such a test will not be easy, much less conflict free. A test has to meet stringent criteria if it is to be accepted as valid and reliable. It clearly must not depend on the assumptions and expected behavior of the paradigm or approach that is being evaluated. If the test incorporates the assumptions of the school of thought that it is testing, it could scarcely challenge that school to which it would be implicitly captive. To minimize circular reasoning, the test should not favor one school over another and evaluate each equally. Showing that states and peoples have been engaged in seemingly ceaseless war, for example, does not necessarily demonstrate that they are unable, as some theorists contend, to resolve their differences peacefully or are incapable of constructing institutions to ensure their collective security. Nor, conversely, does evidence that some states and peoples have learned to live in harmony prove that they will not fall out at a later time.

Especially to be resisted is the seductive incentive to cite biased examples or skewed and incomplete evidence to support a particular view about the tendency of humans and their societies toward conflict and cooperation, while ignoring or suppressing dissonant and dissenting fact and informed opinion. This failing is hardly confined to the non-expert. A much celebrated analysis of how important thinkers through the centuries, including our triumvirate, explained the tendency of humans either toward conflict or toward cooperation showed persuasively that they all made certain assumptions about the inherent goodness or evil of humans and about the impact of their socio-economic and political institutions on their behavior. These first moves or "priors" were stipulated, implicitly or explicitly, but never conclusively validated by these theorists in terms of their presumed consequences. The typical approach of each theorist, as described by Kenneth Waltz in this analysis of social thought, was to provide selective evidence to support a preferred "image" of human conduct and its implications for international security.[1]

We want to design a test that in some way captures the rival assumptions made by competing security schools of thought and their expectations about actor behavior. Yet we want a test that exploits our own

---

[1] Waltz (1959).

observations and interpretations of the "facts" as involved and active participants in defining the scope and significance of security challenges in our lives. In this connection, it is useful to recall Imre Lakatos' prudent advice that one test does not necessarily disprove a theory.[2] We will need a series of competing tests conducted by many researchers over time to strengthen or weaken support for one security theory over another. So the test we devise in this chapter should be understood as an introduction to the complex problem of testing our generalizations about the security behavior of actors, and not a definitive method to determine conclusively which point of view to adopt or reject.

As one proceeds in security studies, reflected in the alternative explanations of security advanced in chapters 4–7, it becomes readily apparent that even the tests constructed to validate propositions are themselves sharply contested matters. Tests of validity are no less open to question and criticism than the propositions they test. The aim, again, is not to develop an infallible test of security paradigms, a currently elusive objective. Our aim, rather, is to acquire the requisite conceptual skills and tools and sufficient historical knowledge and sensitivity to empirical evidence to enter debates over security as an informed participant and evaluator of knowledge and methods of learning in this vital area and as a credible evaluator or arbitrageur of rival claims.

The evolution of the rise and collapse of the Cold War between the United States and the Soviet Union from the end of World War II in 1945 to the implosion of the Soviet Union in 1991 has several properties, aside from those covered in the Introduction, that recommend it as a test of currently contending security theories. First, much of the history of the Cold War would appear to initially conform to the assumptions of our first group of theorists. The struggle for global dominance between these two superpowers and their allies, clients, and satellites generated incentives for the development of state military capabilities unprecedented in human history. Moscow and Washington constructed three mutually reinforcing military systems. Central was what Herman Kahn darkly characterized as two superpower nuclear Doomsday Machines, each capable of annihilating its rival in less than a hour – and of potentially destroying much of human life on the planet.[3] Linked to these Doomsday Machines was the creation of enormous conventional and regional nuclear forces in the center of Europe, where Western democratic armies met those of the Soviet Union to defeat Nazi Germany. These two competitors for hegemony,

---

[2] Lakatos (1970, 1978) and Lakatos and Musgrave (1970).

[3] Kahn (1960). The threat posed by these systems, even in diminished size since the end of the Cold War, still threaten the life of the species, as an eminent British cosmologist argues: Rees (2003).

much like Athens and Sparta in their struggle for leadership of the Greek peninsula, also enlisted or coercively induced other states and peoples into their global alliance structures. These superpower military systems, if unleashed in a spasm, would have moved rapidly toward the Clausewitz notion of pure war. These three, interdependent military responses to their global struggle were rationalized by both states as mutually reinforcing to support their defense, deterrent, and war-fighting strategies. Dominance at each level of armed conflict was conceived as mutually contingent to produce overall strategic superiority; the synergism was widely believed by decision-makers on both sides to be indispensable to win or prevail in the global competition.

Second, the scientific knowledge, technological innovation, and economic resources mobilized to sustain these superpower systems exposed the shortcomings of classic models of security. These dimensions of the Cold War transformed the struggle in at least two fundamental ways. On the one hand, the battlefields of the Cold War extended well beyond the real or possible clash of arms to the creation of self-sustaining and enlarging techno-scientific and economic systems to furnish the military capabilities, trained manpower, and logistical infrastructure to ensure the competitiveness of these superpower military machines.

On the other hand, these taxing requirements were made even more complex by yet another requirement for success in the Cold War. Domestic populations of the twentieth century have sought not only security but also increased material welfare, a product of modernization driven successively by the Industrial and Information Revolutions. States are expected to create the conditions both for security and welfare. Somehow states have to reconcile the competing demands of order and security and the violent capabilities on which they depend with policies that also respond to the expectations and demands of populations for rising and sustainable standards of living.[4]

The Cold War became then a struggle for military dominance as well as a test of two competing solutions to solve the welfare demands of the peoples of two competing coalitions. In its fullest dimensions, the Cold War was a contest between two models for sustained global economic development. The Western coalition offered an open, liberal economic system propelled by global markets and ceaseless innovation as its solution to security and welfare. The Soviet Union and its coalition rested their fate on centralized, state ownership and control of the means of production; bureaucratic, not market, determination of investment priorities and what goods and services would be available to consumers in allocating scarce human and material resources; and coercively enforced governmental

---

[4] Rostow (1971).

regulations, covering all economic activities, ranging from monetary flows and trade to consumer choices and employment.[5]

Third, the Cold War went well beyond the material dimensions sketched in these security and welfare imperatives. It was also a struggle over legitimacy before the courts of national and world public opinion. Legitimacy as a Cold War imperative compelled the superpowers to justify their conflicting solutions to global security and welfare imperatives and their self-assumed roles as leaders of their competing coalitions. They also had to validate the principles of legitimacy that purportedly conferred on them the authority to rule other peoples and their own populations. Joseph Stalin, the Soviet leader during World War II, told Milovan Djilas in 1945: "This war is not as in the past; whoever occupies a territory also imposes on it his own social system. Everyone imposes his own system as far as his army can reach. It cannot be otherwise."[6] The West did likewise in marginalizing the role of Communist parties in democratic coalitions and in undermining Communist or Communist-leaning governments around the world.

Fourth, the Cold War was truly global, even more extensive in reach and impact than World Wars I and II. Engaged and ensnared were all humans, whether by choice or necessity. This was the first instance in the evolution of the species, since its emergence out of Africa over a million years ago,[7] that all the populations of the world had been drawn into the vortex of a global struggle. For the first time, too, the conflict put into question the very future of the human species, quite apart from the localized national, ethnic, communal interests of the peoples and states striving for ascendancy. The scope of the Cold War engaged all of the actors and principal factors identified (albeit differentially) by the security theories to be evaluated in succeeding chapters. States, the system of state relations, global markets, multinational corporations, non-governmental organizations (NGOs), and intergovernmental organizations (IGOs), and most of the world's populations – all were implicated by choice or necessity in the Cold War struggle. The Cold War, if viewed as a set of all conceivable interactions between and among relevant actors engaged in

---

[5] Kornai (1992) provides the most comprehensive treatment of command economies and their shortcomings.

[6] Quoted in Koslowski (1994: 140). The determination of conquering armies to impose their values and way of life on others was not especially unique to the Cold War. It is characteristic of religious wars through the centuries, dating back in Christian times to the Crusades and to secular ideological struggles commencing with the French Revolution. The entire Lebow volume should be consulted for incisive critiques of the failure of international relations theory to anticipate the collapse of the Cold War. Useful, too, is the historical overview of the evolution of the international system since the end of World War II to the present in Keylor (2003).

[7] Diamond (1992).

security relations in international relations, offers a sufficiently inclusive set of data to test the security claims of contending schools of thought.

Clearly, in the brief space available to this discussion, all of these actors and factors bearing on security cannot be exhaustively addressed. What is important for our purposes is establishing the claim that the Cold War seriously challenges prevailing security paradigms and approaches to explain the Cold War. When applied to seven theories or approaches to security in chapters 4–7, the strengths and weaknesses of each perspective is exposed to analysis and evaluation. The Cold War test putatively provides a level playing field on which these contesting models can compete for our assent and support to understand and explain security today. A security theory should be able to provide some plausible explanation for the rise and demise of the Cold War. This challenge is warranted given the global scope of this struggle, the billions of actors engaged, the trillions of dollars expended, the advanced scientific and technological know-how committed, the best and brightest minds mobilized for the conflict, and the tens of millions who served as combatants in the Cold War struggle and in the many local hot wars associated with the conflict. If a theory of security cannot furnish insights about this pervasive confrontation of the world's peoples and states, then it loses ground in the competition of ideas about what explains the security behavior of actors. If a security paradigm cannot explain the Cold War, can it be relied upon to help us explain the dramatic and sweeping changes affecting humans today as they are increasingly entangled in what appears to be inexorable processes of globalization? If the central issue of human security is increasingly enmeshed in these processes of widening and deepening interdependence, then we will have to look farther afield than traditional thought to capture these processes of change and their implications for using, threatening or desisting from violence in getting what actors want from each other.

What appears new to the human condition is the widening scope, intensity, accumulating density, real-time speed and impact, cascading effects and synergisms of human exchanges across the globe over an increasing number of domains of vital interest to humans. The latter pointedly concern the security of persons, property, and the state as well as the very existence of the many and diverse societies of this global society which are largely the pre-global products of their particular histories and social evolution.[8] Under these new and revolutionary conditions, a single test of a security paradigm, however inclusive like the Cold War,

---

[8] The diversity of human societies despite the converging biological evolution of humans around the globe is addressed with remarkable clarity and force in the work of Jared Diamond (1997, 1992).

is the beginning, not the end, of the search for validity and reliability. If we should be mindful of Imre Lakatos' prudent warning that one test is insufficient to reject a theory, we should also be skeptical of any theory that fails to address the Cold War. An explanation of the security behavior of actors risks rejection unless it can generate a research program to compensate for this shortfall in its explanatory power. The Cold War serves as a plausible starting point for testing. Not so much is claimed for this test of validity that it, too, is suspect, but enough – as the justification just outlined claims – to warrant its use for the purposes of this volume.

Organization of the discussion

The discussion is divided into two sections. The first outlines the evolution of superpower military forces at nuclear and conventional levels and the complex global alliances each superpower fashioned, not always with desired results, in their struggle for world hegemony. Since the major actors in security matters remain states, the focus is on interstate security relations as well as on the pressures exerted on states by the Cold War bipolar system – on the superpowers and on other states of the system.

The next section broadens the analysis to describe and explain the transnational and domestic pressures bearing on superpower security decisions and actions. These levels of analysis and the forces and factors associated with them were particularly pronounced in the Soviet Union. Included as a third level of analysis will be the impact of continuing scientific discovery, technological innovation – what Joseph Schumpeter termed "creative destruction" – and global markets.[9] This level of analysis will be important in explaining the security behavior of the superpowers. It is particularly critical to understand why fundamental changes in Soviet security policy were initiated as a precondition for integrating the Soviet Union into Western-dominated global institutions dedicated to scientific discovery, technological innovation, global markets, and democratically determined social change.

The domestic pressures on state leaders to solve welfare and popular demands for a say in their government, the fourth level of analysis, noted in table 1.1, will also be shown to play a decisive role in shaping and shoving the security behavior of states. The break-up of the Soviet Union and its empire pivots critically on the linkage between these domestic pressures and the external forces exerted by Western institutions and practices possessed of global scope and impact. The factors and actors captured by the Cold War test encompass all of the levels of actor behavior with which this volume is concerned. When security is viewed from these

---

[9] Schumpeter (1954: 1026ff.).

four perspectives or levels of analysis, explaining the central decision of security behavior – whether to use force or not in pursuit of security interests – both enlarges the study of security and yet nests this sub-set of human concerns within broader ambit of international relations theory and practice.

I.   The rise and demise of the Cold War: struggle for hegemony[10]

The Cold War continued the Thirty Years War among the big powers for global hegemony bracketed by World Wars I and II from 1914 to 1945.[11] The German imperial bid in World War I for European and world dominance was defeated by a coalition of democratic states, principally the United Kingdom, France, and the United States. The latter's late entry into the war in 1917 tipped the balance against the Central powers of the German and Austro-Hungarian empires. Russia as an Entente power in alliance with the Western democracies withdrew from the war in the wake of the Bolshevik Revolution in October 1917, which created the Soviet Union. A generation later, the Soviet Union joined the Western democracies to defeat Nazi Germany and Japan as challengers for global hegemony. Had the latter won World War II, they would have essentially gained control over most of the world's populations and their resources, replacing Europe's empires by its dominating rule over a defeated United States, Britain and Soviet Union.

The winning World War II coalition was fundamentally flawed.[12] The two superpowers which emerged from the war were unable to reconcile their profoundly conflicting differences. These initially revolved around the question of Germany's political future and whether it would be aligned with one or the other of the superpowers.[13] Also at issue was the seizure of power by local Communist parties throughout Eastern Europe with the complicity of Soviet occupying forces. These disputes were further complicated by differences between the United States and the Soviet Union over the civil war in Greece and Soviet pressures on Iran and Turkey for territorial concessions and increased political influence. The Soviet

---

[10] The history of the Cold War has spawned an enormous and growing literature. The brief presented here is drawn from many sources, the principal elements of which are cited throughout the text of this chapter. See Keylor (2001: 251ff.) and his extensive bibliographic references (568–87). The analogy of the Thirty Years War and the interwar global conflict is drawn from Keylor. Useful for US policy up to the Reagan administration of 1980 is Gaddis (1982). For the Soviet Union, the works of Raymond Garthoff, who chronicles the Cold War from that perspective, particularly with respect to Moscow's geo-political policies, are relevant. See, for example, Garthoff (1995).

[11] Keylor (2001) develops this argument at length.

[12] Kennan (1984a) makes this point.

[13] McCallister (2002).

explosion of a nuclear device in late August of 1949, the loss of China to Communist forces the following December, and the June 1950 attack of Communist North Korea on South Korea – a protectorate of the United States – prompted the militarization of American containment policy and of the Cold War conflict.[14] These discrete conflicts can be understood and rationalized as parts of the superpower struggle for global dominion. As for the military components of this struggle, they evolved simultaneously, if not in synchronous lockstep, on three interrelated battlefields: competition for nuclear superiority, military dominance in Europe, and hegemony over the developing world.

1.   *The global nuclearization of the security dilemma*   The Cold War pivots around the efforts of the superpowers to gain ascendancy by force and coercive threats and to impose their preferred solution to global order and governance on their adversary. The military or coercive limits of the Cold War were defined by the ceaseless and enlarging superpower arms race from the end of World War II in 1945 until the implosion of the Soviet Union in 1991. Central was their nuclear arms competition. Tracing the evolution of US and Soviet strategic nuclear forces during the Cold War is a very complex undertaking.[15] Only highlights can be presented here. Each side sought nuclear superiority, evidenced by the ever-expanding war-fighting nuclear weapon systems they constructed. Neither succeeded in this quest. They also cooperated, as sketched below, to place mutually agreed controls on their nuclear competition. These fleeting and fragile controls did not appreciably inhibit either side from seeking a nuclear breakthrough. Superiority was defined by a competitor's capacity to ultimately win a nuclear war if deterrence of a rival's attack on one's vital national interests failed. Both sides also assumed that political and psychological leverage in their deadly bargaining for advantage would ensue if a dominant nuclear posture could be achieved.

   Given space limits, it may be helpful to start at the end rather than the beginning of the superpower nuclear arms race. Table 3.1 outlines the seemingly inexorable expansion of the strategic nuclear forces of the United States and the Soviet Union during the Cold War. Between 1950 and 1990, the United States arsenal grew from 400 strategic nuclear warheads to over 12,000; missile launchers and bombers also increased in number from 462 to over 1,900. The Soviet Union's nuclear forces jumped from 84 nuclear warheads in 1956 after a late start to over 10,000 four decades later; launchers also increased from 22 long-range systems

---

[14] These events and their implications for militarizing the Cold War are developed in Kolodziej (1966: 33–178) and in Schilling, Hammond, and Snyder (1966).
[15] Ball (1980), Freedman (1989), Herken (1985), Kaplan (1999), and Nolan (1989).

Table 3.1 *US and Soviet nuclear strategic forces: 1950–2000*

UNITED STATES

Year	ICBMs	Warheads	SLBMs	Warheads	Bombers	Warheads	Totals Launchers	Totals Warheads
1950					462	400	462	400
1960	12	12	32	32	1,515	3,083	1,559	3,127
1970	1,054	1,244	656	656	390	3,393	2,100	5,239
1980	1,054	2,144	592	4,896	376	3,568	2,022	10,608
1990	1,000	2,440	592	5,152	311	4,885	1,903	12,477
2000	659	2,325	448	3,616	300	1,578	1,407	7,519

SOVIET UNION (to 1990) RUSSIAN FEDERATION (2000)*

Year	ICBMs	Warheads	SLBMs	Warheads	Bombers	Warheads	Totals Launchers	Totals Warheads
1956					22	84	22	84
1960	4	4	30	30	104	320	144	354
1970	1,361	1,361	317	287	157	568	1,985	2,216
1980	1,398	5,002	990	1,910	157	568	2,545	7,480
1990	1,398	6,612	940	2,804	162	855	2,500	10,271
2000	750	3,444	436	2,024	80	626	1,266	6,094

*excludes 22 launchers and 208 warheads in the Ukraine.
Source: Natural Resources Defense Council, *US – USSR Strategic Offensive Nuclear Forces* (Washington, DC, 1990); Arms Control Association, *Fact Sheets* (2001).

to 2,500 in 1990. If these had been unleashed, all human material interests, political aims and moral purposes would have been sacrificed to a final and decisive nuclear exchange. What hath humans wrought – both by authoritarian command and popular consent? The space potentially occupied by all real or conceivable human exchanges between Americans and Soviets and between their respective states was virtually enveloped by the violent forces aimed by each superpower at each other. The logic of "pure war," depicted by Clausewitz, overwhelmed all restraining or disciplining moral or political interests, aims, or values.

The term "strategic" is often used in security studies. During the Cold War it was typically associated with superpower policies designed to achieve defined military objectives by countering, containing, controlling or eliminating an opponent's military forces. This restrictive sense of the term "strategic" contrasts with this volume's broader understanding of security and, by implication, of strategy as policies calculated to achieve defined political objectives by deliberately choosing to use or not to use force. From the Cold War's constrained perspective, strategic forces are those capable of defeating an opponent's military forces. In the case of nuclear weapons, this would require nothing less than disarming a rival's nuclear forces before he could annihilate all or most of one's own population and territory. Military planners on both sides relentlessly pursued this elusive objective. Table 3.1 traces the technological advances in launchers and warheads that comprised the evolving and expanding strategic nuclear forces of both sides. Warhead explosive power is measured in megatons or millions of tons of TNT. By the end of the Cold War, each side had constructed 2,000–2,500 long-range launchers – ground- and submarine-based intercontinental ballistic missiles (ICBMs and SLBMs) and bombers – capable of reaching targets around the globe in a matter of minutes. These were supplemented by more slowly reacting bomber forces, assigned the mission of destroying targets otherwise missed by a full-scale missile attack.

Military planners and political leaders understood early on that nuclear weapons were weapons of terror and mass destruction.[16] They were not calibrated means to achieve defined political objectives, but a substitute for those aims and the moral claims underlying them. They were no less aware of the difficulty of achieving superiority sufficient to disarm an adversary to dictate the terms of surrender. Even a few surviving weapons would be sufficient to visit so much death and destruction on an aggressor that no conceivable rational political or moral purpose would be served by using these weapons. These limitations, paradoxically, acted more as

---

[16] Brodie (1946).

a stimulus for the arms race than as an invitation to find a non-violent escape from the nuclear security dilemma. For almost half a century, both sides pursued policies, defined by the military plans and nuclear capabilities they developed, that mapped well with the expectations of behavior of the Hobbesian endgame or Clausewitz's conceptualization of "pure war." The political and practical obstacles that precluded the realization of pure war during Clausewitz's lifetime in the early nineteenth century until the first atomic attack on Hiroshima in 1945 were essentially surmounted by the destructive capacity and long-range striking power possessed by each side.

At the risk of simplifying an extremely complex history, critical elements of which are still shrouded in secret government documents, the evolution of nuclear capabilities by each side was decided by sliding and shifting answers that decision-makers gave to the question of "How much is enough?" in the way of military capabilities to ensure an effective deterrent and defense posture.[17] On one side were those who contended that a small, invulnerable force of nuclear weapons was enough to deter an adversary from attacking a state's vital interests. These interests were viewed to extend to the territory and population of a state as well as to the protection of its principal allies. Invulnerable forces were those which could not be destroyed by an enemy attack, even a so-called "bolt from the blue." Submarine-launched missiles, eventually possessed by both sides, were especially suited for this purpose. Surviving forces under this theory of deterrence would be sufficient to inflict losses on an adversary that would far outweigh any conceivable rational gain from attacking a state or its vital interests. Such a force was defined by American strategists as the ability of the nation's nuclear forces to survive a surprise attack and retain enough nuclear striking power to destroy one-quarter to one-third of an adversary's population and at least 50 to 66 percent of his economic infrastructure in the prompt and delayed effects of nuclear weapons.[18] The initial blast and heat generated by a nuclear explosion would largely achieve this level of devastation in the prompt effects of nuclear weapons. Radioactive fallout would subsequently make much of an adversary's territory unfit for habitation for a long period of time. Since both the Soviet Union and the United States were able to build such systems, both were said to have the capacity for mutual assured destruction, or MAD.

Neither superpower accepted these constraints in designing and building its strategic nuclear forces. As table 3.1 recounts, both far exceeded the limits of a MAD strategy and the nuclear forces it required. In contrast to the announced claims of both sides that they were reconciled to a minimum deterrent posture of surviving a nuclear attack and of having

---

[17] Enthoven and Smith (1971).   [18] Craig and Jungermann (1986) and Lewis (1979).

abandoned the search for a force capable of disarming their rival, each worked relentlessly to achieve this daunting strategic objective. In policy circles, MAD was criticized for indiscriminately targeting urban populations. An adversary, they argued, had little incentive to avoid striking its rival's cities under MAD. A 1960 study of the RAND Corporation for the Air Force estimated that a spasm attack by the United States or the Soviet Union would result in 110–150 million US and 40–75 million Soviet deaths.[19] Small nuclear forces on which MAD strategy depended were alleged to be vulnerable to a disarming attack. Vulnerability invited attack. For many throughout the Cold War, the balance of nuclear power was not stable, but fragile and delicate.[20] An adversary was expected to cheat and defect from attempts at cooperation to slow or stabilize the nuclear arms race when opportunity and gain commanded such a move.

Most decisively for partisans of a war-fighting strategy were its purported implications for deterrence. The credibility of an adversary's nuclear deterrent forces was argued to depend finally on its possible use. The stipulation of this assumption forced thinking about actually using these weapons. The principal targets of a war-fighting posture were the adversary's nuclear capabilities. Their swift and sure elimination, if possible, would limit damage to one's cities and military forces. Nuclear superiority would also presumably contribute to the control of escalation if hostilities erupted at a non-nuclear level. Nuclear dominance putatively enhanced the likelihood of bringing a war to a quick conclusion on terms favorable to the stronger nuclear power. Finally, a war-fighting nuclear strategy was supposed to underwrite a superpower's extension of deterrence protection to allies, since it communicated its determination to any would-be adversary that it would risk its own survival to defend the security interests of its partners.[21]

The Soviet Union no less strove for superiority.[22] Like the United States, it sought to develop capabilities to disarm its rival. Both

---

[19] Schwartz (1983: 138–9).   [20] Wohlstetter (1959).

[21] For a critique of this position based on historical analysis, see George and Smoke (1974); for a critique based, respectively, on political and psychological weaknesses of then prevailing deterrence theory and practice, see Morgan (1983) and Jervis, Lebow, and Stein (1985).

[22] The evolution of Soviet nuclear strategy is far more complex and subtle than can be presented here. The accent is on the tendencies of Soviet and American military nuclear systems, comprising delivery vehicles, warheads, and command and control mechanisms, to move toward a pure war model. However much Soviet and American strategists differed, notably in their conception of the relation of political and moral objectives and the military forces needed to sustain them, their actual behavior in constructing and rationalizing strategic nuclear systems can reasonably be argued, as traced here, to move toward a Clausewitz pure war model. For more comprehensive and exhaustive discussion of the complexities of evolving and necessarily changing Soviet strategy, paralleling the surveys of American nuclear doctrine and policies, see Garthoff (1966, 1990, 1995), Holloway (1984), Kokoshin (1995), and Laird and Herspring (1984).

constructed invulnerable weapon systems, notably submarine-launched missiles, to ride out an attack. They both created nuclear triads to increase the targeting problems of their enemy by sea-, ground- and air-based nuclear weapons. It proved impossible to design or raise sufficient nuclear forces that could fully and definitively disarm an enemy's nuclear weapons, because of their sheer number, dispersion, mobility, and concealment. Notwithstanding these daunting obstacles to achieving a winning first-strike, total warhead firepower on both sides progressively increased as well as the speed of launching these weapons and the number of multiple independently targeted warheads that each launcher could carry. Speed in launching warheads and their accuracy on target – in distances measured by the length of football fields over thousands of miles of travel – added to the target capability of these weapons, primarily against fixed, concrete-reinforced targets.[23] Upwards of 40,000 targets were identified by American military planners. Only a small percentage of US nuclear forces were needed to destroy Soviet cities, since less than a thousand Soviet cities had populations greater than 25,000. There were even fewer population centers in the United States. Superpower nuclear triads were centrally controlled to prevent their inadvertent or unintended use and to ensure that the coordinated use of these complicated and widely dispersed weapon systems could be achieved to ensure maximum efficiency in delivering these weapons on target under the disrupting conditions of an enemy nuclear strike.

Even as the superpowers were unable to resist the logic of pure nuclear war, they were also concerned about preventing a nuclear war neither wished. These concerns generated a seemingly paradoxical incentive to cooperate with an untrustworthy adversary. As American and Soviet strategists recognized, an unregulated nuclear arms race would result in the expansion of nuclear weapons and delivery systems on both sides at great cost without any corresponding increase in security or strategic advantage. Acknowledgment of this dilemma did not preclude an obsessive pursuit by both superpowers of a disarming nuclear capability. Any abandonment or wavering of resolve in pursuing this objective was itself viewed as a weakening of the deterrent regime to preclude an enemy attack.

The risks of this counter-force strategy were manifest. In a crisis deterrence might break down when it was most needed. The pressures to act quickly, almost instantaneously, might prove overpowering in a self-defeating attempt to decrease damage to one's forces and population

---

[23] See Ball (1980), Pringle and Arkin (1983), and Rosenberg (1983) for descriptions of US nuclear targeting plans.

centers.[24] "Use them or lose them" was the strategic-planning apho- rism of the time. These mutually understood constraints prompted the contradictory development of arms control and disarmament negotia- tions to cut the costs and risks of nuclear weapons and to lower the risks of unintended, accidental, inadvertent, or pre-emptive attacks. Within the narrow band of these overlapping interests, strategists reasoned that cooperation with an adversary, determined to win or prevail in a nuclear exchange, was still desirable and mutually advantageous; in a word, it was "rational" for both sides, however contradictory in practice, to cooperate with an untrustworthy foe to avoid an unwanted war, yet to continue to defect in developing a war-fighting posture, dedicated to winning a nuclear war if it erupted or at least to cutting losses to tolerable lev- els of deaths and destruction. These problematic aspirations proved well beyond the capacity of either superpower to realize.[25]

Arms control negotiations crystallized in several treaties and accords. The earliest, reached in the 1960s, resulted in agreements to end testing of nuclear weapons in the atmosphere, to create a hotline useful dur- ing crises to prevent an unwanted war, and to halt the proliferation of nuclear weapons or know-how to third states. A second set of treaties and understandings was reached in the 1970s. The most important was the SALT I treaty, arising from the so-called Strategic Arms Limitations Talks. Signed in June 1972, the Anti-Ballistic Missile (ABM) treaty lim- ited each superpower to two (later amended to one) ABM site. It also prohibited the development, testing, or deployment of sea-, air-, ground- or space-based ABM systems. These constraints were designed to assure both sides that their mutual destructive capabilities would survive an adversary's surprise attack. The SALT II treaty signed in June 1979 rein- forced this agreement. It identified an elaborate set of restrictions on the development and deployment of long-range nuclear launchers. Each side was restricted to 2,250 launchers by the end of 1981. This set of launch- ers was further refined to include no more that 1,320 launchers with MIRVed warheads (Multiple Independently Targeted Vehicle) of which no more than 1,200 could be ballistic missiles and of these no more than 820 could be on ground-based ICBMs. This treaty was never ratified.

[24] Morgan (1983, 2003).
[25] The theoretical rationale for cooperating with a nuclear adversary on political grounds was laid early in Brodie (1973, 1946). A much narrower rational choice framework for cooperation was developed by Thomas Schelling over several works, including one with Morton Halperin: Schelling and Halperin (1958), Schelling (1960, 1966). Not everyone agreed, particularly partisans of counterforce theory that strove to dominate the Soviet Union by overwhelming military force. See, for example, Gray (1984) and the position of Richard Perle, an influential policy-maker in successive Republican administrations since the 1980s in Fitzgerald (2000) *passim.*

President Jimmy Carter withdrew the treaty from the Senate in response to the Soviet invasion of Afghanistan in December 1979.[26]

Even if the treaty had been ratified, it would not have satisfied many strategists on either side. The election of Ronald Reagan in 1980 moved the arms race to a new level of competition. The Soviet Union was accused of breaking its promise to observe SALT II limits. Fears were expressed that Soviet ICBMs had the nuclear throw weight, measured by the number of warheads and their destructive power, of potentially destroying US ground-based systems in a surprise attack. The focus in strategic planning shifted toward building invulnerable yet fast-reacting, reliable, and accurate systems that could reduce Soviet nuclear capabilities, notably its MIRVed systems, if war erupted. Arms control negotiations shifted then from cutting launchers to limiting the number and destructive force of warheads. These concerns transformed the SALT talks into the Strategic Arms Reductions Talks or START. These languished until the eve of the Soviet Union's collapse. Meanwhile, the two sides increased their strategic warhead totals over the 1980s by approximately 2,000 warheads. As the strategic offensive nuclear arms race accelerated, it was given increased impulse by the Reagan administration's announcement of its determination to develop a Strategic Defense Initiative (SDI), or what was derisively termed a Star Wars project. The President presented the plan as a way of rendering nuclear weapons "obsolete and impotent."[27] However, Western critics and their Soviet counterparts viewed SDI as a bid for nuclear supremacy. Rather than slow the arms race, SDI generated compelling incentives to increase offensive nuclear arms to overwhelm an ABM system.[28]

2.   *The Europeanization of the security dilemma*   The second battlefield of the Cold War was Europe, where a large percentage of the world's technologically advanced, modernized, and highly educated human resources were concentrated. Which superpower could command these resources would tilt the balance of power in their global struggle decisively in its favor. In sketching the evolution of the strategic and military capabilities deployed by the superpowers and their allies in this region, it is important to underline that this brief overview suggests greater coherence and consistency in superpower and allied policy-making than a careful and painstaking tracing of the actual historical evolution would

---

[26] These elaborate arms control negotiations in the 1970s and early 1980s are covered in Talbott (1984, 1979).

[27] See *ibid.* for a detailed exposition of the SDI, so-called Star Wars, controversy and its impact on the Cold War and the evolution of the US and Soviet nuclear arms race.

[28] Garthoff (1995).

support.[29] It is well to be reminded that the aim of this modeling exercise of superpower security strategies is to identify the direction of that behavior within the conceptual framework of an ideal or pure model; that is, as if the decisions of relevant actors were not constrained or compromised in moving along the path rationally dictated by a pure model of armed conflict. Other, competing political and socio-economic aims and interests, as limits toward the realization of a pure model of war, while identified below, are given less weight in this explanation of the superpower conflict in Europe to pivot the discussion around the key question of using or not using force to advance a state's security interests. This focus will be enlarged in the second section to include economic and national, ethnic, and cultural identity politics, as factors bearing on political legitimacy – central concerns of the Cold War confrontation.

As background to describing this theatre of the Cold War, it is useful to remember that, from the fifteenth century, European states relentlessly expanded their imperial reach around the globe to impose their rule on other peoples.[30] Their local disputes were *ipso facto* globalized, as two world wars and a Cold War made abundantly clear, however much leaders and peoples may have believed that they were struggling for ascendancy only in Europe or however much they may have tried or believed they were limiting their objectives to the European theatre.[31] While the alliance of a Communist Soviet Union and the Western democracies was strong enough to defeat Germany and Japan as challengers for world hegemony, their profoundly conflicting political interests and values could not be resolved after the war. The coalition broke down almost immediately after the close of hostilities. Europe was rapidly divided into two armed camps. An "Iron Curtain," as British Prime Minister Winston Churchill proclaimed, split Europe and Germany into two segments, respectively under American and Soviet hegemony. This division was subsequently militarized and hardened by the unprecedented build-up of conventional and nuclear armaments in Europe. The European theatre of military conflict was fused to the evolving nuclear superpower struggle. The story of European security during the Cold War is a story of the efforts of the coalitions on both sides, notably the superpowers, to harmonize and rationalize their military defense, deterrent, and war-fighting strategies in Europe as integral elements of a global pursuit for dominance.

The military build-up of the superpower coalitions in Europe can be divided roughly into seven periods. Each constitutes a distinct adaptation

---

[29] DePorte (1986).   [30] McNeill (1963) and Watson (1984, 1992).
[31] Taylor (1954) and other prominent historians also adopt this narrower view of the scope of World War I than this discussion that portrays the field of battle in Europe as just the cockpit of what was by any measure a war for global, not just European, hegemony.

between the competing security pressures exerted by the global nuclear and European arms races. The first period extended from the end of World War II to the outbreak of the Korean War in 1950. The Soviet Union's hold over Eastern Europe tightened during this period. The threat to the West was largely perceived as more political than military. The fall of one country after the other to Communist rule in Eastern Europe and the Sovietization of its occupied segment of Germany spurred the Western liberal states to eliminate national Communist parties from entering their governments and to concentrate on rehabilitating their war-devastated economies and societies to blunt Communist influence at the polls, most imminently in France and Italy.

These efforts were critically supported by American Marshall Plan assistance and by the signing of the North Atlantic Treaty in April 1949. The treaty committed its members to assist each other in meeting threats to their security; an attack on one was considered an attack on all. This pledge was particularly important for the United States. For the first time, since the Franco-American security treaty of 1778, the United States committed itself to come to the defense of another state *before* the outbreak of war. This pledge was designed to deter an attack on Europe's democracies. Whereas America's belated intervention in two world wars served to free its allies after their homelands had been destroyed, the American guarantee was supposed to preclude the outbreak of war. In light of the rapid demobilization of US forces after World War II, the American commitment rested almost exclusively on its nuclear guarantee at the time that the Atlantic Alliance was formed.

The North Korean attack on South Korea in June 1950, linked to the Soviet explosion of an atomic device eleven months earlier, opened the second phase of Cold War in Europe. These shocks militarized the Atlantic Alliance and transformed a guarantee pact into NATO, a multilateral military organization under American leadership. American divisions were permanently stationed in Europe; military assistance replaced economic aid to defend Europe; and an American military commander was appointed to head NATO. The initial twelve NATO states also agreed to rapidly enlarge their conventional forces in Europe to counter what was perceived as Soviet military superiority in the region. A plan to raise and equip 96 NATO divisions and to field 9,000 aircraft by 1954 was agreed upon.

To reach those ambitious goals, the United States pressed for the remilitarization of West Germany and the incorporation of its 12 projected divisions into an integrated NATO command. Profound allied reservations about rearming a state, which had initiated two world wars were eventually overcome. West Germany joined the NATO alliance and placed its national military forces under multinational command. The Soviet Union responded by hurriedly organizing the Warsaw Pact to counterbalance the Western move. By 1955 not only was Europe divided politically but its security was framed by the creation of two opposed military blocs and driven by the conventional and nuclear arms competition of these alliances.

The third phase from 1953 to 1960 is marked by the rapid nuclearization of the European theatre. NATO rapidly abandoned the goal of building overwhelming conventional forces to match Soviet forces. The principal constraint was economic.[32] President Eisenhower and his chief advisors were convinced that the United States economy could not sustain a massive conventional build-up in Europe. European states faced the same problem of reconciling military and economic imperatives. NATO and American planning for Europe shifted from conventional forces to a nuclear posture. Tactical nuclear weapons and rocket and missile launchers carrying nuclear warheads were introduced into NATO forces. At their height, some 7,000 tactical nuclear weapons and hundreds of complementary theatre nuclear arms were deployed in Europe. The Warsaw Pact followed suit to meet the NATO challenge. The Eisenhower administration announced a new doctrine of "Massive Retaliation" to rationalize this shift. Under this doctrine, the United States and NATO would rely on nuclear deterrence to counter the Warsaw Pact threat to Europe. As American Secretary of State John Foster Dulles proclaimed, US nuclear strategy would "depend primarily upon a great capacity to retaliate, instantly, by means and at places of (America's) choosing."[33]

From the 1950s until the end of the Cold War, United States and NATO strategy relied on nuclear forces to balance what was perceived in official circles to be Soviet military conventional superiority. Warsaw Pact conventional forces were no less dependent on nuclear power. The nuclearization of Europe was essentially melded with superpower strategic nuclear policies. The credibility of NATO deterrence in Europe pivoted on the credibility of the American nuclear umbrella. That fusion was one of the principal driving forces in the development of the American strategic arsenal to provide what war-fighting advocates insisted were the nuclear requirements of "extended deterrence." The issue of credibility – whether the United States would use nuclear weapons to defend its NATO allies at the risk of its own survival – became a central concern of NATO military planning in light of growing Soviet nuclear parity.

---

[32] Kolodziej (1966).
[33] Remarks of US Secretary of State John Foster Dulles in 1954, quoted in Osgood (1962: 103).

Moscow's explosion of a hydrogen bomb in 1953, less than a year after the United States, and the creation of a long-range bomber and missile force in the 1950s joined this issue.[34]

To address the problem of credibility, whether the United States and NATO had the capability and will to use nuclear weapons to defend Europe, the Kennedy administration ushered in the fourth phase of NATO planning from 1960 to 1972.[35] The doctrine of "Flexible Response" replaced "Massive Retaliation." Secretary of Defense Robert McNamara proposed a major expansion of NATO's conventional forces to counter Warsaw Pact forces at this level of strategic engagement. The aim of this build up was to create an escalation ladder on which NATO could achieve superiority at each rung: to deter an attack; to defend against an attack if hostilities erupted; and to bring the conflict to a quick close on terms favorable to the West. The strategy implied that the United States would use nuclear weapons first, if necessary, to defeat an attack if NATO's conventional forces were overwhelmed. Flexible Response also envisioned a sufficiently prolonged conventional exchange, longer than the "Trip Wire" strategy of Massive Retaliation, to preclude a rapid escalation to a superpower nuclear war.

It is useful to pause briefly at this point to identify the fundamental differences of interest of allied nation-states in light of the conventional and nuclear challenges facing them. For the nuclear hegemons, the United States or the Soviet Union, it was imperative that each dictate to its rival – and to its allies – the decision of whether to escalate a conflict or not, thereby controlling each rung of the escalatory ladder. Conversely, their allies, dependent on superpower nuclear forces for their security, strove to maximize their influence over their superior ally's announced and operational nuclear policies. Driven by the same security imperatives confronting their patrons, they were not prepared to relinquish control over their security interests to another power. The European states resisted not only the burdensome costs of conventional defense but also what they perceived was the greater risk they ran than their superpower protector in limiting a conventional war to Europe. Their homelands would be devastated while the superpowers, through tacit complicity, would insulate their territories from nuclear attack. The European states were no less concerned than the superpowers about the conditions under which

---

[34] There is no comprehensive history of NATO military policies. The following are useful surveys of different periods, including the expansion of NATO to former Warsaw Pact states. See Kaplan (1999), Osgood (1962), Schwartz (1983), Yost (1998), and Kolodziej (2002a).

[35] For a discussion of the origins and evolution of Flexible Response, see Daalder (1991), Gaddis (1982), Kaufman (1964), Kolodziej (1966), and Stromseth (1988).

nuclear weapons might be used in Europe or the prospects of possible escalation to a superpower confrontation in Europe as a consequence of superpower conflicts outside the region.

The tensions generated by nuclear weapons and their incorporation in the posture of Flexible Response had two distinguishable results over the course of the Cold War. First, most of the NATO allies reluctantly accepted Flexible Response as the price of ensuring US protection despite its increased costs and risks for the protection of their security interests. In response to American pressures, the Europeans increased their conventional forces, a burden falling principally on West Germany. NATO forces, while enlarged, were never raised to a level to exclude the possibility of nuclear weapons being introduced into the battle. The credibility of US use of its nuclear forces to defend Europe at the risk of exposing its own territory was reinforced by the deployment of over 400,000 troops and their dependants; these commitments were hostage to the US nuclear guarantee. The Soviet Union was largely spared these tensions. Whereas it could impose its strategic doctrine and practices on its allies, much like Athens on Melos, the United States was compelled to negotiate alliance consensus among the democratic nation-states of the alliance which were at liberty to defect from alliance strategy.

A second consequence of the dilemmas posed by nuclear forces, and closely associated with incentives for defection, was the development of independent nuclear forces by other NATO states and by the efforts of all of these states to gain influence over US strategic policies on which their differing security interests pivoted.[36] Three strategies were pursued. First, France sought leverage over US nuclear strategy by developing its own nuclear forces and by withdrawing from the NATO organization.[37] By remaining out of military planning and war preparations, France sought not only to have a greater impact on US operational policies than it might otherwise have had but also to disengage from alliance policies when it suited its perceived interests.

While France reacted by disengaging from NATO's military organization (but not the Atlantic Alliance), Britain pursued an opposed strategy. It tied its nuclear policies directly to the United States in an effort not only to revive the close wartime collaboration between the two states but also, and more immediately, to have some say over American military planning, nuclear targeting, and operational policies.[38] British leaders convinced their US counterparts to furnish crucial submarine-launched missiles to the United Kingdom to underwrite its submarine nuclear forces. Except in the most dire and extreme of circumstances, the British

[36] Osgood (1962).   [37] Kohl (1971) and Kolodziej (1974, 1987).   [38] Pierre (1972).

nuclear deterrent was essentially appended to US forces and planning. On the other hand, those states without nuclear weapons – notably West Germany, which was precluded by treaty from acquiring them[39] – pressed for consultations on nuclear planning within NATO to inflect American nuclear policies in ways favorable to its security interests.

The 1970s ushered in a temporary respite in the Cold War struggle for Europe, opening the fifth phase of the Cold War in Europe. For a brief period, the United States and the Soviet Union and their allies reached agreement on several key issues. Europe became a zone of peace. The Helsinki accords of 1975 essentially recognized and implicitly legitimated, however temporarily, the privileged sphere of influence of the superpowers in their respective halves of Europe. Reflecting realist assumptions about the possibility of reaching such a balanced compromise, both sides agreed to recognize two sovereign German states and to sponsor their membership in the United Nations. Also created was the Conference on Security and Cooperation in Europe (CSCE). Its members included the states from both pacts. Its objective was to promote the exchange of peoples, goods, and ideas across state borders.

This temporary respite was broken in the late 1970s. In this sixth phase, Europe was increasingly drawn into the conflicts between the superpowers in the developing world, principally in the Middle East, southern Africa, and central Asia. The Soviet invasion of Afghanistan in December 1979 stalled strategic nuclear arms talks and arms control negotiations between the two European pacts. Soviet modernization of European nuclear forces pressured the European states to seek increased assurances from the United States to honor its guarantee to Europe by modernizing its European-based nuclear forces. Pressed by European states, NATO decided to deploy 108 long-range and faster-firing Pershing missiles and 464 cruise missiles in Europe to counter Soviet deployment of MIRVed SS-20 missiles and Backfire bombers in the European theatre.

These actions set off mass demonstrations throughout Europe and the United States against the deployment of new and more powerful US theater nuclear systems in Europe. The latter years of the Brezhnev regime were marked by increased US–Soviet discord over this issue. No sooner had the crisis passed than the Soviet Union under Mikhail Gorbachev launched a radical reorientation of Soviet strategic policy. A series of arms control agreements was reached with the West, capped by an agreement to withdraw intermediate-range nuclear weapons from Europe. These accords, the fruits of a détente process initiated by Gorbachev's Soviet Union, constituted the seventh and final phase of the European Cold War.

---

[39] Kelleher (1975).

The break-up of the Soviet Union in 1991 ended the superpower struggle for European dominance. Ascendant in what is now an emergent global society is the coalition of Western liberal, market democracies. Alone as hegemon within this coalition is the United States, the world's sole military superpower.

3.   *The globalization of the security dilemma*   The superpower struggle in the developing world was the third and, in retrospect, the decisive strategic battleground of the Cold War. On this vast and forbidding terrain the superpowers experienced unrelenting and formidable opposition to their hegemonial aspirations. Despite the expenditure of enormous human and material resources and at great cost to their prestige and reputations as big powers, neither superpower was able to tame the peoples and states of the developing world. Each was also defeated in battle by vastly weaker forces on this inhospitable terrain. Each was compelled to search for ways to reduce the burdens of imperial expansion in response to domestic political and economic demands for disengagement.

The nuclear and European theatres map well with the Clausewitzian notion of a tendency toward pure war in which two actors engaged in a duel to the death – the United States and its NATO allies vs. the Soviet Union and the Warsaw Pact. The seeming simplicity of these balanced military struggles bore little resemblance to the incoherence and complexity of the shifting alignments and alliances between the superpowers and their allies, clients, retainers, and surrogates. The patterns of armed conflicts in the developing world, Vietnam and Afghanistan as prime illustrations, more closely approximated the more robust Hobbesian model of war of all against all than planning for a decisive battle, either a global nuclear Armageddon or a clash of Titans in Europe. The Cold War order in Europe, imposed by the superpowers and sanctioned briefly by the Helsinki accords, contrasted with the anarchy of the developing world whose disputatious and contentious peoples and states resisted superpower pressures and blandishments.

The superpowers were never able to count on the reliability of their changing partners in their fruitless and failed efforts to gain ascendancy over these continents and their warring peoples.[40] The latter pursued their own political interests. As often as not, these were sharply at odds with their superpower partner of the moment. Where their interests clashed,

---

[40] The geo-political and military strategies of developing states, as objects of serious study, have tended to lag behind those of the major powers. For an early attempt to fill this gap, see Kolodziej and Harkavy (1982). The International Institute for Strategic Studies (London) has been one of the leaders in developing this literature in its journal, *Survival*, and in its *Adelphi* series.

the weaker partner could generally be expected to resist subordinating its security aims to those of its more powerful ally. The realism of our triumvirate theorists, applicable to some degree to superpower behavior in the nuclear strategic and European theaters we have been describing, has to be enlarged to encompass the much larger and more dense and complex webs of conflicts of states in the developing world. These emerging states resisted subordination to superpower interests and control even as they strove to manipulate their more powerful ally for their own devices.

The context of the superpower struggle should also be viewed from the perspective of the gradual erosion and subsequent collapse of the European empires in the twentieth century. World Wars I and II sapped the resources and will of the European states to retain their hold over non-European peoples. The ironic legacy of the European states was to impart their principles of national self-determination, autonomy, and state sovereignty to their non-European subjects. The decolonization process required much of the twentieth century to accomplish. Its final chapter may be dated with the collapse of the Soviet Union in 1991 and the end of white minority rule in South Africa a year later. By the end of the twentieth century, the nation-state won out as the principal unit of political organization for a fragmented and fractious world society of six billion people. In their attempts to enlist alien peoples into their struggle, the superpowers unwittingly became the midwives of a global system of nation-states that would fill, but not fully, the power vacuum left by the dissolution of the Eurocentric system.

A Hobbesian model generally applies to many segments of the developing world. The dissolution of Europe's empires and the competition of the superpowers to sponsor statehood for these developing peoples produced multiple centers of power and conflict. The superpowers plunged into this anarchic setting, seeking to control its evolution to suit their rival interests. Much like Athens and Sparta, they sought allies in the developing world – or sought to deny them to their rival – to gain political influence, military commitments and intelligence assistance, bases, logistical support, diplomatic cover, and legitimacy.[41] In turn, developing states worked the superpowers for their advantage. While Israel and Egypt

---

[41] The superpower struggle over four decades in the developing world is obviously too complex and varied to summarize in a few pages. The accent here is on the struggle insofar as it reflects Clausewitz's theory of pure warfare. For probing discussions of Soviet policy toward the Third World, see, *inter alia.*, Dunlop (1993), Korbonski and Fukuyama (1987), Nogee and Donaldson (1992), Rowen and Wolf (1987), Valkenier (1983), and Rubenstein (1988). See also Kolodziej and Kanet (1989), which provides an extensive bibliography, as well as Kolodziej and Kanet (1991). There is no definitive treatment of American Cold War strategies toward the developing world. See Keylor (2001) for extensive citations to specific studies.

readily accepted, respectively, American and Soviet economic and military assistance, both used this assistance against each other rather than serve their superpower benefactor. Similarly, Pakistan and India used the aid and military equipment they received from Washington and Moscow to conduct their wars over Kashmir. In the Horn of Africa, Ethiopia and Somalia switched superpower sides when it suited their interests. Meanwhile, the Soviet Union was confronted by the dilemma of supporting a Marxist regime in Ethiopia against Marxist-inspired rebels in Eritrea opposed to Ethiopian rule. Client states could not be counted on to support their superpower patron if their regional position were weakened by mortgaging their interests to Washington or Moscow.

Surface alignment between a superpower and its client scarcely concealed a broader and deeper pattern of chronic regional defection by an allied state when its interests clashed with those of a superpower – a pattern discernible in differential measure across every region of the world. It was most pronounced in the fallout between Communist China and the Soviet Union in the 1950s and the reversal of alignments between Beijing and Washington against Moscow twenty years later.[42] Strategic imperatives and domestic political exigencies trumped ideological affinity. These dilemmas of power and alignment confronted both superpowers with nettling choices. Both had to be concerned that a regional conflict not get out of hand and escalate to threaten their nuclear strategic and European interests. Despite their global competition the two nuclear giants were induced to cooperate with each other to control their clients to preclude worse happening.[43] Both intervened repeatedly in conflicts in the Middle East and south Asia to restrain their clients. The Soviet Union prevailed on Cuba and the Sandinista regime in Nicaragua to avoid provoking the United States in its sphere of interest; and the United States discouraged both Taiwan and South Korea from developing nuclear capabilities, potentially upsetting to the balances of power in northeast Asia.

The United States signed mutual security pacts with forty-three states around the globe. Besides NATO, Washington entered into a multilateral security treaty with the principal countries of Latin and Central America. Bilateral accords were also reached between the United States and the Philippines, the Republic of Korea, and the Republic of China on Taiwan. Two mutual assistance pacts with which the United States

---

[42] Hans Morgenthau was among the first to predict this break as early as 1951. American politics and US military intervention in Vietnam impeded Washington's exploitation of this split for a generation. See Morgenthau (1951a) for a prescient understanding of nationalism and national interests trumping ideology.

[43] Kolodziej and Kanet (1991) describes US and Soviet Cold War strategic behavior and cooperation in the developing world largely along regional lines.

was associated – the Southeast Asian Treaty Organization (SEATO) and the Baghdad Pact – collapsed under the pressure of decolonization and the Cold War. The Soviet Union similarly entered into multiple defense treaties in what proved eventually in the course of the Cold War to be more a burden than a boon to enhance its power around the globe. Arms transfers and military assistance were the principal policy instruments relied upon by both superpowers to create a network of client states. At the end of the Cold War, the Soviet Union and the United States accounted for 65 percent of the total value of arms transfers, estimated at $248 billion, between 1984 and 1988. Of these the Soviet Union supplied $101 billion, or 41 percent; the United States, $60 billion, or 24 percent.[44]

Both superpowers rationalized their intervention in the developing world in ideological, not strategic power, terms. The United States insisted that its intervention in the Third World was to defend free markets, liberal democracy, and human rights. In 1947, President Harry Truman announced the Truman Doctrine to justify $400 million in assistance to Greece and Turkey to support "free peoples who are resisting attempted subjugation by armed minorities or by outside pressures."[45] Truman directly tied the security of these nations to those of the United States and international security. He argued that "totalitarian regimes imposed on free peoples, by direct or indirect aggression, undermine(d) the foundations of international peace and hence the security of the United States."[46]

The reality was less than met the eye. As critics charged throughout the Cold War, successive American administrations, when forced to choose between supporting these ideological values vs. perceived strategic advantage in aligning with regimes and states opposed to them, repeatedly chose the latter – as realist and Marxist theorists, from radically different perspectives, explained and predicted.[47] In the Middle East, oil and strategic interests aligned the United States with conservative Arab states. In Latin America, Washington supported authoritarian regimes and military juntas over Left or Communist-leaning governments. It intervened covertly in support of anti-democratic factions in Argentina, Brazil and Chile and cooperated with plotters who overturned the government of Guatemala in 1954. It sustained Rightist Contra rebels in Nicaragua against the Leftist Sandinista regime and supported the military throughout Central America. It also intervened in the Dominican Republic in 1965 and Grenada

---

[44] See the annual publications of the US Arms Control Agency for the relevant years until publication of this document was discontinued: US Arms Control and Disarmament Agency (1973).
[45] Graebner (1964: 731).   [46] *Ibid.*   [47] Kolko (1988) and Waltz (1979).

in 1982 to prevent what were viewed as Leftist or Marxist regimes from gaining power. No American administration could politically afford the creation of another Communist Cuba in the Caribbean. No less did the United States support authoritarian governments widely considered to be predatory states, like the Mobutu (a.k.a. Sese Seko) regime in Zaire and anti-democratic rebel forces in central and southern Africa, including the minority white government of South Africa and its Apartheid policies.

The Soviet Union's ideological justification for the extension of its power in the developing world was no more convincing than that of the United States. In the first decade of the Cold War until the death of Joseph Stalin in 1953, the Soviet Union appeared to support Communist elements throughout the globe over nationalist revolutionary forces. Stalin's death opened the way for a fundamental reformulation of Communist doctrine. Stalin's successor, Nikita Khrushchev, proclaimed that there were many roads to socialism. The Soviet Union would therefore support national revolutionary bourgeois movements as a stepping-stone to ultimate Communist victory. This ideological shift to exploit new opportunities for strategic advantage increased, almost overnight, the prestige and influence of the Soviet Union among these emerging states. It profited from their repudiation of Western imperial rule and their lingering antipathy toward their former oppressors. Moscow tolerated crackdowns on Communist parties and partisans to advance its position among these states. Like the United States it was prepared to sacrifice ideological purity and commitment to the Communist international movement for the sake of its national security interests.[48]

The frustrations and mounting costs of superpower intervention reached their height in the 1970s and 1980s. The developing states were as relentless as the superpowers in pursuing their national interests and in asserting their sovereign rights, independence, and self-determination. The United States, after decades of intervention in Vietnam, was forced to withdraw in 1973, setting the stage for the complete takeover of the country by the Communist North in 1975. Viewed as a laboratory, the Vietnam experiment revealed the impotence of external rule over foreign populations, determined to create their own state and own political regimes, however much at odds with the ideological preferences of either superpower.

The Soviet Union learned the same hard lesson, but with more devastating consequences in intervening in Afghanistan in December 1979.

---

[48] This summary cannot, of course, do justice to the tortuous shifts and turns of Soviet foreign policy in the developing world. For more thorough and in-depth commentary, see Korbonski and Fukuyama (1987), especially the first three essays, which masterfully survey Soviet Third World policy.

After a decade of frustrating warfare, it abandoned Afghanistan and its clients who were eventually defeated by local opponents. The apparent successes of the Soviet Union in Ethiopia, Angola, Mozambique, Vietnam, Cuba, and Nicaragua in the 1980s were actually disasters in thin disguise. The weakness and poverty of these allies served only to mire Moscow in costly conflicts that it could ill afford as its economy deteriorated. Among the poorest nations in the world, these clients accelerated the decline of the Soviet economy and undermined its ability to keep pace with the West. Notwithstanding these setbacks and burdens, the Soviet Union had still been able to create a formidable and fearsome military system during the Cold War. Its quest for military dominance balanced the might of the United States and the Western coalition for over four decades. Moscow's power and influence was unprecedented in the history of the Soviet Union or that of Imperial Russia. Yet it imploded at the height of its material power. Its collapse *ipso facto* ended the Cold War? Why?

II.   *Explaining the rise and demise of the Cold War*

There is no simple explanation for the unexpected destruction of a superpower and the abrupt end of the Cold War.[49] Unlike past rivalries for hegemony, the Soviet Union did not implode as a consequence of war. Let's briefly establish some widely accepted facts and events about what happened to create a playing field – a data commons if you will – on which rival theory and approaches to explain the end of the Cold War can contest for our support. These events are all the more surprising since they marked a momentous transformation of world politics and international security whose repercussions have yet to be fully felt or understood. Like an elephant in the living room, these events are not easily ignored. They need to be explained. They are a test of the security theories covered in this volume. The following chapters will interpret these results in light of the competing theories of security vying for our support to explain them and for our adoption of their particular conceptual filter to explain security more generally.

The break-up of the Soviet Union should be understood as a process of crises accumulating in number, scope, and density rather than

---

[49] As early as 1992, 300 books and articles had already appeared to explain these events. Since then, cascades of studies have been published to explain outcomes unforeseen by most observers. See Edelheit and Edelheit (1992) for a listing. Relevant, too, including extensive bibliographic citations, are Carrère d'Encausse (1993), Dallin (1992), Gaddis (1992–3), Kaiser (1994), Mason (1992), Miller (1993), Remnick (1993), and Valkenier (1983).

as a single event, as some prominent theorists would prefer to view its passing.[50] At the core of these mounting crises was the failure of the Soviet Union to sustain economic growth and technological innovation, prerequisites to compete with the West and indispensable to respond to the demands of its own population. Efforts to cure this malaise set in motion irresistible pressures for reform that, in adapting to the Western model of an open political system and global market competition, ultimately destroyed Communist regimes throughout Eastern Europe and the Soviet Union as well as the Soviet state. Rather than arrest the decline of the Soviet Union, the reforms instituted by Premier Mikhail Gorbachev enlarged, deepened, and accelerated the cascading crises besetting the Soviet experiment. Reforms, calculated to save the Soviet state and the Communist revolution at home and abroad, resulted instead in confirming the ascendancy of the Western coalition of liberal, market states as the dominant nexus of power of the post-Cold War global system.[51]

How and why did the Soviet Union fall so far and so fast? The roots of its demise go deep into its history as the product of the Russian revolution. Some scholars argue that it was doomed from the start.[52] Whatever the merit of what are called essentialist critiques of a socialist system, it is clear in retrospect that the Soviet Union, as a revolutionary state, was neither able to transform international relations and world politics to its liking nor to adapt to the West's best political and economic practices – at home and abroad – short of its self-destruction. Among the most powerful systemic forces working to undermine the Soviet state and command economy was the Western alternative of a free, global open exchange system. This system unleashed formidable forces of techno-scientific innovation and human ingenuity that not only afforded the West greater wealth and welfare but also created an irresistible magnetic field that would prompt Soviet reformers to emulate Western institutions at the unwitting expense of their own authority and power.

How this impasse occurred is a long story which unfolded over most of the twentieth century. Only highlights can be touched upon here. The Soviet Union rejected, in principle, the imperial systems of the great powers and the market institutions on which their economies were based. Marxist ideology viewed capitalism as a necessary stage in the historical evolution of the world economy that would eventually be replaced by world socialism. The historical mission of capitalism was to eliminate the

---

[50] Cited in Lebow (1995: 1).

[51] Until recently the domestic factors pressing internal reform have been largely underestimated by analysts. Similarly, the impact of these factors on the foreign and security policies of the superpowers require re-evaluation. See Morgan (2000) for a start.

[52] Hayek (1944, 1988).

feudal system. For inherited property rights based on family and blood relations, capitalism substituted private property and market forces to determine how the world economy would be organized and whose interests would be privileged. Under capitalism, economic priorities were, ideally, established by the free play of supply and demand. What would be offered for sale would presumably be determined by what buyers – individuals, corporations, and governments – would be willing to purchase at prices that suppliers would be willing to furnish. In short, the relative cost both of inputs for the supply of goods and services and the price of output commodities and services in free markets determined the allocation of scarce resources available to a society. The free play of supply and demand would determine the balance between consumption and investment within a national and, more broadly, the world economy as a whole.

Marxist ideology predicted the eventual self-destruction of the capitalist system. Projected was the inevitable expansion of capitalist markets around the globe. This expansion would, according to Communist doctrine, eventually divide the peoples of the world into two warring classes: a working class or proletariat into which the world's masses would be consigned and an ever smaller and dwindling class of capitalists or bourgeoisie. The latter, possessed of most of the world's wealth and controlling its principal commercial, industrial, and financial institutions, were necessarily compelled to exploit an increasingly enlarging and deprived working class to increase their profits and power relative to each other. The competition among capitalists for profits and power compelled them to search for markets beyond their national borders.

According to Lenin, who extended Marxist dogma, global competition led capitalists to the search for empires abroad to dispose of their excess capital. Capitalist expansion, leading to imperial rule and global war, would eventually destroy the capitalist system, paving the way for a socialized world. In Lenin's mind, capitalist competition explained World War I as a struggle among capitalists in control of nation-states for the dominance of world markets.[53] The Russian Revolution was justified then as the rejection of the capitalist system and its exploitation of the world's wretched and underprivileged. The Soviet Union legitimated its revolutionary role in world politics as the vanguard of a global socialist system and as the champion of what were depicted within Marxist-Leninist doctrine as the oppressed masses of capitalist exploitation.

As practiced by the Soviet Union, a socialist economic system had several key characteristics that were inimical to the workings of capitalist

---

[53] Lenin (1977) For a critique that has held up over the years, see Schumpeter (1955).

markets.[54] The state, not individuals or corporations, owned the means of production. This was justified to prevent capitalist monopolists, working through multinational corporations, from using their control over a nation's economy to force wages down and, by the extension of the capitalist competition to the world economy, to reduce most of humanity to subsistence levels. The state under domination of the Communist party was assumed to always act in the interests of the working classes of the world. That historic role could be played, allegedly, only if the state under party control possessed the power and authority to allocate land, capital, and labor, and to control prices by central dictation. To ensure that the economy responded to worker interests, the state was charged with planning and directing all phases of the economy through five-year plans. Scarce resources would be allocated to hit the economic targets set by the Communist party and executed by the state through its industrial, agricultural, and professional sectors. What would be produced for the populace would be determined by bureaucratic, ministerial, state, and party directives. The substitution of a socialist system for capitalist markets *ipso facto* eliminated their exploitation of the world's masses. The superior moral status and equity of a socialist economy would eventually triumph over capitalism and imperialism.

Such was the "ideal," but what was "real" proved fatal to the Soviet state. For several decades after the Russian Revolution, the Soviet experiment could claim solid economic gains. Transformed was a semi-feudal, agricultural society into an industrial giant. Urbanization grew apace; universal education was instituted; and gender equality in the workplace was fostered. The Soviet Union succeeded in sustaining growth despite the determined opposition of Western capitalist states.[55] It also surmounted the massive losses to property and life of World War II. The conflict claimed over twenty million lives. By any measure, the Soviet Union's achievements were impressive in the early decades of its existence: economic growth rates were high; Soviet citizens were assured a considerable and, as seen by many people around the world, a greater level of material security than that provided by the Western states; and income inequality between workers and managers was narrower and more egalitarian than in prevailing Western patterns.[56] Experts estimate Soviet growth in Gross National Product (GNP) in the range of 4.4–6.3 percent per annum between 1928 and 1955. While growth continued between the 1950s and early 1980s, the rate of increase steadily declined. The United

---

[54] These are developed in detail in Ericson (1987), Hewett (1988), Kornai (1992), and Lockwood (2000).
[55] Kennan (1961, 1984b).   [56] Hewett (1988: 37–93).

States Central Intelligence Agency (CIA) reckoned that the Soviet GNP rose about 4.5 times over this thirty-year period, although the quantitative increase was less than that of the United States and most of the other Western states. It was also below what Communist China's economic reforms and those of the so-called Asian Tigers were able to achieve.[57]

These growth rates could not be sustained in the last decade of the Soviet Union's existence. The trend lines of all significant economic indicators pointed downward. This included growth in GNP, personal income, industrial and agricultural production, and labor and capital productivity.[58] These grim statistics could be predicated of the entire Warsaw bloc. In 1960, the Warsaw Pact accounted for approximately 14 percent of the world's Gross Domestic Product, while the Western states claimed 61 percent. Thirty years later, the Western portion rose to almost 75 percent, while the Warsaw Pact was half the 1960 level, with the developing states accounting for an increasingly larger share of the remainder.

Many factors, too numerous to cite here, help explain this decline and their relation to the structural weaknesses of the Soviet economy and its lagging technological development.[59] By the mid-1970s, the gains from transforming an agricultural economy to an industrial base had been largely exhausted. Capital stock was aging. The insulation of the Soviet economy from the competitive discipline of world markets and its relatively small size compared to global output hindered the accumulation or acquisition of investment capital and the creation and absorption of advances in Western science and technology. The gap between command and free markets widened, not narrowed, as the Cold War progressed. What Western technology could be imported was already obsolete. Given the rigidity of Soviet industries – tied to planned, dictated production targets – even outdated technology could not be effectively incorporated into the economy. The hierarchical decision-making structure of a rigidly state-controlled economy fostered inefficient practices and waste in meeting production targets. These were unrelated to the real preferences of consumers who had no effective mechanisms, like market prices, to convey their priorities to planners.

There were few incentives for managers under the Soviet system to incur the risks of innovation. Their personal incomes and status were

---

[57] Communist China announced its intention to adopt capitalist market reforms in 1978; the Asian Tigers include Taiwan, Singapore, South Korea, and Malaysia.

[58] Ericson (1987) and Lockwood (2000) present data for these declines. The complexities of estimating Soviet economic data are explored in Hewett (1988) and Kornai (1992). The special problems associated with spending for defense are covered in Firth and Noreen (1998). Western sources generally estimated these indicators as having positive valences, although they may well have been inflated in light of the unreliable data available for measurement.

[59] See also Aslund (1991, 1995), Berliner (1988), and Goldman (1983, 1991).

measured by their ability to meet planning goals, not by qualitative gains for developing new products and technologies. Since the cost of inputs could not be reliably assessed by the simple device of comparing the relative prices of scarce resources – what markets do automatically on a global scale – industrial managers had every incentive to demand limitless resources to meet planned production goals. Except for selective sectors, notably those associated with military technology, what Soviet industry produced for foreign sale almost invariably fell below global quality standards. Heavy annual defense spending added to these fundamental weaknesses of the Soviet economy. These averaged about 17 percent of GNP vs. 6–7 percent for the United States with an economy at least twice as large as the Soviet Union. The resulting distortion in balanced economic development ensured continued waste and inefficiency and a continuing devolution of the Soviet economy in the absence of pervasive reform.

On assuming office as the head of the Communist party in 1984, Mikhail Gorbachev sought to reform the economy and the Soviet state. He identified three aims to be fostered by increased and sustained economic growth: a more effective response to rising consumer demands and Soviet expectations to match Western growth; a strengthened economy to underwrite Communist party legitimacy; and improved economic performance to meet the Western challenge and preserve the Soviet Union's claim as the vanguard of a socialist revolution.

Four interdependent reforms were initiated and pursued throughout Gorbachev's tenure in office. The most important was economic restructuring or *perestroika*. This term covers a wide, bewildering, and often contradictory number of initiatives introduced between 1985 and 1991 to restructure the economy to equal Western rates of growth. They formed no coherent pattern nor did they admit to any cogent design – symptoms of the mounting crisis and the desperation of the Communist leadership to energize the economy. Worker discipline was addressed in a national campaign against alcoholism and absenteeism; managers were directed to develop strategies to make their sectors self-sustaining with no material assistance from central planners; income differentials were introduced to provide incentives for greater productivity and innovation; and spending priorities were redefined to advance these aims. Defense spending was also gradually reduced, and the defense industries, the leading technological edge of the system, were induced to redeploy some of their resources from arms to consumer goods. Five-year plans were self-defeating, calling simultaneously for increases in consumer goods production and, unrealistically, for greater investment to spur capital formation and technological innovation. Scarce foreign reserves, which might have been used to increase investment and foster innovation, were tapped instead to import a greater range of consumer products to meet pent-up demand, especially of the ruling elite. Wages were increased, but with the perverse result of outpacing lagging productivity, fueling inflation, and deepening the economic crisis.

To mobilize the work force to support *perestroika* and to overcome the resistance of managers and ministries to reform, the Gorbachev regime instituted a program of *glasnost*, or openness. Citizens were encouraged to criticize the failures and weaknesses of state bureaucracies and operatives. They were expected to expose corrupt and inefficient officials and set in motion efforts to replace them. Former dissidents, like Nobel laureate Andrei Sakharov, were released from exile or prison. The media were permitted to report breakdowns in the delivery of state services, the lack of adequate goods, or their shoddiness and unreliability. Information about advances in Western economic growth, open political practices elsewhere, and technological development were circulated to the general population and to professionals eager to incorporate this knowledge into their work. *Glasnost* was designed to strengthen the Soviet system, not to discredit the Soviet experiment, certainly not to undermine the power and legitimacy of the Communist regime or its top leaders – precisely what greater openness did.

Paradoxically, openness was closely linked to a contrived and self-destructive attempt both to democratize the system and to strengthen the authoritarian rule of the Communist party and the Soviet state. To strengthen Gorbachev and his team of reformers in their struggle against entrenched conservative elements within the party, ministries, and managers of industrial units, Gorbachev proposed a major reform of Soviet state institutions. As with *glasnost*, institutional reform was calculated to bolster Communist party rule and the Soviet system, not to undermine its capacity to rule at home or to compete with the West abroad. In June 1988, the 19th Party Conference voted to abolish the Supreme Soviet, the long-standing rubber-stamp Soviet parliament, and replace it with a Congress of People's Deputies of 2,250 members. The Deputies would, in turn, elect a smaller body, which would be responsible for the day-to-day conduct of governmental business. This body would also elect a President of the Soviet Union. In the spring election of 1989, and much to the surprise of the reformers, 20 percent of the membership of the new Congress was elected from non-party members. The Communist party still controlled the Congress, since most of its seats were reserved for party members. The poor showing of Communist candidates, once put to an electoral test, signaled the beginning of the end of Communist party dominance and of the Soviet Union.

To these domestic reforms Gorbachev added a fourth, foreign dimension – "new thinking" about security. A generation earlier, Soviet Premier

Nikita Khrushchev rejected the Leninist thesis of the inevitable armed clash between capitalism and socialism. The struggle between capitalism and Communism was supposed to continue by other means as a competition between two models for designing world order and welfare. Gorbachev abandoned both positions in favor of cooperation with the West and adaptation to Western best practices. Pursued was an active policy of détente and peaceful engagement. For the struggle for Europe, the Soviet Premier promoted the notion of "reasonable sufficiency" as the basis for European security. He heralded the creation of a common European home to surmount the Cold War and the division of the continent into two warring camps.

A key explanation for these radical shifts in Soviet security policy from past positions was their political down payment to the West to gain access to Western technology and investments as a spur to the Soviet economy. In largely insulating itself from the ceaseless pursuit of scientific knowledge and know-how driving Western economic expansion, the Soviet Union and its satellites implicitly opted for internal political control of these processes rather than for technological development and sustained economic growth. The decentralization of decision-making and power as well as the acceleration of freely chosen transnational economic and techno-scientific exchanges between Western peoples and societies could not be tolerated by centralized Soviet institutions. As an alternative model for economic organization, the Soviet system necessarily resisted adaptation to these Western institutions. The Soviet system stagnated and the gap between the economic and technological development of the West and East widened. As Joseph Berliner explained: "Because of the international nature of technological advance, any country that does not participate fully in that international intercourse suffers a disadvantage in the promotion of technological progress."[60] Science, technology, and markets had become globalized by the end of the twentieth century. The evolutionary trajectory of these sources of power pivoted around a global division of labor. The Soviet Union and its dependencies had excluded themselves for seventy years from these dynamic processes at the expense of their technological and economic development. As chapter 5 suggests, Adam Smith, the intellectual architect of global markets, was a better prophet than Karl Marx in defining the forces that would produce *The Wealth of Nations*.[61]

To relax East–West tensions and to establish a new foundation for superpower security relations, the Gorbachev regime announced a unilateral ban on nuclear testing in August 1985. Six months later the

---

[60] Berliner (1988: 212–13).   [61] Smith (1937).

Soviet Union agreed to an American demand to separate strategic and intermediate-range nuclear weapons negotiations. Diplomatic talks throughout 1986 and 1987 yielded an agreement in December 1987 to eliminate land-based intermediate-range nuclear missiles from Europe. These breakthroughs in nuclear talks were crowned by the July 1991 agreement between the United States and the Soviet Union to reduce their stock of strategic nuclear forces by 30 percent. Meanwhile, defense-spending cuts were announced as early as 1987. These moves were followed by Gorbachev's dramatic announcement in February 1988 before the United Nations that the Soviet Union would unilaterally cut 500,000 troops, ten percent of its total strength in Eastern Europe, and withdraw 10,000 tanks from the region. These initiatives opened the way for a solution to decades-long negotiations over conventional arms reductions between NATO and the Warsaw Pact. In November 1990, members of the two military pacts agreed to the Charter of Paris that essentially declared the end of the Cold War. Parallel with these accords, the Soviet Union withdrew the last remaining elements of its troops from Afghanistan in February 1989.

Even more fundamental than these concessions to the West, Moscow set in motion the complete unraveling of the Warsaw Pact and its East European empire. To encourage its East European dependencies to follow its reformist lead and to allay the suspicions of Western skeptics, Gorbachev recoiled from implementing the Brezhnev Doctrine. Fashioned in 1968 in the wake of Soviet armed intervention to reverse a threat to Communist party rule in Czechoslovakia, it justified Moscow's right to intervene to preclude political change in Warsaw Pact states. The doctrine was specifically renounced in a Warsaw Pact communiqué on October 27, 1989.[62]

Communist parties in East Europe were expected to follow Moscow's reformist lead. To foster these efforts among satellite states and to assure the West of the credibility of Moscow's détente policies, Gorbachev approved the entry of Poland's Solidarity movement into a coalition Warsaw government, although it was implacably opposed to the Communist party's monopoly of power. The capstone of these initiatives was the fall of the Berlin Wall on November 9, 1989, and the subsequent integration of the two Germanys into NATO with the victory of the Christian Democratic Party in all-German elections in 1990. The remaining Communist states of the Warsaw Pact, with varying degrees of resistance from the Communist party, broke free of its yolk. In spring 1990 Moscow agreed to withdraw its troops from Czechoslovakia and Hungary. Little but a shell was left of the Communist bloc. In 1991 the Warsaw Pact, the

---

[62] For an overview of this process of Warsaw Pact dissolution consult Chafetz (1993).

military guarantor of Communist party rule throughout the region, was formally dissolved.

Gorbachev's reforms were fatal for the monopoly of Communist rule in Eastern Europe. Through blowback, the unraveling of the Soviet empire in East Europe reinforced the demise of the Communist party rule and the dissolution of the Soviet state. Rather than spur Soviet economic reform and growth, *perestroika* plunged the Soviet economy into deeper crisis. Unable to fully embrace market reforms of free exchange, Soviet economic planners were paralyzed in responding to the clashing cues of a command and open economy. The devolution of the Soviet economy further eroded the legitimacy of Communist party rule.[63] These fueled the self-destructive effects of *glasnost* and democratization. These reforms conspired to complete the job of unraveling the Soviet state. In early 1990 the Congress of People's Deputies repealed the monopoly of the Communist party. The Congress also elected Gorbachev President of the Soviet Union. In counterpoint, Gorbachev's archrival Boris Yeltsin was elected as the President of the Russian Republic over Gorbachev's handpicked candidate. A year later, Yeltsin was directly elected as President, the first such election of a Russian head of state in a millennium. At the height of his formal powers as party and state leader, Gorbachev's real power was at its nadir.

The East European example of national self-assertion emboldened the Soviet republics to assert their authority and independence from the Soviet state and ruling Communist party. Led by Lithuania, Latvia, and Estonia, which had never been reconciled to Soviet conquest of these Baltic states in World War II, the other republics of the Soviet Union pressed for greater autonomy from Moscow control. In March 1991, an embattled Gorbachev regime held a referendum on the question of "Whether the Soviet Union should continue to exist as a united country?" While 75 percent of respondents answered yes, six republics boycotted the referendum. Conservatives within the party and state bureaucracy launched a coup in August 1991, a move aborted by the refusal of Boris Yeltsin, President of the Russian Republic, to submit to the plotters. A month later the independence of the three Baltic states was recognized by what remained of the Soviet state. On December 1, Ukraine voted for independence. The Russian Republic, Ukraine, and Belarus announced the formation of a Commonwealth of Independent States, composed of the former republics of the Soviet Union.

From its inception, the Soviet Union was internally flawed by the conflicts embedded in its diverse national, ethnic, and communal composition. The iron fists of the Soviet secret police and military had held

---

[63] Kuran (1991).

these centrifugal forces together by brute force. Once *glasnost, perestroika,* democratization, and new strategic thinking were introduced, the state's coercive hold on its population relaxed enough for these tribal divisions to overwhelm the Soviet state.[64] On December 25, 1991, Mikhail Gorbachev resigned as President of a now non-existent Soviet Union, already effectively dissolved into its component republics. With the implosion of the Soviet Union, the preceding collapse of the Warsaw Pact, and the subsequent disintegration of the Soviet army, the Cold War abruptly ended. In its wake arose a coalition of liberal Western democratic, market states as the dominant power centers of international relations and a world society of six billion diverse and divided peoples.

What explains the implosion of the Soviet Union, the end of the Cold War, and the rise of the Western coalition?

Clearly no simple response to such seismic events is possible. Let's concede from the outset that the complexity and duration of the Cold War, set against two world wars to decide which states and peoples would dominate international relations and the world society, caution against making rash and sweeping generalizations about the end of the Soviet Union and the Cold War. In briefly recounting a half-century of global conflict and its transformation into what is now a post-Cold War era, we have constructed a "laboratory" to identify and evaluate which actors appear to have been key players and what factors and key events seem to have been decisive in producing these revolutionary results. The Soviet leaders did not intend their own demise, the end of Communist monopoly rule, or the dissolution of the Soviet state. Their reforms were supposed to strengthen their power and influence and to ensure their continued authority over the military, economic, and political institutions they created and over which they presided. How could they have not foreseen their own political suicide by exposing themselves to global forces in adapting the Soviet Union to the West's economic and political institutions, which the Soviet experiment had opposed since its inception? Few had a clue – certainly not Gorbachev and his partisan reformers and most observers in the West – that Soviet reforms were ushering in a tectonic shift in power in global politics with entirely new and daunting security issues for states with socially divided populations, like those in the Balkans, the

---

[64] Kaiser (1994) does a masterful job in explaining the fissiparous force of identity politics in the Soviet Union. For earlier treatment of the nationality problem in the Soviet Union which, typical of other studies, did not foresee the collapse of the Soviet Union into its national republics, see Conquest (1986).

Middle East, and Africa, and for the states of the international system in the post-Cold War era.

In the next four chapters, we will try to evaluate seven theories or approaches to international relations and their explanatory power with respect to international security. No one test of these theories or approaches is sufficient to disprove a particular school of thought. Yet the global scope of the Cold War and the fundamental changes in international security introduced by the abrupt and unexpected implosion of the Soviet Union provide an important, if not fully comprehensive, test of how reliable these schools of thought may be in helping us to understand and solve the formidable security problems confronting the world's populations and states today. To set the stage for this evaluation, it is important to be clear about what criteria we are applying. The next section outlines guidelines for testing security theories and approaches.

Guidelines for testing security theories and approaches

What is the purpose of testing a theory or approach? Our aim is not to confirm or reject definitively one theory or approach over another. That is well beyond the scope of this discussion or, for that matter, any that might be devised or designed in light of the unsettled state of international relations and security theory and the turbulent crosscurrents of behavior of the multiple actors impacting on international security. Our aim is more modest, but serviceable. We want to make sensible and reliable choices about what set of conceptual lenses we wish to wear to explain the bewildering reality of international relations and security. What set of lenses we choose will depend on how we assess the political conditions and context we confront – choices which themselves are not self-revealing and unproblematic. We want to have some reasonable basis for relying on one or more of the theories we will be evaluating to explain important events like the end of the Cold War, the outbreaks of World Wars I and II, the end of Europe's empires, regional conflicts today, the suicidal attacks on the World Trade Center, or the American counter-attack, resulting in the overthrow of political regimes in Afghanistan and Iraq.

Following the lead of Hobbes, Clausewitz, and Thucydides, we want to say something not only about how such security problems arose and evolved but also about human behavior more generally. Security studies, while a sub-field of international relations is almost as wide and deep in scope as the set of actor relations of this larger field of thought, decision, and actor initiative. These cover people-to-people relations as well as the transactions of socially constructed actors. The latter include those between diverse societies, states, international organizations, multinational corporations, and non-governmental associations – e.g., the Catholic Church or the Red Cross – of a global reach. Within this capacious set of real and potential security moves by multiple actors, we are particularly interested in explaining the disposition of humans to use or threaten force – or to resist or reject this option – to get their way in their interdependent, mutually contingent exchanges with others. This theoretical knowledge is a precondition for guiding personal and public policies and strategies in coping with force and redirecting appeals to coercion in human exchanges to less destructive and more productive pursuits.

Testing theories of international relations and security is a never-ending process. As we observe the world and the behavior of different actors, including states, we are obliged to assess whether our observations of their behavior and the conditioning physical and social environment framing their thinking, decisions, and actions conform to our expectations. If they act other than in predictable ways, a disconnect inevitably arises between what we expect and what they do. We can ignore the dissonance; we can deny that our theory is flawed; or we can try to reconcile what we see that is at odds with our theory or expectations. This can be done either by re-evaluating our facts to determine whether they check out or by revising our theories to explain these discordant observations. Failing these moves, we can either look to other theories that explain what we see more coherently and comprehensively or continue to rely on familiar but misleading conceptual maps about the real world, a psychologically comforting strategy perhaps, but intellectually untenable and potentially mischievous and self-defeating if acted upon.

In testing a theory, three considerations should be kept in mind. First, a disciplined, scientific mind, as chapter 1 insists, is never satisfied, but relentlessly strives to *disprove* the theory relied upon.[65] There is a greater probability that a theory we use to account for the behavior of actors around us is valid and reliable if we insist on subjecting it to hard facts and events at odds with the theory. We also want to be alert to logical inconsistencies in the expectations of behavior advanced by the theory that don't add up. If some proponents of a school of thought propose, say, that the balance of power between states encourages peace *and* war, we can readily see that we have a puzzle to resolve. It will take some tall explaining to reconcile the claim that the same cause (balance of power) can have two diametrically opposed effects (war and peace). Falsifying our theories is a tougher test than that of selectively assembling evidence that supports our theory, while ignoring data that cast our knowledge in a dimmer or questionable light.

---

[65] Popper (1963).

Second, to be fair to each theory that we evaluate in light of the Cold War experience, it is important to determine whether the dissonance we detect between facts and theory is simply a failure to connect the two correctly from the perspective of the theory under scrutiny. Specifically, we need to assure ourselves that the theory *excludes* expansion and re-interpretation to explain new facts that we discover. Conventional notions of the theory might not be adequate to determine the actual limits of the theory's explanatory power. As we will shortly see with respect to realist theory, for example, social scientists have been ingenious in reformulating this paradigm to adapt it to new facts and events at the cost, some critics argue, of realism itself as a progressive theory.

The theories we will be evaluating are not a static set of explanations of certain forms of actor behavior, say war and peace. They are research projects with lives of their own. They also reflect deep commitments of researchers, analysts, and policy-makers who have staked their professional careers on these theories and their reliability in practice. For them, it is not enough that, pragmatically, a theory can work in practice. It must work well in theory, too! These theories mutate and evolve as new security issues arise, like global terrorism, or as additional observations and novel propositions are formulated to test and validate actor behavior. Theories cannot be confirmed or rejected either because they succeed or fail to explain a particular set of facts or events. They have to be viewed, if alive and well, as responsive to the creativity and seemingly limitless capacity of humans – the object of study of international relations and security – to change their ways or adapt to new circumstances in their physical and social environments. Trying to keep up with the object of study today is difficult compared to the past since change is endemic to the world society humans have fashioned – and continue to reform and reformulate – to meet their competing needs and wants.

Finally, in the search for reliable security theory, we should try to develop our own theories to suit our purposes and needs. We can't reasonably have a theory for everything. We have to be clear about what we want to know. Boundaries have to be set that make sense to limit our search for understanding and explaining a phenomenon – security behavior in our case – if we expect to acquire rough but reliable knowledge. We are interested in knowing why states and other actors, more generally, use or don't use force and threats. This question is embedded within a larger concern of the proper scope of international relations as a discipline and the identification of the key actors and factors at work in this more encompassing domain of human conduct. In evaluating the relative explanatory power of competing theories of security, these questions and the criteria they imply should be kept in mind. Does the theory we are proposing explain what other theories are able to do? Does it also explain facts and events they do not address, or even reject as amenable to explanation? And, finally, does our theory explain and even predict new facts and events falling within the ambit of its claims?[66]

How then should we compare the strengths and weaknesses of our seven schools of thought to international relations theory: realism, neorealism, liberal institutionalism, classical liberalism, Marxism and neo-Marxism, behaviorism, and constructivism? Each purports to be more than just an image of how the world works. Each attempts to identify key actors populating international relations and world politics, the principal factors animating their behavior, and their relative salience and significance. Each abstracts from the buzzing confusion of the world those actors and factors that each believes are central to a theory of international relations and security. What is of central importance in choosing between these seven contenders are (1) the assumptions each school of thought makes about the make-up and motivation of key actors – individuals, groups, states, etc.; (2) the rationales advanced by each for the key choices made by actors in response to what factors drive their behavior; and (3) the level(s) of analysis at which actor behavior is being observed.

These theories do not pretend to explain all facts and events falling within the set of things relevant to international relations, global politics, and security. They focus on what the theorist believes are most important and necessary for our understanding. Partisans of a particular theory or approach are saying that, if the observer misses the actors and factors identified by the theorists to be driving actor conduct, they are essentially missing what's happening. By simplifying reality, the latter become more accessible. Paradoxically, less has more explanatory power. Details and nuance are lost or blurred. What appears to hold over time and space as true is accented. Parsimony simplifies rich and thick explanations of particular events to produce knowledge of the underlying forces shaping international relations over time, space, and social circumstance. These causal elements presumably play central roles in any theory of security, according to the theorists. What we will try to sort out is the validity of the rival claims of these conflicting positions by assessing their explanation of the implosion of the Soviet Union and the end of the Cold War.

We have been speaking about international relations and security as if they were interchangeable terms. They are not.[67] Typically, international relations refer, as the term suggests, to relations among states.[68]

---

[66] These questions are, as chapter 1 describes, a rephrasing of those advanced by Imre Lakatos (1970) as pertinent in testing theories.

[67] Baldwin (1995) and Kolodziej (2000b).   [68] Morgenthau (1985).

That image is captured by one of the founding fathers of post-World War II realism, Hans Morgenthau, in the title of his widely circulating textbook, *Politics among Nations*. Morgenthau distinguishes between the special aims and interests of states and the wide range of means and resources at their disposal to influence each other's behavior in favorable ways from other forms of politics. Examples abound – American or French domestic politics, family and gender politics, or bureaucratic and office politics – to name just a few at random. The scope of Morgenthau's concern is limited to the particular aims of states as he defines them. This leads to an interest in the means and resources relied upon by states to influence each other's behavior and their environment in favorable ways. Other theorists, while conceding the surface importance of states, believe that their behavior cannot be explained by reference to the states alone or to the condition of anarchy underlying their relations. Some, like liberal economic theorists, cite the constraints of global markets. Others, like constructivists, contend that there are more elemental cultural and widely shared ideas and values informing state behavior. These are alleged to be the primary forces in international politics.[69] Other actors, with their own agendas and power capabilities, may influence what states do. For these theorists, actors, like international corporations, are portrayed as more important than states in explaining the latter's decisions and actions.

Each of these seven positions evaluated in successive chapters purports to be a theory or approach to international relations. Security is a sub-set of concerns within a larger set of objectives and actions that actors might take in getting others to do what they want. The litmus test of security for this volume is the decision of the actor to use *or* not use force to get its way. We made this distinction between all the things an actor might do – say be a patron of the arts or build a road – and those within this set of possibilities that specifically raised the question of whether to use force *or* not to ensure a desirable outcome in exchanges with other actors. Our classical triumvirate is particularly helpful in attempting to theorize about this dimension of actor behavior. Now we want to compare how each of our seven contestants for hegemony in security studies portrays their understanding of international relations and their particular explanation of the tendency of actors to use or not use force. These responses are grist for our mill which seeks to advance thinking in a way, inspired by

---

[69] Interestingly enough, Hans Morgenthau's text explaining state relations from a classical realist perspective has the title *Politics among Nations*, indicating a sensitivity to nationalism as a force impelling state behavior and shaping its value system and interests, a point lost to many theorists, like Kenneth Waltz (1979), who implicitly transform Morgenthau's pre-rational, pre-national, emotion-driven nation-states into cold-blooded, rational entities inured to popular impulse or compulsions.

our triumvirate, that enables us to make generalizations about security across time and space.

As table 3.2 summarizes, we can compare these schools of thought along six dimensions. These include their particular view with respect to (1) the key or central actor(s) in international relations; (2) the key factor(s) driving actor behavior in their exchanges with other actors; (3) the expected behavior of actors, whether to cooperate or to conflict with others, in their transactions and their inclination to use force or threats to get their way; (4) the level of analysis at which these exchanges or transactions take place, whether interstate, systemic, transnational, or domestic and the mutual impact of these levels on each other; (5) the preferred method(s) employed by the theorist in making observations to test theorists against facts or reality; and (6) the policy and normative implications of the theory for actors, principally for states, in addressing their security problems. The differences captured by table 3.2 will become clearer as the discussion proceeds in more concrete detail.

Other dimensions might well be suggested. This might include what each theorist considers "real" about actors – what philosophers would term their ontological composition. Hobbes, for example, suggests that individuals and states are selfish and disposed to violence. Others, like Jean-Jacques Rousseau, dispute this claim. In Rousseau's imagined state of nature, humans are neither good nor bad, neither selfish nor selfless. Rousseau argued that notions of virtues and vices were created as human attributes when free and equal humans entered into society – i.e. sustained, repeated, and replicable social exchanges – to ensure their security and property. Once socialized, their natural freedom and equality were forgotten and subsequently subverted by the political regimes imposed on them without their consent and opposed and unresponsive to their will and preferences. As Rousseau stipulates, "Man is born free, and everywhere he is in chains."[70] Only by asserting their will to rule – a General Will embracing the will of each citizen – can humans, now as citizens of their chosen societies, surmount these social chains, assume self-government, and approximate the "ideal" state of self-possession they previously (and purportedly) enjoyed in nature.

As should be clear already, there never was such a pure state of isolated, free and equal individuals as an empirical fact that could be observed. What Rousseau is positing is a normative standard to answer the classical question of what is the best society for humans. It is one in which the principles of freedom and equality are privileged, honored and pursued. Rousseau's General Will or popular rule within a democracy encapsulates

---

[70] Rousseau (1950: 3).

Table 3.2 *Comparing security paradigms*

SCHOOL OF THOUGHT	KEY ACTOR(S)	KEY VARIABLES	EXPECTED BEHAVIOR OF ACTOR(S)	PRINCIPAL LEVEL OF ANALYSIS	PREFERRED METHOD(S)	NORMATIVE IMPLICATIONS
I. Substantive Theories						
realism	state	violence/military force	conflict/ cooperation with rival(s) possible	state-to-state	historical/ analytical	armed conflict endemic, but managed by balances of power and mutual restraints on force
neorealism	system of states	violence/military force	conflict/ cooperation possible, but not likely	system	historical/analytic	armed conflict endemic, but managed by balances of power
liberal institutional	state bounded by other actors	violence/military force and economic ideas/values marginalized	cooperation	state-to-state/ transnational domestic	historical/ scientific/ analytic/ behavioral	cooperation is likely but armed conflict possible
classical liberal	individual (personal/ corporate)	technological/ economic	cooperation	individual	methodological individualism/ scientific	armed conflict is potentially resolvable
neo-Marxist	corporations	technological/ economic	conflict	system/markets	historical/analytic	armed conflict eliminated with end of capitalism
II. Methodological and Social Critiques of Security Theories						
constructivist	actor as a social construct	ideas/values	cooperation/ (conflict?)	exchanges socially constructed	social and social psychological	armed conflict can be eliminated by will directing reason
behavioral	research dependent	research dependent	conflict/cooperation	all levels/research dependent	scientific bias for modeling & measurement	purportedly value free

the freedom and equality that individuals, now transformed as citizens, enjoy as their birthrights and in society continue to possess and exercise through their participation in creating the General Will.

However important these philosophical and moral considerations might be to an understanding of security behavior – and many more can be identified as the chapters below suggest – they fall beyond the scope of this discussion. These other, possible points of comparison are noted to underscore that there is a lot more work to be done to develop reliable theories of security than this overview can hope to cover. Constructivists covered in chapter 7 are particularly concerned about what they argue are the narrow boundaries defined for security studies by most observers, including the limits I have adopted for this volume, as one sharp critic of a draft of this manuscript was keen to point out. These reservations are again noted in the interests of transparency to disclaim that this discussion has exhausted either the subject or ways of thinking about it. Far from it, but it is a start – an arguably plausible move in making some progress in assessing theories of security along the dimensions examined by this study.

Discussion questions

1. Why are tests needed to validate competing theories of security? Does the Cold War – its rise, evolution, and demise – qualify as an appropriate test of the explanatory power of a theory of security?

2. Describe the three-tiered globalization of the superpower struggle between the United States and the Soviet Union, covering its nuclear, European, and developing world dimensions. Evaluate the proposition that the superpower conflict threatened the security not only of the populations of these states but hundreds of millions of peoples around the world.

3. What is meant by Herman Kahn's observation that the two superpowers built two "Doomsday Machines?" Do you think that this outcome of the strategic nuclear competition between the United States and the Soviet Union has any relation to Clausewitz's notion of "pure war?"

4. What were the factors that drove Soviet leadership to embark on an ambitious domestic reform program? Explain *glasnost, perestroika*, and democratization as key dimensions of this reform program.

5. In what ways did Soviet détente policy toward the West differ from previous Cold War periods of relaxed tensions between East and West? Specifically, what impact did this shift in Soviet foreign and strategic

military policy have on its capacity to control the East European members of the Warsaw Pact?

6. Which of the four major changes in Soviet domestic and foreign policy appears to be the most important in explaining the break-up of the Soviet Union? Why do you believe so?

7. Identify relevant criteria by which to compare and evaluate theories and approaches to international relations theory and explain why they are important in deciding which should be adopted to explain the security behavior of actors.

Suggestions for further reading

Hélène Carrère d'Encausse (1993), *The End of the Soviet Empire: Triumph of the Nations*, New York: Basic Books. This French scholar has an international reputation as one of the most perceptive interpreters of Soviet and Russian politics, notably with respect to their national, ethnic, and religious divisions. This work caps decades of scholarly publications signaling the decline of the Soviet Union as a consequence of these internal splits.

Lawrence Freedman (1989), *The Evolution of Nuclear Strategy*, London: Macmillan. This volume provides a comprehensive survey of the evolution of superpower nuclear doctrines and the evolution of the nuclear arms race.

John Lewis Gaddis (1992–93), "International Relations Theory and the End of the Cold War," *International Security* 17: 5–58. This is a trenchant critique of the failure of international relations theory to anticipate the end of the Cold War, written by an eminent historian of the Cold War.

Marshall I. Goldman (1991), *What Went Wrong with Perestroika*, New York: W. W. Norton. This is an accessible diagnosis of why Soviet economic reforms failed by an accomplished observer of Soviet and Russian economic policies. It is a useful supplement to the scholarly analysis of János Kornoi, cited below.

Robert J. Kaiser (1994), *The Geography of Nationalism in Russia and the USSR*, Princeton: Princeton University Press. This volume details the failure of the Soviet Union to surmount the national, ethnic, and religious divisions within the Soviet state and explains how and why these domestic conflicts proved decisive in the break-up of the Soviet state and system.

William R. Keylor (2003), *A World of Nations: The International Order Since 1945*, New York: Oxford University Press. This is a good place to begin to gain a firm, introductory knowledge of the evolution of the Cold War and the post-Cold War era. It complements the Keylor volume cited in chapter 1. See extensive bibliographical citations in each volume.

János Kornai (1992), *The Socialist System: The Political Economy of Communism*, Princeton: Princeton University Press. This is among the most thoroughgoing critiques of the failure of the Soviet system of economic development.

Richard Ned Lebow and Thomas Risse-Kappen (eds.) (1995), *International Relations Theory and the End of the Cold War*, New York: Columbia University Press. This lively collection of essays provides a still relevant set of explanations for the implosion of the Soviet Union and its empire, viewed principally from political and moral perspectives.

Part II

Contending security theories

4   Realism, neorealism, and liberal institutionalism

Pessimistic realism

The triumvirate of chapter 2 comprises the classical school of realism. As realist theory has progressed over the years, notably since World War II with the 1948 publication of Hans Morgenthau's seminal *Politics among Nations*, the assumptions of traditional theory have undergone substantial reformulation. These revisions have been induced by massive changes in world politics during and especially after the Cold War. These fundamental shifts in power and the rise of new and influential actors on the world stage have been the products of the disintegration of Europe's empires, the expansion of the nation-state to include all peoples of what is now a world society of diverse and divided peoples, the relentless growth and extension of capitalist markets, the rapid diffusion of technology, real-time worldwide communications, the progressive march of democratization, and the rising demands of populations everywhere for a greater say in their government, the protection of civil liberties, and basic human rights.[1]

As international relations have changed so also have realists attempted to keep pace with these "realties," while asserting the relevance of their core concepts as timeless and true. This school of thought embraces a wide range of scholars who often differ, sharply and seriously, among themselves. They are loosely held together and distinguishable from other schools of thought by several key assumptions they share about international relations and security. This chapter will attempt to summarize their converging understanding and approach to theory, while noting key differences between them in order to present as full a spectrum as possible of the shaded perspectives grouped under the realist banner. Self-confessed realists have demonstrated a remarkable adaptability to changing security

---

[1] See Huntington (1991), Kolodziej (2003), and Ignatieff (2001).

issues. However much they are assaulted by numerous critics from the other schools of thought yet to be covered and however much they attack each other, it is still fair to say that they comprise a very large and widely published group of international scholars – arguably still the dominant school of thought today in international relations.[2]

Before the discussion focuses on differences among realists, let's first identify what unites them, relying initially on our triumvirate to show the way. In purest form, realists of different stripes identify the state as the key actor in international relations, whether as a solution to the anarchy of a state of nature (Hobbes) or as the dominant force in the relations of peoples and nations (Clausewitz and Thucydides). There are several reasons for according the state a privileged position.

First, as noted earlier, the state has evolved over several centuries to become the principal unit of political organization of the world's populations. It has triumphed over all other forms of political organization – city-states, feudal principalities, and empires, including the Soviet Union.

Second, and closely related to Hobbesian thinking, the state enjoys a monopoly of legitimate violence. The world's peoples, however split they may be by nationality, ethnic origin, language, religion, and culture, have chosen the state – or have had the state forced on them – to resolve their differences. They also rely on the state to defend their interests against the depredations of other states and international actors.

Third, there has arisen a body of international law over several centuries that recognizes the legal and moral authority of the state to perform its internal and external security functions. States, as actors, typically recognize each other as legal and moral equals, notwithstanding their vastly different material power, communal composition, or regime type. Their mutual recognition of their possession of sovereign or final authority over the territory and populations they control establishes these actors as the central actors in international relations. Groups like the Palestinians or Kurds in the Middle East or the Tamil Tigers in Sri Lanka who want greater political power and independence seek statehood to realize their national aims. For realists, a theory of state behavior in their inter-relations with each other *is* international relations theory.

Of course not all states possess either the material power or the authority to perform the external and internal security functions formally assigned to them. For many reasons, those in control of the government and its military forces and civilian bureaucracies may be unable to command the human and material resources to impose their will on

---

[2] See Jervis (1998) for an overview and the Forum on realism in the *American Political Science Review*, Forum (1997).

resistant populations or formidable elements contesting their power and authority. The state may be subject to chronic internal strife and real or incipient civil war. The flawed social, ethnic, and linguistic fabric of a nation may enfeeble the state, as in Afghanistan, Lebanon, Sudan, or Somalia. These so-called failed states are unable to provide basic order and security, the primary attributes of a sovereign state. Or, the state may fall prey to neighboring predator states. Its own security and existence may well be at stake. Illustrative is the attempted absorption of Kuwait by Iraq in 1990 or the division of Poland among Prussia, Austria, and Russia at the end of the eighteenth century.

For classical realists, these weaknesses and the failure of some states to match the legal and moral definition of a state or its expected capacity to provide for its own security and that of its populations do not obviate the choice to focus on the state as the principal actor in international relations. Just the opposite is the case. No other unit of social organization has been able to successfully contest its monopoly of legitimate violence. Whether a state survives or not depends on its capacity to perform the security roles that it alone can execute. Failure to adapt to the external, environmental imperatives of power imposed by a nation-state system – that is, a system of interacting powerful and independent states – are for realists prima facie evidence of their centrality to international relations and global security. Realists predict that units failing to adapt to these power imperatives will be selected out of the evolutionary process. Absent a ready substitute today for the state to assume its political and security roles, the state becomes by default the principal actor in international relations from a realist perspective and the foundation, however shaky, of international security.[3]

For realists, the key variable or factor driving state behavior is power. The principal form of power is force or military power. This is assumed to be true for two reasons. First, there is the overall distribution of violent capabilities across all states. This changing but inherently unequal distribution of military power is identified by realists as the skeletal structure of the global order. Posited is a direct but still largely unclear and contestable relation between the ever-changing distribution of material power, notably state military capabilities, and the outcomes of the conflicting demands made by states on each other.[4]

Second, the material capacity of a state constitutes its ability to decisively influence not only the behavior of other states but the system or

---

[3] Buzan (1991).
[4] As noted below, Christensen and Snyder attempt to fill the gap between structure and outcomes in Christensen and Snyder (1990).

balance of power prevailing between states itself. Other forms of power or influence, including scientific, technological, and economic power, are viewed as subordinate to, and in the service of, the use or threat of force.[5] So-called soft power, such as the ideals of democratic government, civil liberties, and human rights, are seen to be trumped eventually by the material power of states and their capacity to use violence to impose preferred outcomes on other actors. Realists do not deny the existence or impact of these other forms of power. They readily concede that they determine the outcomes of interstate transactions in many important ways.

Traditional realists reject the notion that these non-violent material and non-material forms of power can eventually surmount the compelling logic of force and the violence wielded by states. On this point up-to-date and classical realists are of one mind. When push comes to shove, realists contend that these alternative forms of power are either supports for the creation of more formidable and effective coercive power or overtaken by the logic of force and coercive threats in regulating the outcomes of interstate relations. All states must be concerned, first and forever, with their power position relative to other states. This imperative arises from two conditions: the anarchy of the nation-state system within which each state must pursue its objectives and the necessary assumption on which each must act, viz., that state preferences are fundamentally in conflict and do not converge, notably in ensuring the security of the state. The anarchical system within which the state is embedded is alleged to generate formidable incentives to induce a state to use or threaten force as a prerequisite of its survival and of its capacity to impose its will on other states and international actors.

As the military power of another state rises, other states are prompted to assess, as an objective imperative and observable and potentially threatening condition, how this change impacts on their survival, security, and interests. Those interests are defined by realists in terms of the state's material power and its relative standing among states along this determinant. To do otherwise than relentlessly to pursue power ostensibly places the vital interests of these states at risk. States must, therefore, develop military forces, strategies, alliances, and weapons acquisition policies to sustain and improve their competitive position. Other concerns and considerations, like wealth or religious, cultural, and ideological values or domestic politics, are necessarily subordinated to the high politics of using force and threats of violence to get one's way and, implicitly, of waging virtual or real war with other states and actors. Protecting and advancing

[5] Nye (1990, 2002).

all of these values depend on preserving or achieving a preferred order. International politics pivots, then, on the fundamental question of war and peace, since war is the final arbiter of a state's claims on other states and international actors.

Borrowing from micro-economic theory, realists portray states and those controlling their resources as rational actors. Stipulated is their alleged overriding concern to maximize their power relative to other states, quite apart from the specific purposes and material aims that they may have. All states and statesmen are assumed to be bound by this constraint. They are led to calculate each move and transaction with other states from the perspective of how the outcome of these exchanges will either enhance or weaken their relative power and position within the state system. States focus on power rather than on their interests, aims, and values because the latter depend for their realization, whatever their composition, on power to get other actors to bend to the state's will, embodied in the violent capabilities at its disposal.

States are expected to choose what they will do and to behave in terms of the costs and risks of using or threatening their power. They are supposed to be especially worried about the military power of other states and about threats to their vital interests as a consequence of fundamental shifts in the distribution or structure of material power across these units. States are never free from assessing and reacting to these power transformations that impact on their interests. Striving to maximize a state's power is predicated of all states and equated by realists with "rational" behavior. It provides the basis for generalizing about the expected behavior of states regardless of regimes or ideological orientation. "We assume," argues Morgenthau, "that statesmen think and act in terms of interest defined as power, and the evidence of history bears that assumption out."[6] Morgenthau echoes a proposition stated a century earlier by another observer of the security behavior of all states, however different and divergent their political regimes.[7] On this score, Hobbes and Morgenthau are of one mind. A sovereign king (the Leviathan) and a sovereign people (popular will as the Leviathan) must act, if rational according to realist doctrine, to balance the countervailing power and potential threats to their interests and security posed by other states.

Realists and neorealists agree that the imperative of pursuing power is imposed on states. It is *outside* the state's capacity to surmount or ignore. It is exogenous to them. States can't change this systemic condition.

---

[6] Morgenthau (1985: 5). See also Allison and Zelikow (1999), Chapter 1, which details these assumptions of the realist paradigm. Also useful for a recent defense of the realist paradigm, see Van Evera (1999).
[7] Maine (1886: 60–1).

States are compelled to adapt to the changing forms and time-bound contingencies of power projected by other states as these arise in their mutually dependent exchanges. The imperative of power is a constraint imposed on states in their struggle to get what they want under the condition of anarchy, which their claims to sovereignty and a monopoly of legitimate violence condemns them to. This condition of anarchy, rooted in the decentralization of power – principally the capabilities of violence in the hands of states – confronts all states with a security dilemma. If they arm too much they encourage other states to match or exceed their efforts. Against their better judgment, they may provoke a cycle of instability that can potentially lead to war and their own destruction. If they neglect this security imperative and ignore the pursuit of power, they do so at the potential expense of their security and interests. What is tricky about this power imperative is that they are supposed to succeed in this endless enterprise without generating countervailing power to offset their efforts by incurring costs and risks beyond the expected gains in the power they seek.

States can attempt to increase their power through their own efforts or through alliances and alignments with other states. The latter are useful to enlarge the material base of the allied states. As the Melian dialogue suggests, alliances are also useful mechanisms to deny allies to rivals and potential adversaries. They can serve, too, to control other states, which might otherwise wish to remain neutral and enlist their resources in the struggle for power against their will and preferences. European members of NATO, for example, sought alliance with the United States after World War II to overcome the latter's isolationist policy toward Europe. From their perspective, the alliance, as many hoped, would keep the United States in, the Soviet Union out, and Germany down. Conversely, some of these states, notably France and Germany, broke with the United States over its decision to overthrow the Saddam Hussein regime in Iraq. Whereas in the Cold War they feared that American power might abandon them, in the post-Cold War era of unipolar American power, they feared that their security interests might be compromised if they aligned themselves unconditionally with American power.[8]

Striving for power and for allies leads logically to the quest for ascendancy and hegemony. This logic is the political complement to the search for the elimination or control of other actors and states by force – the model of pure war stipulated by Clausewitz and implied by Hobbes' endgame. Not unlike the drive for monopoly by economic actors, whether individuals or corporations, under conditions of initially free markets,

[8] Layne (1993) and Waltz (1993).

states under anarchy are engaged in an incessant struggle for power. They have a strong incentive to become monopolists, too. By eliminating or controlling the decisions and actions of competitors, they define their environment in favorable ways and escape or diminish the uncertainty of anarchy. Realists predict that this relentless pursuit of power by states will eventually be futile. States will eventually be frustrated by the countervailing power of other states. States are compelled to balance other states and to form or adapt to changing balances of power to resist the tendencies of a rising hegemon.

According to realists, the striving for a balance of power is a fundamental and permanent property of the state system. To support this proposition traditional realists and neorealists reconstruct the history of state relations largely as a balancing game. Beginning with the rise of the modern state in Europe around the fifteenth century, often dated by the invasion of Italy's city-states by France's King Charles VII in 1495, the nation-states of Europe are portrayed as having been plunged into four centuries of balancing and war. First Spain and Portugal emerged as major powers through the riches they exploited by their expansion into the Americas. By the end of the sixteenth century, their power was challenged by the rising naval power and imperial expansion of England and Holland. Meanwhile, on the European Continent, with the end of religious wars signaled by the Treaty of Westphalia in 1648, European politics was increasingly driven by the rivalry of France and Austria for ascendancy. By the eighteenth century the number of states competing for hegemony and advantage increased to include England, France, Austria, Prussia, and Russia. Through the century, they changed partners to suit their interests and security needs. The reliability of an ally turned on its estimated contribution, not always well reckoned, to the power of a state and the balance of power among rival states.

Realist theorists predict that ideological affinities and treaty commitments will always accede to the logic of power and interest. Cooperation between states is contingent on their success in the competition for power. All alliances are conditional on changing circumstances and the rapport of force among states. Conflict and defection are the expected modes of behavior both for rivals of the moment and for temporary allies. The international law principle that treaties or pacts must be honored (*Pacta sunt servanda*) bows ultimately to the countervailing imperative that fundamental changes in the international environment justify changes, even renunciation, of treaty obligations (*Rebus sic stantibus*). Legal and moral constraints, while provisional limits agreed to by states, are ultimately subordinate to the exigencies of the struggle for power, much as Thucydides recounts in the Melian dialogue, discussed in chapter 2.

New, weak states, like the United States, also played this game by hiding and isolating themselves from Europe's big power game.[9] In 1793, the republican United States renounced its obligation under the Treaty of 1788 with monarchical France, although French assistance had been indispensable to achieve independence from England. Gratitude bowed to necessity. The Washington administration understood that aiding republican France against its royalist opponents risked war with France's enemies, imperiling the survival of the United States. Alliance obligations were vacated because honoring them risked the very life of the state whose existence made their execution possible.[10] That France was now a republic carried no weight in Washington's decision. Worries about survival overrode support for a fellow republican regime.

Realists cite the alliance of the conservative powers of the continent (Austria, Prussia, and Russia) with liberal Great Britain against revolutionary France as further evidence of the balance of power working to check the expansion of a rising power despite the conflicting ideological commitments of the partners. The century of big power peace between the Congress of Vienna in 1815 and World War I in 1914 is attributed to the flexibility of the balance of power and Britain's key role as balancer to restrain Russia in the east and rising German power on the Continent.[11] The Crimean war in 1854 joined previously bitter rivals France and Britain to contain Russian thrusts for power toward Turkey. Thereafter the military dominance of Imperial Germany, growing out of the victory of Prussian arms in wars against Denmark (1864), Austria (1866), and France (1870), was the object of continental balancing and British sea power. The rigid alliances of Germany and Austria vs. Britain, France, and Russia at the start of the twentieth century capped this evolutionary process of the balance of power in Europe. This competition expanded beyond Europe to embrace peoples around the world who were subjected to European rule.[12] The struggle for power in Europe extended finally to Japan in the east and to the United States across the Atlantic Ocean, states previously at the margins of the European balance of power system. These states subsequently became central actors in World War II and in the struggle among the big powers for world hegemony. With

[9] Schroeder (1994a, b) makes clear that more options than simply balancing are open to states, including strategies of bandwagoning, hiding, and attempts to surmount balance of power limitations to promote peaceful resolution of state conflicts.

[10] Corwin (1916).

[11] See Bridge and Bullen (1980), Gulick (1955), and Kissinger (1953) for similar portrayals of the balance of power in operation. Paul Schroeder offers a different view of the Congress of Vienna system, based on mutual regard and a balance of equities, not power. See Schroeder (1994a, b).

[12] Hobsbawm (1969, 1975) and numerous citations therein.

Germany's collapse and Japan's surrender in 1945, the century-long struggle for European and world hegemony passed from Europe's empires to the United States and the Soviet Union.

The neorealist revision

The superpower bipolar system after World War II prompted a major reformulation of realist thinking. Kenneth Waltz is the principal architect of this neorealist revision.[13] Neorealism accepts the principal assumptions of classical realist theory, but narrows the focus of realism and its conception of theory to advance a formal proof for the power-seeking of states. First, it posits the *system of states*, not individual states or the dyadic relations between states, as the principal determinant of state behavior. The decentralized distribution of material capabilities as distinguished from the power of any one state or group of states, including big powers and contending hegemons, is defined as a structural condition of power that "shapes and shoves" states.[14] The system and its structure of material violence is said to induce states to be ceaselessly concerned about their survival and security.

The anarchy of the system is stipulated to compel states to seek power to ensure these fundamental interests over all other competing values. Each is thrust on its own resources. The nation-state is then understood as a self-help system. No state can ever fully trust another to resist encroaching on its vital interests, nor can it rely on other states to come to its aid when their own vital interests, security, and survival are put in peril. This condition of anarchy acts as a cause, generating chronic conflict, overriding the altruistic aspirations and peace pronouncements of state leaders. Anarchy cannot be surmounted since it is daily reaffirmed by the striving for state autonomy and independence. States and the state system form a reinforcing vicious circle of perpetual conflict.

Waltz and his partisans claim to have raised these causal mechanisms to the level of a scientific principle akin to the force of gravity in the physical sciences or DNA in the life sciences. This move was accomplished by severely limiting the capacious scope, flexibility, and range of options open to states to cooperate in pursuit of their competing interests, as delineated in classical realism's conception of international relations and security. Neorealism mortgaged these options to establish its claim to scientific truth. This claim is logically sustainable if neorealism's self-contained, rigorous, and narrow definition of international relations – as

---

[13] Hobsbawm (1969, 1975) and Waltz (1979, 1954, 1964, 1981, 1993, 1997).
[14] Waltz (1986).

the system of state relations defined by the distribution of violence across these units – is affirmed as the appropriate, if circumscribed, domain to theorize about international relations and security. Once its assumptions about the dominating condition driving state behavior are granted, much like points and lines in Euclidian geometry, its conclusions about the concerns of the state for its survival follow inexorably. The neorealist model dictates that states, as units of coercion, are locked in interdependent relations with each other for their very survival. As Waltz insists, "A theory is a picture, mentally formed, of a bounded realm or domain of activity. The theory depicts the organization of a realm and the connections among its parts."[15] Waltz's "picture" of international relations reduces the field of study, solely and exclusively, to the coercive power of states within an anarchical state system. This system is closed, complete unto itself and insulated from all other actors and factors of influence.

The almost infinite number of policies and purposes that a state might pursue other than those defined by neorealism's conception of international relations fall outside the purview of the theory. All other forms of power and influence – scientific knowledge, technological innovation, economic wealth or ideological values – are painted out of the picture. For neorealists these complex sources of power, while acknowledged to be of importance to traditional realist thinking,[16] are marginalized or dismissed as simply irrelevant to the scope of the theory of state behavior that neorealists advance. They are assigned negligible weight, since by assumption – Waltz's "mentally formed" picture – states are unable to surmount the exigencies of force and violence imposed on them by the structure of power of the international system. These other forms of power and the wide and bewildering range of activities and projects pursued by the states, notably their welfare imperatives or concerns about their authority and legitimacy, are consigned to other levels of analysis of state behavior of fundamentally secondary worth and weight.

Neorealist theory stipulates that other domains of state action – say promoting human rights or economic development – can in no way overcome the decentralization of violence in the hands of state units. They ignore at their peril the incentives for coercion generated by this anarchical system. The state system is purportedly self-contained, insular, and non-permeable by other forms of hard or soft power. Other levels of analysis and the international actors associated with them are also excluded from the scope of the theory and the impact that the power they dispose might have on state behavior and on the state system. These include individuals, transnational associations (Catholic Church,

---

[15] Waltz (1997: 913).   [16] Morgenthau (1985).

Human Rights Watch), multinational corporations, intergovernmental organizations (World Trade Organization, European Union, etc.), and social movements, like global terrorist and crime organizations. Neorealists readily recognize the importance of these actors. What they deny is that their power and purposes are within the ambit of a theory of international relations or that they play determinative roles in the state's pursuit of its security and survival.

Second, and in sharp contrast to traditional realists, neorealists identify the security and survival of the state, not power per se, as the overriding, privileged aim of state action. The distinction has crucial implications for describing, explaining, and predicting state action. Whereas realists – classicists like Hans Morgenthau or modern game theorists like Robert Axelrod – envision a wide range of possible ways to enhance state power and to strike bargains and compromises with other states, neorealists stress the decisive importance of insurmountable systemic anarchy and the necessity of the state's military capabilities to ensure its security. The rich and textured pursuits of state power, both limited and driven by competing legal, economic, and moral considerations, drop from view in the neorealist reinterpretation of the state and the material constraints it confronts. For neorealists all forms of power pivot eventually on the state's success in achieving a competitive position in the incessant struggle of states to survive and to preclude any state or group of states from challenging their security interests. Conflict is endemic to state interrelations. Cooperation with rivals or allies is fundamentally temporary and contingent – dependent on changing circumstances.

Under conditions of anarchy, states will always balance each other. Failing to do so imperils their existence. They do not bandwagon, hide or attempt to surmount the system.[17] These are rejected as workable options. States risk being selected out of the struggle for survival. If the United States and its allies balanced the Soviet Union and its partners in conformity with neorealist theory, one should expect the same mechanisms to be at work with the rise of a multipolar world disposing diverse centers of hard and soft power, within a system dominated by one military superpower (United States) in the post-Cold War period. This is seen as assuming either opposition to the United States as the unipolar power of the contemporary system or as an attack on the ascendant Western coalition of liberal democratic states whose techno-economic power vastly exceeds the states of the southern hemisphere among the developing states.[18] Before or after the Cold War, states are still impelled,

---

[17] Schroeder (1994b, 2004).
[18] See, for example, Layne (1993), Mearsheimer (1990), and Waltz (1993, 1997).

according to neorealists, to worry about their relative material capabilities.[19] Economic and technological imbalances of power, not just the erosion of military power, are asserted to be an inescapable imperative.[20]

Third, neorealists argue that bipolar systems are more stable than multipolar systems.[21] The former are purportedly less prone to war. The Cold War bipolar structure was pictured as not only stable but indestructible for the foreseeable future. The military power at the disposal of the United States and the Soviet Union was supposed to be so overpowering that no other state or combination of states could contest or supplant them. Neither superpower, according to neorealist thinking, needed allies. The same could not be said of smaller powers. By definition, shifting alliances would have no effect on the bipolar system, however much it might have implications at the margin for the changing partners of the superpowers. The deck chairs of the superpower transcontinental liners, depicted here as alliance partners, might be reshuffled or some transferred from one superpower liner to the other or cast overboard. The power of the ocean liners and the direction in which they were driving other states and actors would still be unaffected by these surface shifts. No new combination of allies – the shuffling of deck chairs if you will – could undermine the material power of either superpower.

Since each superpower could ostensibly accurately evaluate the power of its rival and since both could be unconcerned about the actions of their allies, calculations of power were presumably more transparent and measurable than those under a more complex multipolar system. The dominant nuclear capabilities possessed by the superpowers reinforced the alleged stability of the bipolar system. Conventional arms, however destructive, could not be focused as decisively or as readily as nuclear weapons. Threats to resort to conventional warfare by the superpowers inevitably raised the prospect of escalation and mutual nuclear destruction. Each could completely annihilate the other state in a matter of minutes. This embedded threat transformed the calculations of the adversaries and advised caution and hence strengthened the incentive for stability on both sides.

The superpowers had an objectively discernible incentive to cooperate to prevent a nuclear exchange and to avoid their destruction. This overwhelming strategic constraint limited how far and wide they would press their interest through force or threats. The kind of gross miscalculations by opponents characterizing the outbreak of World War I and World

---

[19] Layne (1993).   [20] Grieco (1990).
[21] Waltz (1964). For a contrasting perspective, which argues the opposite case, see Deutsch and Singer (1964).

War II, in which Germany mistakenly assumed that it would emerge victorious, might have been less likely if the swift and sure power of long-range, invulnerable nuclear weapons had been available to military planners.[22] Indeed, neorealists pressed for more, not less, nuclear proliferation. Their assumptions about state power and its ceaseless pursuit for security led them to anticipate and predict that states would go nuclear – and, accordingly, advise that they should – since they supposedly had little choice under conditions of anarchy. Such a world, too, would also be more stable; that is, less prone to big wars and more inclined to limit small ones.[23]

After almost four decades of debate, the question of whether bipolar or multipolar systems are more war prone or not remains unsettled.[24] Partisans can be found on both sides of the debate. Both adduce evidence to support their position. The validity of their rival claims depends decisively on reinterpreting the evolution of interstate conflict to fit their prediction of the outbreak of hostilities. Many traditional realists cite the system of overlapping and contradictory alliances, secretly struck by German Chancellor Otto von Bismarck after the creation of the German imperial state in the second half of the nineteenth century, to illustrate how multipolar systems are more stable.[25] When no ally is reliable and everyone is a potential defector, aggressors can neither fully depend on their partners of the moment nor be sure whether they and hitherto neutral states might not join in a coalition against them.[26] With the rise of the United States as the sole military superpower, the debate over the stability of bipolar vs. multipolar systems has been temporarily made moot, but it may again re-emerge, either because American power may overreach, much like Athens in the Peloponnesian War, or because another hegemon or coalition of states is able to challenge the American hegemon.

Ad hoc amendments to realism and neorealism

Some realists, while accepting neorealism's systemic explanation of conflict as verifiable, argue that both classical realism and neorealism have to be enlarged in scope and depth to explain new forms of state behavior. In particular, the conditions of actor choices and behavior need to be better specified to explain and predict state security behavior and policies. These

---

[22] Waltz (1981). For a similar perspective, viewed from the perspective of liberal theory, see Mueller (1989).
[23] See Waltz (1993) in which Germany and Japan are viewed as going nuclear. Mearsheimer (1990) makes essentially the same prediction.
[24] Contrast Waltz's position with Deutsch and Singer (1964). After four decades of research and debate over the question, the issue of whether bipolar or multipolar systems are more or less prone to war remains unsettled. See Midlarsky (1989).
[25] Bridge, particularly, (2003: 260ff.).   [26] Eyck (1968) and Taylor (1967).

scholars seek to test the conditions under which neorealism's thesis can be perfected in specific cases where contradictions seem to arise between what traditional realists and neorealists predict and how states actually behave.

These ad hoc fixes cobbled together to close embarrassing gaps in realist theory and to strengthen the realist paradigm in its competition with other would-be hegemons of security theory have produced several notable departures from classical assumptions and neorealist expectations. The cumulative effect of these adjustments to embarrassing facts and dunning criticism by rival schools of thought is to turn classical realism on its head and to erode the explanatory power of neorealism. These shifts have prompted critics either to dismiss realism as a "degenerating research program"[27] or to ask whether it has simply collapsed into the arms of its competitors to the point that critics wonder whether "anybody today is a realist."[28]

First, there are those who move from the objective conditions of power balances, insisted upon by realists and neorealists, to psychological or subjective variables to explain state actions at odds with balancing behavior. Among these scholars are those who argue that a multipolar system may well be either stable *or* unstable, depending on the military strategies chosen by decision-makers to ensure state security. Whether one or the other outcome obtains turns, according to these analysts, on the perception of ruling statesmen of whether an offensive or defensive military strategy will best serve their state's interests.[29] Leaders who believe the next war will be won by the offense – the assumption generally shared by European military staffs before World War I – purportedly view their states as members of a "chain gang." To avoid losing the war, no ally can be lost. Under these circumstances, the onset of war can be sparked by an ally out of control; it drags its allies into hostilities by pulling on their "chains." For those who perceive the defense as the winning strategy – the case during the interwar period – alliances are invitations to "buck passing." This defecting behavior, in reducing the deterrent impact of an alliance, may also accelerate the coming of war, since a would-be aggressor has less to fear from an opposing but flawed alliance of "buck-passers."

Note the shift in the explanatory power of this revision. Balancing and the reliability of alliance and the issue of war or peace are explained by

---

[27] Vasquez (1997), Vasquez and Elman (2003).
[28] Legro and Moravcsik(1999). This criticism is deepened by the work of empirical, behavioral scholars, addressed in chapter 6, who find multiple disconnects between the claims of realism and the actual behavior of states. See Wayman and Diehl (1994) for a probing discussion of these gaps between fact and theory.
[29] Christensen and Snyder (1990).

the *perceptions* of statesmen.[30] For classical realists and strict constructionist neorealists, the objective conditions of material power always and
ultimately dictate a state's behavior. Certainly there is room for misper-
ceptions and miscalculations of the true power of an adversary and of the
balance of power between states. No matter in the long run. Immaterial
perceptions are no match for material power when put to the test. Stress
on objectively observable, material power clearly distinguishes classical
realists and neorealists from their revisionist colleagues. The former contend that these friendly amendments, wittingly or not, threaten the realist
and neorealist conceptual edifice. Revisionists argue that under the conditions they specify, the *perception* of the distribution of violence across
states and of the material balance of power can be, and often is, more
important than the material balance itself. This line of analysis, if allowed
to supplant the assessment of material power capabilities, departs fundamentally from classical realist thinking and unequivocally from more
narrowly focused neorealist strictures.

This reorientation toward subjective perceptions, as causal, to explain
state security policies is carried even further by other analysts, who still
count themselves in the realist camp. They focus on the psychological
mechanisms by which actors assess the "intentions" of other states and
their leaders. According to this line of analysis, states and statesmen balance according to the *perceived* intentions of other regimes. They do not
balance in response to the material power of other states or even their
perception of the military capabilities and strategies of these potential
rivals.[31] Whether states will balance against a powerful, rising hegemon
or bandwagon with that state will depend on an estimation of how the
latter will use its superior material power. States will not always balance
against the most powerful state. This expansion of realist theory essentially abandons the centrality of military power as the determiner of state
behavior. It relies on a theory of state intentions as the key variable to
determine state balancing or bandwagoning behavior.

Still other self-proclaimed realists believe that even this move is not
enough. For them, moving from capabilities to intentions fails to adequately explain state security behavior, balancing, and alliances, notably
in the interwar period between World War I and II.[32] While the classical
realist assumption of exogenously determined state behavior as a function of the distribution of military and material capabilities remains as an
important factor explaining security alliances, some realists believe that

---

[30] The leading theorist who is principally responsible for introducing perceptions into international relations theory as a perfecting amendment of realism is Robert Jervis. See Jervis
(1976, 1998).
[31] Walt (1987).   [32] Schweller (1998, 1994).

these state groupings and alignments are more fully understood as the consequence of converging state preferences. Choices are made even at the expense of the state's material weakness, depending on whether it is a revisionist or status quo state. Variations in state alignments and in the line-up of alliance rivals depend on differences in the values and preferences pursued by a state, and other domestic societal political arrangements. This extension of traditional realism to fundamentally subjective factors, more in keeping with constructivist rather than realist thinking, robs realism of one of its most fundamental assumptions about ceaseless state power seeking and balancing against the strong. The causal arrows explaining state security behavior are reversed. One friendly realist critic concludes that those holding this position transform "realism into idealism."[33] This criticism does not sit lightly with realist revisionists who rejoin that states will side even with the strong if there is an advantage to be gained, particularly in those cases where powerful states are status quo powers and where weaker states do not view their apparent material weakness relative to a more powerful state as a source of concern or threat.[34]

In this vein, the end of the Cold War, too, is explained by another group of self-proclaimed realist theorists in psychological and normative terms. Gorbachev and other Soviet reformers are portrayed as gradually convinced of the West's non-aggressive intentions. The perceived defensive position of the United States, in particular, is alleged to have conditioned and elicited a détente policy as a precondition of reform. If it were assumed that the West had adopted a defensive posture (contrary to Leninist expectations), then it followed that the West would not exploit détente or the weakness of the Soviet Union during the reform process and its adaptation to prevailing Western institutions, notably global capitalist markets. Gorbachev's reforms, based on his perceptions of Western peaceful intentions, ironically and unwittingly destroyed the Communist regime and his personal power.[35] In this revisionist reformulation of classical and neorealist thinking, the material power of the rivals fades from view as the central driving force of superpower behavior. The explanation of Gorbachev's reform policies and of radical shifts in the Soviet Union's security posture toward the United States depends not only on

[33] Legro and Moravcsik (1999: 32).

[34] For a vigorous and wide-ranging rebuttal by realists to critics who accuse them of abandoning first principles, see Feaver et al. (2000). When states can see gain from aligning with a more powerful state, which is a potential (and for classical realists a real) threat to their power and interests, they can be expected to join that state, contrary to classical and neorealist expectations.

[35] Wohlforth (1993, 1994, 1998).

Gorbachev's perceptions of power but on the analyst's perceptions of Gorbachev's perceptions of Western intentions.

Another, more recent attempt to save a realist (if not a neorealist) explanation of changes in Soviet foreign and security policy under Gorbachev merits attention.[36] These self-identified realist scholars focus on explaining the shift in Soviet policies rather than on addressing the more daunting question of why the Soviet Union collapsed. The latter remains the key event transforming the Cold War and ending the bipolar system. In contrast to classical realism, these researchers focus on the technological and economic shortcomings of the Soviet Union. These constraints are portrayed as forcing wrenching changes in Soviet thinking, including both conservatives and reformers, to opt for a détente policy toward the West. In emphasizing these material, but non-military, capabilities, there is a surface overlap between old and new realists. Material, observable forces are privileged to explain foreign policy changes.

Gone begging in these explanations is the question of why the West chose to rely on an open, transnationally based system of scientific discovery, technological innovation, and expanding global markets to address their economic needs. These choices that can only be partially reduced to strategic power considerations produced the gaps that compelled a change in Soviet foreign and security thinking. What is not explained fully or persuasively are the factors that led to the construction of those structures of power that, more than military force, destroyed the Soviet state (what realists and neorealists assume will not happen to a militarily powerful state) and the monopoly of power of the Communist party in the Soviet Union and throughout its East European empire. Explaining changes in Soviet security and foreign policy cannot be separated from explaining why the Soviet Union imploded and the Cold War ended. The latter outcomes require an explanation outside the limits of a realist paradigm, however imaginatively revised by realist theorists to save the theory.

As one might well expect, hard-core realist pessimists are not prepared to reinterpret realism to include subjective factors or variables, such as perceptions, ideology, intentions or normative convergence between states and leaders, to explain a state's behavior and its security policy. Nor are they keen to accept the claims of scholars pointing to defensive and offensive strategies as necessary either to support or to expand the theory, much less as friendly amendments to neorealism. Friendly amendments to correct perceived realist and neorealist shortcomings risk being transformed into substitute motions. Such motions, if accepted, threaten the

---

[36] Brooks (1997).

realist-neorealist research project, as critics have observed.[37] With friends like these, who needs critics?

Optimistic realism

In varying degrees, and however hard-core realists and neorealists may resist or reject them, these several emendations of classical and neorealist theory can be viewed as conceptual bridges to a more optimistic notion of realism. For these optimists, conflict, power-seeking, survival and opportunistic political gain still inform state behavior. While these limits to consensual cooperation can never be fully and finally surmounted, optimistic realists are more open to the possibility of relaxing these conflictual constraints than their pessimistic brethren.[38] This group of theorists is cautiously expectant about the evolutionary prospects of non-coerced state cooperation. They view states as rational, self-interested actors. Rivals can learn to cooperate for mutual advantage and hold their conflicts in check. From the dismal and pessimistic assumption of egoistic behavior, shared with other realists, these theorists argue that cooperation is possible for sustained, indefinitely long, periods between states under certain definable conditions.

For some, "bounded" cooperation – conflict within limits – can even become the dominant and expected norm between rivals. These lines of analysis are supported by the logic of game theory, experimental laboratory evidence, and historical references to state behavior. Optimists assume that states can learn to cooperate as a function, paradoxically, of their self-regarding pursuits. States can limit their reliance on force and coercive threats in their exchanges for mutual benefit. They can, conceivably, turn the vicious circle of violence and counter-violence projected by classical theorists (and endorsed by neorealists) into a virtuous circle of increasing cooperation and resistance or reluctance to use force as a viable instrument to get what they want.

Opponents, even seemingly enduring rivals like France and Germany after World War II and the superpowers of the Cold War, have incentive to cooperate.[39] In contrast to neorealists, these optimists extend and generalize these incentives both to bipolar *and* multipolar systems. Competing states are expected to eschew using force or employing excessive threats if these moves result in counterproductive reactions from their

---

[37] Vasquez (1997).
[38] See, for example, Axelrod (1984, 1986), Axelrod and Keohane (1993) and Schelling (1960, 1966).
[39] Glaser (1996). Evidence of superpower cooperation at regional levels is found in Kolodziej and Kanet (1991).

rival. If the expected gain from threats or violence is outweighed by the costs and risks of these strategic moves, then it stands to reason, according to these optimists, that states will resist pressuring their rivals, allies, or neutrals.[40] On the specific question of whether to initiate hostilities or not, rivals are expected to do everything possible to control not only their rival's behavior but also their mutual interactions to preclude a war or an armed exchange that neither wants. Such a war might erupt by accident, inadvertence, or unintentionally as the consequence of actions whose repercussions were not fully perceived. Once begun, notably when nuclear weapons might be used, rivals have strong incentive to bring such armed exchanges to a quick close to preserve their societies and vital interests. The expected utility of using or threatening force for probable gains is defined by these putatively shared rational calculations.

Cooperation by rivals to control their armed struggle through arms control and disarmament measures is not necessarily inconsistent with realist precepts. Clausewitz recognized as much over a century ago in defining the use of force *as a political action*. Cooperation between opponents makes sense if their vital interests and very survival are at risk unless they establish limits to their appeal to force to resolve their differences. Presumably, they also want to survive and avoid disastrous outcomes of their violent exchanges. It is assumed by these optimistic realists that states strive to avoid accidental, inadvertent, or unintended warfare and seek to minimize their largely unforeseen and damaging consequences by limiting violence and bringing hostilities to a quick close. World War I is the model for such unwanted outcomes disastrous to all participating states – outcomes that none expected and certainly none willed or wished.

There is also evidence, drawn from experimental findings through simulation studies, that limited cooperation between opponents in one area may spread to other areas of interaction. Through repeated contact and experiences of mutually beneficial cooperation, political learning can reinforce a strategy of cooperation over short-run gains obtained by defecting. To produce this virtuous circle, moving counter to the Hobbesian vicious circle, Robert Axelrod's research suggests that a simple tit-for-tat strategy could evolve into a sustained strategy of consistent cooperative behavior.[41] This strategy immediately punishes a player for taking temporary advantage of a cooperating player. Once the defector returns to cooperation, however, he is rewarded by the mutual gains arising from

---

[40] The theoretical basis for this position was principally established by Thomas Schelling (1960, 1966); See also Schelling and Halperin (1958).
[41] Axelrod (1986), Axelrod and Keohane (1993).

cooperating. The attractiveness of this strategy, according to Axelrod, is its simplicity, absence of vindictiveness, and pragmatic penchant to immediate and reciprocally enjoyed positive payoffs for the players. As Axelrod summarizes, a tit-for-tat strategy is "nice, provocable, forgiving, and clear."[42] Players adopt strategies that have these properties. Cooperation can be started, sustained, and strengthened. Certainly underlying conflict between rivals continues between rivals, but through experience actors learn that they gain more through cooperation, although not necessarily equally, than if they defect for marginal gains at the last exchange with a rival and choose unremitting conflict as their modus operandi. The theoretical basis for the incentive to cooperate is outlined in more detail below when the discussion turns to the Prisoner's Dilemma game as a metaphor of international relations and, specifically, the search for state security and survival.

The implications of Axelrod's theoretical position are that Hobbes' self-interested egoists can cooperate and resist the temptation of temporary and fleeting advantages by exploiting others. The transformation of a vicious into a virtuous circle need not necessarily depend on a Leviathan who stands outside the exchanges of actors over whom he rules. Order can conceivably arise from the initial conflict of interests of the players and be the product of their self-interested moves.[43] The tit-for-tat strategy, employed by one of the players in Axelrod's tournament, won over much more elaborate and complicated strategies to maximize gains in successive plays of the game. The iterative experience taught players that cooperation paid more than conflict and defection.

Several conditions encourage cooperation. The payoffs for the players must be interdependent, that is, mutually contingent. What becomes increasingly clear to the players is that their mutual gains maximize their individual gains through cooperation. To reach this level of conscious "play," they must continue to meet and interact. Their exchange is not a one-time thing. Within this "shadow of the future," as Axelrod suggests, players have the incentive to discount short-term gains by defecting in favor of long-term benefits. The expectations of this game work particularly well if the number of players is small. Confusion and misunderstanding are minimized. Players can form clear and reliable expectations of each

---

[42] *Ibid.*: 176.
[43] Keohane (1984), drawing on neoclassical theory, covered in chapter 5, advances this expectation. See Coase (1937, 1960). A serious problem, signaled by Axelrod and his colleagues, is that the evolution of cooperation drawn from the simulation appears to work best with small numbers. Can it be applied to 200 nation-states and six billion diverse and divided people? It is by no means clear that such voluntary cooperation is easy or automatic without some order in place. This raises the question of the role of coercion in social evolution.

other's behavior through repeated plays of the game. Monitoring expected behavior is easier and less costly than more elaborate strategies to punish defectors; sanctions are more focused and calibrated than the reciprocal moves of the egoists posited by Hobbes.

A second group of friendly realists uses history rather than game theory to argue for the possibility of cooperation among egoists. The English school has been particularly resourceful in expanding the scope of classical thinking about security and order without fully abandoning key assumptions of traditional realism. Partisans of this school share the assumption of self-interested actors, yet rely on their reconstruction of the historical record to underscore evidence of growing cooperation among states. In generalizing across the behavior of states since their inception in Europe,[44] Hedley Bull suggests that states have relaxed the divisive effects of anarchy and partially surmounted this defective condition. They have succeeded in developing a limited order or governance of their interdependent relations. Over several centuries of learning, states have converged on several key, if limited, rules to produce a fragile order and peace. States still support a decentralized system of global order, resting on the sovereign nation-state. The autonomy and legitimacy of states is validated and sustained by implicit accord of the states themselves. States recognize each other as moral equals despite varying differences among them in their power to discharge their internal and external security functions. These properties are embedded and sustained by the nation-states system, resulting in a synergistic reinforcement of state autonomy and sovereignty and the preservation of a system dedicated to these state interests and aims.

According to English school adherents, states have a vital interest in maintaining this decentralized system. It is the best, if scarcely infallibly reliable, guarantee of their survival and independence.[45] The system is also the precondition for the assertion by states of their monopoly of legitimate violence in ruling over populations demarcated by the geographical space over which they preside. A system of states also provides

---

[44] This volume adopts a different notion of the state than Tilly (1975a, b, 1990). It suits the purposes of this discussion to focus on the modern state and its evolution arising out of Europe in the fifteenth and sixteenth centuries. See, for example, Spruyt (1994) and especially Rosecrance (1986), who traces the rise of the trading state.

[45] Bull also makes the paradoxical argument that, sometimes, a state may have to be divided among stronger states if it is incapable of fulfilling its security obligations in order to preserve the balance of power as an institution of interstate governance. The partition of Poland at the end of the eighteenth century between Prussia, Austria, and Russia is cited by Bull (1977) as an example of the contradictory constraints of a nation-state system as a system of governance: a state may be sacrificed to save other states and the balance of power among the predators.

each unit with the capacity to defend its interests and those of its population against outsiders. Bull and his English school partisans contend that, progressively, this system of states in which states took account of the moves and power of their peers gradually evolved into a society of states. As members of a society, states not only calculate how to use their power to shape the behavior of other states in favorable ways but also act on the expectations of shared interests and values in the governing arrangements of the society.

Bull observed that states were actually more at peace than at war over the centuries of their evolution, notwithstanding the obvious carnage of the twentieth century, of which Bull was acutely aware. As rational, prudent egoists, concerned about their own interests and survival, they were increasingly preoccupied with resolving differences peacefully and with limiting violence in settling accounts. The carnage of World Wars I and II or the global competition of the Cold War may have qualified the limits of cooperation among states, but these struggles affirmed, not denied, the underlying condition of implied cooperation to save the society of states and to check aspiring hegemons.

The balance of power among states to prevent any one state from dominating others and turning the system into unipolar rule was equally at work during peace and during these armed struggles. The balance of power was inherent in the state system as its key mechanism of governance. Viewed in this favorable light, balance of power politics strengthened, not weakened, the society of states. Anarchy was not fully surmounted; it remained the natural condition under which states acted. It was defined and, accordingly, limited by the implicit rules of behavior inherent in the balance of power. Anarchy was not, as neorealists contended, a necessarily disruptive condition, nor a causal force beyond the control of the members of this society of states. War, too, was an institution of government, limited in its destructive scope by the implied and mutual benefits enjoyed by states as members of an imperfect society. This view paralleled Quincy Wright's understanding of war as a condition of "imperfect" law between states,[46] not a rupture of underlying "laws" of state behavior, potentially discoverable and verifiable by careful observation and by rigorous and systemic scientific testing.

This society of states stopped well short of the Hobbesian endgame. States were able to agree on the decentralized governance of the society they formed. Its preservation also fostered peace and prosperity. Bull insisted that, if this process were viewed over the long-run existence of these states, what might appear to the untutored eye as a ceaseless

[46] Wright (1965).

struggle for power yielded an evolving but stable balance of power among the members of a society of states. Peace was more prevalent than war. The balance sustained international law and customary practices, moral and normative rules, and international institutions and organizations in establishing a fragile but real and palpable global order. These were critical, self-sustaining, self-correcting, and self-strengthening components of international governance. Hobbes' fear that all commerce, arts, and industry would be impossible unless there were a single awesome power to arbitrate differences appeared unfounded or, at least, unduly pessimistic, when applied to states. The latter could live peacefully under the seemingly paradoxical threat of war. States could also cooperate sufficiently, even in large numbers, to provide an order to encourage economic exchanges and to allow growth to flourish. This was principally due to the peace they were able to achieve as well as to efforts to limit violence when war erupted. A society of states also protected private property and the sanctity of contracts.[47] The order constructed by this society permitted all manner of cross-border exchanges for the mutual benefit of the world's populations. In light of these several dimensions of state cooperation, Bull concluded (in contrast to Waltz) that even under conditions of anarchy, states could fashion a primitive society and minimal order capable of replication over time within which the incentives to use force or threats could conceivably recede, not expand – all without a Leviathan.

This optimistic realist position has since been carried further by some partisans of the English school.[48] The kind of society of states posited by Bull initially emerged among states that implicitly shared a common Western culture. If initially the society of states projected by Bull arose implicitly from a shared Western culture, there is no necessary reason, this realist camp contends, that the rules and norms of a society of states could not be extended to all peoples, however much they were divided by culture, religion, language, and custom.[49] If analysis goes below the surface of the structure of states – a move that traditional realists and neorealists reject as outside the permissible boundaries of theory – it is possible to envision a growing convergence, if not congruence, of the foundational values held across different cultures. The notions of democratization, civil liberties, and human rights, while clearly expressed in

---

[47] Bull asserts this norm of the purported existence of a society of states without much proof or evidence; a more solid historical and theoretical basis for this norm is found in North (1990).

[48] See Buzan (2004) for the most up-to-date position of this school and Martin Wight (1966a).

[49] This position is pointedly rejected by Bozeman (1960). It was later extended by Huntington (1996).

different cultural, national, and ethnic idioms, would appear to be globalizing forces. Gradually and with punctuated and irregular movement, these forces appear to be inducing international actors, notably states, to comply with these norms. The limits of sovereign authority are both being limited and enlisted in defense of human rights.[50] This evolution offers some prospect that it will shape and shove the system of states as it presently exists in world politics into the kind of society of states envisioned by the English school.[51]

Liberal institutionalists

Before a critique is attempted of realist and neorealist theories, it is important to first outline liberal institutionalist thought. Theorists in this school have made a concerted effort to develop a conceptual framework for international relations theory that "subsumes" realist thinking.[52] Institutionalists purport to explain everything that realist theory can explain about the behavior of states and their pursuit of security interests and survival – and, echoing Imre Lakatos, a lot more. The "lot more" principally concerns the priorities of state decision-making that extend well beyond security issues to include the "multidimensional economic, social, and ecological interdependence"[53] of states and other international actors. Institutionalists seek to affirm the centrality of the state while widening the scope of international relations to include interests other than those narrowly related to security, as limiting the downward spiral of conflict predicted by classical realists and neorealism.

The broader scope of institutionalist theory presents a serious problem for theory development. By widening the scope of state interests to explain state behavior, institutionalists must include a larger number of actors and factors impacting on state decisions. They must also add levels of analysis beyond the interstate and systemic levels posited by realists and neorealists. Added, as chapter 1 describes, are transnational and domestic political levels of analysis. Transnational actors (multinational corporations, intergovernmental and non-governmental organizations) and domestic regimes and actors (interest groups, bureaucrats, political parties, the media, etc.) are then brought within the circle of theoretical concern. Parsimony, a key feature of traditional realist and especially of neorealist theory, is sacrificed for relevance and greater specificity in explaining state behavior. Institutionalists devote greater attention to the particular conditions or constraints under which states and other actors interact

---

[50] This proposition is extensively developed in Kolodziej (2003).
[51] Buzan (2004), Buzan, Little, and Jones (1993).
[52] Baldwin (1993) and Keohane (1986).   [53] Keohane and Nye (2001: 246).

and how they make decisions and behave. The widening and deepening effects of institutionalist thinking are precisely what many realists and all neorealists resist in advancing their theory of international relations and security. Liberal institutionalists try to meet this criticism by accepting key assumptions of realist theory, while insisting on a research program that identifies the coercive *and* non-coercive conditions and incentives under which states act.

The state remains the central actor in institutionalist theory. Military power is affirmed as the final determiner of outcomes of interstate relations once it is invoked. The state and its governing leaders are viewed as rational actors. They do not deliberately make decisions or take moves that result in losses or unacceptable risks for themselves. States, like individuals, are also assumed to be selfish egoists. They pursue their interests under conditions of anarchy, marked by great uncertainty about the implications of their behavior; that is, they lack the necessary information to act in ways that they can accurately and reliably predict the results of their mutually contingent behavior with other actors. Unlike neorealists, institutionalists view anarchy in a similar light as English school realists. States have a wide range of choices over different policy domains whether to cooperate or defect. They are not necessarily compelled to rely exclusively, or primarily, on force and threats in conducting their mutually contingent affairs.[54]

Like their realist counterparts, institutionalists portray states as locked into what game theorists call a Prisoner's Dilemma game. In this metaphoric game, which purports to capture the predicament of sovereign states in their exchanges with each other, two prisoners isolated by the police are interrogated about their involvement in a crime. Under the conditions of the game, both could go free if they do not inform on their partner. But if one of the prisoners "rats" on his partner, he goes free in the game and his "sucker" partner gets, say, ten years in jail. In the game, if both "rat" on each other, both get lesser sentences, but neither goes free; say, each gets three years in jail.

Figure 4.1 presents a simple version of this game to simulate the conditions of choice confronting autonomous states within an anarchical international system in which distrust and uncertainty pervade their expectations of their rivals' motives and the likely choices they will make, endangering their interests. Clearly, the prisoners gain most if they opt for box A. But can each trust that his partner in crime won't defect and rat on him, given the incentives of the game? By ratting, the prisoner goes free and the sucker partner gets ten years. If both rat on each other, both get

[54] Milner (1993).

PRISONER I
(vertical)

FREE	FREE	
A	B	
FREE	10 YEARS (SUCKER)	
10 YEARS (SUCKER)	3 YEARS	
C	D	
FREE	3 YEARS	

PRISONER II
(horizontal)

Figure 4.1 *Prisoner's Dilemma*

three years. Given the lack of trust and information by which the prisoners might coordinate their preferences for optimal gains (the police hold each in isolation), each criminal has an apparent compelling incentive to squeal on his partner rather than risk the worst outcome of ten years in jail. Better three years than ten, since neither knows what his partner will do. This is clearly not the optimal outcome for both prisoners, because the move to box A would be best for both. Lacking trust and information, neither can confidently rely on the expectation that his partner will remain silent. The outcome disadvantages both but less so than being a sucker and remaining silent. Both have a powerful incentive to rat on their associate.

States, based on the Hobbesian assumption of rational egoists, are cast in the roles of competing prisoners. They can improve their security as well as gain positive benefits if they cooperate. But they lack the information, reliable institutional mechanisms for coordination, and fundamental trust in each other. They are egoists after all, according to realist and institutionalist assumptions. They have the incentive to defect from cooperation when it appears that they can gain at the expense of other states. When security is at issue and force the currency of the exchange, they have an added call to use or threaten force to compel the cooperation of other states, whether rivals, allies, or neutrals.

At this crucial point in the analysis, liberal institutionalists enter the discussion. They agree with realists of all stripes that overcoming the selfish tendencies of states, especially their possession of a monopoly of violence, is a very real problem. This problem cannot be ignored simply by assuming that the benefits of cooperation are self-evident if states cooperate. Nor can states rely on the good will or altruistic and idealistic pronouncements of states. States always have to worry that they will be disadvantaged because other states and actors might cheat. This concern is embedded in all of their relations. Here again institutionalists and realists agree. Unlike most realists – most notably neorealists – institutionalists believe that the informational and coordinating limitations of state interactions can be relaxed and even surmounted by institutions, created for mutual, if differentially, valued benefits by states. The distribution of benefits to cooperating egoists, like that of silent prisoners going free, can be effectively and equitably maximized to exceed the gain each might achieve through unilateral action and defection at the expense of other states. Cooperation yields optimal gains for all parties.

Institutionalists also still insist that they are working within a "systemic perspective"[55] to achieve a parsimonious explanation of state behavior. Most realists generally reject this claim. In other words, to achieve parsimony, liberal institutionalists attempt to develop a theory of international relations and state behavior by limiting their observations, following the lead of their realist and neorealist counterparts, to the exogenous or exterior relations of states and to key non-state actors. The larger scope of state and actor exchanges is still cast in terms of their effect on state actions and policies. States are viewed as interacting with each other but also, and simultaneously, with other actors at transnational and domestic levels. They are also embedded in a larger and more complex web of interdependent interactions with intergovernmental and non-governmental organizations. Salience is attached to the material conditions of these exchanges.

Non-material ideological and psychological factors are not so much rejected by some institutionalists as subordinated to the workings of the exterior relations of actor behavior.[56] Like realist theory, institutionalists cross this boundary when it suits their purposes, but the thrust of this school of thought is to stay within the limits of an "objective" perspective in theory-building.[57] Ideas and ideology orient actors in their choices and strategies, but their independent impact on state policies is still viewed as subordinate to the material interests of actors – economic and security – and to changing power relationships.[58] Their principal causal role is to furnish "focal points" for cooperative choices between states. Belief in the

[55] Keohane and Nye (2001: 257).   [56] Goldstein and Keohane (1993).
[57] Keohane (1988). See also Nye (1988).   [58] Goldstein and Keohane (1993: 25).

idea of a European Union as the institutional basis for economic cooperation and increased welfare for participating states illustrates this causal role. The repeated affirmation of this belief and the rules and norms associated with its application in the policies and behavior of states institutionalize these beliefs and organize the environment of state interaction in ways favorable for all participants.[59]

Before we turn to what liberal institutionalists mean by institutions, it is important to describe their understanding of the political context within which the state acts today. They replace the realist billiard ball conception of state interaction with an image of multiple, overlapping webs of actor relations across the entire range of policy concerns of states. States are ensnared in these webs. Depending on the policy domain being examined – say the environment or foreign investment – different actors play varied roles in designing and determining the constraints and opportunities for state power and moves. This messy picture, according to institutionalists, portrays world politics more realistically than realist theory. Robert Keohane and Joseph Nye advance a widely cited version of the institutionalist model. It purports to subsume realist thinking within a broader institutionalist framework.[60] They present world politics as a system of "complex interdependence," a view that has attracted a large following and enjoys a leading place in international relations research and theory building.

According to liberal institutionalists, these networks of exchanges between states and non-state actors along which continuing bargaining between them for advantage is conducted have purportedly changed international relations in three fundamental ways. First, these interactions and the diverse interests, aims, and power capabilities of these actors create multiple channels through which they can achieve their purposes. States are not the only channel through which actors can work their will. States, too, use other avenues and rely on other actors than states to achieve their objectives even in relation to other states. Global markets which address state welfare functions and obligations illustrate these

---

[59] *Ibid.*: 1–30, develops the views of these authors about the causal import of ideas. They are more complex than can be described here, but their centrality is still resisted in explaining state behavior. Moreover, state preferences and interests are still stipulated as given, and efforts to link beliefs and values or what the authors loosely identify as "ideas" to the formation of interests is defined outside the scope of theoretical analysis. This move, of course, begs the question of where preferences and interests arise as drivers of behavior, a glaring gap in the institutionalist research project.

[60] This school of thought is more complex and varied than can be fully presented here. See Hall and Taylor (1996) for a review of three orientations, including historical, rational choice, and sociological institutionalism. This discussion has concentrated on the Keohane–Nye group because of its prominence and widespread citation in the literature.

mechanisms.[61] Keohane and Nye summarize these dimensions of complex interdependence and differentiate their conception of international relations from realism, while attempting to incorporate realist assumptions of egoism and anarchy into the scope of their theorizing. Going beyond interstate relations, the singular channel of state interactions assumed by realists, these authors also identify transgovernmental and transnational levels of analysis. As they summarize: "*Transgovernmental* (governmental elites of states bargaining with each other and with their state colleagues) applies when we relax the realist assumption that states act coherently as units; *transnational* applies when we relax the assumption that states are the only units."[62]

Complex interdependence also stipulates that states confront multiple issues simultaneously, not serially and sequentially. These must be solved as they arise, and not as the state might wish. The hierarchical division of high and low politics posited by realists is supplanted by a horizontally defined agenda with multiple, conflicting, and interconnected trade-offs. Except under conditions of clear and imminent danger of war and armed hostilities to fix the attention of state decision-makers – much like hanging confronting a convicted felon – states typically face multiple and diverse issues and hard-choice trade-offs made under conditions of uncertainty in assessing gains and losses across a wide and evolving range of policy problems. Military security normally competes for attention and priority with these non-security issues. State power and decision-making are parceled among these policy domains. Depending on the issue at hand, rival coalitions of actors coalesce within the state, including counterparts at transnational and domestic levels of action in other states, to press for their favored outcome on a particular issue.

The domestic politics of different states are drawn into this sprawling and untidy bargaining process. What appear to be the relations of states with each other at an interstate and systemic level of analysis is actually driven often, depending on the policy domain under examination, by non-state actors at transnational and domestic levels. Thus the actors, issues, power structures, and levels of analysis included within the ambit of complex interdependence and institutionalist theory go well beyond the realist paradigm. These elements are then funneled and focused on state behavior; hence the claim of a systemic viewpoint is affirmed, even as few actors and factors are left out of consideration at lower levels of analysis. The claim of "parsimony" becomes muddied and problematic.

Institutionalists stipulate that state priorities fall along a shifting continuum. Within institutionalist thinking, there is no sharp and distinct

---

[61] Lindblom (2001).   [62] Keohane and Nye (2001: 25).

break between security and coercion, on the one hand, and other state aims and interests and non-coercive power to achieve them, on the other. The distinction between high and low politics made by many realists, as if they were separate and scarcely interacting and interdependent domains, is replaced by a notion of a range of state interests. States use different forms of state power – material or hard power and non-material or soft power – to advance these interests.[63] Under conditions of complex interdependence, non-coercive forms of power and a disposition to cooperate with other states are assigned no less a privileged status than military power in explaining the day-to-day decisions and actions of states. Realists and institutionalists differ sharply in their explanation of the variations in state behavior precisely on this point.

States also confront not only the power of other states but that of other actors, like intergovernmental organizations, actors of their own creation. Intergovernmental organizations (IGOs), like the United Nations, NATO, or the World Trade Organization, are attributed power to constrain states and to have interests in their own right. They orient, limit, and, alternatively, expand the power and interests of state members. These IGOs are complemented by thousands of non-governmental organizations (NGOs). These influence state and IGO policies and behavior. Global markets and notably multinational corporations, the dominant actors within them, further limit *and* enlarge state power depending on the policy domain, say, environmental, health, labor or trade issues. Powerful individuals, too, are capable of influencing state security and non-security interests. These may be influential market players, like a George Soros, who made millions by speculating on fluctuations in monetary rates, or determined reformers, like Jody Williams, who convinced many states to ban land mines. More darkly, private actors can be terrorists, like Osama bin Laden, whose Al Qaeda network reportedly has cells in sixty countries.

Finally, liberal institutionalists argue that the dominance of military power and security is eroded before these other issue concerns and the power of state and non-state actors to dictate desired outcomes. The depreciation of material power and force opens the way to explain and decide interstate relations in terms of other interests and different forms of power. Economic, environmental, and ecological issues are identified as particularly crucial areas of state concern. These cannot be reduced to the realist focus on force and threats. Other forms of cooperation and power are more relevant for solutions to these collective action problems than the assertion of the state's coercive powers. Rival states, for example,

---

[63] Nye (1990, 2002).

which seek increased material welfare for their populations are restrained from using force or coercion to compel a concession or trading privilege. In such a policy setting, force or threats are counterproductive for both sides. Increased economic activity implies rules of law and the free play of market forces, insulated from state intervention.

An important implication of these trade-offs of interests across policy domains is that states are as interested in absolute gains as they are in their relative power standing with respect to other states. Realists insist, however, that states are always and everywhere worried about the relative gains of other states. Institutionalists draw attention to the conditional setting within which states assess relative vs. absolute gains in their relations with states.[64] States, as rational actors, are assumed to make evaluations of their exchanges with other actors to assess whether the gains made by another state, say in its military or technological and economic capabilities, would harm or damage the state's interests. If not, then institutionalists advance evidence to show that relative increases in a state's gains will not necessarily be viewed as threatening. For example, Britain, France, and Israel, allies of the United States, possess formidable nuclear capabilities, yet aspiring nuclear powers, like Iran, Iraq and North Korea, are branded as serious security threats.

There is also the problem of moving from a potential to a clear and present danger. States may intend to use their relative gains in material capabilities to harm another state, but be impeded by a host of factors from carrying out their intentions. There are also data to show that the zero-sum game of Prisoner's Dilemma tends to exaggerate the relative gains of states and emphasize worst-case scenarios.[65] Institutionalists portray absolute gains as typically more important to a state than concerns about its relative power position.[66] These include benefits from more trade and investment or from greater cooperation with other states. Even rivals can gain mutually rewarding benefits through coordination of overlapping, shared interests, such as increased environmental protection for all parties. Institutionalists insist that states will place greater value on the absolute acquisition of more wealth and welfare for their populations and for the state even if other states, including current or potential rivals, actually gain *more* materially from a relative perspective. To relinquish these gains would weaken the state relative to the multiple constituencies it serves. It would also forgo the opportunity to cooperate with other states and to increase their mutual power to address mutually contingent issues, including their security and the coordination of their efforts in pursuit of non-security objectives.

[64] Powell (1991).   [65] Snidal (1993).   [66] Keohane (1984, 1993).

This rich and complex tapestry is the international relations context within which institutionalists attempt to explain why cooperation arises between states in contrast to the realist expectation of chronic conflict and defection. States face trade-offs between strictly security issues and other aims and interests. Security issues pose, as this volume defines security, the question of whether to use or not use force. These security issues rise or fall in salience and immediacy and compete for the attention and resources with non-security issues. These fall along different and varying points along the security/non-security continuum of complex interdependence. Bargaining between states is certainly framed by the underlying anarchy of their autonomous positions, but institutionalists argue that merely acknowledging this condition tells us little about what instruments of power and persuasion states will actually use, given competing incentives to cooperate or defect or to use force or desist. The assumption of anarchy also tells us little about what forms of power are best suited to achieve the objectives being sought. Military force may or may not be relevant to these pursuits, according to liberal institutionalists.

This ceaseless process of new and old issue areas of concern demanding decisions and actions by the state in its relations with other actors prompts the creation of rules, norms, and principles of behavior. States rely on these mechanisms to anticipate the behavior of other states and to guide their own reactions. Repeated adherence to them by states transforms these patterns of behavior and their accompanying and shared expectations by actors into formal institutions. States can rely on these institutions to stabilize and control their political environments in mutually agreeable ways. These institutions gradually become regimes. States are still assumed to have the material power to defect from these arrangements and to be tempted to cheat on other states when the gains from their defection exceed the costs at the margin when a decision to cooperate or not arises. They can ignore or violate established patterns of behavior and well-recognized rules, norms, and principles of action. However, defections come at a stiff price, potentially costly in long-term losses for all parties. Institutionalists claim that the costs and risks of defection have mounted increasingly for states as interdependencies across all important domains of state interest have expanded in scope and number. Institutions become critical values and interests of the state in their own right. Once formed, states increasingly define their interests to maintain and extend these institutions rather than the reverse, wherein interests and power maximization incentives are said to drive institutions.[67] Depending on

---

[67] See the exchange between Mearsheimer (1994) and Keohane and Martin (1995).

the issue area under consideration, institutions can explain and predict state behavior, particularly the inclination of states to cooperate.

But what do institutions *do* to warrant this claim? According to institutionalists, institutions perform several functional roles that encourage cooperation. Shared rules imply reciprocity. Much like Axelrod's tit-for-tat game, institutions communicate to actors, including rivals, the rewards of cooperation and the costs and risks of conflict and defection. If states violate a rule, they risk a countervailing and costly reaction from other states, potentially damaging to their interests. These moves may assume the form of a sanction, such as a stiff and embarrassing note of criticism or an economic boycott or a raising of tariffs on selective products. These moves and counter-moves may escalate to the closing of borders and even an attack on a state's military bases or personnel. The violation of an expected behavior in a specific exchange may undermine the institutional structure itself.

Institutions also provide information to each of the actors to help coordinate their mutually contingent behavior for shared, if not necessarily, equal benefits. This crucial dimension of information is precisely what is absent in the Prisoner's Dilemma game. Knowledge based on the patterned behavior of a state over time allegedly pierces the shroud of secrecy and misperception surrounding state exchanges. Greater transparency bolsters the confidence of decision-makers that cooperation will not be exploited. Standards for monitoring compliance to rules as well as sanctions for penalizing defectors can also be incorporated into the institutions framing state behavior.

Organizations, like the World Trade Organization, NATO, or the European Union, are the concrete embodiment of these evolving institutional structures and processes of decision-making. Proof of the importance of these institutions can be measured by the vast resources, privileged status, and scope of the multilateral decision-making funneled through these organizations. Additional evidence of the importance of institutions is the growth of intergovernmental organizations since World War II, which now number over a thousand. These organizations, like firms in international markets, decrease the transaction costs of doing governmental business and bargaining for gains in relations among states. These bargaining relations and the resulting cooperation deriving from them can be achieved, as institutionalists aver, without a Leviathan or hegemon.[68] The incentives of greater transparency, mutual and reciprocal absolute

---

[68] Keohane (1984). The problem with this position is that the expected decline of US power, viewed by many scholars as impending in the 1980s, belied the actual ascendancy of American power.

gains, decreased uncertainty, and lowered transaction costs make institutions inviting, indeed necessary and increasingly important in ordering state behavior through voluntary cooperation among rational egoists.

Evaluation of realism, neorealism, and liberal institutionalism and the Cold War

How well do these three theoretical positions hold up? How well do they explain the rise and evolution of the Cold War and the US–Soviet global rivalry? How well do they explain or predict – or at least anticipate – the implosion of the Soviet Union and the abrupt end of the Cold War and the bipolar balance that dominated much of the second half of the twentieth century?

One way to organize this critique is to evaluate the responses of realism, neorealism, and liberal institutionalism along the dimensions of comparison outlined earlier. First, let's look at actors and their expected behavior as projected by these orientations. All of these schools focus on the state as the principal actor in international relations. None explains why the state triumphed as the principal unit of political organization of the world's diverse and divided populations. The state is assumed as a given rather than posed as a puzzle and problem to be explained. There is a loud silence about explaining the process of decolonization and the subsequent expansion of the nation-state as the principal unit of political organization of the world's divided and disparate populations. Nor do these three positions envision the dissolution of states, most especially a big power. The continued existence of the state and its perpetuation in much the same form since its inception is implicitly assumed and not questioned, notably by realists. The principal, non-trivial amendment to these state-centric approaches is offered by liberal institutionalism. It departs from its cohorts by widening its explanatory lens of state behavior by including the impact of non-state actors and non-coercive incentives and policy options on the state and on the state system. The state is depicted not only as a vehicle for security but also as a welfare state whose existence depends on its ability to deliver material plenty to its populations at politically ratified and legitimated levels and rates.

Neorealism is particularly vulnerable to criticism. In substituting survival for the less precise notion of state interests as power – Hans Morgenthau's reaffirmation of classical realism – neorealism laid claim to a status on a par with the natural sciences, a position forcefully rejected by traditional realists as possible or even sensible and moral.[69] The neorealist

---

[69] Morgenthau (1951b).

canon ruled out the possibility of a state's dissolution if it met its survival test: sufficient military capabilities to balance those of its rivals. If it met this test, the state would not be selected out of the struggle for survival. It would be the last international actor to be eliminated. Given the military balance at the end of the Cold War between the United States and the Soviet Union and their respective alliances, there was no reason to expect that the Soviet state would collapse anytime soon – or ever.

It can be argued, as neorealists claim in rebuttal, that the Western coalition was gaining ground militarily.[70] Its technological lead in developing new weaponry, from satellite communications to smart bombs and precision bombing and reconnaissance drones, was stealing a march on the Soviets. Nevertheless, the Soviet state at its end possessed the largest ground army in Europe. It could still, if it chose, suppress national uprisings among its satellites, as it had done on three previous occasions (1953, 1956, 1968) or rebellious movements among its many domestic nationality and communal groups. Its massive internal police and intelligence services, which instilled fear and commanded the obedience of the Soviet Union's unruly national groupings, remained intact. It also had a Doomsday Machine equivalent to that of the United States. Yet the Soviet Union imploded, contrary to classical realist and neorealist expectations.

Neorealists and realists do provide what seems to be a convincing explanation of the global struggle for power after World War II at the three levels of military balance sketched in chapter 3.[71] The global superpower struggle for hegemony increased military capabilities on both sides to unprecedented historical levels. The quest for allies was no less relentless. It was as if the Melian dialogue were repeating itself over two millennia later between two powers striving now for global hegemony rather than dominance of the Greek peninsula.[72] The titanic battle appeared to conform to the expectations of these three schools of thought. The ever-expanding growth of nuclear capabilities on each side of the Cold War divide conformed to realist and neorealist expectations.

Liberal institutionalists did not challenge this projection of superpower behavior. Rather, they concentrated on explaining interstate cooperation through bargaining and negotiation between rational actors who would perceive the benefits of voluntarily coordinating their nuclear policies to preserve a stable nuclear balance. Institutionalists and the optimistic

---

[70] Odom (1992).

[71] Mueller (1995) insists that the Cold War can be better explained as a conflict over ideas rather than a struggle for hegemony through the pursuit of material superiority. Most constructivists, discussed in the next chapter, would agree. See, for example, Wendt (1992) and Kubalkova (2001a).

[72] Fliess (1966).

branch of realism offered a reasonable explanation for the superpower to cooperate at all of these levels on arms control and disarmament issues. By focusing on their mutual interests, and not just on survival, these theorists introduced a wider range of security concerns into the calculus of states and their leadership than is available by strict adherence to a neorealist conception of international relations. Theorists Thomas Schelling and Robert Axelrod, who began from tough-minded Hobbesian assumptions of self-interested and egoistic actors or states, were able to define wide areas of accord between even implacable rivals. Nuclear war advised caution and cooperation through negotiated transformations of the military balance to stabilize the military environment and to discipline allies from precipitating a superpower confrontation.

Institutionalists strengthened this line of analysis. Greater transparency arising from improved satellite intelligence and increased confidence in national means of verification underscored the institutionalist emphasis on information about an adversary's capabilities as an incentive for cooperation. Trust could be fostered by greater transparency and verification. A negotiated nuclear and conventional environment also responded more sensitively and discriminatingly to the conflicting interests of Moscow and Washington than unilateral efforts to surmount the military balance between them.

What liberal institutionalists had difficulty explaining were the persistent, unilateral and decidedly non-cooperative efforts of each superpower to surmount the constraints of the military nuclear and conventional balance between them throughout the Cold War, as realists and neorealists predicted. States were still assumed to seek maximum material power in order to dictate their security preferences to adversaries and allies. The American proposal to build an anti-ballistic missile system fits this model. Technological advances generated incentives to change the quantitative and the qualitative balance of forces on each side. But barring a breakthrough that was never clearly on the horizon, the incentives for limited cooperation were sufficient to explain the political constraints imposed on the Cold War conflict, much in line with the expectations of Clausewitz's notion of war as politics by other means and in accord with realist expectations.

All three schools expected the superpowers to pursue hegemonic objectives and, in turn, to be checked by a countervailing balance of power. Neorealists stipulated a bipolar power balance as more stable, although they offer no explanation for its emergence other than citing the large and ever increasing nuclear capabilities of the superpowers as demonstrable proof of bipolarity. Neorealism has no theory – or apparent interest – in explaining change either as a function of domestic politics or in relations between states other than by reference to a rigid bipolar system that has since (and inexplicably) collapsed. The observation of bipolarity constituted an explanation by hindsight. Neorealists were confident, too, that bipolarity would endure almost indefinitely because of its posited (if not demonstrated) stability. Neither traditional realists nor institutionalists challenged this expectation, although bipolarity existed only a brief four decades.

Neorealists could explain their behavior if they were in power, but not the behavior of actors under their scrutiny. Acting implicitly against its own long-term interests, the United States helped rebuild the economies of its former foes in implicit violation of neorealist dogma that assumes a search for survival and security through preponderant power, a critique only partially offset by the looming struggle with the Soviet Union. Although a superpower was not supposed to worry about an ally under a bipolar system, the United States still consulted its partners on key security issues impacting on their mutual, if not fully congruent, security interests – behavior at odds with neorealist strictures.[73]

The leadership of the Soviet Union also fundamentally violated neorealist rules of big power behavior. First, Premier Gorbachev made substantial unilateral concessions to destroy all intermediate nuclear weapons in the European theater as a down payment on negotiations leading to sharp cuts in the strategic nuclear arsenals on both sides. Second, and more significantly, he announced major cuts in Soviet armed forces. Conventional arms control talks, stalled for decades, were given a kick-start. Third, he announced that the Soviet Union would not intervene to protect the Communist regimes of the Warsaw pact. This promise was largely kept, notwithstanding the failed attempts by domestic conservative rivals to force Gorbachev's hand by intervening in the Baltic states to bring them into line. Lacking effective Soviet military power to back their rule, none of the Communist regimes in power was able to withstand popular demands for democratic reforms or resist the destruction of their monopoly of power. Finally, the Soviet Union conceded what had been thought unthinkable until then, namely, the destruction of East Germany as a state and its peaceful reintegration through free elections into a united Germany under democratic rule within the NATO alliance.

None of these schools of thought offers a satisfactory explanation of these radical departures from their expected scripts for superpower or state behavior. To their partial credit, institutionalists opened the door to other actors and factors to explain these changes. They include other levels of actor engagement with states than their neorealist or many of

---

[73] These points are developed at length in McCallister (2002).

their realist cohorts. They introduce transnational and domestic levels of state and non-state interaction into their research programs to explain state behavior.

With some notable exceptions,[74] institutionalists have not systematically exploited the implications of this opening either to lower the privileged position assigned to the state relative to other actors or to develop a coherent and more conclusive explanation for outcomes of international actors' exchanges. Institutionalists have largely confined their focus to state behavior and to their self-defined problem of reconciling their notions of complex interdependence with realist and neorealist assumptions. Their concern has served more to develop a common theoretical framework of analysis for theorizing about state behavior and the international system than to break out of this conceptual box when countervailing evidence fails to fit a realist or neorealist straitjacket.[75] The state and the state system are depicted as departing from the projected patterns of action of strictly applied realist expectations, but never to the extent that institutionalists feel impelled to put into question – that is to problematize – the state or the state system as a consequence of the pressure brought to bear by non-state actors, by the structures of power and incentives associated with global markets or by identity politics. Demands for national self-determination and legitimacy in regime composition and rule drop out of consideration. These powerful forces and the actors associated with them are largely absent from conceptual prisms through which these theorists approach security.

At a transnational level, realists and neorealists concede that big powers have to compete for relative power not only on the dimension of military capabilities but also on the battlefields of scientific discovery, technological innovations, and sustained economic development. It is, therefore, consistent with realist expectations that a Soviet Union, which was losing ground rapidly on these critical fronts, would seek some respite in the superpower struggle. From the perspective of these realists, the détente policies initiated by the Gorbachev regime can be viewed as a strategic move to slow down the arms race; this would permit the shift of scarce techno-scientific and economic resources to strengthen the Soviet Union's economic growth and to enhance its competitiveness.

Expected Western concessions to relax the Cold War struggle would also open the way to Western technology, markets, and investment. These benefits could also be viewed as a tactic to disarm opponents to Gorbachev's domestic reforms, to enlarge public debate and transparency

---

[74] Goldstein and Keohane (1993) and Keohane and Milner (1996).
[75] Baldwin (1993).

(*glasnost*), to restructure the economy and shrink the public sector to the benefit of an enlarging civil and private society (*perestroika*), and to democratize Soviet governing institutions as a check on entrenched conservatives and bureaucrats. From the narrow focus on these three schools of thought on state survival and on the imperative of maximizing power in pursuit of state interests, these changes in Soviet strategic behavior and economic policy can be viewed as in the service of high politics. Economic or welfare demands on Soviet leadership are conceived as instrumental and subordinate to these security imperatives. They are not interpreted per se as sufficiently compelling to be accorded a status in leadership decisions equal to the security objectives of the state, nor of sufficient weight, once addressed, to threaten the very existence of the state itself and the power and privileges of its leadership, too.[76]

Neorealists and pessimistic realists agree that states that fail to compete with rivals will eventually be selected out of the process of survival of the fittest. Thus states are always supposedly concerned about their relative material power relations with competitors. This concern extends both to military and to the techno-scientific and economic dimensions of the rivalry. What appears no less true is that states that fail to respond effectively to the demands of their populations for greater material welfare are also threatened with extinction. The Soviet leadership may, arguably, have been moved by strategic objectives in shifting to a détente posture as the precondition for domestic economic reform. That reform was essentially cast in terms of adapting the Soviet Union and its economic bloc partners to the power of Western global capitalist markets as drivers of ceaseless civilian and military technological innovation. The Soviet state's military prowess was irrelevant to this adaptation process except insofar as cuts in defense spending might have facilitated the transformation of the Soviet economy.

As Joseph Schumpeter recognized, well before the outbreak of the Cold War, capitalism and the imperatives of market exchange for maximum profit induced private entrepreneurs to engage in "creative destruction."[77] Worldwide markets and the incentives for profit and prestige they generated by winning in this global game drove technological innovations. They created new products and services only to have them "destroyed" by more effective and efficient substitutes or surmounted by the creation of new markets for previously unimagined goods for hire or sale.

The Soviet Union's command economy could not match the incentives for innovations and profits of global markets and their capacity to stimulate the creation of more and better products and services. Whereas

---

[76] Brooks and Wohlforth (2000/2001).   [77] Martinelli (1994).

it was still able to match the West in military violence, it was increasingly clear, even to those elements of its most conservative and ideologically committed elites, that radical economic reform had to be undertaken. The Soviet experience suggests the proposition that states, to survive in light of the expectations of their supporting populations for "more now," must address this welfare imperative or risk withdrawal of popular support and, worse, the very existence of the regime and state, too. That is precisely what happened when Soviet leadership attempted to adapt the Soviet command economy to an open, free market system. The more the Soviet Union adapted to the power structures, institutional rules, and demanding discipline of global markets, the more its leaders unwittingly hastened its demise.[78]

Institutionalists make some provision for the workings of this welfare imperative, but scarcely enough to incorporate this global power structure into a plausible explanation for the break-up of the Soviet Union and the end of the Cold War. The scope of their conception of international relations and security falls short of fully embracing the force of this welfare imperative and its impact on transforming the Soviet state. Absent fundamentally transforming systemic weight assigned to these economic and welfare demands, animating the aims and actions of governing elites and their populations, and the capacity of the global techno-scientific and market institutions fashioned by the Western liberal states over centuries to satisfy them, a persuasive explanation for the self-destruction of the Soviet state purely on strategic military grounds or realist expectations is difficult, arguably impossible, to mount and sustain. Neorealists can certainly argue that states which are unable to address the security threats posed by other states will be selected out of the power struggle. This Darwinian principle also worked in reverse to spell the end of the Soviet Union. Interstate cooperation, not conflict, was the long-term basis for state survival, security, and the wealth of nations – a lesson learned too late by the Soviet regime.

Other theoretical perspectives than those of realists and liberal institutionalists will have to be invoked to fully account for the Soviet Union's collapse. Economic liberals who are discussed in the following chapter do pursue the logic of the efficiency of markets. They expose the dependence of state survival on a global market system fostering voluntary exchanges between buyers and sellers and on a global division of labor

---

[78] Kolodziej (1997) develops this point. Brooks (1997) and Brooks and Wohlforth (2000/ 2001) provide data to support this proposition, although the authors interpret their data to show that economic reform was instrumental to security imperatives, and not driven by the demands of the Soviet populations and ruling elites, a curious deconstruction to save traditional realist theory.

to ensure sustained economic development and innovation for state survival.[79] The explanatory weight they assign to these forces marginalizes the state's coercive powers. Whatever the shortcomings of a "pure" theory of the market may be, based on liberal economic assumptions, the state's dependence on technological innovation and global markets underscores its dual and mutually dependent security and welfare functions. These are ignored or slighted at the peril of the state's survival and that of its ruling regime and governing elites. The classical economic liberal position provides greater purchase than the three theories under examination to explain the end of the Cold War as a direct result of the failure of the Soviet Union to adapt successfully to the global economic and techno-scientific forces of a modern and modernizing global economy.[80] Liberal institutionalists open international relations theory to a transnational level of analysis, but stop short of attributing systemic causal effect of the power of actors working at this level of global exchanges on the state and the state system. They fail to connect the "causal dots" linking the powerful incentives of the market and the demands of populations for greater material wealth and welfare. They limit, if clearly do not eliminate, appeals to force or violence in realizing these compelling aims.

It is no accident that Kenneth Waltz, neorealism's leading theorist, devotes considerable thought to dismissing economic explanations of state conduct. He rejects both a Marxist and a classical liberal explanation of state conduct, while adapting, methodologically, the "pure" models of these economic positions and applying the logic of his pure model to the stipulated impact of a system of violent capabilities distributed across state units to explain their behavior.[81] Within the cramped ambit of its posited assumptions, the neorealist explanation of state security behavior is unassailable since it is essentially tautological. The glaring vulnerability of this position is that the "pure" neorealist state exists largely in the mind of neorealist partisans. The states we experience in the Cold War depend for their survival on the expectations and support of those whom it serves. These expectations are certainly rooted in security and survival, but these central state interests are not attainable exclusively by appeals to force and violence. They are equally driven, compellingly so under the circumstances of the last days of the Soviet Union, by demands of restless populations, elites and masses, for economic development and for a release

---

[79] Lindblom (2001).
[80] See Kornai (1992) and the detailed data and citations in Brooks and Wolforth (2000/2001) which argues that Soviet elite perceptions of the decreasing material capabilities of the Soviet Union shaped the economic ideas and ideology which drove reform, and not the reverse.
[81] Waltz (1979).

from the burdens and costs of empire. These pressures set off a seismic tremor strong enough to destroy a superpower. So much for the durability of superpower military prowess and the stability of the bipolar system.

Liberal institutionalists also concede, more than realists and neorealists, that domestic politics and the actors associated at this level of analysis can have a significant impact on the capabilities of a state and its external behavior.[82] But, again, liberal institutionalists are so closely joined at the hip to realist assumptions of the autonomy of the state that they are self-constrained from fully exploiting this insight. There is every reason to believe, and research findings support this position, that Gorbachev's reforms were not only directed at matching the military and economic development of the West but also at improving the material lot of Soviet elites and the Soviet people.[83] The radical shift of Soviet foreign policy toward détente with the West and a negotiated end of the Cold War can be viewed as instrumental to the objective of preserving the Soviet Union's big power status and Communist party rule.

These moves can also be interpreted as motivated by the need to install free market practices and to fundamentally transform domestic politics to mobilize and enlist support for a peaceful solution to regional and global conflicts with the West. Once these reforms were set in train to respond to internal pressures for greater and sustained economic well-being, they accelerated the pace of decomposition of the Soviet political and economic system. A purely instrumentalist interpretation of economic reforms in the service of narrowly conceived security imperatives makes no provision for such state- and system-destroying outcomes. Neither Gorbachev nor liberal institutionalists fully appreciated – and realists and neorealists not at all – the powerful systemic force of global market competition and technological innovation as autonomous structures of power beyond the capacity of the state's monopoly of violence to fully manipulate and control.[84] To work effectively and efficiently these structures had to rest on free choice, not coercion. They depended on the unfettered communication of preferences in open and transparent markets, defined by universal prices, and by the unhindered flow and diffusion of scientific and technological knowledge – institutions and mechanisms incompatible with an authoritarian regime and a command economy.

The decomposition of the Soviet state and the bipolar system was also driven by yet another force, filtered out by the conceptual lenses of the

[82] Keohane and Milner (1996).   [83] Brown (1996) and Hough (1997).
[84] A partial exception to this generalization is Brooks and Wohlforth (2000/2001) but these authors do not sufficiently accent the structure of Western science, technological innovation, and markets as *systemic* structures of power apart from the possession of these capabilities by specific states.

three theoretical positions under scrutiny. National, ethnic, and communal divisions, always just below the surface of Soviet political life, were magnified in the ensuing disruption provoked by domestic political and economic reform and by détente with the West. Russian nationalism could no longer be tapped to preserve the Soviet Union. The costs of empire, including Moscow's dominance of the Soviet Union's fifteen republics, its East European satellites, and a gaggle of unruly allies and clients abroad, proved too burdensome to carry any longer. The reformers around Gorbachev clearly sought to lighten and offload these obligations.[85]

These national pressures eroding Soviet state power and legitimacy were joined in the struggle between Gorbachev, as champion of a decaying Soviet Union, and Boris Yeltsin, as defender of Russian national interests. The conflict split the Soviet Union apart more decisively than all of the military power of the West or, arguably, the force of economic globalization. These material constraints conditioned but did not dictate the choice of the Soviet peoples to redefine their political loyalties by reference to their disparate national, ethnic, and communal identities. These essentially subjective, centrifugal forces overwhelmed the progressively weakening centripetal material power of the Soviet state to coercively fashion a new socialist man who would eventually subjugate and efface these assertive parochial identities. As the socialist man shattered into national, ethnic, and communal shards, so also did the unity of the Soviet Union fragment into its component, nationally defined parts. There is little or no room for these decisive forces of identity to express themselves in realist and liberal institutionalist thinking, much less so in neorealist theory.[86]

In contrast to the Soviet Union's centralized solution to identity politics, the Western states built their security alliance on *nation*-states. They rested their security and the survival of their political regimes on maintaining specifically the loyalties of their peoples. The Gaullist challenge to the United States and its refusal to submit French military forces to NATO and to American command were motivated by the conviction that the French contribution to Western defense ultimately rested on reattaching the French people to their military and to a renewed commitment to

---

[85] Kanet (1989) and Kanet and Kolodziej (1989).

[86] There have been some *ex post facto* ad hoc attempts among realist theorists to incorporate nationalism within a realist framework: Posen (1993) and Van Evera (1994). This poses a serious problem for realism and its partners since identities and the subjective values and preferences of actors are not entertained by the positivistic rules of evidence on which these exogenously driven theories rest, nor is the level of analysis of actors at a domestic level viewed as fundamental to a theory of international relations and state security.

the French nation after a long recessional from big power status through-out the century.[87] Whatever the tensions between NATO states, notably between the United States and France for most of the Cold War, the coalition held together because the member states and their populations consensually affirmed their participation in the alliance. French President Charles de Gaulle's attack on the hegemonic proclivities of the United States and his rejection of the superpower bipolar system were driven by his conviction that neither would prevail in the face of national sentiment and self-interest.[88] Unlike their East European counterparts in the War-saw Pact, the European members of NATO could have left the alliance and assumed a neutral stance without suffering an armed intervention by the United States to keep them in. France's withdrawal from the military integrated NATO system under American leadership but not from the Atlantic Alliance testifies to this larger range of alignment choices avail-able to Western allies. Similarly, Germany's reintegration, symbolized in the toppling of the Berlin Wall on November 9, 1989, dramatized the invisible but crucial importance of national loyalties and identity under-lying the unity of the modern state. Unlike Soviet Premier Gorbachev, the leaders of the East German regime were acutely aware of the adverse con-sequences of Moscow's decision not to intervene to compel the obedience of the East European populations to their Communist governments.

The Soviet state could neither supplant the contesting power of national identities to state power nor substitute the monopoly of power of the Communist party for the legitimacy accorded the state by national pop-ulations whose interests the state is expected to represent and reflect and to which it is supposed to be held accountable. It is no accident of speech that has occasioned the Hobbesian state to become a *nation*-state. Indeed, as one important study of the evolution of the nationalities problem in the Soviet Union suggests, the Soviet Union's efforts to create a new socialist identity had the ironic effect of supporting local elites whose power base rested more on their ethnic, communal, and national con-nections with local populations than on the surface controls exercised by Moscow within a nominally unified state rapidly unraveling along nation-alist and communal fault lines.[89] Over what Fernand Braudel terms the *longue durée* of history,[90] local identities ultimately overwhelmed Soviet state power, not the reverse, and co-opted its coercive power for their particularistic interests.

If the survival of the Soviet state and, *ipso facto*, the continuation of the Cold War depended on meeting security, welfare, and legitimacy

---

[87] Kolodziej (1974, 1987).   [88] Kolodziej (1974, 1987).   [89] Kaiser (1994).
[90] Braudel (1980).

imperatives, then the conception of the state itself will have to be redefined in ways that go well beyond realist, neorealist, or liberal institutionalist understanding of the state and the breadth and depth of its security functions. None of these theories addresses these profound questions, posed by globalization and the creation of a world society for the first time in the evolution of the human species. In light of the Soviet experience, theory about security must extend to the protection of free market exchange and the expression of popular sentiment, values, and identity. The Hobbesian conception of the state, modernized by Max Weber, as the repository of monopoly of legitimate violence, captures a necessary property of the state as it has evolved over the past several centuries. The Hobbesian state, central to realist theory, obviously lives on. Indeed, the peoples of the Soviet Union were so attached to the notion of the state that they formed fifteen states.

This faint praise for the Hobbesian state still falls short of an adequate explanation of the fatal weaknesses of the Soviet state and the failure of the Communist experiment. Nor does this realist response explain the subsequent behavior of the Soviet Union's successor states to adapt in varying measure to the ascendant Western model and to welcome (again at different rates and varying scope) the best technological and economic practices of Western societies. The modern state is expected to help, not hinder, the economic well-being of its populations. States are also supposed to represent the national and communal identities over which they rule in the society of states of which they are members. Increasingly, they are being pressured to protect and advance civil liberties and human rights as normative imperatives of their mandate to rule with authority. The implosion of the Soviet Union as a consequence of its failure to meet, simultaneously and synchronously, the competing tests of security, welfare, and legitimacy advises a re-examination of what a state is and its prospects beyond narrow security concerns of using or threatening force. At this juncture in the evolutionary development of these research programs, it would appear that these three theories (and their several mutations) are more fixed on preserving their paradigmatic borders from invasion, even as they violate their own boundaries, than on opening them to cooperation with the other paradigms and approaches covered in chapters 5–7. This effort would require a rethinking of disciplinary boundaries to respond to the unprecedented conditions of a global society and the new, novel and challenging security challenges that it poses, even as those still unsolved from the past persist.

If serious challenges can be raised about the choices these three schools of related thought have made with respect to key actors, their motivation, their expected behavior, and the levels of action to which they are confined by these theorists, problems also arise with respect to the methodological constraints imposed by these researchers on themselves. The surface strength of these three schools in their purest, classical forms is their attempt to describe, explain, and predict state behavior independently of the subjective and psychological factors impacting on individuals or groups in command of the state. Largely military constraints and the distribution of these capabilities across actors are stipulated as the bedrock on which to develop a potentially objective, empirically verifiable theory of state behavior. There is much to be said of this approach to match the rigor of the physical and biological sciences. The problem confronting these theorists, reflected in the ad hoc amendments to realist theory or the guardedly widening interest of institutionalists in domestic politics and ideational explanations of state behavior,[91] is that the actors whose behavior they are explaining refuse to be limited by the circumscribed visions of these three schools. The effort to include psychological, ideational, and domestic political variables into their analyses has had the unintended effect of eroding the explanatory power of the classical statement of these positions in their pure form. The ad hoc attempts to "save" realism and its companions has prompted some severe critics to reject the entire realist and neorealist project and, by implication, to impugn theorists, like liberal institutionalists who are striving to reconcile their amendments to realist theory.[92]

The realist-neorealist-institutionalist attempt to make international relations a science, however laudable, has not fully succeeded as these defections from the positivistic canon of these theorists suggests. Widely disputing theorists like Robert Keohane and Kenneth Waltz, as champions, respectively, of liberal institutionalist and neorealist thought, agree that they are seeking to surmount the problems associated with theories rooted in the subjective states of mind of ruling elites and populations. The collapse of the Soviet Union and the end of the Cold War challenge realist, neorealist, and liberal institutionalist thinking, since these momentous systemic changes are not easily squared with the methodological and evidentiary limits imposed by these schools of thought on themselves. The amendments of fellow travelers, calculated to expand the explanatory scope of these orientations, have served more to blur the clarity and coherence of these schools of thought. On the other hand, they do serve as a bridge to other theorists, who will occupy our attention in the next chapter.

---

[91] See Christensen and Snyder (1990), Goldstein (1993), Keohane (1996), Posen (1993), Schweller (1994), Snyder (1991), Van Evera (1994), Walt (1987), and Wohlforth (1994).

[92] See Vasquez (1997: 899–912) for an update on the realist debate. Also Legro and Moravcsik (1999) and Wayman and Diehl (1994).

Discussion questions

1. What assumptions about the expected behavior of states do all realists accept? How do they explain the pursuit of power by states and its uses? Are their conceptions of state behavior and power consistent with those of classical realist thinkers?
2. What are the functions of alliances, including their formation and dissolution, and the balance of power in realist theory?
3. How does neorealism differ from realism? How are they the same? Evaluate the neorealist claim that it is more scientific than classical or contemporary realism.
4. What ad hoc amendments have been progressively added to realist and neorealist assumptions to explain the changing conditions of state behavior since World War II? Do these conceptual shifts strengthen or weaken the coherence of realist and neorealist theory?
5. Distinguish between pessimistic and optimistic realists. What factors appear to induce states to cooperate rather than defect and resort to force to get their way in their interactions with other international actors?
6. In what ways does liberal institutionalism converge and diverge from realism and neorealism? Can liberal institutionalism be viewed as a paradigm of international relations and security theory or should it be more properly understood as a supplement or ad hoc qualification of realism and neorealism?
7. Evaluate the capacity of realism, neorealism, and liberal institutionalism to explain the rise, evolution, and collapse of the Cold War bipolar system.

Suggestions for further reading

Robert Axelrod (1984), *The Evolution of Cooperation*, New York: Basic Books. This is now a classic work in security studies and the most elegant, accessible, and theoretically sophisticated representations of optimistic realism.

David A. Baldwin (ed.) (1993), *Neorealism and Neoliberalism: The Contemporary Debate*, New York: Columbia University Press. This set of essays, written by leading international relations and security theorists, is an excellent introduction to the contesting claims of realism, neorealism, and liberal institutionalism.

Forum (1997), "Forum on Realism," *American Political Science Review* 91: 899–935. This forum presents contesting views of the status of realism and neorealism as research projects. Particularly insightful is the critique by John Vasquez and the counterclaims of prominent realist theorists.

Robert O. Keohane (ed.) (1986), *Neorealism and Its Critics*, New York: Columbia University Press. This set of essays marks one of the first major attempts to bridge the theoretical divide between realism, neorealism, and liberal institutionalism, edited by a prominent liberal institutionalist.

Jeffrey W. Legro and Andrew Moravcsik (1999), "Is Anybody Still a Realist?" *International Security* 24: 5–55. This article is friendly to classical realism and sharply criticizes those realists who stray from its central tenets of the rational behavior of states, as central actors, under conditions of anarchy and ceaseless conflict, in which exogenous distributions of material capabilities drive state security policies.

Hans J. Morgenthau (1985), *Politics among Nations: The Struggle for Power and Peace*, New York: Alfred A. Knopf. There is no better starting point to understand contemporary realism than by reading this classic in the field. Noteworthy, too, is the capacious understanding of power presented by Morgenthau that, while privileging material power and the struggle for power among states, alerts the demanding reader to the influence of diplomacy, political bargaining, legal rules, and moral norms on state behavior.

Kenneth Waltz (1979), *Theory of International Politics*, Reading: Addison-Wesley. Once Morgenthau's work is under control, the reader should tackle this founding statement of neorealism and compare the two with respect to their differing conceptions of state power and the political, legal, and moral contexts within which states act.

Frank W. Wayman and Paul F. Diehl (eds.) (1994), *Reconstructing Realpolitik*, Ann Arbor: University of Michigan Press. Behavioral, empirical tests are applied to realism and it is found wanting. This work should be read in tandem with chapter 6, which introduces readers to a behavioral approach to international relations theory and security.

5 Economic liberalism and Marxism

Introduction

This chapter evaluates liberal economic and Marxist theory and their relevance to international relations and security studies. The first section focuses on liberal economic thinking, the second on Marxism. A concluding section assesses their explanatory power with respect to the Cold War.

Including liberal economic theory in the pantheon of relevant security paradigms would appear at first glance to be a mistake. Many liberal economists would be equally puzzled to be among the likes of realists, neorealists, or institutional liberals. They would insist, and not entirely without justification, that they are principally interested in discovering and testing economic laws and how they explain the production and distribution of material wealth and welfare. They would contend that liberal economic theory focuses on the behavior of economic actors. Power and politics are excluded by definition.

These disclaimers scarcely square with the multiple impacts of liberal economic theory *and* methods on security decision-making by international actors, most notably states. The discussion below first outlines the key methodological contributions of liberal economic theory to security. These have had a profound influence on how strategic security theory and practice is conducted around the globe by analysts and practitioners concerned with the effective and efficient use or threat of force or its limitation.[1]

These methodological tools are equaled in importance by liberal economic theory's significant contributions to substantive security theory. These are of equal importance to its methodological tools used widely and extensively by strategic analysts and decision-makers. Liberal theory offers a powerful explanation for why individuals and states do *not*

---

[1] Allison and Zelikow (1999: 3–142) explicate this point with reference to the Cuban missile crisis. The distinction between *strategic* studies vs. *security* studies, the latter as a branch of international relations theory, is crucial. The debate is joined between these two positions, respectively, in Baylis et al. (2002), Gray (1999), Baldwin (1995), and Kolodziej (2002b).

resort to force to get their way. These contributions make liberal economic theory a serious contender for primacy among competing security paradigms. It can explain the economic reforms of the Soviet Union as an adaptation to the compelling incentives generated by the Western market system. Once the Soviet Union embarked on *perestroika* and installed the initial elements of a market system, these reforms accelerated the process of internal instability already far advanced and the eventual breakdown of the Soviet command economy. The crisis destroyed the Soviet Union as it collapsed on its member republics and their supportive national identities.

Whereas realism and neorealism focus on why actors do or don't use force as a derivative of the expected gains or losses of overcoming countervailing force, liberal economic theory explains why actors might prefer not only consensual cooperation over coercion in coordinating their relations with friends and foes but also work to create voluntary social institutions, principally markets, that surmount the play of countervailing force in eliciting reluctant and resistant cooperation. This perspective goes well beyond liberal institutionalism, with which economic liberalism is sometimes associated. The conceptual horizon of institutionalism is limited by its affirmation of the Hobbesian assumption of violence as the ultimate arbiter of actor preferences and differences. An economic liberal model posits a "perfect" or "ideal" assumption of human choices. Self-interested competitors voluntarily coordinate their interdependent but not necessarily convergent aims in their exchanges for mutual if differentially valued material gains. Theory and practice proceed as explanations of deviations from this perfect model of shared information between competitors and the costs and benefits of all conceivable moves.

METHODOLOGICAL CONTRIBUTIONS OF LIBERAL ECONOMIC THEORY TO STRATEGIC STUDIES

Economic man as rational actor

First, as chapter 4 delineates, the liberal economic assumption of the rational, self-interested actor is widely relied upon in military strategic and foreign policy decision-making.[2] The object or value to be maximized is radically different between these two disciplinary groups. They converge

---

[2] Classical security theorists also relied upon this model. Hobbes' and Clausewitz's endgames were implicitly the logical consequences of reducing rivalries exclusively to the countervailing use or threat of violence to resolve ceaseless conflicts between adversaries, whether individuals or states. See Wrong (1994) who makes this point for Hobbes. For a general review and evaluation of the rational actor model and competing organizational and bureaucratic politics models, see Allison and Zelikow (1999).

on the method of analysis drawn from micro-economic theory. Whereas economists assume that rational actors seek to maximize their wealth and welfare by assessing the material costs and gains from a transaction in the absence of duress, security theorists and military strategists substitute power as the maximizing goal of actors; the latter are expected to use force or threats to influence the behavior of opponents and allies and to structure the security system within which they act in preferred ways.

Examples of purported strategic rational behavior in using or threatening force abound. Germany's absorption of Czechoslovakia's German-speaking Sudetenland in 1938 was but one early phase of its imperial plan to subjugate Europe. The Japanese attack on Pearl Harbor in 1941 was designed to force a division of the eastern and western Pacific between Japan and the United States into spheres of interest, granting each hegemony within its domain. The Soviet decision to deploy nuclear weapons in Cuba can be viewed along several lines of rational behavior, ranging from a move to equalize the "balance of terror" with the United States to the support of an important ally. The American invasion of Afghanistan in 2001 aimed not only at destroying terrorist camps under Al Qaeda's control but also at precluding the re-emergence of any Afghan regime willing to harbor terrorists threatening to US security interests.[3] These examples illustrate the dual dimensions of state use of force for particular gains (or for precluding losses) *and* the tendency of states, underlined by realist expectations of rational state behavior, to shape their security environment in desirable ways to constrain both adversaries and allies – if they believe they can at acceptable cost and risk in minimizing or eliminating security threats or attacks on their vital interests.

Over time, rational actors are expected to identify all possible moves to reach their goals. They will then, according to the model, choose those strategies best calculated in allocating their scarce resources to maximize gains at least cost and risk. This model of rational behavior is stipulated to produce strategies that most efficiently and effectively advance an actor's aims. Any deviation from this perfect model is by definition less than optimal.

These are heroic assumptions of actor behavior, as more than one critic has pointed out.[4] The model assumes perfect, omniscient knowledge about the consequences of all actor choices. For theoretical purposes – immediate policy concerns aside – partisans of rational actor approaches concede what we all know from personal experience and casual observation: that actors make choices in most cases under conditions of

---

[3] See n. 1 and, specifically, Baylis et al. (2002) and Gray (1999).
[4] George and Smoke (1974), Green and Shapiro (1994), and Simon (1975, 1986).

uncertainty about the consequences of the choices before them. Uncertainty is endemic in responding to complex policy problems and at work in constraining political and bureaucratic settings. Information searches to narrow uncertainty is rarely, if ever, a free good. It is acquired only by expending scarce human and material resources to estimate the consequences of acting (or not), even as the context for action may be changing rapidly with little or no warning. Meanwhile, costly and time-consuming bargaining and negotiations have to be conducted with other actors with their own interests within policy and bureaucratic decision-making circles. As Herbert Simon, a Nobel Laureate in economics, argues, these are formidable constraints. They are never fully surmountable obstacles to fulfilling the exacting criteria of rational actor behavior.[5] Recall the catastrophic failure of Soviet economic reforms that undermined the regime they were designed to save. Meeting rational actor standards is made all the more problematic by the "fog of war."[6] Note the costly miscalculations of the American and Soviet interventions, respectively, in Vietnam and Afghanistan. Or, recall the unexpected resistance to the American occupation of Iraq after the announcement by President George Bush in May 2003 of "Mission Accomplished."

Rational actor analysts reject the criticism that they should be expected to identify all of the many contingent and circumstantial conditions shaping an actor's specific decisions in the pursuit of long-term goals and interests. They rejoin that their task is to project the logical and expected consequences of a course of action, defined by its means-end effectiveness and efficiency for the actor's maximal material gain (liberal economists) or power (realist security theorists/strategists).[7] The actor, assumed over time to be omniscient, will eventually engineer around contingent impediments to rational choice and their logical outcomes. What they don't expect the actor to do – whether an individual or state – is to deliberately act contrary to what it wants. They expect, instead, that actors will strive to acquire the knowledge they need to make "rational" decisions, those that project the likely outcomes of choices and that yield the highest payoffs. These moves conform or at least approximate rational actor criteria. From this "ideal" or "pure" perspective, rational actor theorists and practitioners rationalize their choice of this approach. (They, too, are rational actors, after all!)

What is less obvious in the comparison of economic and security theorists – and what this chapter tries to clarify – are the conflicting implications of this shared analytic framework of rationality, when applied

---

[5] Simon (1975, 1986).   [6] Keegan (1978).
[7] Friedman (1996a, b: 1–24). Also Rogowski (1978).

by both groups of theorists and practitioners to their objects of study. Economists assume that under the pure or "ideal" conditions of *free and non-coerced* choice and of full information available to all participants about the consequences of their interdependent choices, actors will cooperate *consensually* for mutual, if differential, material gains to maximize their wealth and welfare. They will cooperate voluntarily because defections from expected behavior or established rules, notably those imposed by the market, will result in lower levels of material gain for all participants. Why would rational actors choose less over more?

As we have seen, strategists who affirm Hobbesian assumptions about actor behavior, principally realists and neorealists, stipulate the opposite: that actor exchanges are *never* free or voluntary. They are always cast within an implicit or explicit order defined by force and threats. Even the most open society conceivable in theory or genuinely dedicated to the Rousseaunian ideal of general consent to public policies and order must still confront Hobbes' security imperative. As many democratic theorists reluctantly admit, free and open societies dedicated to fostering maximal consent to public policies cannot escape Hobbesian limits.[8] Rousseau also rejected the notion that his solution for peace within a community – the General Will – could be generalized to relations between different communities, peoples, and states.[9] At a global level he was as pessimistic as Hobbes about the prospects for peace between states and between discrete, autonomous human societies.

More from the economist's tool chest

A few words should also be said about the importance of the widespread use of other conceptual tools developed by economists in security decision-making besides the rational actor model as the centerpiece. Short of writing a text on economics, cataloging and commenting on all of these tools is obviously impossible in the scope of this discussion. Only a few can be described here to provide a sufficient foundation to appreciate the scope of liberal economic theory and its relevance to security. Viewed from the widespread use of economic theory throughout the Cold War and no less today, it is difficult to exaggerate the impact of economic concepts as tools of the trade for practicing security theorists and strategists.[10]

---

[8] This conundrum is conceded by many democratic theorists as a limit on free government. See, for example, Mansbridge (1996).
[9] Hassner (1997).
[10] The work of Thomas Schelling (1960, 1966) and Schelling and Halperin (1958) is illustrative.

A key point of intersection in the use of economic tools is the assumption of scarce resources made by economists and strategic decision-makers. While the implications of this assumption for the security behavior of states cannot be extensively explored here, three illustrations may suggest the significance and salience of this assumption in security decision-making. These illustrations highlight what is often neglected by the security theorists covered in chapter 4. Liberal economic theory tells us a lot about why actors – individuals, groups and especially states – choose *not* to use force to get their way in their exchanges.

First, there is obvious and much discussed tension between "guns or butter." Even a military superpower like the United States cannot acquire all of the weapons or maintain its forces at levels desired by its military. Under the condition of scarce resources, "managers of violence"[11] must choose, say, between more special forces over regular infantry personnel or between more land- over carrier-based aircraft. These competing aims cannot be easily accommodated at the same time. More importantly, all nations, however rich, must choose between their strategic military and welfare aims by assessing their trade-offs in lost gains – what economists term opportunity costs in favoring one competing goal over another.

The tension between "guns and butter" was at work throughout the Cold War. For the superpowers engaged in a global struggle for dominance, economic tools appeared ready-made to handle the question of "How much is enough?"[12] to defeat or deter an adversary. The Truman and Eisenhower administrations of the 1950s were acutely concerned that excessive defense spending might undermine the American economy and weaken the nation's ability to meet its security imperatives.[13] A generation later, analysts worried that the American economic hegemony was gravely on the wane. They worried, too, about what they viewed as its diminishing capacity to meet the Soviet military challenge.[14] Some predicted its demise – for some sooner than later.[15] What few expected, as chapter 3 describes, was the collapse of the Soviet Union, partially attributable, as liberal theorists claimed, to its failure to resolve the guns–butter dilemma as well as the Western states.

A second use of economic reasoning concerns the choice of force levels, weapons systems, deployment options, and technologies to respond to security imperatives. Given the countervailing material power of adversaries – note the capacity of the Soviet Union to match the nuclear and conventional forces of the United States – Cold War strategists were

---

[11] The term is Huntington's widely quoted characterization of the military function.
[12] Enthoven and Smith (1971).   [13] Kolodziej (1966).
[14] Gilpin (1987) and Keohane (1984). For a contrasting view, see Nau (1990).
[15] Kennedy (1987).

obliged to choose among these competing components of military planning to meet the nation's real or perceived threats, ranging from guerrilla warfare to World War II massive clashes of conventional forces or to "bolts-out-of-the-blue" nuclear attacks. At each decisional point, meeting these threats always exceeded the human and material resources available to either superpower or their allies.

Rational actor criteria, finally, are useful as a basis for evaluating the alternative benefits, costs, and risks of competing solutions to these problems. Do you get "more bang for the buck," as Eisenhower administration decision-makers asked in the 1950s, if the nation put more resources into nuclear as opposed to conventional weapons?[16] Or, in fighting a ground war, should more be spent on air-strike forces or long-range air transport? Would heavier or lighter tanks and armor work best to defeat opponents in different regions around the globe? If more money is spent on naval or ground forces within a fixed budget, what are the lost benefits or opportunities of lower air and ground force capabilities? These are stock economic questions posed within the rubric of assessing the destructive capabilities available to the state to "get ordnance on target,"[17] the principal criterion dictating the planning and decision-making of military planners, as Samuel Huntington suggests.[18]

Substantive contributions of liberal theory to security studies

First, pure models of rational economic behavior advanced by liberal economists put force and coercion outside the scope of their theorizing. By that token, it opened the way to thinking about how actors could get their way by resisting appeals to force or coercion in their interdependent exchanges with other actors. Over time through evolutionary trial and error and learning, liberal economic theory came to assume that actors will opt for non-coercive cooperation to achieve their competing but still converging preference for material gains.[19] This will be true even if the actors do not gain in equal or equivalent measure. Of course they know full well that intimidation and duress enter into human decisions. What they seek to know are the full range and array of possibilities of voluntary cooperation, even if humans may not opt for this solution to competing actor aims. Liberal economists focus on the absolute gains of their exchanges rather than on the relative and unequal material portions they receive. Given the ideal of maximizing material gain, economists

---

[16] Kolodziej (1966: 180–253).   [17] Hitch (1960) and Gansler (1989).
[18] Huntington (1957).
[19] Note the parallel between liberal economic theory and Axelrod's (1984) explanation of cooperation beween egoists, notably those trapped in a security dilemma.

assume that actors, however much they may have competing economic interests, are playing – or can choose to play – a win-win game. This will necessitate their mutual confirmation of free market rules and discipline as the most efficient and effective strategy to enlarge the production of economic wealth – the "Golden Straitjacket" to use Thomas Friedman's widely cited metaphor.[20]

Second, the "pure" model of economic behavior stipulated by practicing economists is bolstered, as a contribution to security theory, by the history that this ideal has enjoyed in practice. The compelling incentives of material gain driving the liberal economic model have inspired countless partisans to apply its expectation of actor cooperation to security policy and policy-making. The likelihood that free economic exchange promotes peace has a long tradition in economic theory and in the commercial practices of states. Recent research findings lend guarded support for these expectations. The idea of open and free markets as a global strategy to create "perpetual peace" can be traced back at least two centuries to Immanuel Kant. In the midst of a quarter-century of revolutionary wars convulsing Europe and its dependencies, Kant still argued that "the *spirit of commerce* sooner or later takes hold of every people, and it cannot exist side by side with war. And of all the powers (or means) at the disposal of the power of the state, *financial* power can probably be relied on most. Thus states find themselves compelled to promote the noble cause of peace, though not exactly from motives of morality."[21]

The policy of free trade was embedded in the foreign and strategic policy of Great Britain throughout much of the nineteenth and early twentieth centuries. Implicitly or explicitly, it drew its rationale from the supposed creation of a virtuous circle of non-coercive choices. An open, free, voluntary global market system would animate economic actors to achieve ever-increasing material wealth *and* peace.[22] These expectations were projected in American security policy in Woodrow Wilson's vision of a peaceful and prosperous world through unfettered, global commerce and the universal spread of democratic regimes. The realization of this vision of peace was initially frustrated by the United States' rejection of the Versailles Treaty and by its refusal to join the League of Nations after World War I. The Wilsonian vision re-emerged after World War II with US sponsorship of the United Nations and its construction of a liberal trading system and expansion of democratic regimes around the globe through the Truman Doctrine and Marshall Plan assistance.[23]

---

[20] Friedman (2000: 101–11).   [21] Kant (1991: 114). Italics in the original.

[22] Cain (1979), Irwin (1996), Hobson (1919), and Howe (1997).

[23] Levin (1968), Acheson (1969), Cooper (1968), Ruggie (1982), and Mandelbaum (2002: 17–44).

Third, the classical economic model, whatever its shortcomings and self-denying limitations as a paradigm for security, helps explain the impact of global capitalistic markets on the decisions of most Communist states, notably Communist China and the Soviet Union, to abandon their command economic systems and to adapt to a Western model of open market exchange. Even though these states resisted embracing liberal democratic political principles, they did reform their economic command systems on the Western model to harness the proven power of open global markets as the motor force for sustained economic growth and technological innovation. The implosion of the Soviet Union and the end of the Cold War can be traced in discernible measure to the incentives of "commerce" generated by global capitalist markets. Two centuries earlier, Immanuel Kant already foresaw at the dawn of the Industrial Revolution the potentially powerful workings for peace of free economic exchange.[24]

Contrasting implications of strategic and economic rational actors

Strategic and foreign policy decision-makers rely heavily on the elaborate conceptual and methodological apparatus developed by economists in pursuing their discipline. What is often overlooked in this interdisciplinary transfer of concepts, and what this chapter underlines, are the contrasting expectations of individual and state behavior driving economic vs. Hobbesian or realist-directed models of behavior. The competition of "pure" models of security around which this volume revolves should not obscure or minimize the useful exploitation of economic tools to service both of these models despite their divergent endpoints. There is less of a paradox than meets the eye in this observation. It is important to remember that the rational actor model is an analytic construct. The substantive values or incentives that propel the model and its results depend on the actors chosen for study by the analyst and values assigned to their behavior. On these crucial points, economists and military strategists part ways.[25]

Economists explain how actors allocate scarce land, labor, capital, knowledge, and entrepreneurial resources to supply as many goods and services as consumers are prepared to buy. They assume that actors are engaged in *voluntary* exchanges through open, free markets. Under conditions of increasingly integrated, globalized markets, buyers and sellers adapt their behavior to each other without central direction by adjusting

[24] Kant (1991: 114).
[25] See table 1.1, which contrasts realists and liberal economic theory.

to the relative prices for goods and services signaled by markets. The focus is on making and creating material plenty at levels of supply in quantity and quality agreeable to buyers and sellers defined by prices as registration of convergent preferences.

On the other hand, military strategists ask how might a state choose from a menu of coercive options, including the manipulation of threats, to elicit the desired behavior of friends and foes to ensure its security preferences at least cost and risk. How can a state's "killing, hurting, and maiming" capacity be efficiently and effectively employed to influence an opponent's behavior in favorable ways, as one widely quoted strategist posed the means–end problem.[26] Whereas the "ideal" market system is fundamentally consensual and rules are reciprocally defined by the participants in pursuit of their self-interests, security systems are involuntary as a function of the coercive relation defining the exchange between the rivals.

This latter use of the rational actor model narrowly frames the security problem confronting a state. Ruled out are strategies of non-use of force to surmount differences. In choosing from a menu of violent capabilities available to a state by its own means or by access to allied assets, an economic question of potential mutual benefit is transformed into a strategic military problem of mutual losses. These are estimated by how much hurting, maiming, killing, destroying are needed to prevail in an exchange or conflict. In other words, what set of capabilities and strategies is best calculated to deter an adversary from doing what I don't want – say, attack an ally – to defeat him if he strikes, or to compel him to do what I wish. Or, how can force or threats induce a rival to stop producing weapons of mass destruction, conducting campaigns of ethnic cleansing, or harboring terrorists? Use of economic concepts for these destructive purposes contrasts sharply with their use by economists. The currency of exchange is not mutually satisfying economic gains, but the actual or threatened destruction of what the opponent values. The operational focus is getting or threatening ordnance on target. Rational behavior is reckoned in deaths and material losses rather than material gains or personal satisfactions.

As the evolution of the US–Soviet military struggle illustrates, answers to these instrumentally posed questions were neither obvious nor uncontested over almost a half-century of Cold War struggle. Rationality, as chapter 3 describes, paraded simultaneously under the competing banners of Mutual Assured Destruction (MAD) and a nuclear war-fighting or utilization (NUTS) strategy. The defense of Europe prompted conflicting

---

[26] Schelling (1966: 1: 1–34) on the diplomacy of violence.

strategic postures of large conventional forces vs. proposals for trip-wire strategies and early use of tactical, theatre and long-range nuclear weapons. The Vietnam and the Afghanistan wars joined the issue of whether all superpower confrontations were causally linked – to lose one ally signaled the fall of allied dominoes everywhere – or whether regional gains and losses were of unequal measure in forming moving global balances of power between the superpowers. The game was zero-sum, not win-win.

The uncertainties surrounding these strategic choices did little to shake the use of "pure" or "ideal" economic models and their associated conceptual and methodological tools in framing and in driving these debates. Nor were decision-makers inhibited in implicitly justifying their decisions as applications of rational choice in response to real or anticipated adversary military moves. The seemingly compelling logic of the rational actor model had the effect of blurring or minimizing the costs run in responding by force to worst case scenarios. The very conceptualization of a security problem was itself a factor explaining actor choices. Once posed in these polarizing terms, uncertainties were dispelled by the analyst and policy-maker. Actors were assigned values and commitments to make the models work. The admonition of British Prime Minister Winston Churchill that the adversary must always be taken into account in terms of *the rival's* assessment of *his* strategic problems and of *his* likely armed solutions tended to be slighted or ignored in the thinking of many modelers. They were moved – as many critics suggested – by the pure workings of the rational actor model rather than by a dispassionate, empirical examination of adversary power, intentions, and behavior.

This tendency to err by over-reliance on pure models of rational decision-making – that stipulate rather than empirically verify the assumptions and objectives of adversary strategic thinking, decisions and actions – has already been described as an obsessive driver of the superpower nuclear arms race. The competition can be explained more by the excessive pursuit of pure logic hinged to worst case scenarios and applied to the stipulated deterrent capacity of nuclear weapons than to the actual utility of these weapons, if used, or the likely behavior of rivals when confronted by the threat of these weapons.[27]

The same tendency to ignore the adversary by positing what the analyst or policy decision-maker might do rather than what the adversary was

---

[27] See chapter 3 for these critiques of the rational actor model for its failure to account adequately for the psychological make-up of rivals and how they process information about adversary behavior and react to their psychological, not necessarily rational or logical, perceptions of threats: George and Smoke (1974), Morgan (1983, 2003), Jervis (1976), Jervis, Lebow, and Stein (1985), and Lebow (1981).

willing to do to win a war was particularly acute in American policy in the Vietnam war. Because American analysts and decision-makers presumed that both sides understood what acting rationally implied, American decision-makers believed that both sides were acting on the same assumptions to form what one prominent analyst termed a coherent "idiom of military action."[28] It seemed reasonable, contrary experience and observation notwithstanding, that what would motivate American decision-makers to act or not in the face of coercive threats or military force would also produce a similar response from an adversary. Projected onto the opponent was a defined and limited range of analyst scripted choices available to the adversary which were assumed by the decision-maker to exhaust the feasible or "rational" range of adversary responses to differentially applied forms of "killing, hurting, and maiming."[29]

But what if the adversary had an entirely different set of assumptions about the value and stakes of the conflict and of the range of feasible military strategies, some deemed too costly or risky by the initiator of coercive diplomacy? Who blinks first when two clashing "rational models" are in play? One consequence for American security policy in Vietnam was to systematically underestimate the determination of North Vietnam and its leadership to absorb losses valued as "irrational" by American decision-makers, reacting to their own conceptions of rational behavior.[30] The reasoning is circular. The adversary is conveniently excluded from the exchange of threatened "killing, hurting, or maiming" in calculating his reactions. Instead, the aims, interests and levels of tolerance for being hurt are imposed by the strategists on the rival as if their aims, interests, and tolerance levels were congruent. The model rather than experience then drives analysis and policy-making.

CLASSICAL ECONOMIC MODEL AS A SECURITY PARADIGM

Freedom vs. coercion

Before the classical economic model is evaluated to explain the rise and demise of the Cold War, some attention must first be given to its key assumptions and conceptual tools as they pertain specifically to the maximization of wealth and welfare. Already introduced are the notions of egoistic, self-interested rational actors making decisions in pursuit of their

---

[28] Schelling (1966: 146–7).
[29] Halberstam (1972) exposes the costly repercussions of this mode of analysis when applied to the Vietnam conflict.
[30] Fitzgerald (1972) and Halberstam (1972).

interests, aims, and values under the constraint or the limit of scarce resources. These need more elaboration. Absent some initial, if necessarily incomplete, understanding of the implications of these assumptions and concepts, it will be difficult to appreciate the impact of liberal economic thinking on security theory and practice.

What Thomas Hobbes is to realism in propounding a theory applicable to the power of states, Adam Smith is to economic liberalism in explaining *The Wealth of Nations*, his most celebrated work.[31] Smith advanced an entirely different yet putatively no less universal notion of what it means to be human than Hobbes. He foresaw far more brilliant and beneficent prospects for this thinking and linguistically talented species than Hobbes and the latter's pessimistic partisans. No less committed to rational thinking than his realist counterpart, Smith simply began at a radically different starting point of rationality. What is "real" for Smith contradicts what is "real" for Hobbes and for most of the theorists already discussed. Based on his observation of human behavior, Smith concludes that humans seek "opulence" or, simply, wealth and material welfare.[32] Smith stipulated that opulence-seeking was more effectively pursued by consensually, not coercively, induced cooperation. Voluntary, free, and mutually adaptive exchanges were the key to expanding material plenty. For Smith, the human "propensity to truck, barter, and exchange one thing for another" distinguishes humans from all other animals. According to Smith, this propensity is "the necessary consequence of the faculties of "reason and speech," a stipulation that lies at the foundation of modern rational actor theory in economics.[33]

Smith assumed that self-interested individuals, his unit of analysis much like Hobbes', entered these exchanges for their mutual material benefit but from different vantage points. Smith's benevolent egoists possessed varying personal endowments – intelligence, imagination, creativity, dexterity – accumulated resources (land, capital, and knowledge) and developed habits of diligence and discipline. In contrast to animals, Smith contended, humans who truck, barter, and trade surmounted the limitations of an animal which is "obliged to support and defend itself, separately and independently, and derives no sort of advantage from that variety of talents with which nature has distinguished its fellows."[34] "Among men, on the contrary," Smith concluded, "the most dissimilar geniuses are of use to one another; the different produces of their respective talents, by the general disposition to truck, barter, and exchange, being brought, as it were, into a common stock, where every man may

---

[31] Smith (1937). [32] Smith (1937), especially book I: 3–21. [33] *Ibid.*: 21.
[34] *Ibid.*: 16.

purchase whatever part of the produce of other men's talents he has occasion for."[35]

Smith postulated, further, that if these materially driven actors cooperated in applying the principles of a division of labor and specialization, collective *and* individual wealth would be enlarged. Smith's celebrated story of the pin factory illustrated these principles of social behavior as sources of increasing wealth. He observed that by dividing the tasks of making pins – drawing, cutting, sharpening, and grinding – ten men could make upwards of 48,000 pins a day. "But if they had all wrought separately and independently, and without any of them having been educated to the peculiar business, they certainly could not each of them have made twenty, perhaps not one pin in a day . . ."[36]

The principles of the division of labor and specialization, once installed and globalized in social relations through cross-national markets, fostered skill and dexterity. Time and transaction costs were reduced, since workers would not move from one operation to another in producing goods.[37] Innovations could be expected from experts with a practiced eye to spot ways to improve production within their area of specialization. These efficiencies would be diffused throughout the domestic and world economy. The synergisms arising from the mutual reinforcement of these beneficent properties of specialization would boost wealth even more for all those implicated in the market system.[38] Collective wealth would be maximized for the greatest number. The portions divided among those engaged in these exchanges, however varying in worth the allotments, would be larger for each contributor than acting alone or in partial and constrained concert, exemplified by monopolistic guilds. The pie would get bigger. Individual slices, while slimmer, would still be larger as a consequence of the workings of the division of labor, increased specialization, comparative advantage, and the enlargement of increased exchange through expanding markets within and between nations.

Beginning with a different standard human model – nice economic, not nasty power-hungry, man – Smith arrived at a more optimistic vision of limitless plenty than his Hobbesian counterparts. Postulating the assumption of free choice to pursue selfish desires for material gain by exploiting the endowments and resources at their disposal, egoists would simultaneously advance their own interests and those of others. Smith's vision of the convergence of personal and collective good, if freedom is given full reign to egoists in making their *social* choices, is clearly described in this much cited passage:

---

[35] *Ibid.*   [36] *Ibid.*: 4–5.   [37] Williamson (1975) and North (1990).
[38] Irwin (1996: 75–86) usefully summarizes Smith's views about the benefits of free trade. Also Smith (1937: 9ff.).

But man has almost constant occasion for the help of his brethren, and it is in vain for him to expect it from their benevolence only. He will be more likely to prevail if he can interest their self-love in his favour, and shew them that it is for their own advantage to do for him what he requires of them. Whoever offers to another a bargain of any kind, proposes to do this . . . It is not from the benevolence of the butcher, the brewer, or the baker, that we expect our dinner, but from their regard to their own interest. We address ourselves, not to their humanity but to their self-love, and never talk to them of our own necessities but of their advantages.[39]

Here Smith broke decisively with centuries of Western economic think-ing and practice. The implications for a theory of security were no less pro-found. Ancient Grecian, Roman and Western medieval societies resisted freeing commerce from social, political, and moral constraints. Other cultures and civilizations did likewise.[40] Traditional societies feared what they believed would be the socially costly consequences of free and unfet-tered economic exchange. They foresaw increased conflict with other societies as economic competition arose. They especially feared the effect that unbridled pursuit of material gain would have on the stability of society and its capacity to perpetuate its values over generations. The promotion of personal and individual self-regarding interests and rights undermines the practice of civic virtues in the service of societal ideals.[41] Personal material gain would be privileged over service to societal ideals.

There was also the widespread belief, experienced by these societies,[42] that the unchecked pursuit of wealth and its unequal accumulation, widening the gap between the rich and the poor, would incite class conflict, concerns that the discussion below of Marxist and neo-Marxist thinking reaffirm today. It is difficult for the modern mind to compre-hend that Sparta's militarized and anti-commercial society was more admired than Athens' democracy and its promotion of commerce.[43] Anti-democratic Sparta restrained what were widely believed to be the cor-rupting social practices of permissive societies. These conservative social values were at the base of medieval Christendom's social system for a millennium and animate today much of the non-Western world, however much modernization may be impacting on these resisting societies.[44]

---

[39] *Ibid.*: 14.   [40] Polanyi (1968), Polanyi, Arensberg and Pearson (1957).
[41] Rahe (1984).
[42] The *Federalist* papers, written to defend the American constitution, are very much con-cerned with this perceived threat to democratic rule. See especially No. 10 written by James Madison, *Federalist* (n.d.: 53–62). See also Pearson (1977) and Polanyi (1968).
[43] Rahe (1984, 1992).
[44] The tension between modernization and tradition was first developed by Ferdinand Tönnies (1957). His insights have since been echoed by a procession of commentators over a century, not always with attribution to source. For modern updates, see Barber (1995) and Friedman (2000).

Later mercantilist writers of the post-medieval period, while favoring international trade, also objected to free trade and unfettered commercial exchanges for many of these same reasons. They were convinced that such a libertine policy would result in "a disharmony between private and public interests."[45] They favored the coercive intervention of the state to prevent a misallocation of resources and the distortion of prized social values over what liberal economic theorists posited as individual rights and interests.[46] They advocated tariffs on imported goods and the protection of home industries to foster a favorable balance of trade, to increase the flow of gold into state coffers, and to promote internal economic development and employment.[47] While the merchant class rose in status and stature in the thinking of mercantilist writers, the latter displayed no inclination to give priority to commercial exchanges over other social values, most notably the power and interests of the state. Their policies were keyed to augmenting the monarch's revenue, raising rents on land, and employing the poor at what were subsistence levels.

Smith advocated radical changes in state economic policies. These constituted the creation of an entirely new global system of decision-making dedicated to the production and diffusion of wealth – a fundamental revolutionary change in international relations and global politics when compared to the mercantilist system that it eventually supplanted. Less, not more, state intervention was advised in favor of increased individual and social reliance on the maximum extension of the institution of free, open, global markets. Free markets would ensure *The Wealth of Nations* by unleashing the creative energies and endowments of self-interested individuals. Oblivious to state boundaries, markets were suited to exploit the benefits of the division of labor and specialization.

Markets as a social institution and the incentives they generated would best respond to the special knowledge of individuals – their own priorities in their trucking and bartering.[48] They knew best what they wanted, what no state or planner could ever divine, since their preferences were fundamentally subjective and personal. Only individuals knew their wants. Unlike command economies, voluntary markets could objectify these subjective preferences through prices that, theoretically, could extend around the globe. Individuals had a self-interest to use their endowments, resources, and knowledge to best advantage to bolster their material positions by responding to market cues. Free markets performed the Herculean task, unmatched by nation-states – and less so empires – of

---

[45] Irwin (1996: 44).   [46] *Ibid.*: 10–44.   [47] *Ibid.*: 27–44.
[48] For an update on Smith's thinking in accessible form, see Lindblom (2001).

consensually coordinating daily the exchanges of billions of buyers and sellers effortlessly, effectively, efficiently – and peacefully.

As later classical theorists were to insist in following Smith's lead, individual human self-interest and freedom of choice, when mediated through the rigorous competition afforded by global markets, promised the greatest good for the greatest number of people.[49] The promise was not limited to Englishmen or Europeans, but extended to all people engaged in global markets regardless of religion, culture, ethnicity, race, or language. To increase the wealth of nations, the wealth of individuals had first to be augmented. That would be best achieved, as Smith argued, by leaving the individual

perfectly free to pursue his own interest his own way, and to bring both his industry and capital into competition with those of any other man, or order of men (thus foreigners, too). The sovereign is completely discharged from a duty, in the attempting to perform of which no human wisdom or knowledge could ever be sufficient; the duty of superintending the industry of private people, and of directing it towards the employments most suitable to the interest of society.[50]

Smith extended this prescription to the relations of states and peoples. He had no truck for empires – Western or non-Western – as solutions to national wealth. Their economic performance was inevitably suboptimal. They fostered privilege and preferences for the few at the expense of wealth and welfare for the many, including ironically the few advantages by imperial economic systems (as later Soviet elites discovered). Empires discouraged creative enterprise and resourcefulness and exploited foreign and domestic labor rather than relying on the workings of the division of labor at work in competitive global markets. No less did he oppose domestic corporate monopolies or labor guilds as restraints on free exchange.

Freedom of choice, theory of markets, and peace

So what does this brief review of key concepts of classical economic theory have to do with security? Liberal thought explains why humans have powerful reasons and incentive *not* to use force to get what they want. It addresses the conflict-reducing or peaceful propensities of peoples and states that clearly fall within this volume's conception of the set of choices and actions constituting the phenomenon of security. Liberal economic theory posits the properties of freedom, creativity, self-interest, rationality, and linguistic capability as distinguishing features of human make-up.

---

[49] Hayek (1948, 1960, 1988).   [50] Quoted in Irwin (1996: 84).

These properties, when focused on the pursuit of material gain, produce harmony, according to liberal thinkers. The classic tension between self-interest and social good is relaxed because a system of voluntary exchanges, advanced by global markets, is based on self-interest; the voluntary social system associated with free markets works and channels egoism to yield unintended but positive social benefits that could not otherwise be fostered or realized by coercion or moralistic dunning.

Smith divined that ever-enlarging markets, as humanly constructed social systems, would automatically coordinate the exchanges of self-interested economic actors for their good and others. The individual actor was "led by an invisible hand [the market, its rules and institutions] to promote an end which was not part of this intention. Nor is it always the worse for the society that it was no part of it. By pursuing his own interest he frequently promotes that of the society more effectually than when he really intends to promote it."[51] Harmony is produced through experiential learning – initially more by trial and error than by deliberation and planning. Humans can achieve their personal strivings for wealth by freely cooperating within the market system. If free and open, the wealth of their nations would increase and multiply.

The specific material interests of actors do not necessarily converge under conditions of free and open competition. What actors can be expected to agree upon – and do – is a preference for a social system based on market principles and norms of freedom. On this score, there is a convergence of interest, reinforced by the beneficial experience with institutions nurturing and protecting free exchange. Under the assumption of "pure market operations," liberal economic theory contends that no other socio-economic system is capable of producing wealth as efficiently or effectively to meet incessant demands for "more now" by the world's populations. Economic liberals reject the Marxist critique that the system is fundamentally inequitable. Rather, it is contended that it promotes equity through the application of the principle of quid pro quo.[52] They dismiss the Marxist prediction that support for the market system will eventually be withdrawn by a growing, underprivileged class as a consequence of the unequal and inequitable distribution of wealth. What is a fatal weakness for Marxists is a profound strength for economic liberals. Why, the latter ask, should equal wealth be doled out to all at the expense of those who contribute more through their hard work and industry as well as through their discipline, creativity, innovative enterprise, and resourcefulness?

The problem of overproduction would also not result because the market is self-regulating over time in matching demand and supply. The

---

[51] Smith (1937: 423).   [52] Lindblom (2001) makes much of this point.

pursuit of material gain through trucking and bartering is assumed to be without discernible limits under changing but never fully surmountable conditions of scarce resources.[53] Human ingenuity, fueled by limitless material appetites, once freed through the incentives and workings of global markets, continually create new labor- and capital-saving technologies and efficiencies as well as products and services. These are diffused through new markets created by resourceful entrepreneurs. Left to their own dynamics, markets in league with global systems of scientific discovery and technological innovation move inexorably (and rationally) toward ever-greater worldwide economic integration, a spur to sustained economic growth and development.

Smith and later writers perfected this "pure" or "ideal" picture of prosperity by identifying the political preconditions for the realization of these benefits. First, the state's capacity to confiscate private property and to impose onerous regulations on free market exchanges, skewing and frustrating actor preferences, had to be curbed. The liberal state is then the least intrusive state. For the liberal theorist and practitioner the state's coercive powers must be limited if the free market model is to work to produce the greatest material good for the greatest number. The state must then be subject to popular will and electoral accountability, defined fundamentally by its adherence to market rules and discipline, the protection of private property, and its free disposition. Second, state–supported monopolies or wasteful subsidies to sustain uncompetitive industries must be ended. These run afoul of the efficiencies of competitive markets since prices are set by fiat and coercion and not by the free exchanges of buyers and sellers in the market. Finally, obstacles to commercial exchange across state boundaries, notably tariffs, had to be eliminated to ensure the unimpeded workings of the principle of comparative advantage between trading peoples and states.[54] Otherwise, those engaged in the market would not enjoy the full benefits of the division of labor and specialization, keys to economic plenty.

Harmony arises from the enlarging recognition of humans that greater wealth and welfare depend on these free exchanges. These values hinge on the construction of a social system dedicated to their preservation and promotion. The principles on which markets and the market system rest as a social system – freedom of individual choices – run counter to those on which the modern state and the prevailing state system are founded.[55] Simply put, freedom and coercion, as contesting principles underlying markets and states, respectively, are fundamentally incompatible in theory, if provisionally accommodated in practice. Yet both institutions, as Smith conceded, responded to human needs and

[53] Alchian and Allen (1969: 2–37).   [54] Rosecrance (1986).   [55] Lindblom (2001).

demands. Hobbes' world of Leviathans possessing a legitimate monopoly of violence created a political order that left all states to defend themselves by their own violent means in advancing their interests.

Whereas Smith confronted the dilemma of balancing freedom and coercion as equal if contending claims as the bases for human institutions, responding, respectively, to welfare and security needs, realists and especially neorealists, like Kenneth Waltz, recoil from confronting this daunting dual problem of balancing these rival claims in developing a coherent and capaciously explanatory theory of security. Rather than recognize, as Smith does, that each is indispensable for social order and public welfare, these security theorists define the dilemma away. An abstract, parsimonious model of security is conceptually stipulated as having an autonomous existence from the observed interdependent clash of freedom and coercion reflected in the conflicting choices made by actors embedded in state and market systems. Sidestepped then at the risk of falsifying the *real* problem confronting human societies is the reconciliation of the rival claims of these social systems simultaneously, not serially and sequentially. Distinguishing between low politics (economics) and high politics (security) fails to confront the contesting imperatives of societal order, survival and replication and those of socio-economic development posed by the conflicting incentives these social systems as power structures generate and impose on human choice and public policy. Each system and power structure, their competing demands notwithstanding, are necessary if not sufficient for the replication of a liberal global order.

From a Waltzian neorealist perspective, it makes sense to attack the economic theories of Karl Marx and Adam Smith and banish them from security studies. Both project a wider and deeper understanding of human societies and their governing institutions as critical to the defense and replication of those societies. These theorists scarcely converge on what social systems best promote their economic theories. Their opposed evaluation of the beneficial social effects of global markets is the obvious and most significant point of division. Yet they implicitly agree that the scope of realist and neorealist theory of security is too confining and ultimately indefensible on theoretical *or* policy grounds as an accurate representation of actor behavior. Their expectations of increasing and widening economic interdependence of the peoples and states of the globe fundamentally challenge the relevance and reliability of realist and neorealist theory to accurately map what's real about actor behavior. They reject this exclusionary claim to explain the security behavior of individuals, nations, or states simply by reference to force and violence.[56]

---

[56] Waltz (1979: 20ff.).

According to Smith, the self-interested pursuit of material gain is a universal and irresistible force – a *force profonde* as the French might say – if given free rein to express itself in markets or, more generally, in *voluntary* associations of all kinds that compose domestic, international and civil societies. If, initially, few recognized that global markets had the unintended but beneficent consequence of creating collective wealth for all nations, Smith's great intellectual breakthrough was to give permanent voice to what could be socially created by the power of reason and reflection. While it is important to emphasize that Smith affirmed the need for state power to ensure domestic order and external defense, it is no less crucial to stress that voluntary systems of free exchange crowded out the incentive to use force in the transactions of individuals and states in their quest for personal and collective wealth and welfare.[57]

Smith never drove the implications of his economic theory and the principle of freedom on which it rested to its logical or "pure" endpoint. In extending great latitude to the state to intervene for the sake of domestic peace and external defense, he allowed that the liberal state would actually enjoy more revenue for these purposes than a mercantilist state that interfered with free exchange.[58] Free market exchanges increased the size of each nation's economic pie, measured by real goods and services. As with individuals, as the national economic pie grew larger, the proportional slices afforded the restrained, liberal state were smaller than those of mercantilist or authoritarian states, but the absolute size of the slice was larger. Smith anticipated this ironic outcome wherein a less powerful state could increase its power by profiting from the free exchanges of its citizens. The findings of economic historians lend evidentiary weight to this insight.[59]

This counter-intuitive outcome has much relevance in applying liberal economic theory to the end of the Cold War and to the ascendancy of the United States as the sole superpower. In general 4 percent of its growing Gross National Product is currently needed to sustain its global military reach, which is second to no other power or even group of leading powers. It spends more on defense than the combined totals of the members of the UN Security Council, NATO, and the European Union. More generally, the attraction of free markets eventually proved compelling to Soviet and Chinese Communist decision-makers. Their ideological and even their personal political interests proved wanting in resisting the pull of this

[57] Smith (1937).
[58] See book V: 653–900. Economic historians affirm Smith's prognosis. Jones (1988, 1987) and North and Weingast (1989).
[59] Jones (1988, 1987).

socially constructed power system, built in theory (if not always proved in practice) on the principle of consent, not coercion.

Smith's liberal successors pushed his reasoning beyond the Hobbesian limits he acknowledged. This erosion of Smith's legacy progressively marginalized Hobbesian theory in accounting for economic practices.[60] For our purposes, the body of theory that post-Smith liberal theorists developed forms what this chapter presents as the "pure" liberal economic model, purged largely of Smith's insistence on the centrality of the state's security role and of its obligation to supply collective goods like roads, bridges, and education – let alone the modern state's welfare responsibility to furnish safety nets, social security, and health insurance to its citizens. It is this "pure" model, a purification of Smith's initial position (which arguably he would have rejected), that constitutes the liberal theory both of economic development *and* security. There is justification in including this "pure" liberal model as a security paradigm, since the social requirements to make the model work to multiply plenty constrain and, for many liberals, theoretically negate the incentives to use force or violence in social relations, most notably those dedicated to the production and exchange of wealth. For these "pure" liberal theorists, the coercive state is a predator,[61] a position not all economists would endorse.

Later liberal thinkers moved Smith's views to an endpoint that in its ideal form was decidedly anti-Hobbesian. Unlike realists and neorealists who eschew any notion that their theories have implications for socioeconomic development, many of these thinkers argued that the pursuit of freedom and the market ideal of consensual and cooperative exchanges between individuals were the roads to peace. They advanced an entirely different conception of how security might be achieved than by using or threatening force or by pursuing realist balance of power policies. For these theorists and activists, free, open, global markets were not only necessary for the wealth of nations but also for the peace of nations. They fleshed out Immanuel Kant's insight about the peace-promoting properties of commerce by building on Smith's conceptual edifice. For these inheritors of Smith's mantle, promoting economic exchange is ipso facto promoted peace. This case was not made in a day, but required two centuries to build. It continues to be extended and revised today.

---

[60] As more than one eminent liberal economic theorist has reluctantly acknowledged, the creation of a pre-existing social order and the proper definition of property rights by the state are pre-conditions for the wealth of nations. See especially the work of Douglass North (1986, 1990; also North and Weingast [1989]). North initially attempted in his 1973 book with Robert Thomas to explain economic growth by reference solely to market exchange: North and Thomas (1973). He subsequently modified this view in his later writings that won him the Nobel Prize for economics. See also Lindblom (2001).

[61] See, for example, Tilly (1985), Olson (1982), and Buchanan and Tulloch (1965).

Tracing the gradual and punctuated evolution of liberal security doctrine over two centuries is well beyond the scope of this discussion. One way to solve this problem is to highlight the thought of several celebrated liberal activists and theorists and identify the key links they forged between economic exchange and peace. These still have explanatory power and purchase among many theorists and practitioners today.[62] The first group consists of political activists and publicists – Richard Cobden, Norman Angell, and John Hobson. The second consists of two of the most celebrated economists cum philosophers in the twentieth century, viz., Joseph Schumpeter and Friedrich von Hayek.

Richard Cobden worked tirelessly to put Smith's liberal principles into practice. As a member of the House of Commons and later as a minister of state, he strongly supported the end of tariffs on food imports into Britain. As a parliamentary minister, he also promoted free trade and fostered free trade treaties between states to liberalize global economic exchanges. These were designed to create an increasingly dense socio-economic network to reinforce the mutual interdependence of peoples across state boundaries. The latter expectation draws on Smith's belief that economic actors would naturally coordinate their efforts as by a hidden hand, if not hindered by state coercive policies. The Industrial Revolution spurred Cobden and his liberal allies to advocate free trade and apply its alleged benefits to transform the war-propensities of states. As the world's industrial leader, Britain's interests in free trade corresponded to its ascendant competitive position. What was good for British commercial interests was projected to be good for the world's populations, too. What is significant for our purposes is the forceful argument of economic liberals, like Cobden, that global commerce ensures plenty *and* peace, central components of the liberal economic paradigm for security.[63]

Cobden marshaled Smith's conceptual arsenal to promote his cosmopolitan notion of a global "commonwealth of voluntarily co-operating individuals" as the foundation for perpetual peace.[64] As an ideal to be

---

[62] Mueller (1989).

[63] These notions were widespread throughout Europe. See, for example, the economic views of Jean-Baptiste Say, whose theory of economic growth and peace formed a single, coherent doctrine. Silberner (1946: 69–91). Journalists like Thomas Friedman suggest as much in noting that nations with McDonald hamburger outlets don't fight. See Friedman (2000: 248–75), for his "theory of peace" where McDonald's "Golden Arches" appear.

[64] Note that Immanuel Kant (1970, 1991: 41–53, 93–130) rejected this solution to perpetual peace on the grounds that national and linguistic differences precluded its emergence. Instead, his solution to the problem of peace was the creation of a coalition of republics. Kant's position is the basis for the currently widely held behavioral proposition that "democracies don't fight." For a recent review and critique of the vast literature devoted to this proposition and an attempt to provide a theoretical basis for this observation, see Lipson (2003).

pursued, it would arise independently and autonomously as a social institution that would transform the state and the state system of armed competition, balances of power, and war.[65] The state would be relegated to
the protection of private property and the enforcement of contracts consensually agreed upon by freely acting individuals. The coercive power
of the state, expressed in wars, would gradually fade from view and be
replaced by a free and peaceful global liberal society. Karl Marx shared
this vision of a peaceful world, although as we will see for entirely contradictory reasons. Whereas the liberal ideal was projected as a world
population of freely standing, autonomous individuals, Marx envisioned
a stateless, socialist world ruled by a global working class.

Cobden expected that ever-increasing economic interdependence
would generate enlarging world support for the expansion of open markets, a virtuous circle of self-propelling force. In contrast to a system of
property-exploiting states, as the basis for domestic and world economic
development, an emerging global civil society comprising Cobden's
commonwealth of enlightened individuals, joined by their shared humanity and not divided by their national, ethnic, religious, or cultural differences, would privilege the voluntary peaceful propensities of free economic exchange and constrain the coercive power of the state and check
the war-propensities of the state system. People would gradually understand that "war and its accoutrements were incompatible with the new
economic interdependence."[66] The theory of markets and the pursuit of
material betterment dictated this logic as a lesson drawn from the evolution of human societies.

Cobden blurred the distinction between domestic and international
economic policy that most of the security theorists discussed until now
insist upon. His commonwealth of cooperating individuals testified to
his vision of the predicted outcome of his economic free exchange ideas.
At home he opposed the political power of the British landed aristoc-
racy which monopolized positions of authority in government, military,
diplomatic service, colonial and ecclesiastical life.[67] Ending tariffs on corn
with the repeal of the Corn Laws in 1846 and the freeing of British markets from state control were expected to break the coalitional monopoly
held by these groups. A global market system was invoked to undermine
their hold on domestic power. The release from their oppression was also
expected to weaken the interest of those groups favoring colonies and

---

[65] Contrast this vision of global governance with that of Kant and Hedley Bull (1977:
chapter 4).
[66] Cain (1979: 240).   [67] Ibid.: 233ff.

empire as a solution to Britain's quest for economic wealth and welfare. Global, capitalist markets would make costly imperial preferences and burdensome colonies, held down by the boot rather than uplifted by the ballot box, unnecessary and redundant. British economic policy, guided by Cobden's liberal principles, would ensure its security if other states followed Britain's example. They would follow if the logic of free markets were pursued as a superior solution to global order and welfare instead of the then existing balance of power system.[68]

World War I delivered a devastating blow to liberal theory. Cobden's extension of liberal economic theory to peace appeared illusory, even mischievous, when applied to national security policy. On the eve of World War I, Cobden's liberal successor, Norman Angell, misguidedly affirmed Cobden's conviction that war was not possible between increasingly economically interdependent states because of its cost.[69] No less heeded by the states of Europe was John Hobson's argument that Europe's empires were wasteful and a central source of conflict and war.[70] Instead, the major European powers relied on empires as indispensable in the struggle for hegemony in Europe and the world. The developed states of the globe, centered in Western Europe and North America, were never more economically interdependent in their history, measured by trade and all forms of economic exchange, including investment and the movement of national populations across state boundaries, yet they plunged into a global war.[71] What went wrong?

The response of liberal thinkers has been that the fault does not lie in liberal doctrine. Much as George Bernard Shaw said of Christianity, liberals insisted that liberalism was not wrong; it was just never fully applied. Conflicts arose and wars erupted because liberal practices had allegedly not been sufficiently employed to produce the harmony, which liberals predicted between "producers and consumers, a harmony that will supersede any temporary conflict of interest."[72] This liberal response to war in the twentieth century is not easily summarized. Liberal theorists, like those in the realist camp, assume a wide variety of positions even

---

[68] Since this volume is concerned with exposing the ideal or pure properties of rival security paradigms, it cannot dwell on the actual history of their application in policy. For the British case, see Irwin (1996), Howe (1997), and Semmel (1970). Britain pursued a policy of the open door up to World War I even though its competitors increasingly moved to protect their home industries through restrictive economic policies and to insist on imperial preferences. Semmel and Howe describe Britain's policy of free trade imperialism. For a neo-Marxist critique, consult Hobsbawm (1975, 1969).
[69] Angell (1909).   [70] Cain (1978).   [71] Hirst and Thompson (1999).
[72] Gilpin (1987: 30).

though they share key assumptions about human nature, the relation of the state to civil society, and the logic and workings of markets.[73]

For purposes of brevity, two liberal theorists – Joseph Schumpeter and Friedrich von Hayek – whose work is widely acknowledged as among the best of this school of thought, may be singled out as representative of this position. Schumpeter defended capitalists and capitalist markets as sources of peace and plenty against the claim of V. I. Lenin, discussed below, who insisted that capitalism drives imperialism and produces global class conflict and war, notably World War I. Schumpeter located the roots of imperialism elsewhere than capitalism and defended the expansion of markets as antidotes to these scourges. Friedrich von Hayek, in turn, focused his attack on the threat to human freedom – economic and political – posed by revolutionary Communism after World War I. Together, their voluminous writings are among the most powerful defenses of liberal doctrine and profound critiques of the explanations of global conflict advanced by realism (joined to nationalism) and Marxism.

Schumpeter identified imperialism as the principal cause of World War I. In contrast to Lenin, he defined imperialism as "the objectless disposition on the part of a state to unlimited forcible expansion."[74] It was sustained by two principal elements. The first arose, according to Schumpeter, from the rise of aristocratic elites who had a class interest in war. They created and sustained military systems that perpetuated their dominant social status and power. They exploited and destroyed the productive capital and labor available to society. They survived and perpetuated themselves by preying on the social economic capital of a society. They also incited vestigial "social atavisms" in the mass of the population. These Schumpeter associated with the virulent nationalism that drove Europe's populations to war to impose their national wills on other imperial European states and on subjugated populations around the world.

The global socio-economic and political system inspired by liberal capitalism opposed the dominance of aristocratic classes, holdovers from a feudal past, and the military systems that underwrote their domestic and international power. Businessmen, according to Schumpeter's

---

[73] As Robert Gilpin observes, liberalism assumes many forms: "classical, neo-classical, Keynesian, monetarist, Austrian, rational expectation, etc. These variants range from those giving priority to equality and tending toward social democracy and state interventionism to achieve this objective, to those stressing liberty and noninterventionism at the expense of social equality" (*ibid.*: 27). For a range of opinion, see Friedman (1962), Friedman and Friedman (1980), Keynes (1936), Hobson (1902), and Mill (1848a, b).

[74] Schumpeter (1955).

conception of their "ideal" role in market operations, were expected to be primarily interested in peace, not war; in open, free markets, not in domestically subsidized monopolies. Much less did they have an interest in imperial expansion. That solution to domestic welfare led to costly colonies, squandered resources more profitably invested in civilian projects, large armies to suppress local populations, and suffocating civil bureaucracies to administer them. These resources could be better deployed to production and innovation and to enhance the wealth of the nation and all of its citizens.

War also impeded technological development. The efforts of entrepreneurs fostered by market incentives for profit were frustrated by war preparations and armed conflicts. The ideal of liberal economic exchange made no distinction between the national, ethnic, religious, or cultural properties of buyers and sellers or of consumers and producers. Markets as a social system and capitalism as their driving force dampened and diminished the self-destructive atavism of antagonistic social groupings. In theory, all individuals were free and equal when bargaining in the market on a global level across state and national boundaries. "Pure" economic exchanges, consistent with liberal theory, stripped away the relevance of all other properties or characteristics that humans might create or invent in fashioning their identities – religion, culture, ethnic, national and tribal origins, or language. If the individual was reduced to "economic man" and citizens to consumers, the conflicts incited by these social differences were also diluted and dissolved. Not that these non-material claims on human freedom should be discarded: rather, they should be enjoyed by excising their impact on the efficiencies and effectiveness of capitalist markets to create wealth as an essential precondition for these freedoms to flourish.

Hayek relentlessly attacked central state planning.[75] Interstate conflicts would be significantly reduced – potentially eliminated – according to Hayek's reasoning by the incentives of open markets. Free and voluntary cooperation through market transactions by rational and informed individuals would produce optimal use of economic resources and promote and sustain valued collective goods. There was no need for a planner's hand or a state's directive power to reconcile the diverse interests of individuals. Whereas Hobbes insisted that only a focused monopoly of violence in the Leviathan or state could solve this problem of non-converging interests, Hayek and liberal adherents envisioned a non-coercive solution for coordinating conflicting human preferences through the creation and fostering of global markets and a global market system.

[75] Hayek (1944, 1988).

Hayek transformed Hobbes' security dilemma into what he believed was a solvable economic problem. The challenge of a rational economic order was given by this Hayekian formula: "Put at their briefest, (the conditions) are that the marginal rates of substitution between any two commodities or factors must be the same in all their different uses."[76] In other words, the material resources available to individuals could be put to an almost infinite number of possible uses. Each choice necessarily implied opportunity costs of what would have to be incurred in choosing one course of action over another to advance a particular interest. How then could society sort out these divergent and clashing individual interests in a way that would yield the greatest benefit to the greatest number of individuals *as these individuals conceived their particular interests?*

Hayek argued that this social problem could only be solved by discovering some way for the free choices of individuals to express the knowledge of their interests as only they, alone, could know and express them. The dispersal of this knowledge within the subjective states of mind of individuals precluded the possibility – theoretically and practically – that planners could know those interests. Much less could a state, especially a state that owned the means of production, solve this social problem. Imposing its will was testimony enough of its failure. The state's monopoly and control of a nation's economic resources would inevitably constrain, distort, and skew both the economic and political choices of individuals and falsify the expression of those interests and frustrate their realization. Only free, open markets could meet this knowledge test.

Consumers and producers could express their conflicting interests to determine the value of their competing claims in the form of prices. Individual knowledge of interests was transformed into potentially globally integrated market prices for the realization of those material interests. This signaling was instantaneous and, theoretically, global. Favorably quoting Ludwig von Mises, a fellow liberal thinker, Hayek argued that only competitive markets could solve the social economic problem he posed of coordinating the conflicting preferences of individuals under conditions of scarce resources. All other coercive or directive solutions would always lead to less than optimal results: "The essential point on which Professor Mises went far beyond anything done by his predecessors was the detailed demonstration that an economic use of the available resources was only possible if this pricing was applied not only to the final product but also to all the intermediate products and factors of

[76] Hayek (1948: 77).

production and that no other process was conceivable which would in the same way take account of all the relevant facts as did the pricing process of the competitive market."[77]

This line of reasoning was then extended to political decisions. These referred not only to support of market solutions to the central problem of reconciling divergent interests with scarce resources non-coercively, but also of defining the conditions of human freedom and choice in public life. These implied more than the freedom of consumer choices or employment, restricted under authoritarian systems. These freedoms would be guaranteed wherever free markets reigned. They were also the preconditions for preserving free choice because their realization would require the ownership of private property and its unfettered use and disposition. Absent these conditions of free choice in using his material resources as he chose, the individual would lack the means to limit state coercive power.

Like prices in the market, votes in free and fair elections became the expression of individual interests.[78] Since there was no scientific method to decide what values should be accorded privilege in social, economic, and political spheres, free markets and free elections provided better solutions to these social problems than alternative systems rooted in coercion. Rational actors, on reflection, could not agree on what interests, aims, and values they held dear, but they could agree to affirm the pure or ideal model for making social choices and providing collective goods advanced by Hayek and liberals. This was a vision of convergence at least on the rational rules by which an individual's economic and political interests were to be expressed: through free markets and free and fair elections. Free markets led to free political regimes and democratic rule; both joined to produce peace and prosperity. Paraphrasing Smith, it was not the selfless inclinations of states that produced peace, but their egoistic pursuit of wealth and welfare spurred by the populations to which they are accountable, that promoted peace through prosperity.

The Marxist and Leninist challenge to the liberal ideal

There would appear to be even less justification for including the theories of Karl Marx and his many followers in this evaluation of security paradigms than those of liberal economic theorists. After all, many might ask, "Who is a Marxist today?" – a rhetorical question that, as the discussion below suggests, is prematurely posed. It is also true that liberal

---

[77] Quoted in Hayek (1948: 143). See also Mises (1922, 1949, 1956).
[78] See Buchanan (1959, 1988); also Buchanan and Tullock (1965).

economic theory can at least claim to have won the minds, if not the hearts, of many peoples and states by default.[79] China, the Russian Federation, the other republics of the Soviet Union, and all of the East European members of the former Warsaw Pact have abandoned the Communist experiment of centralized, state-run economies. The three Baltic republics of the former Soviet Union are scheduled, along with most of the former Warsaw pact countries, to enter the European Union, the largest regional market grouping in the world.

It is difficult to exaggerate the implications for international security of these defections from command economic models and adaptation to the liberal economic model – a crucial point in the discussion below in assessing the liberal paradigm's explanation for the end of the Cold War.[80] Except for Communist regimes in Cuba and North Korea or predatory states, like Myanmar, the populations of the world and their representative states would appear to be clapping with one hand as they applaud the global capitalist system and don what Thomas Friedman calls the "Golden Straitjacket" comprising its rules and regulations.[81] The prediction of Karl Marx that the Communist revolution would destroy capitalism, a boast echoed by Soviet Premier Nikita Khrushchev during the Cold War struggle, has proven to be simply wrong.[82] So what can be learned about security by examining a Marxist model and its proliferating offshoots?

The voluminous scholarly writings about Marx and Marxism provide prima facie evidence that the exclusion of Marxist theory from security concerns would be a serious mistake. Two considerations – one conceptual, the other political and practical – are particularly relevant to this discussion.[83] First, Marx advances a theory of conflict, revolution and armed struggle that still has some discernible explanatory power in the post-Cold War era, notably in civil strife and war in the developing world. If the roots of violence and the use of force or coercive threats by rival classes and states are wider and deeper than those identified by Marx, notably in his exclusive attribution of global conflict to the expansionist and predatory proclivities of capitalism, his stress on the exploitation

---

[79] For example, see Gilpin (2001), Soros (2000), Friedman (2000), Gill (1997), and Levy-Livermore (1998).

[80] Realist and neorealist theorists would disagree with the assessment. See Kenneth Waltz's (1979: 20ff.) rejection of Marxist theory in his exposition of neorealism. For a sympathetic reading of Marx from a liberal perspective, see North (1986).

[81] Friedman (2000: 101–11).   [82] Kornai (1992).

[83] Studying Marxist theory and practice is a life's work. Highlighting some of Marx's key concepts that bear on security scarcely scratches the surface either of his voluminous works or the mountainous commentary on them over a century. Illustrative are the following, which also provide extensive bibliographic references: Cohen (2000), Elster (1985, 1986a), Giddens (1971), and Elliott (1981).

of the many by the few continues to have relevance for many people as rationalization of their poverty and privation.[84] Whereas global capitalist markets are expected to free individuals from traditional taboos and state predations, Marxist-inspired theorists contend that capitalism and the multinational corporations dominating global markets are the new imperialists. This is the firm conviction of many influential neo-Marxists today.[85]

Marx and Marxists of all stripes not only deplore economic inequality and the vast disparities of income within and between states, but they also purport to show that these conditions are the inevitable consequences of capitalism as a social system. According to these critics, these inequalities of economic wealth and welfare and political power produced by the market system generate continuing conflict between classes. These conflicts drive international politics and explain domestic revolutions and international wars as components of a system in chronic crisis. Marx's critique of capitalism as the principal source of group and state conflict and violence remains among the most penetrating and pertinent explanations of why peoples and states use force and coercive threats to advance their economic and political interests and moral imperatives.

Second, the many, glaring flaws of Marxist economic theory should not obscure the continuing powerful attraction of Marxist doctrine for millions of people around the globe.[86] Its explanation of social conflict and the eventual supplanting of capitalism by Communism worldwide cannot be falsified simply by citing the collapse of the Soviet Union or the abandonment of the socialist model. As long as a distant future is posited as the eventual outcome of the contradictions within capitalism, Marxist assertions remain unfalsifiable, however much they may appear to be at odds with current experience.[87]

If Marxist theory and logic is circular and, accordingly, problematic as a convincing explanation of how capitalism works and how it creates a security order to protect and promote its interests, it is still persuasive as an *ideology*. It is still capable of mobilizing millions to challenge capitalism's post-Cold War ascendancy. It provides a body of doctrine that

---

[84] Much of the backlash to the globalization of capitalist markets relies on Marxist assumptions, updated in reaction to the new forces driving advanced capitalist markets. Illustrative is Sassen (1998). Many partisans of global markets and capitalism, some like George Soros, who have profited handsomely from their skilled entrepreneurship, are concerned about the staying power of markets. See, for example, Rodrik (1997), Gilpin (2000, 2001), Soros (2000), and Stiglitz (2002).

[85] See Hardt and Negri (2000, 2004) and Harvey (2001, 2003).

[86] For an exposition and critique of Marx's work, see Elster (1985). For a more sympathetic treatment, see Elster's (1986a) later work and especially G. A. Cohen's (2000) defense.

[87] Gilpin (1987) makes this point, in chapter 2: 25–64, a critique equally applicable to liberal economic thought.

rallies popular sentiment and demands for a more equal and equitable division of the world's wealth than can be achieved by the prevailing rules and institutions of capitalist markets. As an ideology (whose persistence and attractiveness has to be explained, too), Marxism provided a rationale for Communist regimes in the Soviet Union and China. Until the internal flaws of a state-centered, bureaucratically dictated economy were revealed in the second half of the twentieth century, Marxism as a justification for state ownership of the means of production was arguably the leading social force throughout the developing world during the first generation of decolonization after World War II.

The mutations of Marxism into a body of doctrine challenging capitalism testify to its political power if not to its coherence as an economic theory. In this ideological guise, as a rejection of the prevailing Western liberal, capitalist security order on which global markets depend, Marxist tenets have to be reckoned as a vital force in any effort to theorize about international security. Its mobilizing power of popular sentiment and will across the globe, ebbing and flowing for over a century and half, becomes one of its principal justifications as a security paradigm, quite apart from whatever errant claims it may make as a social or economic theory. As an ideological and moral critique of the failures of capitalism to address a wide range of glaring inequalities and injustices, Marxist theory reveals its capacity to enlist groups around the world opposed to the prevailing international security order and its interdependent entanglement with global capitalist markets.

In the brief space available to cover Marx and Marxist thinking, emphasis will be placed on what unites the many contending viewpoints within this tradition. Quite simply, it is impossible even if more space *were* available to satisfy either Marxists or their critics that there exists a singular body of doctrine that conclusively interprets the writings of Karl Marx. Disentangling the empirical and social scientific contributions of Marx from their policy prescriptions is no less a daunting task. Since Marxism continues to inspire peoples around the globe to seek fundamental changes in their socio-economic and political conditions and to impel some to use force or threats to effect these changes, Marxist doctrine can, through blowback, explain the behavior of these activists or states. Paul Samuelson, a leading neo-liberal economist and Nobel laureate, dismissed Marx as a minor post-Ricardian economic theorist.[88] While Samuelson may well be right that Marx was no equal to David Ricardo as a liberal economic theorist (and why would Marx deny that?), his derisive observation misses much of the mark of Marx's significance, notably

---

[88] Singer (2000).

for security studies. If Marx clearly is outside the pale of prevailing liberal economic "theory," the problems he raises about the conflict-producing effects of economic inequality, an inescapable product of free markets, remain a non-trivial problem of great concern to capitalist partisans. Marx's Philippic against capitalism also inspires formidable challenges to the preservation and extension of the market system and the current international order on which it precariously rests.[89]

The discussion is divided into two sections. The first reviews Marx's theory of socio-economic change with special reference to the implications of his thinking for security theory and the incentives of market outcomes to induce appeals to force and threats. The second moves beyond Marx to V. I. Lenin, who extended Marxism to explain World War I as the inevitable result of capitalist imperial expansion and internecine conflict. The multiple mutations of Marxist and Marxist-oriented thinking are loosely held together by the conviction that the uneven, unequal and inequitable economic development of the world economy arises from fundamental and insurmountable flaws within the capitalist system. The evident disparities of material welfare between the Western developed world and the vastly greater developing world purportedly create the moral and political conditions for Marxist theory and ideology to flourish. Chronic and what are alleged to be growing gaps in wealth between haves and have-nots galvanize relentless efforts to radically reform or overturn what is charged to be an unjust socio-economic and world order. If we are to give a full account of the sources of international insecurity, these challenges must be included as grist to the security mill we are constructing.

Marx and the violent overthrow of capitalism

Like Adam Smith, Marx privileged the economic dimension of human make up. Unlike Smith, he rejected the liberal model as a prescription for peace and plenty. Marx portrayed the pursuit of material wealth and welfare as a social or collective enterprise. It was not viewed as an activity conducted by Smith's egoistically motivated individuals. Marx conceded that humans "truck and barter," properties most directly associated with capitalism, but these proclivities were incidental to what he portrayed as but the expression of a social evolutionary process creating progressively more efficient means of production in the material progress of humans and human societies. Whereas liberals begin with the assumption of rational individuals capable of making economic choices in the marketplace to maximize their material wealth with socially beneficial

---

[89] This argument is developed in Gilpin (1987, 2000, 2001).

effects as largely unintended byproducts of their efforts, Marx posited the human species as a materially motivated social actor whose destiny, guided by Marx's claimed social scientific discoveries, was to capture and control the material forces shaping human evolution. The driving object of species behavior was its material betterment. That was dictated by an evolutionary process in which increasingly more powerful means or forces of production were discovered and applied as best social practices. Within a Marxist frame of analysis, rationality expresses itself through time, space, and historical circumstance as a social, not individual, process of choice and action.

Frederick Engels, Marx's patron and collaborator, summarized what he believed was Marx's contribution to explaining social evolution and, implicitly, social conflict:

Just as Darwin discovered the law of development of organic nature, so Marx discovered the law of development of human history: the simple fact . . . that mankind must first off eat, drink, have shelter and clothing before it can pursue politics, science, art, religion . . . that therefore the production of the immediate material means of subsistence and consequently the degree of economic development attained . . . during an epoch form the foundation upon which the state institutions, the legal conceptions, art, and even the ideas on religion, of the people concerned have been evolved, and in the light of which they must, therefore, be explained, instead of vice versa, as had hitherto been the case.[90]

Marx's conception of the evolution of historical materialism,[91] as Engels explained, distinguished between primary forces of production in response to inescapable and ineluctable human bio-economic needs and the human relations of production between consumers and suppliers arising from evolving and increasingly more technologically sophisticated forms of production. Primacy was assigned to "forces of production" or what contemporary theory largely conceives as scientific discovery transformed into a ceaseless if not linear process of technological innovation. These modes of production, in turn, created hierarchical power structures astride which sit those classes owning and controlling these modes of production. Similar to liberal economic theory that stipulates that rational economic actors will always maximize their material gains under conditions of scarce resources, Marx asserted that mankind would always choose the more productive system.[92] On this score, liberals and Marxists agree. The quest for better means of production was stipulated by

---

[90] Elliott (1981: 334).
[91] Marx's conception of historical materialism evolved and changed over his lifetime, eventuating in internal contradictions that remain unresolved as Elster (1985) exposes in painful detail. For a more accessible and sympathetic presentation of Marx's theory of historical materialism, see Cohen (2000).
[92] This point is made by Singer (2000).

Marxists to be embedded in human social evolution rather than directed by the individual choices of selfish, creative egoists.

Humans enter into social relations to adapt and to exploit these forces of production in the quest for ever-greater material plenty. These forces of production evolve over time to ever more efficient and effective levels. This bio-economic drive animated humans everywhere, regardless of time or spatial circumstance. Evolving processes of production were conceived as the motor of social change. Successive economic systems were created and advanced less by conscious or deliberate choice (at least until Marx's theoretical discoveries according to Engels) than by instinctive human adaptation to the dominant material conditions defining their existence. Marx was among the first theorists to recognize the implications of the Industrial Revolution as a spur to the unprecedented spread of global markets and Europe's imperial expansion. The asymmetries of economic and political power occasioned by capitalist markets constituted an entirely new and revolutionary condition in human social evolution.[93]

If the progressive material development of mankind was inevitable as superior forces of production replaced lesser mechanisms, no less inevitable was a process of social development motored by a class struggle between haves and have-nots arising from these productive forces. These classes arose from the struggle between old and newer forms of production. These changing forces of production in each epoch of the material evolution of mankind generated a complex set of *social relations* of production that exploited these new and more efficient modes of production. These relations of production became what can be termed a social system that was compatible with the substrata of material conditions of production. The resulting superstructure of power decided whose preferences would be privileged and who would acquire more wealth than others in human societies.

Those occupying positions of authority in these superstructures, resting on the foundation of a given evolutionary state of material development, constituted a ruling class. Local and global politics and conflicts might appear on the surface to be moved by the considerations attributed to humans by realists or liberal institutionalists, but these surface phenomena, Marx contended, could be more accurately linked to underlying and increasingly powerful global forces of production. These, he alleged, were the basis for a science of human societies, the point stressed by Engels. Once a given superstructure, rooted in less efficient and effective ways of making material wealth, came into contact with a superior system of production, a clash of social forces or relations of production would

---

[93] Marx and Engels (1948).

arise until the latter, more innovative system eventually triumphed as the foundation for a new social order.

Political conflict and revolution were driven by the tension between one form of production and its supporting superstructure and new forms of production and their corresponding and competing social structure. Each structure of power has its own, appropriate and preferred security order. Each supports and protects either that class which is in power but whose control is waning since it is tied to a decaying system of production or that rising class associated with the new epoch of productive power. Politics and armed conflict are joined in the clash of these rival classes whose interests are inextricably tied to a certain stage of the material evolution of human societies. In its progressive form, politics as a struggle for power promotes the new system of production; in its regressive form, it sustains a system that is no longer optimal and condemned eventually to be overthrown and discarded. The property rights and ruling authority on which the latter system rests delays but cannot stay the dissolution of the old order. The new forces of production, as Jon Elster, a leading scholar of Marxist theory, observes, "will, inevitably, will out."[94]

Marx succinctly captured this process of material evolution and the clash between contending forces of production and the political supports and security orders associated with them in his *Preface to a Contribution to the Critique of Political Economy*. It is worthwhile to quote Marx at length, since commentary cannot improve on his exposition of Marxist theory:

In the social production of their existence, men enter into definite, necessary relations, which are independent of their will, namely, *relations of production* corresponding to a determinate state of development of their material forces of production. The totality of these relations of production constitutes the economic structure of society, the real foundation on which there arises a legal and political superstructure and to which there correspond definite forms of social consciousness. The mode of production of material life conditions the social, political and intellectual life-process in general. It is not the consciousness of men that determines their being, but on the contrary it is their social being that determines their consciousness. At a certain stage of their development, the *material productive forces* of society come into conflict with the existing *relations of production* or – what is merely a legal expression for the same thing – with the property relations within the framework of which they have hitherto operated. From forms of development of the productive forces these relations turn into their fetters. At that point an era of social revolution begins.[95]

---

[94] Elster (1986a: 142).
[95] Marx (1970: 3–4). Italics added. See also *The Eighteenth Brumaire of Louis Napoleon*. Elliott (1981: 399): "Men make their own history, but they do not make it just as they please; they do not make it under circumstances chosen by themselves, but under circumstances directly encountered, given and transmitted from the past."

Marx attempted to give concrete expression to this abstract rendering of historical materialism. "The handmill," he noted, "gives you society with the feudal lord; the steam mill, society with the industrial capitalist."[96] The handmill was a metaphor for the productive forces associated with European feudal society based on land and agriculture. The lord of the manor who owned an estate controlled serfs who worked the land under his management. Serfs also had rights tied to the soil. They, typically, could not move to other manors nor rise above the social station to which they were born. Lords bore allegiance to each other as a guarantee for their mutual protection. This superstructure, resting on the transfer of political authority through blood and custom and on the productivity of land, human energy, domesticated animals, and manual tools for economic survival – owned and controlled by feudal lords – formed a decentralized and localized security system as a defense against exterior attacks and as the guarantee of local peace. Technological innovations and the rise of capitalist markets would challenge and ultimately transform this diffused and conflict-prone system of security into a global capitalist imperial system, the organizer and forerunner of a global socialist order.

Once the steam engine, as the metaphor of European industrialization, supplanted the handmill, associated with feudalism, as a principal means of production, a new capitalist class emerged to challenge aristocratic power. Both the English and French revolutions were portrayed by Marx as a struggle between these classes and the rival superstructures to which each was tributary. The factory system could not exist within the constraints of private property defined by the rigid codes to which lord and serf were bound. Labor had to be alienated from the land, made mobile, and subject to flexible pricing to respond quickly and efficiently to the rapidly changing demands of capitalist modes of production deriving from industrialization, technological innovation, and globalizing markets. The factory system on which capitalist expansion depended could come into existence only with the elimination of feudalism, serfdom, and slavery and the emergence of "free" labor as a commodity to be bought and sold in the marketplace.

The rise of a capitalist class in possession of these new means of industrial production gave rise to a working class. The struggle between these two classes ushered in for Marx the final stage of historical materialism. All history was funneled through class struggle: "Freeman and slave, patrician and plebeian, lord and serf, guild master and journeyman – in a word, oppressor and oppressed – . . . carried on an uninterrupted . . . fight that each time ended in a revolutionary reconstitution of society at

---

[96] Quoted in Singer (2000: 49).

large, or in the common ruin of the contending classes."[97] Marx predicted the same fate for capitalism and the capitalist class; he (and his followers) worked ceaselessly to ensure his prediction, evidencing why Marxist and neo-Marxist doctrine is so powerful and persuasive a political force. Joined are predictions of the future ascendancy of socialism as a system of global governance and the obligation to bring about this prediction.

What was unique about capitalist modes of production, as Marxist and non-Marxist recognized, were the incentives they generated to integrate mankind within a single and unified system of economic production. This would be accomplished, as Adam Smith had already foreseen, by the creation of global markets. Capitalism thrived by "trucking and bartering" and by expanding the outlets of its ever-enlarging productive capacity through markets that would eventually encompass the globe. Capitalism's historic role was to create this new social system and structure of power. Marx welcomed British imperial rule in India as the fulfillment of material progress. It supplanted India's feudal system based on a rigid caste system and destroyed its cottage manufactures and, specifically, its cotton industry by flooding its markets with inexpensive British goods.

But according to Marxist theory, capitalism, like feudalism, which it supplanted, was doomed to collapse because of its very success. This ironic result allegedly arose from the contradictions within capitalism as a social system. Capitalism was prone to overproduction. Rather than clear the market by cutting prices and absorbing losses, capitalists were predicted to behave in self-destructive ways by exploiting labor. A falling rate of profit and an increasingly alienated class of workers worldwide, unalterably opposed to capitalist rule and dedicated to its overthrow, created a permanent state of crisis for the capitalist system. Exploitation derived from what Marx charged was the capitalist system's inherent structures and incentives to reserve for capitalists most of the material value of goods and services created by labor. Marx insisted that the creation of economic value was defined solely to the input of labor, not to capital, techno-scientific knowledge, or entrepreneurship as drivers of production and innovation. Since workers were denied the fruits of their labor, capitalism would destroy itself through cutthroat competition of worker exploitation and alienation. While liberal theorists also postulated the value-creating capacity of labor, it rejected the Marxist refusal to include land, capital, technological innovation, knowledge and entrepreneurship into the equation of value-added.[98]

For Marxists, unbridled competition led to the concentration of capital as those unable to maintain the pace of economic rivalry went bankrupt and swelled the ranks of the working poor reduced to subsistence and

---

[97] Quoted in Elliott (1981: 29).   [98] Schumpeter (1954).

destitute poverty. Pressures built up to find markets abroad to offset these rapacious capitalist proclivities. This deepened the crisis which moved then inexorably from a national to a global level. The exploitation of labor, now extending around the globe, enlarged the number of disaffected workers, while reducing the number of capitalists and their economic and political power. Eventually this system of economic relations would be toppled by these supposed internal contradictions. What would arise would be a socialist world order in which the means of production would be owned and controlled by an ascendant working class. A global socialist economic system would *ipso facto* be a world security order, ruled by the Communist International on behalf of the interests of a global proletariat or laboring class.

The role of the state in the revolutionary process: Lenin's extension of Marxist theory of conflict and revolution

Marx's theory of conflict, rooted in his conception of historical materialism, confronted two challenges – one theoretical, the other political. The first concerned the failure of the socialist revolution in advanced industrial states; the second, the decision of indigenous national socialist movements to support their states in World War I rather than foment a global socialist revolution. Until the outbreak of the war, Marxist theory viewed these nationally based socialist parties as the vanguard of the revolutionary struggle against capitalism. The revolutions of 1848 convulsing Europe, which prompted Marx and Engels to herald the coming Communist utopia in their *Manifesto of the Communist Party*, actually consolidated authoritarian rule on the continent. The uprising of the Paris Commune of 1870 in the wake of France's defeat in the War with Prussia was decisively defeated by what emerged as the French Third Republic. Enhanced, not diminished, was the control of the state by the bourgeoisie and capitalist class.

This was no less true in Germany, which was rapidly establishing itself as the leading industrial state on the Continent. Germany's socialist party, the largest in Europe, adopted a conciliatory posture toward the state and capitalist interests, seeking power by ballots rather than by bullets. These setbacks at domestic socialist reform, confounding Marxist theory, were compounded by World War I. National loyalties shattered the solidarity of the socialist internationale. Instead of universally opposing the war as a derivative of their class interests, workers supported their nations in the conflict of Europe's empires for world hegemony.

These gaps and contradictions in Marxist theory largely revolved around its underdeveloped conception of the modern state. Marx initially conceived the state as little more than a "committee for managing the common affairs of the whole bourgeoisie."[99] Unlike realists, Marx did not assign the state an independent existence apart from the class struggle as the driver of conflict of international relations. This raised an important question: Why didn't capitalists seize the state when they apparently had a chance in 1848 and 1870 – and thereafter? Why did the workers support the war between the European imperial powers? V. I. Lenin provided politically persuasive, if not empirically convincing, answers to these questions in his *Imperialism: The Highest Stage of Capitalism*, published in 1916 in the midst of World War I.

Lenin rejected the position of moderate socialist theorists, like Karl Kautsky, that capitalism could reform itself, surmount the class struggle, and stay its historic execution by violent overthrow. Cooperating with capitalists was not the answer to the ascendancy of the working class. Lenin ruled that option out on theoretical and practical political grounds. Compromise would only delay the inevitable victory of the proletariat. Better to accelerate, not retard, what Marxist theory predicted was the inevitable march of history. Cooperation between socialist parties with capitalist-dominated states, other than tactical arrangements of contingent utility, was viewed as theoretically impossible given the systemic contradictions of a socialist and capitalist world system.[100]

Lenin also dismissed the view that the war was a global conflict for hegemony among the great powers. He extended Marxist thinking by advancing the view that capitalism had reached a new and higher state of conflict than Marx had envisioned. He agreed with Marx that capitalism as an economic system had achieved the underlying final social outcome of historical materialism by socializing the global production of goods. He added, moreover, that increasingly the struggle for raw materials and markets under conditions of falling profits and worker exploitation of labor dictated the capitalist search for markets, colonies, and empires abroad. This expansion of state power and its imperial rule over the world's populations, including workers in advanced Western industrial societies, was portrayed as falling progressively under the control of large financial conglomerates. They were charged with using the coercive powers of the state to sustain their global competition for markets and power. Workers were duped into the belief that World War I was a struggle between states and national peoples rather than the last stages of a global class struggle between finance capital and a potentially united proletariat.

Lenin summarized his explanation for World War I and justified his prediction that capitalism would eventually collapse as a consequence

---

[99] *Manifesto of the Communist Party.* See also Elster (1985: 298–458, 1986a: 141–167) for an extensive critique of Marxist theory about the state.

[100] This assumption is still held by neo-Marxists. See Hardt and Negri (2000, 2004).

of the global struggle for imperial control of the world: "Imperialism *is* capitalism in that state of development in which the dominance of monopolies and finance capital has established itself; in which the export of capital has acquired pronounced importance; in which the division of the world among the international trusts has begun; in which the division of all territories of the globe among the great capitalist powers has been completed."[101] What may have appeared to be a struggle for global hegemony among nation-states, as depicted by realist theory, was in reality for Lenin a façade for the continuation of the class struggle under a different guise. Finance capitalists in control of the coercive power of the great powers sought through world war to ensure their monopolistic positions.[102] Lenin's addendum to Marxist theory was designed to accelerate the social learning process of workers and to increase their consciousness of the class struggle by renouncing the war as the pursuit of national rather than class interests.

Evaluation of liberal economic and Marxist paradigms

How do these two paradigms fare in explaining the rise and demise of the Cold War and the collapse of the Soviet Union? At this juncture in the evolution of the international system, liberal economic theory would appear to have the better of the argument between them. Liberal economic theory also poses a significant challenge to realist, neorealist, and institutionalist theory. Ironically, the rational actor model used by these latter security theorists and widely employed by strategic analysts is drawn from prevailing liberal economic theory. By simply substituting the maximization of material gains for strategic military and diplomatic power, liberal economists advance a plausibly necessary if not sufficient explanation for the end of the Cold War. This line of explanation, however, is less persuasive in explaining either the implosion of the Soviet Union as a state or its disintegration into its constituent republics, hitherto the Kremlin's pawns. These two interdependent outcomes should be distinguished to properly assess the capacity of liberal thought to explain these momentous results.

Realists interpret the economic reforms instituted by the Gorbachev regime as a state power move, not as a response to the wealth and welfare imperative advanced by liberal economic theorists and practitioners.

---

[101] Lenin (1977: 89). Italics added. This view of Lenin's explanation contrasts with that of scholars who allege that Lenin "substituted a political critique of capitalism in which the principal actors in effect became competing mercantilistic nation-states . . ." See Gilpin (1987: 40).

[102] See Schumpeter's (1955) critique, noted earlier, based on liberal economic theory.

Viewed in this narrow framework, détente and economic reform are viewed as little more than attempts to increase the long-term military capabilities of the Soviet Union in its competition with the West. The détente policies, sketched in chapter 3, are portrayed as strategic ploys in the ceaseless struggle of states for power. From this perspective there was no expectation that the Soviet state would implode or that the Cold War would soon be over. Indeed, economic reforms are understood to ensure the continuation of the Cold War for an indeterminate future in keeping with big state rivalry. That did not happen.

Liberal economic theory explains Gorbachev's détente policies and the disintegration of the Warsaw pact as a response to the constraints and challenges posed by free markets as a *system of power*. Relaxing the military conflict between the West and East and cutting defense budgets were pre-requisites for transferring scarce national resources to civilian economic needs. Ending the burden of empire by withdrawing from Afghanistan and cutting aid to weak, failed states abroad would release additional resources to implement domestic economic reforms. Cutting the costs of maintaining a command economy and control over socialist regimes and their failing economies in Eastern Europe set the stage for market forces to work across national boundaries within the Soviet sphere of influence. More importantly, détente encouraged Western trade and investment in a Soviet Union tamed to market rules. Western technology would also be transferred as economic exchange grew apace.

Absent these profound political changes and economic reforms, the Soviet Union would continue to be isolated from the wealth-producing forces of global markets and competition. The pursuit of wealth and welfare, as Soviet leaders recognized, was no less a state imperative in its own right as security. The Soviet regime was compelled to choose between continued high-intensity strategic conflict within the constraining bipolar framework of the Cold War or economic development – "guns or butter," if you will. An increasingly disenchanted Soviet elite confronted by the monumental failure of the socialist experiment and mounting popular disaffection with economic stagnation conspired to swell pressures for reform. Soviet reformers opted for the radical adaptation of the Soviet economy to the West's market system.

But why did the Soviet state then implode? Why would a rational, experienced policy-maker like Gorbachev, who had through wit and skill navigated his way through treacherous political waters to assume control over the Soviet Union, install economic policies and advance political reforms that would unwittingly lead to the demise of the Communist party and the Soviet state which he headed and on which his personal power and authority rested? That would not appear rational. Nor was Gorbachev's behavior consistent with the expectations of the rational actor model. It predicts that the actor will assess the consequences of his actions and choose optimal moves and strategies to maximize his interests. These heroic assumptions were clearly beyond realization by the Gorbachev regime.

Informed foreign observers of the Soviet economy were no less surprised than realists by the swift destructive impact of economic reforms on the Soviet states.[103] On the one hand, the *economic* rational actor model reveals the compelling logic of economic reforms and the decisive pressures these engender to open a state to free, open global markets to realize its security aims. On the other hand, the model, as an analytic tool, falls short of providing a plausible explanation for the implosion of the Soviet state into its fifteen constituent republics. The liberal model cannot account for the ethnic, national, and religious conflicts released by the collapse of the Soviet Union and their eruption throughout the former territories of the Soviet Union.[104] Under liberal theory these rivalries are supposed to fade away with the extension of global markets (or, if a Marxist model is invoked, the imposition of a socialist system).[105] Much less can liberal theory explain the violent national and religious wars of the Balkans in the 1990s, which, arguably, were checked by Titoist Communist rule and the pressures of the Cold War conflict.

To its credit, and in counterpoint to realist theory, liberal economic thought can argue, based on empirically tested theory, ample experience, and supportive practice, that any people or state that resists adaptation to market economic institutions, to the rigors of global competition and the division of labor, will lose in the race of the swift. But liberal theory has neither a coherent nor compelling theory of the state, nor a theory of its coercive power, more generally, other than a tendency to depict the state as predatory and socially dysfunctional.[106] Since these concerns are banished from the scope of classical liberal thinking (Smith excepted) – i.e. why and how the state was formed and what are its critical socioeconomic roles[107] – liberal economic theorists are no more equipped than their realist-neorealist-institutionalist competitors to explain the collapse of the Soviet state. They can explain why pressures for economic reform proved irresistible to prevent the Soviet Union from losing the

---

[103] Kornai (1992).   [104] An exception is Carrère d'Encausse (1993).
[105] For dissenting views challenging the utopian vision of liberal economic theory, see Chua (2003) and Saul (2004).
[106] Tilly (1985) and Olson (1982). Certainly not all liberal economists hold this view. Adam Smith did not, but there is an underlying suspicion of power in liberal thought, including its economic component, as Lord Acton observed: "Power tends to corrupt and absolute power corrupts absolutely."
[107] Of course not all liberal theorists can be charged with this criticism, including Adam Smith, who had a healthy understanding of the importance of a strong, if not overweening, state as a key support of the market system.

race for survival, but not why the Soviet Union imploded the way it did – into national units which were themselves internally divided into conflicting identity groups. Nor is liberal theory useful on the timing of these revolutionary transformations. Absent a plausible explanation of state formation or collapse, liberal theory cannot adequately explain why the Cold War ended – and so abruptly and unexpectedly. It can reasonably claim to be a part of the necessary explanation for these momentous events, but other forms of "rationality" must be invoked for a satisfactory explanation, since other actors and factors were at work that challenge the liberal paradigm and its realist competitors.

What can be properly attributed to liberal theory is the prediction that a planned economy will eventually be forced to adapt to the rigors of the market model or be "selected out" in the evolutional social process. Indeed, and in marked contrast to the realist and neorealist expectation that a state would be "selected out" if it failed to successfully adapt to the strategic power threats posed by its rival, the Soviet state was "selected out" because it failed to successfully adapt to the discipline of free market practices. *Perestroika* unleashed powerful forces that placed unbearable strains on the Soviet economic and political regime. Until now, Beijing has managed to contain the political forces let loose by its own restructuring. Its police and military forces have not been divided or dismantled by privileging political reform and openness over economic development. Witness the crushing of popular revolt in the Tiananmen Square massacre of spring 1989. The powerful glue of national and racial identity, absent in the Soviet case, also inhibits the shattering of the Beijing regime into the national, ethnic, linguistic, and religious divisions that persisted throughout the brief history of the Soviet Union.

None of the paradigms examined so far – clearly not Marxism – can account for the staying power of identity politics and its continuing capacity to incite religious, cultural, national, ethnic, and tribal conflicts. These enduring rivalries were either temporarily contained or absorbed by the Cold War conflict. It should have come as no surprise – although it did to many – that these conflicts would reappear once the constraints of the superpower, bipolar system had disappeared.[108] The Cold War did not create these rivalries, many of which preceded by centuries the emergence of the Cold War.[109] There is evidence to suggest that the superpowers controlled and contained these underlying rivalries to prevent their

---

[108] Authors concerned with ethnic conflict were quite aware of these divisions. Their voices could not be heard above the din of Cold War rhetoric. See, for example, Gurr (1993), Jones, Connor, and Powell (1991), McNeill (1986), Smith (1937), Smith (1981), and Gellner (1983).

[109] Goertz and Diehl (1993).

escalation into a global conflagration, even as Moscow and Washington sought allies, clients, and surrogates to bolster their relative positions in their Cold War.[110] Domestic insurgencies which now plague the Russian Federation and many other former republics of the USSR were suppressed by the authoritarian Soviet state. Civil war currently racks the Russian Federation after a decade of failed efforts to check the Chechen rebellion. Georgia and most of the Muslim-populated republics – Uzbekistan, Turkmenistan, Kyrgyzstan, and Kazakhstan – are in latent or open civil war. Armenia and Azerbaijan remain bitter enemies. The Balkan wars, occasioned by the breakup of Yugoslavia, have been arrested only by the massive intervention of NATO bombing and military occupation. And Czechoslovakia dissolved into its contending parts as the Czech and Slovak Republics.

The paradigms covered so far are even less helpful in providing much insight into the conflicts inflaming large segments of the developing world during and, most conspicuously, after the Cold War. The list of armed struggles between peoples of clashing social identities is long and bloody at this writing: Sri Lanka (Buddhist vs. Tamils), Rwanda and Burundi (Tutsis vs. Hutus), Sudan (Muslims vs. Christians and animists), and the Congo (tribal divisions). To these must be added the struggle between Israelis and Palestinians and the deep splits within the Muslim community between Sunni, Shi'ite and other splinter communal groups, stretching from North Africa to southeast Asia. Also to be included is over a half-century of armed struggle and arms races – and now a nuclear stand off – between India and Pakistan over Kashmir, rooted in two incompatible notions of state legitimacy.[111] The dispute pits two contradictory principles of political authority and sovereignty – a secular India vs. a Muslim Pakistan. In northeast Asia, bitter strife splits the two Koreas, and the two Chinas, more by class and regime differences than ethnic, racial, or linguistic differences. In the Horn of Africa, there is the puzzling case of Marxist regimes at odds with each other.

Marxism fails on the qualitative measures either of identity politics or of regime conflicts over legitimacy. Soviet leaders sought to surmount these historically determined differences by producing the "new socialist man."[112] That socialist man proved "hollow" once put to the test of the unrequited political aspirations of the many peoples composing the former Soviet Union. Among the most powerful of the latter were groups associated with national, ethnic, cultural, and religious identities striving for greater autonomy and independence. They resisted the authority

---

[110] Kolodziej and Kanet (1991) make this case.   [111] Kochanek (2003).
[112] Kaiser (1994) and Carrère d'Encausse (1993).

of central leadership and the imposition of a homogenized citizenship consistent with socialist doctrine.

Appeals to class solidarity or division have little or no discernible relevance in efforts to explain the break up of the Soviet Union and the end of the Cold War. Where such appeals had some effect were during the first stages of decolonization. Elites used Marxist dogma to mobilize their populations in the fight for national independence and to hold on to power through the state's coercive power until the promises of a better life were forfeited by counterproductive economic policies. This pattern roughly followed the process of sovietization in the early days of the Bolshevik revolution in Russia. Marxist doctrine galvanized hundreds of millions to oppose Western power. To this degree, Marxism as an ideology and political force contributes to an explanation of the initial evolution of the Cold War, but adds little or nothing to an explanation of its rapid and unexpected passing.

Similarly, now that the Western capitalistic model of economic development has become ascendant, the Marxist expectation of a global socialist revolution would appear to be permanently frustrated. Western capitalism, whatever its flaws, has demonstrated remarkable restorative powers when challenged by restive populations. Buried for the time being is any prospect of a worldwide workers' revolution. There is also no perceptible limit to continued scientific discovery and technological innovation, driven by the prospect of enormous gains to be made by selling new products on a world scale to potentially reach six billion consumers, with the world population expected to reach nine to ten billion by mid-century. Rather than pave the way for socialism, capitalism's dynamism, its incentives for innovation, and increasingly integrated markets (defined by a uniform and global price system) would appear irreplaceable as a social system dedicated to the wealth of nations – its many and glaring shortcomings to the contrary notwithstanding.[113]

Given these setbacks to Marxist ideology and socialist practice, it would be tempting to dismiss Marxism as a worthy contender to explain international conflicts and armed struggles. The seeming convergence of former command economy states on the Western market model and the latter's adoption by many developing countries would seem to herald Marxism's death knell. However, announcement of its demise would appear to be premature. Not unlike the resilience of the paradigms already discussed when confronted by new facts, Marxist thinking has

---

[113] The debate about the social benefits, burdens, and failures of the market, as a social system, is vast, sprawling and inconclusive. For a start, see Lindblom (2001) and citations.

arisen like a phoenix from its own ashes but in a different form from its classical roots. If classical Marxist-Leninist theory and its predictions of the globe's socio-economic development have been overtaken by events, the Marxist critique of the shortcomings of capitalism continues to spawn mutations that have implications for the development of security theory.

Modern World Systems (MWS) theory is illustrative. This Marxist-inspired hybrid posits the existence of a world capitalist system, incorporating global markets, nation-states, and cultures. As Immanuel Wallerstein observes, "Capitalism and a world economy (that is, a *single division of labour* but multiple polities) are obverse sides of the same coin. One does not cause the other. We are merely defining the same indivisible phenomenon by different characteristics."[114] From this perspective of a total system and a division of labor organized and propelled by the incentives of capitalist markets working through time and space across national boundaries to transform regimes and cultures to do its bidding, the Marxist critique is redirected and amplified to challenge the capitalist system. The MWS critique does not spare the nation-state as a prop for the world system, nor the ideology and culture constructed to legitimate it.[115] MWS theory divides this power structure into three segments: a dominant core, a semi-periphery, and a periphery. The core of capitalist states, with the United States and the European Union (and Japan) in the ascendancy, manipulate the periphery and control the semi-periphery through global markets on behalf of dominant capitalist interests. MWS concludes that this global socio-economic condition permanently exploits underdeveloped peoples and holds them back from developing their economies. The result is chronic and unrelieved poverty, and a progressively widening gap between haves and have-nots. These disparities in resources as well as in capital, technological, and productive capacity create the conditions for persistent and unremitting class conflict. These conditions generate incentives that prompt exploited and disaffected populations to resort to force, violence, and terrorism to destroy what is perceived as an oppressive system.

While Marxism, Modern World Systems, and other Marxist mutations have lost crucial rounds since the end of the Cold War in the fight for ascendancy as the dominant security paradigm, the shortcomings and failures of the capitalist system to adequately address the demands of

---

[114] Quoted in Brewer (1990: 176) who develops a systematic critique of the principal mutations of Marxist theories of imperialism (italics added). Writers in the Modern World Systems school include Wallerstein (1974), Frank (1969), and Baran (1958). Gilpin (1987: 67–72) provides a useful summary.

[115] Robbins (2002).

populations for sustained economic development, a greater share of the world's wealth, and a closing of the welfare gap and digital divide between rich and poor provide ammunition for the Marxist attack. These inequalities and associated inequities are cited as sources of instability and conflict and threats to global security.[116] If the twentieth century is viewed as a laboratory in which command and free markets were tested for their capacity to increase wealth and distribute welfare, it is clear that command economies failed the test. What is less clear is whether the solution of free, open markets will meet the test to forestall global social discontent, dissension, conflict, and armed struggle within a globalized and globalizing world. Partisans of a free, open global capitalist system are no less concerned than their opponents with finding solutions to these shortfalls in liberal economic theory.[117] This analysis of security paradigms cannot address these issues within the space of this discussion. However, the future development of security theory will have to confront these challenges to the scope of its concerns. Otherwise it will fail to account for why peoples around the globe, notably in the developing world, are prompted to use force to get their way and say, when deprived of the economic security to which they increasingly believe they are entitled.

Discussion questions

1. The rational actor model of decision-making is used extensively by security theorists and practitioners to explain actor behavior, notably that of states. What are the distinguishing properties of this conceptual and methodological tool and how does its application differ when used by security analysts and economists?
2. What role does the assumption of scarce resources play in strategic and security policy-making? How does this constraint apply to choices affecting levels of spending for defense and the development of weapon systems and forces levels? How does it apply to the traditional trade-off between "guns and butter"?
3. In what way did V. I. Lenin amend Marxist theory of global armed revolution against the capitalist system? And how did Joseph Schumpeter attempt to rebut Lenin's position and explanation for World War I?

---

[116] See Kolodziej (1992a, b) and especially the views of security specialists from around the globe and the priority they assign in these symposia to economic disparities, underdevelopment, and poverty as the foremost security threat confronting nation-states, the nation-state system, and the populations of the world.

[117] See, for example, Krugman (1990), Soros (2000), Stiglitz (2002), Strange (1986, 1988), Thurow (1996), and Lindblom (2001).

4. Compare the assumptions of human behavior of Adam Smith and the classical security theorists covered in chapter 2. What roles do they respectively assign to the state? Relate their thinking about security to the understanding of security and security studies advanced by this volume.

5. Evaluate the capacity of economic liberalism and Marxism to explain the rise, evolution, and collapse of the Cold War bipolar system.

Suggestions for further reading

Friedrich von Hayek (1948), *Individual Freedom and Economic Order*, Chicago: The University of Chicago Press. Hayek's brief for markets rests squarely on his contention that they promote human freedom. Only individuals, argues Hayek, know their preferences and "pure" markets composed of voluntary exchanges between actors are said to objectify these preferences through prices, providing knowledge to interdependent actors about what each is willing to pay for goods and services and the expected return on labor, land, and capital for those providing these material benefits.

V. I. Lenin (1977), *Imperialism*, New York: International Publishers. Lenin's extension of Marxist theory to explain World War I in economic, not political or military strategic, terms, had a profound impact on twentieth-century thinking about conflict and merits reading both as a polemic and as a theoretical rending of Marxism that still has intellectual sway among intellectuals and policy-makers despite its shortcomings and rejection by most states and their peoples in the wake of the collapse of the socialist experiment.

Charles E. Lindblom (2001), *The Market System: What It is, How It Works, and What to Make of It*, New Haven: Yale University Press. This is a brief, accessible depiction of how markets work, a non-technical evaluation of their impact on human welfare, and a balanced critique of their strengths and weaknesses as a social institution.

Karl Marx (1970), *A Contribution to the Critique of Political Economy*, Moscow: Progress. The introduction to this volume of less than ten pages summarizes Marx's theory of historical materialism and its implications for the evolution of capitalism and the projection of a worldwide socialist revolution.

Dani Rodrik (1997), *Has Globalization Gone Too Far?*, Washington, DC: Institute for International Economics. Although the socialist experiment in its Soviet form is bankrupt, there is rising criticism of global capitalist markets as a solution to the welfare demands of the world's populations. This volume, while cast in prevailing liberal economic theory, identifies some of the key shortcomings of exclusive reliance on unregulated markets to provide for the material needs of billions around the world.

Joseph A. Schumpeter (1955), *Imperialism*, New York: Meridian. This volume responds to Lenin's theory of imperialism from a liberal economic perspective by one of the most distinguished economists of the twentieth century.

Peter Singer (2000), *Marx: A Very Short Introduction*, Oxford: Oxford University Press. This short outline of Marx and Marxism summarizes key Marxist concepts and their impact on Western thought. It is a useful beginning for what is a lifetime project for the serious Marxist scholar.

Adam Smith (1937), *An Inquiry into the Nature and Causes of the Wealth of Nations*, New York: Modern Library. There is no substitute for reading Smith in the original. This chapter cites relevant pages as a start. Smith's capacious perspective includes both markets and the state, an institutional approach that is neglected in mainstream liberal economic theory.

Part III

Validating security theories

6   Behaviorism

Chapters 6 and 7 depart from the previous discussion. Behavioral and constructivist research programs are better described as "approaches" than as "paradigms." Partisans in both camps believe that they are carving new paths in developing international theory and in security studies.[1] Both schools include a broad, varied, and disputatious array of scholars and analysts. The members within each camp are more linked by the methods they use and the evidence they rely on than by the assumptions they make or share about any fixed notion of human behavior or nature. The paradigms covered in the preceding chapters stipulate, implicitly or explicitly, certain, defined interests and preferences of actors and assume certain persistent tendencies or patterns in human choices and behavior. These are conceived as endemic to the make-up of individuals or actors (realists and classical liberals) or embedded in the social structures of which individuals or collective actors are members (neorealists, liberal institutionalists, and Marxists).[2]

Although their methods could not be more at odds with each other, practitioners of behavioral or constructivist research implicitly agree that, if there is a core to being human, it remains to be discovered, not postulated. The notion of a definitive human nature is viewed either as unknowable (scientific behaviorism) or problematic, depending on the social exchanges of conceptually capable, linguistically skilled, creative, free humans and their agents who infuse meaning and significance into their relations and are the authors of their social make-up or construction (constructivists).

Chapters 6 and 7 identify the principal properties of these two contrasting approaches, beginning with the behavioral research program. Each

[1] This claim is made by James Fearon and Alexander Wendt (2002), who represent behavioral or rational and constructivist approaches to security.
[2] Waltz (1959) condenses the debates among philosophers and social scientists over two millennia with respect to their contending explanations of the sources of human conflict and cooperation, dividing these theorists into three schools of thought, each with its own distinct image of human behavior, derived, respectively, from individuals, from domestic socio-economic and political structures, or from the decentralized state system.

school of thought will be evaluated with respect to its contribution to security studies. As a matter of equity, each will be assessed initially on its own terms as well as in terms of the criteria invoked in this volume, viz., its capacity to explain the end of the Cold War.

The reader should be under no illusions that this discussion of behavioral or rationalist approaches to security will be comprehensive or conclusive. This cautionary note is dictated by the very volume and broad scope of the research programs grouped under the behavioral banner. A survey of behavioral research about war and armed conflict in 2002 contained 1,300 citations, compared to 700 in a similar survey in 1989.[3] As chapter 7 notes, the volume of constructivist scholarship has not been expanding at the same rate, but the trend lines remain upward and strong.[4] Given this volume and complexity of output, some discrimination and selectivity is advised even if any choice, however justified, cannot be fully fair in the eyes of all of the partisans of a behavioral or constructivist persuasion.

The strategy adopted by this discussion is to identify a widely recognized representative of behavioral research and to rely on this elected surrogate as a model for this camp. For the behavioral approach, the research program of power transition (hereinafter PT) theory will be evaluated as a stand-in for a behavioral or, as some prefer, a rationalist approach to security studies. Power transition research attempts to explain why global, systemic-wide war, notably between big powers, breaks out – a question of obvious centrality to security concerns.

Three considerations advise this selective choice. First, the PT research program does not dwell on anarchy or assume non-converging and insurmountable big-power conflicts over preferences. These are key differences with respect to a realist and, especially, a neorealist position. PT provides a useful point of comparison between these rival schools of thought. In principle, power vacuums do not exist in PT research. Those that might temporarily appear are quickly filled by states competing for hegemony. Power, like nature, abhors a vacuum. War between big powers is explained by different power configurations between dominant powers and contenders for ascendancy and by dynamic rates of change in the material assets of these competitors as a function of their internal, domestic capacities to mobilize human and material resources in their competition with other states. These configurations and the internally

---

[3] Midlarsky (1989, 2000).
[4] See the following and voluminous citations: Adler and Barnett (1998), Katzenstein (1996), Ruggie (1998), Wendt (1999), Adler (1997, 2002), and Fearon and Wendt (2002).

generated power transformations within them create a structure of power that either encourages or discourages war.

Whether war will erupt between the challenger and the dominant power, given a certain condition or threshold of material power between them, will depend, according to PT theorists, on the challenger's evaluation of whether its interests are served by the existing system. This subjective assessment of the positive value of the status quo by the challenger decisively influences the political and security implications of the material distribution of power between these rival states. That assessment is viewed either as a threat to, or as support of, the challenger's central concerns and preferences, whatever they might be. As a major proponent of power transition theory explains,

(P)ower transition is fundamentally different from realist thought. Specifically, realists believe that the international system is anarchic, and that all actors react identically to a given stimuli [sic]. In contrast, power transition posits that states will not react to international imperatives in the same ways unless they share similar evaluations of the status quo ... This important emphasis on status quo evaluations clearly distinguishes power transition from realism, and it links domestic and international politics within a single perspective.[5]

In causally associating the material conditions of power between challenger and hegemon and the subjective evaluation of the balance of power between them in the service of challenger's interests, the PT research program is potentially a bridge between behavioral or rationalist research and constructivism – two approaches that appear at first glance to be so much apart. In incorporating the notion of "satisfaction into its concerns," PT and constructivism acknowledge "ideas," a subjective variable, as a key driving force of state behavior.[6] As the discussion below explains, this bridge has yet to be built, but a conceptual foundation is being laid to erect such an edifice.

Power transition theorists claim that they provide more explanatory power for war – or no war – than realists who fix on a supposed international condition of permanent and putatively insurmountable anarchy both as a cause and as a condition of state behavior. In contrast, PT theorists view domestic and international politics and their mutual regulation and governance as very similar and, theoretically, as potentially forming a unified field of action for the state. Both imply the existence of a power hierarchy. "Power transition theory's hard core assumes," as one

---

[5] Kugler and Lemke (2000: 133).
[6] Interestingly enough, James Fearon and Alexander Wendt, who, respectively, represent the two opposed camps, are also optimistic that bridges can be built between these two approaches; primarily by way of methodology and a shared interest in the questions each group poses for study: Fearon and Wendt (2002).

perceptive commentary observes, "that the hierarchically organized international order contains rules similar to rules of domestic political systems 'despite the absence of an enforceable code of international law.' "[7] An analogy is drawn between groups jostling for power within a domestic regime and states in a ceaseless struggle for power, pelf, and privilege. In both instances challengers arise to threaten the existing structure of power and those in the position of ascendancy within each domain. This potential harmonization of domestic and international politics departs sharply from the realist dichotomy between these two realms.[8]

Second, and building on the integration of domestic and interstate politics, PT research can conceivably be extended to actors and factors working at systemic and transnational levels of analysis – i.e., to all the levels of actor initiative sketched in chapter 1. PT theory focuses on the relations of big states and on conflicts between the hegemon or dominant state and its rivals, depending on the historical era under examination. The measures employed to track this competition pivot on techno-economic material power *and* the subjective estimation of state actor satisfaction levels within a prevailing international order. These dimensions – objective and subjective components, respectively, of power transition concern – essentially encapsulate state behavior at all four levels of state behavior of interest to this volume. Big-power war is necessarily global or systemic since international order is the stake. There is an implicit convergence between the potential scope of the PT research program and this volume's characterization in chapter 3 of the Cold War as a struggle between two superpowers to define the international system and global politics to their liking. Their fated, if not fatal, conflict was *ipso facto* a contest to impose their conflicting preferences for world order and rule on each other and on other peoples and states.

The changing interstate relations of big powers define a particular order in history and the unique dynamics and structure of power of the era under observation. The domestic politics of a state are the crucibles in which are determined a state's satisfaction or dissatisfaction with a particular world order and the threats posed by the prevailing hegemon. The principal measure used by power transition theorists to explain war depends on the amount and rate of change of technological and economic power acquired by states. Although not a part of PT theory (and a shortcoming to be explained below), the realization of increased material

---

[7] DiCicco and Levy (1999: 585). See also Kugler and Lemke (1989: 172) and Lemke (1996: 8).
[8] The blurring of domestic and international politics under conditions of anarchy is examined in Milner (1993).

resources hinges critically on the exploitation by a state of what is increasingly a globalized, transnational economic system. This is the fourth level of analysis by which a state's behavior, including its security policies, can be observed and explained.[9]

Third, PT theory is a coherent, focused, clearly delineated, and (arguably) progressive research program. This assertion is supported by a growing body of confirming data and published research in support of PT claims.[10] These attributes qualify PT as a model of behavioral research, particularly with respect to structural theories of international relations and security. The latter identify the material conditions – techno-economic and military capabilities – between dyads of states. Observations of these distributions and the expected behavior of states form the basis of structural explanations of why states do what they do. Specifically, PT theory relies on its replication of these data to assign probabilities of war between dominant and challenger states.

Mention should be made of other important behavioral research programs that meet the three tests applied to PT for its candidacy. Correlates of War (COW) research, for example, has made extensive contributions to the measurement and probability of war between states.[11] While PT researchers often rely on COW data and indexes, COW researchers do not accent the crucial significance of "satisfaction" or "dissatisfaction" with the status quo as a key indicator of war between dominant and challenger powers. This is PT's "value-added" to behavioral war and peace studies.

Similarly, the much-debated proposition of the "democratic peace" could have been chosen as the stand-in for behavioral research.[12] While initial research stressed the relation of democratic regimes and peace, more recent research and publications address the four levels of state and actor analysis to provide a more comprehensive context within which to assess the weight of democratic rule as a key determinant of peace.[13] The

---

[9] Wendt (1994). Of course other research programs of behaviorism and constructivism might well be reviewed if space constraints did not dictate otherwise. For other relevant approaches consult n. 1.

[10] Aside from references to A. F. K. Organski and Jacek Kugler throughout this discussion, see Lemke (2002) for a summary of this growing supportive literature, including his own work.

[11] Geller and Singer (1998), Singer and Diehl (1990), and Singer, Bremer, and Stuckey (1972).

[12] Doyle (1986, 1983).

[13] Russett (1993), Russett and Starr (2000), Russett and Oneal (2001). Russett's *Triangulating Peace* is especially relevant in its effort to link democratic regime make-up (ideological and institutional) to transnational economic exchanges of an open trading system and international institutions dedicated to the peaceful resolution of interstate conflicts.

unsettled status of this research program among its partisans and critics, turning on the issue of whether the observation of non-violent resolution of conflicts between democracies over a limited time span constitutes a theory, reduces its value somewhat for this discussion until this internal debate is more definitively resolved.[14]

Note, too, that a large number and wide variety of *strategic* research programs might also have been employed to illustrate a behavioral approach. In contrast to structural approaches, like COW and PT, strategic research programs focus on the decision-making of actors who depend for the realization of their competing, complementary, or converging preferences on their mutually contingent choices and behavior. The research program of Robert Axelrod, described in chapter 4, illustrates this form of behavioral or rationalist research.[15] "In contrast," as one PT scholar explains, "structural theories focus on physical realities without explicit consideration of how decision-makers calculate how they should react to those physical realities. Power transition theory is a structural theory because it hypothesizes that given certain structural regularities in the relations between a pair of states, certain foreign policies are expected to be observed."[16]

Remember we are primarily concerned with presenting the behavioral approach, not in reviewing all of the many research programs that might qualify for candidacy as our surrogate. The alternatives, suggested here, underscore the converging aims of behavioral research despite their different starting points, methods, and evidentiary preferences. Space requirements limit our choices, and choosing one approach has the advantage of a focused discussion. Fortunately, there are several edited volumes that go into greater depth than this volume can to identify the range of research programs under this rubric and to highlight the strengths and weaknesses of these behavioral or rationalist approaches.[17]

This volume's discriminating (and potentially discriminatory) strategy, adopted out of convenience to characterize and assess the behavioral approach, is obviously an imperfect solution to the goal of adequately portraying the contributions of this orientation to security studies. It is

---

[14] Lipson (2003) reviews and evaluates critics of the democratic peace thesis and advances a vigorous defense of its explanatory power on theoretical grounds.
[15] Other important examples of this style of research, associated with game theory, are Brams and Kilgour (1988) and Bueno de Mesquita (1981). This form of strategic research should not be confused with strategic policy-making in which the aim is directing the use or threat of force to compel an adversary to bend to an actor's will. For this limited conception of strategy and strategic thinking, see Gray (1999).
[16] Lemke (2002: 38–9).
[17] Comprehensive surveys and analyses are found in the following: Breecher and Harvey (2002), Carlsnaes, Risse, and Simmons (2002), and Midlarsky (2000, 1989).

sufficient for our purposes if the discussion establishes that PT, as a research program, has an explanatory power, whatever its failings, that is not otherwise available by relying on the paradigms already reviewed. This assessment creates a presumption that, taken together, behavioral research programs – structural or strategic – can challenge for hegemony in security studies. PT theory and behavioral research merit serious consideration if this survey and evaluation of security studies is to be complete. At a minimum, the behavioral approach provides important critical tools to evaluate prevailing international relations theories and their policy implications by submitting these rivals to rigorous empirical tests for validation.

The behavioral approach: the scientific study of war and peace

Behavioral research attempts to apply the model of the physical and biological sciences to individual or collective international actors under investigation. International actors as units under investigation are not ascribed any pre-determined or prescribed tendency to act in a certain way. Observations are counted upon to supply answers once tested for their validity through replicated runs of a given research design or project. Hypotheses or propositions are advanced, but there is a deliberate decision within the scientific protocol to eschew presumptive expectations about actor behavior before all of the evidence – supportive and contradictory – is in.[18] In applying a rigorous scientific standard to security studies, behaviorists resist assuming beforehand what might be the make-up of humans and an explanation and prediction of the predilections of international actors – whether toward peace or war. That is what scientific research is supposed to discover.

Of course behavioral scientists implicitly assume that humans can be studied by the same objective methods used by physical or biological scientists. Some analysts, notably constructivists, find this assumption to be misleading, presumptuous and potentially mischievous. They charge that this approach reduces the study of humans to the inanimate or sub-human objects studied by physical or biological scientists and restricts the study of human behavior to the methods of observation and validation of these researchers.[19] They object that the assumption of uniformity

---

[18] On this score, see the debate between Hedley Bull (1969) and J. David Singer (1969), who, respectively, present the cases for classical and scientific approaches to international relations. See also Kenneth Waltz's critique of the inductive, propositional approach of Singer and his behavioral cohorts as non-theoretical: Waltz (1979: chapter 1).
[19] See, for example, Onuf (1989) and Walker (1993, 1989).

across human and non-human objects of study falsifies and wittingly, but unjustifiably, depreciates the unique properties – speech, ideas, learning, and value creation – that distinguish humans and their societies from the non-reflective and non-reflexive objects around them.[20] They also have serious reservations, as chapter 7 delineates, about the bias of behavioral research in marginalizing or ignoring the diverse and contending socio-economic and politico-moral contexts that enable actors to act as social units or constructs in time, space, and historical circumstance.[21]

Rather than interrupt this discussion of behavioral research further by a lengthy critique of the starting points or assumptions underlying a behavioral approach, let's give these scholars and analysts a chance to justify themselves through their contributions to security studies on their own terms. Applied by the behavioral social scientist, the scientific approach seeks to detect patterns in the behavior of the actors being studied, much like the aim of the triumvirate in chapter 2. The difference between them is not the object of their inquiries but the methods they rely upon to discover general tendencies in human and social behavior. Both are guided by a nomothetic, not an idiographic approach (i.e., history). The latter seeks to recount events, typically sequentially, in precise and detailed fashion – say those leading to World War I or II. These are carefully recorded rather than a theory propounded of why these events occurred that might apply to other similar cases or conditions.[22] For those social scientists pursuing a nomothetic approach, these patterns of actor behavior identify underlying "laws." These govern or guide the decisions and actions of the social units or actors under examination. These patterns or laws or covering rules "explain" what drives the actors.[23] The goal is to generate generalizations or hypotheses about the actors under observation either within the limits or parameters defined by the researcher or, more ambitiously, as potentially predictive of actor behavior regardless of differences of time, space, or circumstance.[24] Behavioral social scientists,

---

[20] From different but converging perspectives, these social theorists advance this criticism. Giddens (1984), Morgenthau (1951a), and Weber (1958).
[21] Some behavioral scholars would disagree. See Goertz (1994).
[22] Schroeder (1997) elaborates on this distinction and division of labor between historians and social scientists, as do the other articles in this *International Security* symposium. Too much should not be made of the distinction between nomothetic and ideographic approaches since social science laws must necessarily be historical in content.
[23] See Kenneth Waltz's (1979: 1–13) critique of the search for patterns or laws of behavior rather than for an explanation of why these patterns emerge.
[24] An example of the latter would be Adam Smith's theory of markets or the hypothesis of Jared Diamond (1997) that a necessary, if not sufficient, explanation for the differentials in power that we observe across human societies and states today arises from their geographic position around the globe.

like their counterparts in the physical and biological sciences, typically abstain from making moral evaluations of the behavior they observe. The focus is on the "what is" of that behavior, not "what ought" to be the actor's choices and behavior. Just call it "as you see it."

The contributions of an early proponent of scientific social science applied to the behavior of states and, specifically, to their penchant to conduct war illustrate the search for underlying principles or laws of behavior. Quincy Wright's magisterial study of war, a forerunner of postwar behavioral research on armed conflict, sought to discover the underlying rules directing or deflecting states from war within the larger context of global and domestic politics and the socio-economic and cultural forces within which a state acts.[25] These regularities were viewed as laws. Trained as an international lawyer, Wright reversed the logic of applying written, textual laws to resolve conflicts over interests or values by seeking to determine the factors and forces that created these laws. These were more fundamental and profound "laws" or patterns in human thought, decisions, and behavior than scripts manipulated by lawyers.

In this vein, it was then not surprising that Wright should redefine wars as imperfect forms of law whose "perfection" presumably would be achieved under conditions of peace as a social state of affairs. He stipulated the possibility that, increasingly, conflicts could be resolved by appeals to prevailing international law and order founded on a natural or scientific understanding of human behavior. This idealized state of law of nature or pure peace, no less an ideal than, say, the pure endgames of Thomas Hobbes and Adam Smith, would move the imperfect law of war to the perfect law of peace in which conflicting human values and preferences would be compromised or converge by employing non-violent means and reason, guided by the results of scientific investigations. Peace would be defined not by force or threats but by mutual consent to laws and norms binding human communities and states together in conformity with what Wright supposed would be the social scientist's discovery of order in nature – inanimate, animate, and human.

Wright defined war as "a state of law and a form of conflict involving a high degree of legal equality, of hostility, and of violence in the relations of organized human groups . . ."[26] This constitutes an attempt to define

---

[25] Wright (1956, 1942). Note that many behaviorists cite Lewis F. Richardson as an early pioneer of this approach rather than Quincy Wright. Richardson's work focuses sharply on measuring arms races and deadly contests between states by relying on the technique of differential equations. His work pays little attention to the contexts within which states behave. Given its broad scope, Wright serves this volume better than the narrower concerns of Richardson (1960a, b).

[26] Wright (1942: 13).

"war" in such a way that it can be used by other researchers as a potentially universal definition of war. This so-called "operational definition" to guide research was designed to organize a research program that others could join and work on together to accumulate knowledge about war and its properties. The latter included those factors pushing states or "organized groups" to war or peace, the patterns of armed exchanges that war assumed once engaged, and the factors and forces required to return states and groups to a condition of peace in which laws and norms might once again regulate their relations.

Wright's definition of war implied that "organized human groups" had significant influence over what "laws" would define their mutual relations. Nature might well constrain human choice and possibilities but the species was not subject to necessity as forces in the physical universe or as lower animal species might be. If scholars could all agree – no small problem – on what they were studying – war and peace – they could presumably discern and record regularities in the onset, conduct, and termination of wars between states, human societies, and groups. These observations would presumably stand apart from what scientists might feel emotionally, politically, or morally about what they observed. For Wright, behavioral research could claim that its findings are "scientific" in the same way that explanations of rabies, as a disease, is independent of our feelings about animal carriers.

Pursuing knowledge about why and how states act rather than why and how we might conjecture or wish them to behave, behavioral research seeks, implicitly, to move state policies toward peace and away from war by applying this knowledge to influence state relations.[27] On this score it purports, like the schools of thought already discussed, to be a tool of decision-making and improved public policies. Once laws are discovered, as embedded in the behavior of states or of "organized human groups," then states and other international actors can be guided in the measures they can effectively take to prevent war or control its damaging effects. In commending Wright's example for emulation, a proponent of a scientific approach to the study of war and peace observed: "War, to be abolished, must be understood. To be understood, it must be studied. . . . Quincy Wright's book marks the beginning of much that nowadays has become known as 'peace research.' "[28] These causes or conditions of war, if validated by scientific methods, could then be presumably manipulated to

---

[27] For a reiteration in more modern dress of the debate, noted above, between Bull and Singer, see the exchange between James Fearon and Alexander Wendt (2002).
[28] *Ibid.*: xii; observations of Karl Deutsch, a pioneer in the scientific study of war and security.

end war or ameliorate its damaging effects, much as the medical sciences depend on knowledge of biological functions to intervene to prevent and eradicate disease.

Following the lead of the hard sciences, behaviorists invite other, like-minded social scientists to reproduce their observations and to validate their generalizations in the same way that physicists or biochemists would expect others in their disciplines to replicate and verify their evidence and findings. Social scientists are expected to set down – clearly and precisely – the methods they use to make their observations and the rules of evidence for collecting data. They are obliged, too, to rigorously and meticulously confine their generalizations to the evidence they've assembled and to the tests they have applied to their measures. They do not work alone. They consider their research to be a component of a research program shared by other investigators. Like Wright, they expect this joint enterprise to accumulate knowledge.[29] For example, note as a model the discovery of the DNA molecular chain as the building block of life organisms. This breakthrough laid the foundation for the construction of the human Genome a half-century later as a biological road map and reference to assist scientists in their efforts to explain life processes. On the strength of this accumulated knowledge, hard scientists have the database they need to develop ways to cure diseases and physical impairments.

Finally, behavioral scientists try to formulate their questions and research projects in ways that can be answered by observations of the behavior of the units under examination. These observations are not made in a conceptual or methodological vacuum. They depend on operational definitions of the unit under investigation in order to have a standard or generic actor, like the state, capable of reproduction in the investigations of other researchers. The nature of these units or actors – like states, consumers, international organizations, etc. – are defined by cooperating scientists. These working understandings and intersubjective agreements about how to conceive "reality" putatively inoculate them from injecting their values and biases as observers into their research. Data or evidence are then arrayed in measures or indexes that aggregate, as appropriate, the frequencies and intensity of actor behavior.

Throughout these investigations, scientists are obliged to think of tests to falsify what they have discovered as a check on their results and to ensure that they submit their research to tough and exacting testing. The falsification of hypotheses or propositions is especially critical in social scientific research concerned with security. Much of the evidence and

[29] Zinnes (1976).

observations relied upon is largely historical and the units of analysis are collective bodies. Given the kind of observations most readily available to researchers, security studies and international relations are more akin to geology or astronomy than biochemistry or physics. These latter disciplines depend heavily on controlled laboratory experiments to validate propositions or hypotheses about the behavior, for example, of light or electricity, or about the properties of proteins and their biological functions.

Certainly the experimental method has a useful and respected place in international relations. It is especially appropriate for psychological research, game theory, and simulations.[30] This said, the fact remains that the vast volume of research in international relations and security studies, in particular, is historical in content. As often as not, the actors observed no longer exist. Nor are the actors whose behavior is being observed in real time easily susceptible in most cases to the experimental methods of the laboratory. The behavior of these actors can scarcely be controlled in the same way expected of experiments in the physical, biological, or psychological sciences. Actors, like states, IGOs, NGOs, and other collective bodies or institutions – political parties, social movements, or domestic regimes – are not amenable to direct researcher-imposed controls except those defined by the researcher in his protocols constraining his observations.

Given these constraints, it is important that the units being observed be strictly defined – for example, "big powers," "hegemon," or "democratic regimes" – and that the evidence and procedures related to the behavior of these actors be precisely set down to permit replication of these trials and the falsification of results. There is always the temptation that scholars will selectively cite data and observations that support their hypotheses, while neglecting or rejecting countervailing evidence.[31] As suggested earlier, the paradigms of the preceding chapters are vulnerable to the attack that none is conclusively falsifiable since their partisans are ingenious in posing ad hoc explanations for their shortcomings or posit an indefinite future as the eventual validation of their explanations and predictions of state behavior.[32] Devising falsification tests and searching

---

[30] Axelrod (1984) used game theory simulations to great effect. For a sympathetic critic of experimental laboratory methods, see Levy (1992a, b).

[31] Examples abound since it is more the exception than the rule that in advancing an opinion or social value for adoption in public debate, opposed views and countervailing evidence are rarely cited. See Jervis (1976), which surveys these failings, notably the selective citation of historical data to bolster a problematic point.

[32] Gilpin, especially (1987: 25–64).

relentlessly for disconfirming evidence are checks on the temptation to "cook the data" to suit pre-ordained conclusions.

Power transition research program

Power transition researchers, as already noted, reject the notion that they are an offshoot of realism, with which they are often, and mistakenly, associated.[33] Rather than rely on realist assumptions revolving around endless competition for power between states and shifting and ceaseless balance of power maneuvers, power transition theorists characterize their research as modeled after the hard sciences. Their approach is putatively falsifiable and "rational."[34] PT researchers insist that, as a scientific enterprise, their work constitutes a progressive research program. As two of the leading contributors to power transition theory claim: "In a Lakatosian sense, power transition may be the most productive research program, or paradigm, available for international relations researchers."[35] It presumably explains what other theories don't, and a lot more; putatively, it also generates new projects consistent with its research program that uncover new facts or events neglected by other theories. What does transition theory contribute to security studies that warrants this expansive self-appreciation?

Power transition theory poses a narrow but important question: When and why do big power conflicts erupt into war? PT challenges realism's balance of power model. It dismisses the realist model as outdated and out of joint with the contemporary working of the international system, however much it may have served specialists and practitioners of international relations before.[36] It allegedly ignores or slights the new conditions of power driving state behavior of the modern era. The realist balance of power model posits peace as the function or derivative of a balance of power between the major states. Wars won't happen if states maintain a rough balance of power as a check on any state or alliance of states seeking

[33] Lebow (1995), for example, conflates these schools of thought.
[34] Kugler and Lemke (2000). Three perceptive commentators on PT theory agree with the self-assessment of PT scholars that their work constitutes a research program distinguishable from realist scholarship: Vasquez (1996) and DiCicco and Levy (1999).
[35] Kugler and Lemke (2000: 160).
[36] Organski and Kugler (1980: 14). This summary of power transition theory is a composite of several key sources. To avoid excessive citation, the principal contributions are identified in chronological order: Kugler and Organski (1989), Kugler (1990), Lemke (1996), Kugler and Lemke (2000), and Tammen et al. (2000). See these publications for additional citations and those noted below. Especially useful are the critiques of Vasquez (1996) and DiCicco and Levy (1999).

dominance by disrupting the balance.[37] Parity prompts peace. The evolution of international relations is conceived as propelled by the ceaseless pursuit of balances by big states. These are formed by joining the internal power of big states with that of allies against rival arrays of state power to guarantee the survival of the alliance. The outcome of these repeated moves is a decentralized state system as an institutional guarantee of the autonomy and independence of the states of the system.[38]

A. F. K. Organski, who first formulated PT theory,[39] argued that balance of power models, however formulated, could not explain big-power war – or peace.[40] While agreeing with realists that states are the primary actors in international relations, PT theory views the balance of power model as particularly faulty under contemporary conditions of relentless, worldwide modernization and industrialization. All states are portrayed as undergoing these processes of transformation in greater or lesser degree and at different rates of change. The power capabilities of states are, therefore, constantly changing as a consequence largely of their *internal* development. These shifts in the material capacity of states at a unit level, principally in the techno-economic capabilities they are able to internally generate, produce changes in power distributions across states within the system. These changes crystallize in a hierarchy of power, not a balance of power characterizing previous centuries of interstate relations in a premodern era. Within the purview of PT theory, the hegemon of an epoch and potential rivals are the central concern of international relations and security research. PT theory directly challenges shifting alliances, dear to realism, as sufficient to explain peace and minimal international governance and order under the relentless pressures of modernization, sustained economic growth, and ceaseless and rapid technological innovation. Preponderant power prompts peace.

A quick glance at the evolution of the international system over the past two centuries illustrates the PT brief. In the nineteenth century, Britain arose as the dominant power in international relations thanks to its initiation and lead in the Industrial Revolution – its techno-economic

---

[37] The most recent rehearsal of these arguments is found in Vasquez and Elman (2003), which interestingly enough devotes almost no attention to the PT challenge and includes articles that essentially dispute the claims both of balance of power and PT's focus on hegemonial power as the keys to explaining war and peace. See Schroeder (2003).

[38] Bull (1977) summarizes the realist position and its explanation of international order and governance as based on the balance of power, the foundation for international law and moral conduct between states.

[39] Organski (1958: 338–76).

[40] Organski's followers are no less adamant in their insistence about the utility of PT theory for policy-making. Kugler and Lemke (2000) are devoted to establishing this claim.

dominance – and the translation of these capabilities into unrivaled naval power. By the middle of the twentieth century the United States had replaced Britain as the dominant world power, fending off challenges from Germany and Japan in World War II. It subsequently ascended to sole superpower status with the self-destruction of the Soviet Union.

PT's line of analysis is particularly pertinent today and furnishes an additional justification for focusing on PT theory. There is no state or alliance of states capable of currently challenging US military power or the current array of its techno-economic capabilities in the post-Cold War era. PT insists it has something new and compelling to say about such hegemonic moments in the relations of states and peoples, a claim weighed below.

Three variables are cited as the determining factors of a state's material power: size of population, techno-economic productive capabilities, and the mobilizing capacity of a political state to harness these human and material resources in its competition with other states. These factors converge to produce a hierarchy of powers to form the skeleton structure of an international order akin to domestic regimes. Below the United States, which now commands the heights, are the so-called great but still lesser powers of China, Japan, Germany, the European Union (if truly federated and integrated), and a potentially re-emerging Russia at some later time. China, and possibly India, are identified as the next possible challengers to American power, but not until they register higher marks on the measures around which PT theory pivots in order to position themselves as a challenger to American hegemony. Lower down the pyramid are France, Italy and Brazil, and well below them most other states of the international system – all small powers by PT standards.

PT researchers have carefully plotted these three variables and measured their changes over a century and a half since the end of the Napoleonic wars (a period when relevant economic data became increasingly available). They compare the relative changes in power of the great powers by examining pairs or dyads of great-power relations over this time period. Of particular interest are the rivalries between dominant and challenger states in each historical era, specified by the research design. The challenger is defined by a quantitative measure capable of replication and verification by other researchers. A state becomes a challenger to the existing dominant power and hierarchy when it acquires 80 percent or more of the material capabilities of the dominant state.[41]

---

[41] The most explicit presentation of the initial PT model is found in Organski and Kugler (1980: 13–63).

This potentially measurable power relation is crucial for the theory. Organski and associates explain peace or the absence of war as a consequence of these measures of hegemony. The decided and discernible imbalance of power possessed by the dominant state defines the international order. As long as that imbalance holds, defined by the 80 percent threshold test, no war occurs. However, once a challenger approaches or passes that mark, a necessary if not sufficient condition is created, objectively, for the possible onset of a systemic, global war. Power imbalance, not balance or parity, keeps – and has kept – global peace. PT research findings, tested by standard statistical methods, yield evidence that there is a significant correlation and presumed causal connection between peace and the presence of a hegemon. This correlation arises from an observation of state behavior and changing power relations between the great powers since the Congress of Vienna in 1815 to the present.

According to PT theory, whether war would actually erupt depends on one additional crucial variable besides the material measures of hegemonic power already noted. A rival (or, arguably, an alliance of rival states) might well meet the 80 percent test and still decide not to challenge the hegemon. This added variable pivots around the satisfaction of the rival (or the potential rival alliance) with the order created by the hegemon. The challenger would have to be dissatisfied with the status quo, which presumably privileges the hegemon's interests under the prevailing international order resting on its power. PT theory predicts that war would be highly likely between big powers if a challenger were rapidly overtaking a dominant power *and* was dissatisfied with its position under the hegemon's rule. To avoid war, the hegemon would be obliged to accommodate the challenger or face the prospect of war. As long as its dominance was not in question, there would be no war. As a rational actor, the challenger would have no hope of prevailing. Conversely, the hegemon would have little incentive to attack a potential challenger. Why attack when the dominant state is on top? An interesting finding of PT research is the differential impact of incentives for war on the dominant and challenger power. The evidence marshaled thus far by PT researchers suggests that the challenger is more likely to initiate hostilities than the targeted hegemon.

Aside from rejecting the balance of power models of realist theory, PT theory also disputes the sources of change that give rise to war. These are principally rooted in internal processes by which states acquire techno-economic capabilities. The diffusion of power through the international system principally derives from changes in the material capabilities of states, and not from alliances. The resulting hierarchy of power that domestic-driven changes in state capabilities induces poses a strategic choice for the challenger, viz., whether the leadership of the challenger state determines it is satisfied or not with the status quo. Realism assigns the sources of conflict to the power drives of states in their interstate relations. Domestic politics and techno-economic development are black boxed out of consideration. Neither domestic politics nor the subjective states of mind of state rulers figure in classical or traditional realist thinking as central and critical drivers or determinants of state behavior, notably between the hegemon and the potential challenger.

PT theory specifically singles out and faults Waltzian neorealism for its failure to provide an explanation of power shifts and its concentration during the Cold War on the supposed stability of the bipolar balance of power, a charge to which neorealism is particularly vulnerable.[42] Neorealism is unconcerned with changes in material capabilities at an interstate or unit level, although its definition of the state system depends on autonomous units and the distribution of violent capabilities across these units. Moreover, PT adds the dimension of satisfaction, a fundamentally subjective value. This variable is excluded by most realists as "unrealistic" and an impediment to the objective appraisal of state behavior. Preferences are not crucial to the theory, since to get what an actor wants, it is obliged to seek power. Preferences thus are neutralized. They don't count as crucial factors shaping and shoving state behavior.[43] For neorealists capabilities trump good intentions or the specific preferences attributed to rivals.[44]

In contrast to these schools of thought, PT asserts that its findings are confirmed by a research design that meets rigorous scientific tests. Only some of the features of that design can be described here. It conforms to scientific protocols that require careful specification of the scope of the scientific investigation; precise determination of the units (states); and the replication of observations of the behavior of states and of their mutual and repeated exchanges. These research tasks are preparatory to delineating the measures relied upon to estimate the dimensions of the behavior of states and their propensity to war: power differentials; the probable tendencies of varied power configurations to move toward war or peace; the satisfaction levels with the status quo of potential rivals; the speed of the potential challenger's rise to challenger status; the flexibility of the dominant power to adjust to changes in the distribution of power; and the mutual confidence of the big-power rivals to accommodate their shared

---

[42] For example, Waltz (1964).   [43] For an alternative view, see Moravscik (1997).
[44] Alert readers of chapter 4 will detect that this assumption is rejected by some realist theorists who stress intentions over capabilities in explaining alliances; for example, Walt (1987).

and conflicting interests.[45] As already noted, parity is defined by a test of a challenger's possession of power equal to at least 80 percent of that of the dominant state. Overtaking "occurs when a rising power enters the steep growth portion of the endogenous growth trajectory and develops economically at a faster rate than the dominant power."[46] Note the salience that PT assigns to internal processes over external or exogenous factors to explain state behavior and the presence or absence of security threats and war.

War itself is neither self-evident nor self-explanatory. It also has to be defined to distinguish great-power struggles from conflicts between lesser powers, however intense and destructive the latter may be. These are limited in the PT research design to wars between powers in which "battle deaths reached higher levels than in any previous war,"[47] and the vanquished state suffered a loss of territory or population. *The War Ledger* research design, developed by Organski and Jacek Kugler, introduced still other precisions to generate a data set of state relations that could be statistically tested in a way to falsify the PT hypothesis. The general point to emphasize again is that behavioral research demands specification of what units, observations, and proposed explanatory causes are to be tested and how these research operations are to be conducted. These methods and the amenability of a research question to be designed in a way that evidence, measures, and tests can be replicated by other researchers are crucial criteria to meet the demanding requirements of behavioral research.

The evolution of PT theory research, since its initial formation almost a half a century ago, suggests that it is a progressive research program. While its initiators (Organski and Kugler) hew closely to their view that their research only concerns great powers and, within that set, dominant and challenger states, many partisans of PT research insist that the model can – and should be – applied to all state dyads.[48] Douglas Lemke has made the longest strides in extending PT theory to smaller states and regional hierarchies. In an elaborate reformulation and development of the PT model,[49] Lemke identifies 21 local hierarchies of dominant and challenge states in South America (4), the Middle East (3), the Far East (5), and Africa (9). These regional hierarchies form a complex structure of multiple hierarchies bounded by a dominant system. Each

[45] These complex measures and calculations are discussed at length in the citations to PT theory herein. They are sententiously reviewed and evaluated in DiCicco and Levy (1999).
[46] Tammen *et al.* (2000: 23).   [47] Organski and Kugler (1980: 46).
[48] Houweling and Siccama (1988).   [49] Lemke (2002).

local hierarchy is defined operationally (and without reference to variable state preferences or regimes) by their *potential* capacity to launch military operations against each other. State capacity is measured by modifying Bueno de Mesquita's adaptation of Kenneth Boulding's "loss-of-strength gradient." This yardstick measures a state's power, which is assumed to diminish or decline over distance.[50]

Lemke observes patterns of war and peace over his four regions that confirm PT expectations for big powers, although Lemke estimates that the probability of war differs across these regions. Whether war or peace will be the outcome of a dominant challenger dyad is measured (a) as a function of the distribution of power between these smaller powers within the regional hierarchies and (b) of the "dissatisfaction" of the challenger with the status quo putatively imposed by the dominant power within each hierarchy. Power capabilities are measured by Gross Domestic Product and by COW indexes of power; "dissatisfaction," by increased rates of spending on military capabilities as a harbinger of a challenger state's intention to launch war to assert its dominance.

Critique of power transition: as science and as an explanation for the end of the Cold War

This evaluation seconds the assessment of PT critics and partisans that PT has contributed to the behavioral study of security and, with the Lemke study as evidence, that it is a progressive research program by Lakatosian standards.[51] PT's challenge to balance of power models and its rigorous research findings have inspired a growing number of younger scholars to broaden and deepen this research project.[52] PT theorists have extensively tested their model to show a robust correlation between parity and war, a challenge to realist theory that has yet to be adequately addressed. PT research has also brought to light the importance of the *rate* of power shifts as a critical factor explaining the onset of war. Also of significance is the stress PT places on the subjective evaluations by challenger states of how well their interests are protected and how much their influence counts as subordinate members of a hegemonic system.

As one widely respected scholar of war concluded in evaluating PT research:

---

[50] See Boulding (1962) and Bueno de Mesquita (1981).
[51] Relevant are Waltz (1964), DiCicco and Levy (1999), Midlarsky (2000), and Vasquez (1996).
[52] The joint authorship of an update of PT theory is illustrative: Tammen *et al.* (2000).

(A) great deal has been learned about parity and war through use of the scientific method. . . . *The War Ledger* and the thought of Organski and Kugler have played a major role in this effort by setting out a scientific research program that has helped us to remove much that is confusing in the power politics and capability approaches and to identify the role power transitions play in conflict and the onset of war . . . (T)heorizing associated with the power transition thesis continues to produce new insights, new findings, and new research proposals. Given the still early stage of our peace science, little more can be asked.[53]

This cautious testimonial points to problems with PT theory on its own terms, as the sympathetic critics discussed below make plain. To their credit PT theorists are among the harshest critics of their work. Only the highlights of these criticisms can be sketched here. These set the stage for evaluating the relevance of PT theory to the Cold War.

First, there are problems associated with the scope and the small sample size that the original research project of *The War Ledger* developed. As already suggested, there is no theoretical reason why PT should not be applied to all competing dyads of competing states, as Lemke and associates contend. The sample of great powers and dominant–challenger dyads are necessarily limited over the research period that is examined, constrained by the variables of economic development as a key determining PT factor. These constraints limit what generalization can be generated across time and circumstance. This limitation is underlined by the applicability of PT to World Wars I and II. Neither war began as an attack by the challenger (Germany) on the dominant state (Britain), but on other, smaller states and then spread to the major states.[54] The exclusion of the United States as the real and eventual target state of German power, given its ascending economic and military power, is also puzzling. The Soviet Union also drops out of sight in this analysis. By World War II, both rising superpowers were challengers for hegemony. These exclusionary rules, invoked by *The War Ledger* research program, unduly narrow the research design and the scope of its potential applicability.

Other findings than PT may explain war (or peace) between great powers. Wallensteen reports that he could find no causal relation or correlation between war and PT in a systematic examination of paired states between 1816 and 1976,[55] although PT data, equally plausible, find otherwise. More testing is needed to arbitrate these conflicting claims. In this vein, comparing Organski and other PT researchers' findings creates additional puzzlement. While Organski can explain war in five or ten power transitions, Houweling and Siccama,[56] using a broader definition

[53] Vasquez (1996: 53). See also (1993: 98ff.).   [54] Vasquez (1993: 103–4).
[55] Wallersteen (1981).   [56] Houweling and Siccama (1988).

of big states, identify eight power transitions which result in war, and nine which do not. With such mixed, statistically significant results, there is a strong possibility that other factors than those relied upon by PT theory are at work to explain the onset of war. This circumstance does not negate PT as an explanation so much as problematize and dilute its ability to integrate security and international relations theory. These weaknesses also raise questions whether there is a strong causal connection between war and PT or whether the relation is, as a friendly critic of PT theory suggests, "random and spurious."[57]

While much can be said for rigor and parsimony in modeling challenger–dominant state conflicts – prized attributes of behavioral research – the capacity of PT research to capture historical contexts accurately and their relevance in explaining security behavior remains a serious drawback of this research program, as the criticisms already noted underscore. The determined focus of the PT model on interstate war falls short of the ambitious standard set by the triumvirate of theorists in chapter 2. They are not only interested in interstate and inter-societal wars (Clausewitz and Thucydides) but also why all actors – not just states – either use or renounce force to get their way in their interdependent and mutually contingent exchanges with other actors (Hobbes). The disciplined concern with modeling only interstate relations leads, as some PT scholars acknowledge,[58] to anomalous conclusions, such as Africa being labeled a zone of peace because of the low level of interstate war on this continent. Integrating the many widespread and continuing violent struggles in Africa into a PT research program would require a major reformulation of the PT model, potentially risking its internal integrity through ad hoc adjustments. In making PT more relevant, one would be implicitly reducing its precision and relaxing its exacting rigor. Currently lost from sight is an explanation for large-scale deaths and injuries to millions of inhabitants trapped in pervasive civil conflicts in Sudan (over one million deaths), Congo (over three million), and Rwanda and Burundi (over one million), not to mention hundreds of thousands more in conflicts in eastern, western and southern Africa.

In its present form, PT has not devised a way to address civil conflicts, which increasingly dominate international politics in contrast to the receding instances or likelihood of interstate wars. Under the condition of a globalizing world that blurs the distinction between domestic and international politics, this is a major weakness of PT's explanatory power of war and violent conflicts – or their absence. In some sense, this is an ironic lapse, since PT does link domestic capabilities and changes

---

[57] Vasquez (1996: 44).   [58] Lemke (2002: 161–206).

in these forms of material power to international conflict. It also introduces the intriguing variable of "satisfaction" or "dissatisfaction" into the calculus of states as a key determinant of war and peace. These notions and perceptions of legitimacy to which they are implicitly related would appear to be amenable to expansion to non-interstate armed conflicts.

If "satisfaction" is granted as a central variable, its satisfactory measurement remains beyond the current reach of PT research. Pending further study and more convincing measures of a potential rival's "satisfaction" with a hegemon's rule, this gap in the PT research program needs to be filled if PT theory is to claim greater explanatory power and to win wider currency among security analysts. PT partisans concede this shortcoming.[59] Where advances in measuring dissatisfaction have been made, the results have thrown further doubt on PT emphasis on material factors to explain war. For some PT researchers, measures of challenger dissatisfaction with the status quo appear to be more important than power transitions per se in predicting the onset of hostilities. These conflicting findings are reported by Woosang Kim in a series of carefully drawn calculations of alliance transitions and equality between rivals for dominion.[60] Using different but comparable measures from those used by *The War Ledger*, Kim's research, as he observes, "supports Organski's contentions that rough equality of the sides and more dissatisfied rising states increase the chance of war. His other hypotheses do not fare as well . . . Transitions themselves have no effect on the probability of war."[61] Kim's research constitutes a potential break with PT assumptions. If confirmed by more research and testing, it might well challenge PT itself.

John Vasquez's evaluation of PT appears to have merit. PT is a necessary but not sufficient explanation of wars. Its applicability, even to great powers, is problematic.[62] PT partisans acknowledge these criticisms but view them as a challenge for future research rather than as an inherent weakness of the theory. They are aware, too, of additional puzzles.[63] Why should a threatened dominant state reject preventive war to arrest a challenger before the latter grows too powerful? Or, why isn't a challenger satisfied with the status quo when it achieves parity and even predominance? The cases of the Soviet Union under Stalin and the United States in the post-Cold War era raise these questions. Pending the ability of PT theory to address these concerns, these lines of critique limit PT's explanatory power. They do not void its claim, however, that, as an important, if circumscribed, research program, along with competing schools of thought,

[59] Kugler and Lemke (2000: 136–7).   [60] Kim (1991, 1996), Kim and Morrow (1992).
[61] Quoted in Vasquez (1996: 46).   [62] Vasquez (1996).
[63] For an excellent summary and evaluation of the generic attacks on PT theory, see Lemke (2002: 27–35).

it must be taken into account – no small achievement – to estimate the probability of whether certain types of war will occur.

Power transition and the end of the Cold War

What does PT have to say about the end of the Cold War? The rivalry for a half-century between the United States (as hegemon) and the Soviet Union (as challenger) would appear to qualify PT as a contender to explain the rise, evolution, and abrupt end of the Cold War. PT is a partial antidote to the paradigms of chapter 4, especially neorealism. It depicts international relations as a dynamic process rather than as a static system captured by still photos of state material capabilities seemingly frozen in time and space. PT portrays the exchanges between big powers as a continuing process and seeks to measure this evolutionary development. It resists the easy (and misleading) assumption that the superpower struggle – or the competition between any challenger or hegemon – can be reduced to a single data point.[64]

PT stresses the dynamic, continuing, and changing relations of power between hegemon and challenger, traced by their techno-economic competition and the transformation of these primary components of power into military capabilities. If that is the case, then why didn't the challenger (the Soviet Union) initiate hostilities as PT theory expects? While PT theorists do not directly examine this question, their response would presumably be defined by the assumptions underlying their research design of what constitutes a challenger and a dominant power. The obvious reply is that the Soviet Union never attained an 80 percent level of techno-economic power to qualify as a worthy challenger. This does not explain why it broke off its challenge, which had begun as early as the Bolshevik Revolution in 1917. Conversely, the Soviet Union might never have reached the stage of being a worthy challenger. In that case, *The War Ledger* would not fit the Cold War experience and in principle would have limited explanatory power – even relevance.

On the other hand, it is important to emphasize that the Soviet Union's military power was still sufficiently formidable that an all-out nuclear attack would have destroyed the United States as a viable human society. On this score, it would appear that it met the 80 percent measure. Of course the Soviet Union would have been destroyed by a US nuclear counter-attack since America's invulnerable forces could not be disarmed by a Soviet first-strike. PT theory is robust enough to explain away the Cold War by invoking its economic capability measure. The Soviet Union

---

[64] Lebow (1995) makes this criticism.

simply did not have sufficient material wherewithal to challenge the American hegemon and was rapidly falling behind.

This line of interpretation explains too much and, therefore, too little about what we need to know about the end of what is still the most profoundly threatening conflict to the existence of the human species in the evolution of interstate conflict. PT critics, like Vasquez, charge that it falls short of a reliable theory to explain why wars occur. In the case of the Cold War, its shortcoming, like most of the theories covered in the preceding chapters (liberal theory excepted), is rooted in its inability to explain why peace broke out – suddenly, abruptly, and unexpectedly. In focusing on the onset of war, PT theory does little to inform us of the international conditions and mechanisms or internal decisional processes that bring about peace and the resolution of conflict except indirectly, viz., a challenger's power is measured to determine if it is positioned to qualify for a fight with the hegemon. As Manus Midlarsky observes, in comparing PT theory, as a structural approach, and game theory, as a strategic research program: "A focus on power transition reveals a gap in theory. Whereas the power transition typically focuses on shifts in power between the challenger and dominant power, a game-theoretic perspective reveals the importance of concessions needed to accommodate the challenger peacefully. The value of war and the value of concessions need to be compared by all parties to a dispute, yet PT theory specifies only the former."[65] Such comparisons would require assessments of regional state preferences – a variable that falls outside the boundaries of the classic PT model, and only recently addressed in recent scholarship.[66]

PT's notion of "satisfaction" does not square with the evidence of "dissatisfaction" among elites within the Soviet Union either as a state, a regime or a model for economic development. What is interesting to observe, and what PT theory in its present form neglects, is the dissatisfaction of a leading segment of the Soviet elite with the rigidity of Communist rule, the mounting burdens of its empire, and the lagging performance of a command economy. Focusing on a disaffected but still powerful elite faction unhappy with its failed power position, dissatisfaction as a key variable explaining change (and the end of the Cold War) moves research and analysis to a more discrete and discriminating level of analysis than the positing of a collective dissatisfaction attributed by PT to a state rather than to the ruling coalitions *within* the state. Under this aspect, the "challenger" would be disaggregated into warring factions within the Soviet state, each vying for power and control of the state's coercive authority and material capabilities. This internal conflict would

---

[65] Midlarsky (2000: xvii).   [66] Tammen *et al.* (2000) and Lemke (2002).

then define the state's satisfaction level. Indeed, and in contrast to those realists who view group conflict as a driver of imperial over-expansion and war, a fragmented elite – the Soviet case is illustrative – can be said to be the unwitting driver of peace, not war.[67]

As liberal economic theory explains, rational actors – and PT theorists by their own self-definition are rational choice analysts[68] – will always opt for more over less material wealth. They will adapt to best techno-economic practices to ensure maximum wealth and sustained economic growth. Liberal theorists predicted that eventually the Soviet Union would be obliged to adopt the Western model of open, free markets to compete. PT can measure power capabilities, since this is a straightforward economic exercise of relying on readily available, if sometimes contested, data describing the evolving size of a nation's Gross Domestic Product. What PT cannot easily explain, nor has much interest in addressing, is why the market system became the dominant power system for global economic development. And how and why the globalized Western market system fatally absorbed the Soviet state and its command economy into its maw.

The market system is posited as a given rather than viewed as a puzzle to be explained and as a power structure itself impacting on state choices, quite apart from the nation-state system. If a Marxian or neo-Marxian or liberal economic perspective is introduced,[69] the market system can be conceived as the driving force of the international system. This system of power and choice, as these theorists explain, can be distinguished from the results of the system, viz, its material output.[70] PT theory effectively relies on GDP measures in identifying hegemons and challengers and the conditions affecting the outbreak of war. GDP as a measure is more a condition than an explanatory cause of the social processes of actor choices associated with free markets, as liberal economic theory explains. The GDP measure is dependent, then, on this more primal variable of social structure for its explanatory power.

PT theory portrays the evolution of a state's power as autonomous and independent of an increasingly integrated market system. Its policies and responses are unrelated to the incentives generated by this global social system. The market system constrains state choices and induces conformity to market rules, if economic growth and technological innovation are to be fostered. We owe these insights to liberal economic theory. Even casual observation of the workings of global markets and their extension to every important segment of economic activity provides daily evidence of

---

[67] Snyder (1991).   [68] Kugler (2000: 129–63).   [69] Hardt and Negri (2000).
[70] Lindblom (2001).

the strong pull of the global market system. PT research partially responds to this criticism in positing domestic or internal economic change as a crucial determinant of state capacity and behavior as well as the workings of the state system – in sharp contrast to the constricted research design of neorealism. It falls short, however, of telling us why a state should reform its very internal political regime to acquire the material capacity to keep abreast of a dominant state and why, paradoxically, in adopting its rival's economic practices, it should by that token adapt to a status quo it had hitherto opposed.

We learn little from PT theory about the mechanisms, incentives, and processes of decision-making or the direction of putatively rational choices that move regimes to transform themselves and the power arrangements and distribution of influence and power of domestic actors in the bargain. These elites, no less than states, are competing for domestic hegemony. PT offers no conceptual bridge at this point in its development of this research project between these two levels of elite and state competition. To explain the rise and demise of the Cold War, PT theory will be obliged to go beyond its self-limiting research boundaries.

Since most PT research assigns preponderant causal force to the objective conditions of relative and transitional power configurations, the behavior of the Soviet regime in its death throes runs contrary to the expectations of PT research. Soviet Premier Gorbachev's self-initiated disarmament of Soviet military power, the dissolution of the Soviet empire in Eastern Europe, and the renunciation of military intervention abroad are at glaring odds with the predicted behavior of big-power states engaged in profound rivalries for dominance of the international order. They presumably seek nothing less than to remain abreast of their rivals and to impose their order on the global system.

These dramatic departures from PT expectations bespeak, as critics suggest,[71] a transformation of basic political values and interests among a significant portion of the Soviet elite. This value transition is not easily explained by reference simply to power transitions. PT also presents a puzzle for the post-Cold War era. The Russian Federation as the rump successor of the Soviet Union continues to display serious dissatisfaction with American hegemony, although its ruling elites abandoned the Soviet Union's challenger role despite its possession of formidable military and police powers. Witness the Russian Federation's intense and continuing resistance to NATO expansion eastward to incorporate the former republics and satellites of the Soviet Union, to Washington's unilateral renunciation of the ABM treaty, and to the US war on Iraq.

---

[71] See chapter 7.

There is just too much to explain – or to explain away – for PT to help in understanding the end of the Cold War: formidable Soviet military parity with the United States squandered almost overnight without a fight; renunciation of its right to dictate the strategic realignments of its Warsaw pact satellites; abandonment of big-power status and influence; the self-dissolution of the Soviet state, regime, and empire; the downward spiral to economic dislocation and chaos; and the subsequent plunge of the Russian Federation and some of its former republics into civil war. PT may address these shortfalls at some later date, as a progressive research program, but there appear no immediate breakthroughs on the research horizon of PT scholars to fill these gaps.

There is reason to believe that the Soviet Union might well have persisted as a rival state despite its adoption of the Western market system. This leaves the troubling question of why Communism collapsed and the Soviet state imploded. These hard facts and their explanation lie outside the scope of PT theory. PT has no theory of the state any more than the schools of thought covered so far, nor (as this criticism contends) a theory of the market system that generated the economic capabilities that under-girded American hegemony, PT's focus of explanation. PT just assumes the existence of these structures of power, as if they were frozen in time, although PT theory insists that these dynamic forces portray international politics better than (changing and conflicting) realist conceptual maps.

PT addresses the important but fundamentally secondary question of explaining power shifts and big-power conflicts as a function of the level of the subjective "satisfaction" of the challenger state with the status quo. Regime preferences count, and how they are created and evolve beg explanation. These questions are largely "black boxed" by PT research except for what is still a failed search for surrogate measures of "satisfaction" or "dissatisfaction," independent of the substantive content of these central, multiple, changing, and determining preferences.[72] The Soviet Union might well have continued as a challenger under a liberal political regime, but it did not. Then why did it implode even as it adapted to a Western economic and political model of power?

This is the Achilles' heel of PT theory. If PT theory fails to address the need for a theory of the state or the market system, it is no less uninterested in explaining the emergence of social identities as a foundation of why political communities and states emerge, evolve, fade, and pass away. This hole in PT theory is suggested in its elliptical explanation for the demise of the Soviet Union as a challenger: "the inconsistencies of

[72] For an elaboration of this point, see Moravscik (1997).

central planning and the many failings of the Soviet political system have removed Russia from consideration as a contender, at least in the foreseeable future."[73] Note the elision between the Soviet political system and Russia. Between these two nouns lies the collapse of the Soviet Union into fifteen republics and their almost instant transformation into fifteen independent nation-states. Once the Soviet Union shattered into its previous integral components, the Cold War ended and American hegemony was confirmed. Sheer military or material power does not adequately explain the transformation of global politics. Some deeper and more convincing understanding of "dissatisfaction" needs to be explored and appropriate measures fashioned that do better than abstract appeals to so-called state dissatisfaction with the international order.[74] In this case, peace, not war, would appear to have broken out as a consequence of several converging dissatisfactions: a substantial component of the Soviet elite with authoritarian rule and a quest for more personal and group freedom; the human and material burdens of empire; the demands of suppressed nationalities for self-determination, including ironically the Russians themselves; rising and increasingly compelling demands from Warsaw pact members to regain their independence as sovereign states, most urgently pressed by the Baltic states and Poland.

This brings the discussion to a final conundrum. It impacts not only on PT theory but also on all of the paradigms of this volume. What explains a dissatisfied hegemon? The latter by definition gets its way. It defines the international order in terms of its interests and privileged status. Then how can the post-Cold War unilateralist thrust of American security and foreign policy be fully understood in terms of the challenger–hegemon conception of international relations and security theory?[75] Since the end of the Cold War, successive American administrations have contributed to what is now an expanded and growing record of a dominant power fundamentally dissatisfied with the international order. The United States seeks fundamental changes in international order and in the internal regimes of targeted states at odds with American policies and its announced security interests. Military interventions have been registered in Central and South America, Asia, Africa, and Europe, notably in the Balkans. Note, too, US rejection of multiple multilateral treaties conflicting with professed American national interests. The latter include the Kyoto protocol

---

[73] Kugler and Lemke (2000: 146).
[74] Timor Kuran (1991, 1995) offers a path toward empirical research of the subjective support of individuals for regimes that is promising in his explanation for the surprising breakdown of Soviet and Communist rule of the Warsaw Pact satellites.
[75] The rationale for unilateral use of military power either to pre-empt an attack or, as in Iraq, to mount a preventive war is spelled out in United States (September 2002).

on global warming, the comprehensive test ban treaty, bans on land mines, international accords to check the production of bio-chemical weapons of mass destruction, and the establishment of an International Criminal Court.

These rejectionist positions have been capped by the pronouncement of a doctrine of pre-emptive and preventive military attack to head off anticipated security threats from whatever quarter, state or non-state, that might arise around the globe.[76] This strategic doctrinal position is not a set of empty words or merely the reassertion of a right claimed by all sovereign states. The American-led invasion of Iraq, opposed by the United Nations Security Council and by some of the principal allies of the United States in NATO, aims at transforming the Iraqi regime and, more broadly, Middle East politics to American liking or satisfaction. These hegemonic moves to solidify and expand American global rule may usher in a radically new era of interstate politics and pose entirely new forms of international security threats. Until now, theorizing has revolved around notions of balance of power multipolarity or bipolarity during the Cold War period. The agenda for research in international relations and security must now address the logic of a potentially unipolar power and its implications for the governance of states and peoples around the globe.

If the United States is understood as a *revolutionary* power rather than as a status quo and satisfied global hegemon, then PT theory (and the paradigms of chapter 4 and 5) will have to expand its (their) research agenda(s) to explain its expansionary behavior.[77] A revolutionary power seeks more than the status quo ante. It strives for a fundamental change in how the relations of peoples and states are governed. Despite its overwhelming techno-economic and military power, the United States wars on smaller powers, like Iraq, and threatens other states, even former allies, with retribution, if they do not conform to its announced determination to change both the external power relations of state and the state system to its liking. No less critically, it exercises its coercive power to reform regimes to suit prevailing preferences of the domestic ruling coalition. A shared ideological thrust and a belief in American exceptionalism

---

[76] *Ibid.*

[77] The provocative insights of the historian William Appleton Williams (1972, 1973, 1978, 1980) on this point are relevant, if overlooked, in explaining American expansion first to the West and then to the world. Williams' explanation turns on the force of ideology that, according to his analysis, pushed Americans who were otherwise politically divided to pursue expansionist policies, because they shared the view of America as the model for the world – whether by the consent or coerced acknowledgment of other peoples. Some indirectly supportive evidence for Williams' thesis of ideologically driven imperialism is found in Louis Hartz's (1955) thesis of American exceptionalism.

rather than elite competition would seem to have some purchasing power in explaining American imperial expansion than internal hyper-powered group competition for power.[78] The United States justifies its actions both in terms of the *macht* or power politics of the traditional realist doctrine of national security and the lofty aims of spreading global markets, democratic values, and human rights around the globe.[79] It is as if Thomas Hobbes, Adam Smith, and Immanuel Kant were marching under the same banner and to the same drumbeat. In its current form as a research program, power transition theory is presently incapable of accounting for the paradox of a dominant power or hegemon dissatisfied with its own success. Other paradigms and approaches fare little or no better.

Discussion questions

1. Why is a behavioral or rational and constructivist explanation of security better characterized as an approach than as a paradigm for international relations and security studies?
2. Distinguish between realist and power transition explanations for peace and war.
3. What are the principal components of the research design of power transition theory? Explain why this research project meets the tests for behavioral research parallel to inquiry in the physical and natural sciences.
4. In what ways do behavioral or rational approaches fall short of a research model drawn from the hard sciences?
5. Can PT theory be considered a progressive research program in terms of Imre Lakatos' understanding of theory? Do you agree that it meets Lakatosian tests?
6. Evaluate the capacity of power transition theory to explain the rise, evolution, and collapse of the Cold War bipolar system.

Suggestions for further reading

Walter Carlsnaes, Thomas Risse, and Beth A. Simmons (eds.) (2002), *Handbook of International Relations*, London: Sage. This volume, divided into the principal sub-fields of the discipline, evaluates the current state of international relations theory. The essays by James Fearon and Alexander Wendt on rationalist and constructivist approaches and by Jack Levy on war and peace are essential reading for any serious student.

---

[78] For a contrasting view, see Snyder (1991).   [79] *Ibid.*

Michael Breecher and Frank P. Harvey (eds.) (2002), *Millennial Reflections on International Studies*, Ann Arbor: University of Michigan Press. This edited volume is readily accessible to budding theorists and wannabe practitioners. The section on security studies is of particular interest.

Jonathan M. DiCicco and Jack S. Levy (1999), "Power Shifts and Problem Shifts: The Evolution of the Power Transition Research Program," *Journal of Conflict Resolution* 43: 675–704. This chapter greatly relied on this informed and constructive critique of PT theory.

Daniel S. Geller and J. David Singer (1998), *Nations at War: A Scientific Study of International Conflict*, Cambridge, UK: Cambridge University Press. This is an excellent review of Correlates of War research by two of its leading proponents.

Jacek Kugler and Douglas Lemke (2000), "The Power Transition Research Program," pp. 129–63 in *Handbook of War Studies II*, edited by Manus I. Midlarsky, Ann Arbor: University of Michigan Press. This brief essay neatly summarizes what power transition researchers believe is their contribution to international relations theory and security studies.

Douglas Lemke (2002), *Regions of War and Peace*, Cambridge: Cambridge University Press. This work extends PT theory to four regions of the world and provides evidence of PT's capacity for progressive expansion.

Manus I. Midlarsky (ed.) (1989), *The Handbook of War Studies*, Boston: Unwin Hyman; (ed.) (2000), *Handbook of War Studies II*, Ann Arbor: University of Michigan Press. These two volumes are excellent reviews and critiques of behavioral research.

Bruce Russett and John R. Oneal (2001), *Triangulating Peace*, New York: W. W. Norton. This work introduces students to the democratic peace thesis that sets this proposition within the larger context of international, transnational, inter-governmental, and domestic politics.

Ronald L. Tammen *et al.* (2000), *Power Transitions: Strategies for the 21st Century*, New York: Chatham House. This edited volume presents a broad spectrum of power transition research and findings, which is linked to the policy implications of this research.

John A. Vasquez (1993), *The War Puzzle*, Cambridge, UK: Cambridge University Press. Vasquez reviews and critically evaluates the behavioral research on war and peace in this volume. It is a useful preparation for his probing critique of the power transitions research project in "When Are Power Transitions Dangerous? An Appraisal and Reformulation of Power Transition Theory," pp. 35–73 in *Parity and War: Evaluations and Extensions of the War Ledger*, edited by Jacek Kugler and Douglas Lemke, Ann Arbor: University of Michigan Press, 1996. This critique complements that of Jonathan M. DiCicco and Jack S. Levy, noted above.

Quincy Wright (1942), *A Study of War*, Chicago: University of Chicago Press. Wright is a pioneer in creating the field of security studies, notably from the perspective of peace studies, in which he attempts to explain war and armed conflict as a precondition for discovering ways to limit or eliminate this institution to solve conflicts.

7   Constructivism

Can a constructivist approach explain state security behavior and the workings of the nation-state system better than its rivals? Can it provide theoretical insights and practical policy guidelines to relax or surmount the security dilemma confronting peoples and states in ways beyond the scope of prevailing paradigms and behaviorist approaches? What is the "value added" to security studies that constructivism brings to the table?

Many constructivists are themselves unsure about what their responses should be to these questions. They are agreed that prevailing theories are wrongheaded and potentially mischievous as guides to security policy-making. The thrust of their work, however, is more to question prevailing theories than to advance an alternative paradigm for the study of security and international relations. As Nicholas Onuf, one of the leading founders of this school of thought, observes, "Constructivism is not a theory."[1] It is an approach to social inquiry. It is especially relevant and pertinent as a tool of criticism of widely held empirical and normative theories.[2] Viewed in this way, as Onuf insists, "Constructivism applies to all fields of social inquiry" and "is a way of studying social relations – any kind of social relations."[3]

In keeping with constructivist practices, the discussion below problematizes Onuf's claim to assess what "value-added" constructivism brings to security studies and international relations theory. If constructivists eschew what they are doing as "theory," in the sense understood by theory in chapter 1, it is also clear that constructivist scholarship has had – and continues to have – a great impact on how social inquiry is currently being conducted. Increasing numbers of academic analysts swell its ranks. Their papers multiply in research panels at professional conferences. Some of its harshest critics now concede a place for this approach, raising it to the level of one of the top three paradigms in international relations,

---

[1] Onuf (1998: 58).
[2] Wendt (1999) develops this point in excruciating detail. Emmanuel Adler's (2002) probing review and evaluation of constructivist research concedes the same point.
[3] Onuf (1998: 58).

along with realism and liberalism, despite the fact that constructivists reject having created a new paradigm.[4] Going well beyond the scope of dominant theories of security today, constructivism has been especially important in portraying individual and state security as social constructs susceptible to limitless reformulation over time by willing and willful actors rather than as a static concept fixed to definable and unchanging conditions, as realists and neorealists are wont to assume. Increasing numbers of international relations theorists and practitioners rely on constructivism's conceptual tools, particularly its departure from conventional notions of causality and empirical theory, when they think about international politics and security. So the up-to-date security analyst is obliged to seriously examine its claims.

Many – arguably most – constructivists, are skeptical that their approach and the corpus of their work constitute a "paradigm."[5] Most partisans are happy with "approach," partly because many are suspicious of *any* claim to "knowledge." For many, constructivist claims to special or theoretical knowledge are simply "speech acts." These attribute a privileged position or status to the speaker. Constructivists doubt any claim to special knowledge – including their own – that might empower one person or group over another. Theory, as a cluster of speech acts, is not viewed simply as a way to explain social behavior or as some form of objective truth. Rather, many constructivists reduce theory to speech acts questing for power. Theory and its claims to "truth" are then an invitation to constructionists to expose and resist the power aspirations of rival schools of thought. Many constructivists doubt, too, whether a theory of international relations of the kind pursued by most of the theorists and analysts discussed so far is even possible.[6] Whether constructivism is a paradigm or not is less important at this point in our discussion than acknowledging the contributions that constructivists have made to security and international relations theorizing by their unswerving dedication to problematizing all claims to theoretical "knowledge." Among these, those who attribute to the state a monopoly of legitimate violence come under particularly close scrutiny and sharp attack. Constructivism's

---

[4] Walt (1998).   [5] Onuf (1998, 1989).
[6] See chapter 1 for a brief description of what is stipulated as the elements of social theory within which this volume is largely cast. While this volume, and particularly this chapter, is sympathetic to the constructivist project and welcomes its insights, it remains tributary to the possibility of an objective, if not disinterested, social science, a proposition rejected by many constructivists. As the discussion below suggests, this volume sees value, limited by the reservations developed below, in the constructivism of Alexander Wendt and of Peter Katzenstein and his associates – so-called "light" rather than the "heavy" constructivists. See Katzenstein (1996) and Wendt (1992, 1994, 1995, 1999, 2000).

"value-added," as a way of understanding security, centers principally on its challenge to other schools of thought – and, paradoxically, its own claims to knowledge.[7]

Constructivist scholarship identifies an enlarging number of socially constructed rules orienting the behavior of individuals, groups, and states. This corpus of studies provides accumulating empirical evidence, largely in the form of descriptive narratives, to support the proposition that shared norms, which actors themselves author, both constrain and enable them to act. These internalized, actor-validated norms are said to account in some significant measure for behavior and outcomes of social trans-actions, quite apart from the influence of material conditions impact-ing on actors.[8] These disparate findings still do not add up to a theory of constructed rules and institutions that structure and inform societal organization and actor behavior across human societies through time and across space in ways paralleling the sweeping ahistorical claims of realists, liberals, and Marxists. Conversely, the countervailing data and counter-factual reconstructions of history advanced by constructivists can't easily be ignored by contesting schools of thought simply because they may fall short of paradigm status or outside the confining scope, methods, and evidentiary tests of existing security theories.

Constructivists claim to explain or at least provide provisional evi-dence to show how political actors – you, me, states, political par-ties, international organizations, *et al.* – acquire their identities and, more pointedly, how these identities generate the material and non-material interests of these actors. Whereas realists argue that state inter-ests are fixed and timeless, constructivists rejoin that the latter respond to changing actor identities, including those of states viewed as rei-fied actors. Constructivists contend, notably Alexander Wendt, whose work will be reviewed shortly, that states can have different identities and, correspondingly, varying interests. The state is, therefore, not a given, but itself a social construct. If constructivism could explain the causal (not just asserted) connection between identities and interests and how this connection impacts on security policy in the thinking of actors or agents in their mutual communications and social prac-tices (e.g., states signaling war or peace or raising military forces and

---

[7] The internal quarrels among constructivists form a growing body of literature. See, for example, Kubalkova (2001a, 2001b), Kubalkova, Onuf, and Kowert (1998) and Fierke and Jorgensen (2001).
[8] Finnemore (1996) and Klotz (1995) describe, respectively, how norms influence actor behavior in defining national interests and in undermining the South African system of racial apartheid. See Ruggie (1998: 862–9) for a lucid sketch of key case studies as well as Katzenstein (1996), Fearon (2002), and Wendt (1999) throughout. Space constraints limit the discussion of these studies.

defending territories), it would make a significant contribution to security studies and international relations theory. To achieve this level of
explanatory power, constructivists would have to show what still remains
problematic: that their explanations of social events and actor practices
trump alternative interpretations drawn from competing international
relations and security paradigms.[9]

To grasp, at least provisionally, the impact of constructivist scholarship
and theorizing on international relations, politics, and security, we need
some understanding of the complex (and very much contested) conceptual apparatus developed by constructivists. Some acquaintance with this
apparatus is a prerequisite for hazarding an evaluation of constructivism's
"value-added" to security studies. Space limits preclude a comprehensive review of the diversity of constructivist opinion and of its mounting
literature.[10] This task is further complicated by the deep splits among
constructivists about what precisely they are doing and how to do it. To
partially relax if not surmount this constraint, the discussion will initially
highlight the approach and contributions of Alexander Wendt, one of constructivism's leading lights. An understanding of his elaborate conceptual
apparatus to explain international politics provides a useful introduction
to constructivist thinking and its relevance to security. Specifying the key
elements of Wendt's thinking is also a precondition for accurately nest-
ing Wendt's approach and contributions, as a surrogate for constructivist
thinking, within this larger, sprawling and expanding field of analysis. In
the interest of full disclosure (but at the risk of undue complexity) the
strenuous objections of fellow contructivists against relying on Wendt as
a worthy representative will be summarized below, and their alternative
conceptualization of the constructivist project will be delineated.[11]

His constructivist critics aside, Wendt's value derives precisely from
his attempt to bridge constructivist thinking and the other paradigms
and approaches discussed in this volume. This syncretic effort is rejected
by heavy or "ideas-all-the-way-down" constructivists. The latter view this
move as intellectually misguided largely because Wendt chooses to join
the issue of the state and explanations of its behavior as an ontological,
not as an epistemological, problem. Heavy constructivists focus primarily, some exclusively, on *knowing* what *is* real rather than positing without
question that the state is real. They insist that the first task of constructivist

---

[9] This point goes to the heart of the rationalist (behavioral) vs. constructivist debate.
[10] The citations in this chapter provide but a sample of this growing literature.
[11] Wendt (2000) acknowledges as much, but without apology. See ns. 5 and 7 for serious
objections to Wendt's constructivism and its alleged compromise with prevailing rationalist thinking. Specifically, see the critique by Maja Zehfuss (2001). See also Zehfuss
(2002) for an extended analysis and critique.

analysts is to address what is yet the unresolved question of how actors know themselves and their social environments and how they act on these ideas or conceptualizations.[12] Words as speech acts that create knowledge and rule-binding human actions are viewed as more telling and explanatory than stipulated identities, like Wendt's states. Knowing how humans know themselves and how they create their social conditions and other actors, like states, is viewed as the proper first move in analyzing political phenomena and, specifically, in exploring issues of security. Epistemology thwarts conventional notions of what is real (states) or ontology. Wendt's self-proclaimed "via media" works in this discussion, however uncomfortably for heavy constructivists, since he remains within the ambit of the contending theories and approaches that currently dominate thinking about security, the principal interest of this volume.[13]

Implicitly following a Lakatos prescription for validating theory, Wendt's aim is more to enlarge the scope of explanation of actor behavior, notably the state, than, unlike heavy constructivists, to reject prevailing theories or behavioral approaches. Wendt's announced objective is to subsume this body of scholarship within what he contends is the broader scope and deeper penetrating explanatory power of constructivist theorizing. What he proposes to do is to change the direction of the causal arrows of ascendant empirical theories. Power, interest, and material forces driving human and state behavior, are still portrayed by Wendt as central concerns of international and security theorists. While acknowledging that "power and interest are important factors in international life," he argues that "since their effects are a function of culturally constituted ideas, the latter should be our starting point."[14]

Wendt is especially keen to draw swords with neorealism. Note the title of his major volume, *Social Theory of International Politics*, an obvious play on Waltz's *Theory of International Politics*.[15] As a bridge to mainstream thinking, Wendt's challenge is also a point of departure to understand the claims of "ideas-all-the-way-down" constructivists who reject Wendt and the mainstream. The student is presented, then, with a three-way debate between Wendt, rationalist schools of security theory, and fellow constructivists who reject both his work and empirical theory. In this complex debate, it is important to keep in mind that Wendt's brand of constructivism purports to be more comprehensive and inclusive as an approach to theory, practice, and research than alternative schools of

---

[12] Campbell (1992). See also his critique and those of the following: Campbell (2001), Doty (2000), Smith (2000), and Adler (2002).
[13] Wendt (2000, 1999).   [14] Wendt (1999: 41).
[15] Compare Wendt (1999) and Waltz (1979).

thought about international relations and security but not an outright abandonment of these positions, much less the insights they afford.[16]

Constructivism and its critics

Why did constructivism arise to challenge prevailing theories? What separates constructivists from the schools of thought already covered in this volume? How do they go about their work in explaining how actors are socially constructed and how and why they think and behave the way they do? And what do responses to these questions have to do with security as constructivists understand this problem?

In responding to these questions, it will be abundantly clear to Wendt's sharpest constructivist detractors that for several reasons beyond space constraints their positions will not have been fully covered. The constructivist project is a work in progress. The learning issues raised by heavy constructivists, quite frankly, have also never been resolved to the satisfaction of scholars and theorists since they were first raised by the Greeks over two millennia ago.[17] So they can be scarcely resolved here. What the discussion can do is join some of the key points of controversy among these conceptually warring opponents to allow indulgent readers to make up their own minds.

The discussion seeks to provide wary students with usable conceptual tools to permit them to compare constructivist assumptions with those of rationalist and behavioral rivals to highlight the constructivist claim to be a radical break from dominant theorizing in international relations. This move will facilitate evaluation between the competing conceptual "wares" offered by each school for sale in the marketplace of ideas. The general thrust of this discussion – extremist positions among practitioners notwithstanding – supports the constructivist claim to be a worthy, if still coming, contender for hegemony in understanding and explaining international politics and security. Once this conceptual framework is up, the specific structure of Alexander Wendt's constructivism will be sketched, followed by an assessment of his contributions to constructivist thinking, including the reservations of his constructivist critics. As with all of the contenders for hegemony, the discussion will assess the range of constructivist thinking as a contribution to an explanation of the Cold War and its passing.

---

[16] This note of compromise is especially evident in Fearon and Wendt (2002).

[17] Emanuel Adler and Michael Barnett (2002), James Fearon and Alexander Wendt (2002), and the Forum (2000) organized by the *Review of International Studies* on Wendt's *Social Theory of International Politics* provide useful and informed introductions to these debates.

It is important from the start to understand what constructivists mean by causality and to assess their claim that they offer a deeper, more profound, and fundamental explanation for the social exchanges of actors than alternatives. In its most extreme, post-modernist, heavy form, constructivism puts into question – that is, problematizes – all knowledge, especially social knowledge. Those in this branch of constructivism dismiss the insistence of most other social scientists that the knowledge they discover and advance can be objective and independent of the interests and biases of the observing "scientist." They reject the notion that knowledge can be divorced from the observer. For them, knowledge, created through language by humans, is inevitably and inherently tainted by privilege, power, and self-interest. This charge is even leveled at the physical and biological sciences. Unlike Wendt, these heavy constructivists insist that all knowledge is relative and depends for its provisional validity on its social construction. They reduce the pursuit of knowledge to an incessant struggle in which those in control of the linguistic tools to dictate the course and outcome of the battle gain power and privilege over others.[18] Words, as symbols of meaning and authority, count decisively for constructivists. The physical, biological and social universes which humans inhabit are mute until they come alive when given voice by humans. For "ideas-all-the-way-down" constructivists these voices never ring "true"; they are always "off key," servicing the interest they favor.

The issue of causality raises next the problem of distinguishing between the causal import of agents and the socially constructed structures enabling them to act in certain ways. For constructivists, actors or agents and the norms, rules, and institutions they construct enable them to act. Both are mutually constituted; both are simultaneous and instantaneous in their workings. Grasping the import of these assertions captures a critical dimension of the constructivist approach and project. There is no easy way to summarize all of the relevant elements of this presently intractable problem of how actors and structures are created, nor do justice to the divergent positions held by constructivists and their opponents about this process.[19] Formulating the problem as a question may at least join the issue: Can "social facts" be explained solely by reference to the thinking and actions of putatively independent and autonomous *agents* or actors that produce these social facts, like buying and selling in global markets or going to war. Or are theorists and observers obliged to posit the existence of collectively shared and actor-affirmed ideas – *structures* of ideas

[18] Foucault (1980, 1982).
[19] A relevant introduction to this problem is found in Giddens (1984, 1993), Dessler (1989), Wendt (1987, 1999), and Carlsnaes (1992). In the latter citation, see chapter 4: 139–93 and works cited therein.

and knowledge – to understand and explain actor thinking and behavior? Depending on the constructivist under examination, this chicken–egg problem is typically resolved more by stipulation than by compelling or persuasive proof advanced by the analyst.

In conformity to the Lakatosian test of validity of competing schools of thought, it is relevant to remember that the constructivist project has roots deep within Western social thought. Max Weber and Emile Durkheim paved the way for constructivist thought over a century ago. Weber implicitly posed the agent–structure problem in insisting that humans are "*cultural beings* endowed with the capacity and the will to take a deliberate attitude towards the world and to lend it *significance*."[20] The physical and biological world comprising the setting for human exchanges is deaf and dumb. This environment and the objects of which it is composed have no meaning or significance in and of themselves except insofar as humans infuse then with social value. The value, meaning, and significance attached to this natural environment and to social exchanges constitute the process of creating "social facts." These facts suffuse our daily social exchanges and thinking whether we are consciously aware of their impact on us or not. Of particular importance is the realization that, while the natural environment would exist whatever meaning we might impart to it, that is not the case with respect to social exchanges and their significance. The latter include religious and cultural values, shared national and ethnic identities, profoundly held notions of political legitimacy and principles of state sovereignty and security. They extend, too, to more mundane matters, like sporting events, family traditions, or the annual rhythms of holiday celebrations.

Neither Weber nor Durkheim believed that social facts and practices could be adequately explained or understood simply by reducing them to the thinking and actions of individual agents. Individuals are embedded in ideational, value-infused structures. These inform their thinking about the world and themselves. These prisms of social value render the physical and social worlds around them with a refracted array of significances. In turn, these "arrays of meaning" generate incentives for action. Weber contended, for example, that the Protestant Revolution and its new mindset, linking human freedom to moral obligation – a sense of personal autonomy and corresponding responsibility for one's own salvation – were a necessary, if not sufficient,[21] explanation for the spread of the

---

[20] Quoted in Ruggie (1998: 856). This discussion draws on Ruggie's informed understanding of the evolution of constructivist thinking and on the author's own reading of Weber and Durkheim. See especially Weber (1968) and Durkheim (1984, 1993).

[21] Weber (1958). Needless to say, but Weber's hypothesis remains highly contested. See Mommsen (1992) and Swedberg (1998).

market system and of capitalism around the globe. According to Weber, the new and widely accepted value of individual autonomy and responsibility, promoted by the Protestant break with Catholicism in positing a direct tie between man and a supreme being, created the conditions for the effective workings of markets. Adam Smith's benign egoists, as a social construct, secularized the Protestant notion of the good Christian who, although driven by personal material and millennial gain, had an implicit obligation to provide collective goods for others. Thus, as chapter 5 describes, Hobbes' coercive, command system would be transformed into a Lockean consensual, market system in which private and public goods would be harmonized by the "hidden hand" of the market.

Durkheim, in extending Weber's insights, advanced the notion of a collective conscience, a set of shared ideas and beliefs that informed the thinking and behavior of members of a given society. These were embodied in the very identities of the members of a society and their conceptions of each other, including their relative power, authority, and status. These collective understandings shaped how others were perceived and evaluated. These "ideas" and "beliefs," however they may have arisen, essentially formed a structure no less real or compelling than the material conditions limiting or facilitating human thinking, choices, and action. These notions and associated social practices were reflected and reaffirmed as socially created "facts" in language (the autonomous individual), shared practices of social conduct (global market exchange through price mechanisms), adherence to norms (human rights), and accession to prevailing social institutions and the power and authority they conferred on individuals and groups (family hierarchy, professional roles, state legitimacy, etc.). These collective ideas were detectable, if invisible and non-material, social forces, enhancing the power of actors and driving their behavior – what Rousseau might have earlier termed the general will.

Building on the contributions of Weber and Durkheim to social thought, constructivists, whether they acknowledge their debt or not, have fashioned new conceptual tools to probe and expose these collective structures of ideas. They remain focused on explaining how actors, possessed of intelligence, self-reflection, and reflexive capacity (acting on themselves), create and are created by these social facts so unlike the inanimate or non-human sentient bodies composing the natural universe. Answers to these daunting questions supply, according to constructivists, new insights in the causes and conditions of war and peace.[22]

---

[22] Ruggie (1998) usefully roots constructivist thinking in the contributions of these early founders of sociology. Searle (1995) elaborates on these links. For an analysis of the implications of constructivism for security, see Katzenstein (1996) and Adler and Barnett (1998).

Shared constructivists tenets

With this all too brief background, we can identify several key and widely shared constructivist tenets. First, all knowledge is socially constructed. Knowledge of nature or of social meaning and the significance of social exchanges depends on some knowing human being. What is known is, therefore, socially and collectively constructed and does not rest inherently in the objects – inanimate or social – to which it is associated. Second, the social relations constructed by humans *are* social knowledge on which thinking, reflective, and reflexive agents rely in adapting to their social and physical environments. As Emanuel Adler explains, "This means that different collective meanings are attached to the material world twice, as social reality and as scientific knowledge. In other words, knowledge is both a resource that people use in their day-to-day life for the construction of social reality, and the theories, concepts, meanings, and symbols that scientists use to interpret social reality."[23] The early Greeks had intuitively grasped these elements of the human condition in their assertion that "Man is the measure of all things." Unless there is a human to hear a tree fall, it did not fall as a *social* event or fact. The notion of "tree" is not given by the tree or the meaning of its physical impact on earth as a function of gravity. These "ideas" arise by way of the agency of hearing and thinking humans. Similarly, the notions of "good" or "bad" are not inherent in the physical or biological universe or in social relations, as such, apart from the significance and meaning imparted to them by humans. These are the elemental particles, if you will, of human identities as social constructions.

Wendt adds a third and fourth dimension to these widely shared tenets. He insists that the structure of human relations – whether between individuals, groups, or states – is primarily the result of shared ideas rather than of material forces, as Marxists would claim. This assertion directly challenges all of the schools of thought covered so far. Wendt argues that human associations and exchanges are principally defined by human ideational conceptions of their material circumstances, whether violence, economic resources, or technology.

Perhaps two contemporary examples may illustrate Wendt's position at a general level of analysis, quite apart from his attack on Waltz's neorealist thinking. Thousands of years of accumulated human knowledge were needed before a grain of sand could be recognized as the host of a computer chip and thereafter as a key link in a global communications system. No less creative and subject to human ideas was the construction

[23] Adler (2002: 95).

of a society sufficiently modernized, industrialized, and technologically sophisticated that it could produce a Bill Gates whose universally adopted word processing program could advance the material welfare of billions of people. These material conditions were in Wendt's world driven by non-material "ideas" that informed and shaped the material conditions of social life, a position in marked contrast to Marx.

This evolutionary process also reveals a fourth tenet of constructivism, the creation of new identities. Changing ideas about who actors believe they are define their interests, not the reverse, as much of social science theory postulates. Identities and interests are constructed from shared ideas. They are neither given by nature nor timeless and unchanging. To wit: no new ideas, no new identities, no new social constructions, no new interests in innovation and material acquisition, no computer industry, no Bill Gates.

In contrast, what distinguishes most of the theorists of this volume from constructivists is their stress on the material conditions of choice confronting actors or agents rather than on the ideas or ideational structures of knowledge that actors construct to explain and thereby to infuse value into their social and natural environments. Constructivists claim that it is this "knowledge" that actors rely upon to guide their decisions in adapting to these settings.[24] Human agents both construct their identities that enable them to act and are simultaneously constrained by these identities. The latter, in turn, are defined by the rules, norms, and institutions affirmed by actors. These ever-changing agent–structure modalities evolve through an endless process of affirmation, rejection or social mutation by which agents redefine themselves and revise the structures which both enable them to act in the here and now and limit their range of freedom at the same time.

This is not to say that the theorists covered earlier discount or trivialize ideas or beliefs as key determinants of actor behavior. They insist, rather, that material factors can explain variance in human and agent behavior in more conclusive and definitive ways than appeals to what Calvin in the comic strip "Calvin and Hobbes" calls "No-See-Ums." For the positivistically and empirically inclined social scientists these "No-See-Um" ideas refer to unobservable, largely unknowable or inaccessible social data. Falsifying the claimed causal effect of these factors beyond the pale of observation and empirical testing is difficult, arguably impossible, for many of a non-constructivist persuasion. Most rivals of constructivism privilege material forces and external conditions as "shoving and shaping"

---

[24] Giddens (1984, 1993) develops this socialized adaptation process in excruciating and repetitive detail.

actor behavior, as Kenneth Waltz insists. Realists and neorealists principally rely on force to explain actor choices and behavior; liberals and
Marxists, on bio-economic needs under conditions of scarce material
resources and given states of technology; and liberal institutionalists, on
shared norms to facilitate the adjustments of self-interested egoistic actors
in pursuit of mutual if differentially enjoyed *material* gains.[25]

The constructivist critique of prevailing paradigms

Constructivism arose largely as a reaction to what were viewed by many as
fundamental shortcomings in prevailing theory about international politics and security. These shortcomings are alleged to inspire explanations
of actor behavior – i.e., conventional knowledge – that, potentially, are
morally mischievous since they tend to affirm power relations already in
place. The state and those in possession of its monopoly of violence are
priority targets of the constructivist attack. Prevailing theories in international politics posit the existence of the state as a given requiring no
explanation. This widely accepted (but under-studied) Weberian "idea"
of the state and its coercive trappings is advanced without explaining its
social origins or justifying its claims to authority and power. Liberal economic theorists, who stipulate a pre-social or asocial individual as the
primary unit of social analysis and by assumption a self-evident reified
actor, also encounter constructivists' fire and ire. Markets and egoists
who make them work are viewed no less as social constructs than states.
These social units are no less problematic than their state counterparts.
Similarly, Marx's economic man as a social construct is not necessarily
determined beyond reform or repair as a consequence of technological
innovation and changes in property rights. Identities are not pre-formed.
They are not beyond the capacity of the agent to recast and, by that token,
to redefine what it means to be human. Ideas inform technological change
and economic practices.

Constructivists object to the choices made by rival theorists in defining the make-up of the actors and the systems they study. The latter
are criticized for failing to develop a theory of how different agents and
their interests arose. Problematized are the notions of a rational actor,
viewed either as the autonomous, calculating, egoistic and potentially
omniscient individual actor or state. Whether explaining the market or

---

[25] Some theorists object to the constructivist charge that ideas are marginalized in contemporary international relations. See Robert Keohane's insistence that ideas help actors
link their preferences to effective strategies; choose between alternative strategies; and
create norms and institutions to facilitate future exchanges. See Goldstein and Keohane
(1993) and Keohane's (2002) critique of Wendt, and Ruggie's (1998: 866–7) criticism.

the state system, the actor is stipulated to have an interest, respectively, in maximizing wealth or power. The state system is reduced to the behavior of states; the market system to the action of individuals, as if these were self-explanatory. These unexamined assumptions, challenged by constructionists, beg the question of the social make-up of these preferred units of analysis of prevailing theories; how the actors are to be studied (individuals or states or other agents); how they acquired their current identities and interests; and how these latter properties change over time.

For constructivists of all stripes, dominant social science assumptions – static and unchanging identities and interests and the stipulation of a pre-determined trajectory of behavior – severely limit social inquiry to means–ends or narrow and self-serving instrumental thinking. Explanations become circular: actors change their preferences in response to the functional, instrumental utility of such shifts in servicing fixed state or individual interests and identities. What is most important about the actor under examination is dismissed out of hand: how these *actors were socially created, how they understand themselves, how they relate to each other as possessed of mutually constructed identities, and how their interests are formed and generated in response to these identities.* These constructed identities and their corresponding interests are fundamental matters to be explained, since responses to these questions necessarily precede strategic analysis and means–ends thinking. And the construction of these starting points – changing actor identities and differentiated interests – are always open to question and, accordingly, problematic.

Constructivists reject the "as if" thinking of prevailing social theory. Actors are assumed without evidence or explanation "as if" they were moving in a fixed and rigid trajectory to get what the analyst (rather than the subject of investigation) stipulates as their preferences. Realists and their fellow travelers assume that states in a decentralized state system will seek power to get what they want, to survive and thrive. Unable to surmount this posited security dilemma, a condition stipulated as embedded in the state system, states will act out these strivings "as if" these constraints were timeless and irrevocable.

Classical liberals, like realists, assume, too, that individuals will act "as if" they were egoists. Whereas realists are unable to envision the convergence of private egoistic and collective preferences, liberals are convinced that convergences can be achieved by voluntary social mechanisms. Following Adam Smith, they expect smart egoists to surmount the conflicting preferences through an ever-expanding market system and, where they initially converge, to coordinate their efforts for joint gains. Egoists will exploit the principles of the division of labor and comparative advantage to produce wealth at the least cost with maximal benefit and sustained innovation over time for the greatest number. Individuals will act this way "as if" Smith's reformulation of human nature were "true," defined by the stipulation of an allegedly inescapably compulsive attribute "to truck, barter, and exchange." Marxists, too, believe in the inevitable march of technological change, making humans who they are and setting (albeit contingent) boundaries to the social identities they can construct.

Constructivists underline what they insist are the enormous costs to knowledge of bounded "as if" thinking. Profound questions go begging about who humans are, how and why they behave, and their prospects as species. These shortfalls are especially acute and significant concerning coping with challenges to personal and state security. "What if" states were able to cooperate and surmount their posited egoisms, and to do so because they believe not only that cooperation is instrumentally beneficial but also a positive political good that is valuable in its own right?[26] As Wendt argues in the discussion below, the state system and the roles that states play within it today evidence a gradual weakening of the Hobbesian world posited as unchangeable by realists and neorealists. Similarly, "what if" thinking opens the observer to the possibility that individuals often – arguably most of the time – act in counterpoint to the liberal economic expectation of egoism and selfish acquisition of material wealth?[27] For many neo-liberal economists to act out of a selfless or altruistic frame of mind would be tantamount to acting irrationally,[28] defined by the stipulated expectations of the liberal model of the standard economic, materially driven rational man.

Or, "what if" Marx, too, were wrong? What if the incentives for capitalistic exploitation and imperial expansion, posited by Marxist theory, could be checked by domestic and international political and socio-economic reforms, like those initiated immediately after World War II by the liberal democratic states, which adopted an open trading regime?[29] And from a radically contrasting perspective, why assume, according to constructivist thinking, that human evolution follows some principle of historical determination and that this process is dictated by a rational, instrumental, functional imperative and concern for efficiency? The Australian Aborigines successfully replicated their way of social life for over

---

[26] Schroeder (1994b, 2003, 2004) argues that the European states and statesmen not only understood that war was threatening to their states and regimes but also that peaceful solutions to state and regime conflicts were beneficial in their own right in creating a European security community bent toward consensual over coercive cooperation.

[27] Frank (1988). Frank's dissenting voice is scarcely the dominant position in conventional economic theory, but it is gaining ground. Also relevant are the earlier critiques of liberal economic thought by Polanyi (1944, 1959) and Durkheim (1993).

[28] For a dissenting view, consult Frank (1988).   [29] Ruggie (1982) and Cooper (1968).

forty millennia. Within constructivist thinking they acted as rationally as any modernized human today. There exists no one immutable and universal form of rationality, but the prospect, conceivably, of countless rationalities, created and constructed by actors as provisionally bounded systems which implicate their variable identities in structures of meaning that constrain yet enable them to act socially in what is for them sensible and rational ways.

Constructivists are largely persuaded that opening up research on the composition of agents and their social construction will privilege "what if" questioning over "as if" thinking to explain how human agents define "security." Counterfactuals defeat factual approaches in the constructivist approach because they more closely approximate, as a methodology of analysis, the creative, reflective, reflexive capacities of human agents possessed of unique linguistic and conceptual skills. In other words, constructivists insist that what they see as "real" is, potentially, the limitless malleability of actor identities and interests and the social structures that inform these actors and to which their behavior conforms. This "shadow of the constructivist future," to borrow from Robert Axelrod,[30] affords more explanatory power of actor behavior and opens research to a greater range of prospective change than prevailing static "as if" theories allow. Posing agent make-up and choices in this way problematizes and challenges existing power structures and the valued positions of privileged actors the latter support.

Constructivists claim that their interpretation of "reality" trumps conventional explanations of actor behavior and of the rise and demise of all social systems, including the practices that sustain or erode them. The range of actor choices and possibilities of transformation are simultaneously (and paradoxically) always limited, yet open to limitless reformulation. As Wendt (following Anthony Giddens) observes, "in both social and natural science observation of the world is affected by our theories, but social scientific theories alone have the potential to become part of their world as well. Such transformations violate the assumptions of the causal theory of reference, since reality is being caused by theory rather than vice-versa."[31]

If humans are free to construct the world as they wish and will, as most constructivists maintain – reaffirming what Rousseau asserted over two centuries ago – and if states, too, are free to make of anarchy what they want, then this "knowledge" of the make-up of actors (ontology) and their conscious grasp and capacity for limitless re-creation of this "knowledge" (epistemology) conspire to privilege "what if" thinking and action over

---

[30] Axelrod (1984).   [31] Wendt (1999: 76).

"as if" theory and practice. Jean-Jacques Rousseau's celebrated and much repeated ontological (and moral) stipulation of the human condition at the opening of the *Social Contract* – that humans are born free but are everywhere in chains – is reaffirmed and presented both as knowledge and as a guide and prompt for action to transform these words into reality.[32]

The constructivist critique of "as if" thinking leads logically to a unique constructivist understanding of causality, principally with respect to explaining social change. Constructivists distinguish between causal and constitutive explanations of actor or agent behavior. In conventional causal analysis there is an assumption that when we say, as Wendt observes, that "X causes Y, we assume that (1) X and Y exist independent of each other; (2) X precedes Y temporally, and (3) but for X, Y would not have occurred."[33] This characterization essentially replicates Robert Dahl's widely quoted attempt to operationalize the concept of "power" as what causes A to do something A would not otherwise do in the absence of the power exercised by B.[34] This way of thinking certainly applies to statements about the natural physical and biological world. It also exemplifies the epistemological assumptions of behavioral theory. Constructivists argue that this understanding of causality, applied to human, social relations and agent behavior, misleads and falsifies how social knowledge is constructed and how agent behavior is to be accurately and appropriately explained.[35]

Constructivists argue (Wendt's reservations below notwithstanding) that agents and their social constructions are not independent and autonomous of each other. They are mutually constituted by the meanings and ideas that compose them. These ideas form social structures that define the identities and interests of these actors or agents. Conventional social science largely reduces these posited constructivist structures to common or shared cultural knowledge. In contrast, constructivists invoke what they term as collective knowledge that defines the identity and interests of agents. The latter are free in their mutual relations and practices to affirm, modify, or reject these collective structures of knowledge over

---

[32] Rousseau (1950).   [33] Wendt (1999: 79).   [34] Dahl (1957).
[35] This volume, as chapter 1 explains, adapts a broad and capacious conception of empirical or behavioral causality. It allows for a greater range of human activity to be observed and counted as explanatory of human thought and action. It stipulates the importance, often determinative, of the causal role of values, ideas, and subjective states of mind in explaining what actors do, and why and how they do it. This is particularly pertinent for understanding what actors mean by security and how they cope with this notion and the knowledge appropriate to addressing this imperative. These assumptions about causality clearly fall well short of the position of "all-the-way-down" constructivists, some of whom reject the possibility of an objective social science capable of accessing the subjective states of mind of actors from the biases of the observer.

time. This process of affirmation, replication, mutation, rejection, and change of identities and social structures is mutually constituted. It cannot be located or reduced to discrete cause–effect or means–end chains as depicted in conventional social science, in which, as with Waltz, the structure dictates actor (i.e., state) behavior or the rational choices of individual actors in pursuit of material gain (liberal economic theory) crystallize into recurrent patterns or market structures.

The properties of agents do not exist apart from socially constructed norms, rules and institutions that inform them. This rule-based construction constitutes social knowledge and defines who agents are as social constructs, as expressed in appropriate social practices consistent with their identities. These agents are fully party to their own social constructions, whether they are consciously aware of their roles or not in "constructing" or in transforming themselves. Constructivists thus challenge two key assumptions of prevailing causal logic. First, X and Y conceived, respectively, as discrete variables do not exist independently of each other. Second, the relation between these variables is not sequential, but simultaneous and mutually constitutive.

An example may help illustrate the constructive claim of "value-added" in explaining agent behavior by positing the mutual social construction of agents and structure through collective ideas and knowledge. Take the socially constructed distinction between master and slave. Once these social facts and relations are set in motion and institutionalized in the linguistic speech acts and practices of actors and agents as continuing elements of their social interactions, they essentially define the identities and interests of master and slave. The thinking and actions of these actors can be explained by way of the socially constructed meanings attached to their social conditions.

These social constructions and the roles assigned to actors within them can be further illustrated by two examples. George Orwell's essay, "Shooting of an Elephant" portrays this process of identity-interest creation as a function of social interaction. Orwell, the author of *Animal Farm* and *1984*, recounts his experience as a British civil servant in south Asia. He describes how he was expected by the local population under his rule to kill what they insisted was a rogue elephant. Despite his personal reservations about killing the elephant, he believes he had to act in line with the expectations of those ostensibly subordinate to his command. To do otherwise would have violated the shared communal view of Orwell as representative of the ruling British Raj and the identity and roles assigned to that position, ironically, by the Raj's Indian subjects.[36]

---

[36] Orwell (1954).

There is also the example of the French General who was court marshaled by the French Gaullist Fifth Republic for his complicity in a failed coup attempt. His defense parallels Orwell's rationalization of what he was about to do against his better judgment. The general told the court that he was the leader of his troops, and he had to obey what they demanded. A roughly accurate paraphrase of the general's justification might be put this way: "I was the chief. Therefore, it was imperative that I follow them."

Reflect for a moment on the American Civil War. Can it be understood in constructivist terms? At issue were the continuation of slavery as a legitimate social practice and the authority of the several states to preserve this institution vs. the authority of the federal government and the union of the American people to eliminate what many believed to be a morally heinous institution. These claims as social facts and as competing and irreconcilable forms of meaning, significance, value and beliefs – as knowledge – were joined in a civil war struggle. In constructivist thinking, these mutually constructed agents and structures in opposition to each other render the enormous physical damage and slaughter meaningful and rational. This is not, of course, the instrumental, means–ends rationality of much of prevailing social science inquiry. It is the *substantive* rationality of a profound commitment by actors to what agents construct as fundamental social purposes – ending or preserving slavery. This new meaning attached to American identity of the fundamental equality of the races generates changes in social practices and in shared notions of what norms, rules, and institutions are to be valued as legitimate. These new "ideas" and the changed social practices associated with them are putatively better guides for explaining the behavior of actors than appeals solely to the instrumental calculations of actors about the efficiency and functional utility of their actions. Constructivists stress instead the "appropriateness" of actions relative to agent identities, not the means–end *consequences* of their choices and strategies.

In constructivist thinking the Union's victory set the American republic on an entirely different course than that of the original Constitution. It ended slavery with the passage of the thirteenth, fourteenth, and fifteenth amendments to the Constitution. It also set in train the elimination of state-supported discrimination among the races. It sparked a civil rights movement that continues until today. As the identity of Americans moved from notions of racial, gender, and ethnic inequality to the equality of all citizens, this newly founded identity generated rules, norms, institutions, and practices to put this social construction into play. Sequentially realized, a particular agent–structure composition at a given point in time is the product of a seamless process of ceaseless construction, whether viewed as the replication, mutation, or transformation of a defined social set.

The explosive expansion of human rights claims around the globe ushered in by the French Revolution and the proclamation of the rights of man would also appear to be relevant to the constructivist position of mutually constituted agents and structures producing social facts. Chou En-lai, the Chinese Communist leader who had been educated in Paris, was allegedly asked what he thought of the French Revolution. He was supposed to have replied that "It's too early to tell." The significance of this observation is that the ideas of liberty and equality are putatively universal properties. Humans are presumably invested with these rights simply because they are human. This redefinition of human rights has evolved over two centuries to become one of the most dynamic forces driving international politics.[37] If the idea of human rights assumes different forms across diverse and divergent societies, it was no less evident that it is also what the French call a *"force profonde."* In constructivist terminology, this *force profonde* has increasingly become a global social fact that informs the cultural knowledge of thinking, reflective, reflexive rational agents and structures their behavior across all human societies as a seemingly irresistible global movement.[38]

Human agents have progressively become aware of their collective and common values as humans. Pressures continue to mount worldwide for the protection and exercise of these rights,[39] as peoples everywhere work to transform their socio-economic and political settings to conform to these new ideas about what it means to be human. This is not to say that the expansion of these newly cultural values will be "instantiated" in social practices universally. Note the Chinese Tiananmen Square massacre of 1989, Rwandan and Bosnian genocides, and continuing civil war in many parts of the globe – in Sudan and central and western Africa, where conflict approaches a Hobbesian endgame. The point here is that, according to constructivist tenets, neither ideas about human rights nor the evils of slavery and genocide nor the elimination of these practices can be easily or plausibly attributed to the existence of autonomous, independent, and socially disconnected individuals – a major contention of constructive thought.

Bridging the gap: Wendt's world[40]

Let's now turn to more probing examination of a closely argued and exhaustively presented constructivist position, viz., that of Alexander

---

[37] Searle (1995).
[38] This line of analysis is developed in the author's edited volume, Kolodziej (2003).
[39] For supportive evidence, see Kolodziej (2003), *passim*.
[40] The subtitle is borrowed, with thanks, from a critique of Wendt's light constructivism by a "heavy," "all-the-way-down" constructivist, Steve Smith (2000).

Wendt. Wendt's constructivism responds to three challenges. The first is Kenneth Waltz's neorealism, the touchstone for Wendt's form of constructivism. The second is Wendt's critique of prevailing social science paradigms and his attempt to subsume this body of scholarly research within the broader scope of the constructivist project. The final challenge arises from many of his fellow constructivists who believe, as suggested earlier, that he concedes too much to prevailing theoretical positions. In tracing the development of Wendt's responses to these three groups of critics, while fending off their attacks, some sense of the intensity of the debate and sharp differences between and among these opponents may be captured. Some appreciation may also be elicited for Wendt's erudite effort to navigate these turbulent waters and steer what he terms a "via media" between them, much to the chagrin of his constructivist skeptics.

Wendt applauds Waltz's structural theory of state behavior, as a right step in the wrong direction. He affirms the explanatory power of a structural approach but rejects Waltz's material conditions for the causal impact of structure on agent (i.e., state) behavior. Specifically, anarchy is rejected both as having causal force and as a condition preceding sequentially the construction by states of their mutually recognized (and changing) identities and interests. Wendt views anarchy as an empty vessel, bereft of any significance absent human meaning and resulting practices that define this condition. Focusing on the state, and not individuals, as many of his constructivist partisans would prefer, Wendt portrays states as having "constituted" their relations in terms of shared ideas about what a state is and, accordingly, on what its interests are. Waltz's structure of power – a decentralized distribution of capabilities for violence across states – and his attribution of a ceaseless and unrelaxed concern for survival and security is, in Wendt's critique, "underspecified."[41] The importance of Wendt's attack is that it is mounted on Waltz's home ground, and not launched from a vantage point outside the scope of Waltz's neorealist framework. States are not stuck in a Waltzian mold. They can break out and make of anarchy what they wish and will.[42] Conceivably, within Wendt's world of states, they can even surmount realism's security dilemma.[43]

Wendt maintains that states have a wide range of choice before them in relating to each other. Waltz's characterization of the system of decentralized states fails to distinguish or provide any guidance in choosing which set of anarchical relations to pursue. For example, states may believe their

[41] This point is also made by two realists. See Christensen and Snyder (1990), but from a strategic rather than a systemic perspective.
[42] Wendt (1992).   [43] Wendt (2003).

survival requires a status quo posture. Here deterrence and accommodation are appropriate rational strategies and practices. Or, their fear of perceived enemy states may be so overpowering that a revisionist posture of expanding their power and eliminating their adversaries and of permanently quashing threats through military force may be the preferred – and perceived rational – strategy. Waltz's rigid separation of structure and state, as independent and dependent variables, respectively, inexplicably rejects any causal connection between the distribution of capabilities as structure and the changing material capabilities arising internally within states as inherent in the evolving composition of these material structures of violence.

Extending this line of analysis, Wendt contends that Waltz covertly smuggles into his structure of power properties of states – such as their shifting identities and interests – that actually do the explanatory work attributed to anarchy. The role of self-help, the attitude of self-regarding egoism toward other states, and the search for security constitute a particular conception of anarchy, as posited by Waltz. These properties of Waltzian anarchy drive the system and state behavior. Since in constructivist thinking these properties or ideas about the state define the identity of states toward each other, they create a non-material structure of ideas, which mutually constitute them. This structure is embedded in the very identity of states – what makes them real – and is more powerful and compelling than Waltz's material constraints, which appear beyond manipulation or transformation. Agent and the structure of ideas animating and informing the actor are not separate and distinct from each other, with structure "causing," as it were, state behavior in response to eternal interests in survival. Viewed from Wendt's world, Waltz's depiction of anarchy represents only one of three possible forms of cultures or structures of ideas and knowledge potentially available to states to choose among. Wendt portrays states as perfectly free to create whatever form of anarchy they please. These forms can range from incessant conflict to perpetual peace, from Hobbes through Locke to Kant.

Each can be distinguished from the other in terms of the mutual perception or conception of states of each other as enemies (the Waltzian analogue), rivals, or friends. These conceptions of identity of states as enemies, rivals, or friends are not dictated by a uniformly composed anarchy. The specific anarchical structure is the mutually constituted product of the interactions of states. The crystallization of these constructions into ideational structures assumes, simultaneously, a causal role in this circular and iterative process of persistent and replicated exchanges. As ideal types, each form of culturally created anarchy has a distinct logic of state identity, interest, role, and the appropriate use of hard and soft power.

The Hobbesian culture of anarchy compares favorably to the Hobbesian model already described at considerable length in this volume. Wendt contends that, while the state system may well have arisen out of Hobbesian anarchy, the state system has evolved currently to a Lockean system where states view themselves more as rivals than as enemies.

The logic and behavioral effects of a Hobbesian and Lockean system may well overlap during an epoch as states may career from armed hostilities and war to peace and cooperation and back again. The process of change in state identities, interests, practices, and of appropriate rules, norms, and institutions is depicted as decidedly more dynamic and fluctuating than Waltzian analysis allows. This underlying and ever-shifting body of ideas on which states act can ostensibly be discerned both by the states which produce them and by the acutely sensitive outside observer (Wendt and fellow constructivists) both as a form of knowledge and as an explanation of state behavior.

According to Wendt, states under conditions of Lockean anarchy accept the status quo and respect the sovereignty of other states. Revisionism is precluded as a strategic option and practice. With greater margins of freedom to cope with or surmount threats to their security or influence and less concern that their sovereignty may be eroded, states can take more risks in cooperating with other states, value future interactions with other states (as Axelrod predicts),[44] and choose absolute over relative gains (as Keohane insists).[45] Military force gradually cedes to non-military force and what Joseph Nye terms "soft power" in a Lockean system of increased interdependence.[46] If war erupts, states can expect mutual constraints in the exercise of violence and be guided by moral strictures, such as Just War theory,[47] both to limit the use of force, notably against civilian populations, and to resist the total defeat and state collapse of adversaries.[48]

These tendencies are illustrative, not conclusive, since we are, after all, describing a process of potentially ceaseless change, mutation and evolution, not an endgame. A Lockean anarchy is sufficiently different from its Hobbesian counterpart of a war of all against all to constitute an entirely distinct culture of anarchy with its own, unique distribution of ideas and, correspondingly, a corpus of knowledge to guide states in their interactions, defined by their mutually constituted identities, interests, and power arrangements. The shift to a Lockean or a Kantian anarchy is not prompted or occasioned by the efficiency of new ways of action,

---

[44] Axelrod (1984).   [45] Keohane and Nye (1984).
[46] Nye (1990) and Keohane and Nye (1989).   [47] Walzer (1974).
[48] Wendt (1999: 282ff.).

but driven by entirely different conceptions of what a state *is*, what it *should do*, and what expectations states can have of each other in terms of their shared norms and the strictures these imply for behavior. In Wendt's world war and security concerns are not necessarily urgent or overriding.

In *Social Theory of International Politics*, Wendt speculates (and concedes he lacks conclusive evidence) that the state system is moving toward a Kantian endgame.[49] Within such a system, states would view each other as friends. States, identifying themselves as friends, generate entirely new interests. Calculations about state behavior would radically change, too. States could then accept wider margins of risk that states might defect and injure them. As competitors in a Lockean system to which states are dedicated, they would not be in perpetual fear of being made a "sucker." Cooperation, not conflict and defection, become more salient expectations. As Karl Deutsch first posited of the emerging European Union, states within a pluralistic security community would see their interests as converging. When clashes might erupt, all could still expect that differences would eventually be resolved peacefully. The security dilemma endemic to Hobbesian anarchy and still lurking below the surface of a Lockean system logic would be surmounted or, at least, substantially relaxed to a point of marginal concern in a Kantian order.[50] Most constructivists, who might not share Wendt's explanation of state security behavior, do affirm his optimism and discern the emergence of "we feeling" and community among states in other regions, too.[51]

At this point, however, Wendt parts company with many constructivists. While sympathetic to the point of view of "ideas-all-the-way-down" constructivists and their shared skepticism about the real or potential evils of the state and the need to surmount them, Wendt's principal aim is to explain social reality as the main goal of social knowledge rather than to address the more daunting problem for which no definitive solution has yet been found of how this knowledge is constructed and acquired. These are questions of epistemology, the central concerns of heavy constructivists, and not of ontology or what's real. Wendt accepts states as given and thereby commits, according to heavy constructivists, the grave error of reifying the state. Rather than problematize the state, as his critics advise, he problematizes Waltz's notion of anarchy and posits a morphology of state identity transformations from which flow appropriate

---

[49] His speculation at this time of writing goes well beyond a Kantian anarchy as the endgame of the state system. His current thinking, which has not been incorporated into this discussion, envisions the possibility eventually of a world state, Wendt (2003).

[50] Deutsch (1957).

[51] Adler and Barnett (1998) and Katzenstein (1996).

and quite different and contradictory interests than those described by Waltz as timeless and unchanging state attributes.

In stipulating states as real, Wendt seeks to keep constructivism within the broad scope of prevailing international relations theory. He brackets (i.e., puts aside) the question of the state's unconditional claim to be preserved and replicated in some singular form. He avers that the observer and theorist, while a participant in the social theory he is constructing, can still generate knowledge that meets the tests, as modified, of the natural sciences. Heavy constructivists, on the other hand, are largely concerned with creating social knowledge that emancipates humans from "oppressive structures."[52] How knowledge of social relations is constructed thus becomes a key concern and a challenge not only to Wendt's brand of constructivism but also, and more broadly, to the claims of prevailing social science theory. The priority assigned by "heavy" constructivists to epistemology puts them at odds with Wendt and at fundamentally opposite poles to most empirical, rationally directed social scientists.

Wendt's stipulation of the state as a self-organizing unit possessed of a monopoly of legitimate violence sits uneasily with "heavy" theorists. For them Wendt's formulation of the constructivist project concedes too much to the power of the state. His compromise hinders the search for alternative mechanisms of rule and social order. If the state is an idea, it can be changed through voluntary and deliberate transformation – a prospect that Wendt affirms in principle but is skeptical about its likely realization anytime soon. This tolerant view of the state, as Wendt's critics charge, effectively divides the state as agent from the structure presumably constituting the state. This move presumably concedes too much conceptual ground to other security and international relations theorists, notably to realists, liberals and liberal institutionalists. By that token Wendt is accused of privileging the claims of authoritative knowledge to these schools of thought. The implication of this concession is that Wendt's reification of the state unwittingly validates its claims to a monopoly of legitimate violence – precisely the attribute brought into question by heavy constructivists.

In attempting to bridge behavioral or rationalist social science and constructivism, Wendt's pragmatic approach acknowledges that the state is going to be around for a long time. There is no replacement for this unit of political organization and no world order in the wings. The state's material capabilities and the loyalties it commands, Wendt assumes, cannot be willed away very easily, if at all, in the foreseeable future. Indeed, Wendt

---

[52] Adler (2002: 107). He provides an excellent, pithy critique of the criticisms of "heavy" constructivists of Wendt's "via media".

views the security roles that the state plays as essentially timeless. These roles can be distinguished from any particular social unit over the evolution of human societies. What is key is the creation of social units, like the state, that can use overwhelming and legitimate violence to arbitrate social conflicts in their particular eras or epochs. The word "state" is less important than the capabilities it has at its disposal, which humans are perfectly free to invest in other socially created units assuming multiple forms and modalities through time and space.

This defense of Wendt's position will hardly sway "heavy" constructivists. As a fellow constructivist complains: "Why did Wendt settle for such a limiting constructivist theory? As a constructivist, Wendt should have been aware that constructivist theories ought to leave room for new and unexpected structural possibilities. Instead he offers a theory and a portrait of agency and the state that locks in politics as the study of inter-state relations and ultimately gives up on bringing into the theory *the ultimate constructor of worlds* – by which I mean the thinking, often reasonable, sometimes surprising, and even at times creative human individual."[53] This brief review cannot definitively settle this internal constructivist quarrel. The aim of this discussion is to join key issues among rivals to allow the reader to make an informed choice.

Constructivism and the cold war: Wendt and his uneasy allies

Until now, Alexander Wendt's constructivism has served as the surrogate for this complex and contentious school of thought. Many constructivists, including one of the anonymous evaluators of this volume, vigorously object that Wendt does not represent their positions. Some are even prepared to vote him out of this school of thought. Evaluating his explanation of the Cold War, as if it were *the* constructivist position, would then dismiss his constructivist critics out of hand without giving them an opportunity to present their conceptions of this school of thought. At the risk of unduly complicating the discussion, and to be fair to constructivists of all stripes, two alternative constructivist explanations for the end of the Cold War are summarized and evaluated. Together with Wendt's account, these can be said, arguably, to cover the principal factions within

---

[53] Adler (2002: 108). Italics in the original. As already suggested, the ferocity of the debates among constructivists and the sweep of their philosophical concerns, particularly with respect to their opposing views over fundamental issues and questions of ontology, epistemology, methodology, rules of evidence, cognitively discovered or socially constructed knowledge, etc., go well beyond the scope of this discussion and conventional social science research.

the constructivist project with respect to international relations theory and security.

The first alternative or "light" constructivist position will focus on Friedrich Kratochwil and his associates. Kratochwil drops below Wendt's analysis pitched at a systemic level to that of foreign policy analysis and to the domestic politics of the Soviet Union. In exploring these levels of analysis and the actors or agents appropriate to these perspectives, constructivists purport to probe deeper for more primary causal structures not only to explain the end of the Cold War and thereby to undermine realist, neorealist, and liberal institutionalist theory into the bargain but also to establish these heavier forms of constructivism relative to Wendt's. Fundamental changes in actor identity working within domestic politics and within the mind-set of leading Soviet reformers are advanced as a more convincing explanation for the end of the Cold War than changes in the material capabilities, principally military forces, of the superpowers. These lines of analysis also challenge Wendt's focus on anarchy and narrowly conceived reformulations of state identity as a function of the interactions of these reified units. Both Wendt and partisans of this extended version of constructivism can agree on what change occurred. Where they differ is in identifying the specific driving forces for change that in the post-Cold War era allegedly transformed international politics and surmounted the superpower and Cold War security dilemma that most non-constructivists posit as endemic to interstate relations and to the nation-state system.

The final constructivist position to be examined, associated with heavy or "ideas-all-the-way-down" constructivism, insists on key principles, relaxed or ignored by Wendt and light constructivists. They affirm that no objective, ahistorical generalizations about actor behavior are possible; that there exists no covering rule for actor and agent behavior beyond social construction of these rules; and that actors are capable of redefining their identities even, paradoxically, as an unintended and ironic consequence of their actions.[54] This latter outcome is precisely what Gorbachev is alleged to have unwittingly accomplished in embracing "New Thinking" with the unintended consequence of destroying the regime reforms were supposed to preserve. All constructivists might agree that Gorbachev

---

[54] Onuf (1998) is especially insistent that agents act always under conditions of uncertainty and that these actions or practices lead to unintended and unforeseen consequences. See also his foundational work (1989). Onuf's hedge poses problems for constructivists, since they also assert that the competent actor relies on his social constructs to adapt to his social conditions. Moreover, how does the all-knowing constructivist observer know when the actor is acting with deliberation and knowledge of the consequences of his decisions or unwittingly with unintended and unforeseen outcomes as the result? See Giddens (1984, 1993), who stresses competence over chance.

ended the Cold War through "New Thinking," but they scarcely share the same understanding of what the content or the consequences of "New Thinking" were.

Wendt focuses on challenging Waltz and neorealism and on reversing the causal arrows for change to the linkage of ideas to identities to interests. The distribution of material capabilities across states is subject to the ideational chain of causality rooted in the changing identities of states. States make of anarchy what they want and will; they have choices about who and what they will be since they are the handmaidens of their social construction. A structure of ideas about state identities and interests appropriate to both rather than a static structure of violent capabilities and their distribution across states, as given, determine state behavior.

Liberal institutionalism, which stresses norms, rules, principles, and institutions as constraints on states, and not simply the material differences between them, also come under Wendtean scrutiny. This position is charged with failing to adequately explain the self-limitation that states impose on themselves in using their material power to get what they want or in choosing cooperation over defection in their exchanges with other actors when they see an attractive advantage by breaking an accord or norm. The liberal institutional concession that ideas count in assisting states to make decisions where alternative (game-theoretic) "equilibria" are possible is still not sufficient within Wendt's critique for social science inquiry to be able to understand and thereby explain state identities, interests, and practices, or the significance attributed to hard or soft power by these actors. The instrumentalist, egoistic conceptions of state behavior of liberal institutionalists prevent them from reaching Wendt's hypothesis that states can ultimately surmount the incentives for defection to form a community of identities and interests that progressively marginalizes to a point of extinction notions of enemies or rivals.[55]

Given the scope of Wendt's ambitious theoretical objectives, it is not surprising that he does not dwell on the Cold War. This broader aim does not prevent him from making sweeping claims about the relevance of his constructivism to explain why the Cold War ended and why his approach is superior to alternative interpretations, including those of rival constructivist critics. Like the other two constructivist position to be discussed, Wendt begins with Soviet "New Thinking" in the 1980s. "For four decades," he notes, " . . . the Soviet Union treated the Cold War as a given. Then in the 1980s it engaged in 'New Thinking,' an important outcome of which was the realization that aggressive Soviet foreign policies contributed to Western hostility, which in turn forced the Soviets to

[55] Wendt (2003).

engage in high levels of defense spending. By acting on that understanding to conciliate the West, the Gorbachev regime virtually single-handedly ended the Cold War."[56]

In a later chapter in his *Social Theory in International Politics*, Wendt rejects materialist explanations for the end of the Cold War, asserting that:

> those wedded to the blind forces model (of Waltz)...will say that the Soviet leadership had to change its politics because of its declining relative power position...However, a structural pressure theory alone cannot explain the form the Soviet response took (ending the Cold War rather than intensifying repression) or its timing (the material decline had been going on for some time). And it also ignores the role that the leadership's realization that its own policies were part of the problem played in conditioning that response. Structural conditions did not force self-awareness on the Soviets. Soviet behavior changed because they redefined their interests as a result of having looked at their existing desires and beliefs self-critically. The reflective model of international explanation captures this process more naturally than the blind forces model.[57]

Soviet self-knowledge and acknowledgement of the negative impact of Soviet foreign and security policies on its Western rivals – in pursuit of Hobbesian strategies of incessant struggle and balance of power politics – purportedly prompted a reassessment and transformation of Soviet identity. By that token Soviet state interests changed, too, from relying on force to get its way with enemies to seeing other states as Lockean rivals with which conflicts could be resolved by non-violent means for mutual advantage.

In the conclusion to his volume, Wendt reasserts these propositions: "Gorbachev's new thinking was a deep, conceptual reassessment of what the US–Soviet relationship 'was.' It was constitutive theorizing, at the lay level, and based on it the Soviets were able to end, unilaterally and almost overnight, a conflict that seemed like it had become set in stone."[58] The notion of conflict as set in stone does not derive from the seeming intractability of the conflict itself. Rather, the notion derives from the human meaning infused into the conflict to make it hard and seemingly resistant to change. Stones can be turned to dust by agent power armed with new ideas about constructing a new identity.

For Wendt to establish his particular constructivist "theory" for the end of the Cold War, he would be obliged to show either (a) why his explanation for the origin, evolution, and, most notably, the end of the Cold War is more convincing than alternatives, or (b) that his position (given the understanding of theory of this volume) is falsifiable. His say-so, however

---

[56] Wendt (1999: 76).   [57] Wendt (1999: 129).   [58] Wendt (1999: 375).

elaborate his conceptual apparatus, is not enough. Since Wendt does not attempt to apply these twin tests, the skeptic is entitled to draw on his constructivist critics as well as the paradigms and approaches covered in this volume to evaluate his constructivism in light of the Cold War laboratory test. Light and heavy constructivists, *inter alia*, extend Wendt's analysis to domestic politics and to the psychological make-up of Soviet reformers like Gorbachev. As noted earlier, these agent and structure dimensions are "black boxed" by Wendt. Light and heavy constructivist critics of his position insist that these levels of analysis and changing actor ideas and identities fundamentally shape and shove the three (or conceivably more) anarchical state systems or societies of states described by Wendt. What's inside the box marked Hobbes, Locke, and Kant is what makes the box, not the box (or state) itself.

Light constructivists and the Cold War

"Soviet New Thinking" has a different, arguably deeper, significance for light constructivists. Rather than stipulate that the Soviet regime under Gorbachev's tutelage moved Soviet foreign and security policy from a Hobbesian to a Lockean and, incipiently, to a Kantian form of anarchy, as Wendt outlines, light constructivists, like Kratochwil and his associates, probe deeper than Wendt into Soviet domestic politics, East European bloc relations, and the psychological state of mind of Soviet reformers and Gorbachev for answers to explain systemic change.[59]

These light constructivists view the Cold War through the lens of an ideological struggle between the Soviet Union and the West. Ideas and the identities they constructed drive the conflict and shape the state practices of containment and balance of power politics. Whereas Wendt stipulates a change in New Thinking, Kratochwil reviews the sources of preceding Cold War thinking, viz., in the ideological competition of East and West. Stalin is said to have abandoned the traditional view of interstate conflict. He substituted, according to Kratochwil, an international politics that effaced the distinction between domestic and international politics. In the postwar world, the coalition of Communist parties of the Eastern bloc formed an imperial unity. Within this system the Communist party enjoyed a monopolistic control over state authority. The material power of the Soviet Union kept this system intact through serial interventions into the domestic politics of Eastern Europe states whenever local Communist

---

[59] Koslowski and Kratochwil (1994) and Lebow (1995). Some of the contributors to the Lebow volume, notably Kenneth A. Oye and Jack Snyder, would not include themselves among constructivists, especially not "heavy" constructivists.

party rule was under threat. The Brezhnev doctrine, which legitimated Soviet intervention as a state practice, was the logical consequence of Soviet thinking under Stalin and his successors.

Then why did the Soviet Union under Gorbachev renounce the Brezhnev doctrine? Its nullification spelled the demise of Communist party rule in Eastern Europe, the dissolution of the Warsaw Pact, the reunification of Germany, the end of bloc politics in Europe, the passing of the Cold War, the implosion of the Soviet state, the ascendancy of the Western coalition, and the transformation of the bipolar system into a unipolar American system. The state system was transformed from an ideological struggle in which domestic and international politics were different aspects of the same phenomenon to what Kratochwil characterizes as the "Austrianization" of the Soviet empire in Eastern Europe, of the Cold War superpower struggle, and of international politics more generally. These changes in the Eastern bloc, the reintegration of the two Germanies, and a softening of US belligerency could come about only by the mutual consent of all parties. That implied a decisive shift from balance of power politics toward the politics of consensual multilateralization of all state exchanges and the peaceful resolution of interstate conflicts in the post-Cold War era. In the post-Cold War world constructed by Soviet reforms, Kratochwil projects a world politics where "virtually all actors have rejected the generative logic of the system that made a balance-of-power policy with shifting alliances the paramount political maxim. Instead, states, whether great, middle-sized, or small, have opted for some form of multilateralism. They also preferred solutions predicated on integration – both in the areas of low politics (economics) and in the vital area of security – to those based on internal balancing."[60]

Kratochwil's construction of the context and content of Soviet New Thinking that produced these changes differs sharply from Wendt's. New Thinking responded allegedly to the crisis of legitimacy of the Communist party in the Soviet Union and in Moscow's East European satellites. Gorbachev attempted to re-establish the frayed and broken bonds between these parties and their national populations. In renouncing the Brezhnev doctrine, he is viewed as seeking to regain lost Communist party legitimacy, not questing for a Lockean system. Set in train then was the dissolution of power of these national Communist parties, the break-up of the Warsaw pact, the reuniting of Germany on Western terms, the end of the superpower confrontation, and the rejection of balances of power and terror. A new international politics arose from the redefinition of Communist ideology and Soviet identity as a consequence of political

---

[60] Koslowski and Kratochwil (1994: 133).

pressures from within the Soviet Union at the very top of the leadership tier and from within the Warsaw pact. Realist accounts are rejected as insufficient to explain these radical shifts in identity, since military capabilities on both sides of the Cold War divide were roughly balanced. Changes in Soviet foreign and security practices, viz., the renunciation of the Brezhnev doctrine to repair the flawed legitimacy of Communist party rule, is assigned the "heavy" lifting to explain the end of the Cold War. Still left unexplained is why Gorbachev embarked on self-destructive reforms that would result in his downfall, the loss of the Communist party's privileged status, and the dissolution of the Soviet state.

Heavy constructivism and the Cold War

A heavy constructivist position rejects Wendt's reification of states and their construction as a self-explanatory given. States which are "real" for Wendt are problematic for heavy critics. The approach of heavy constructionists is decidedly epistemological. To understand Gorbachev's New Thinking, heavy constructivists insist that he has to be accepted on his own terms rather than those imposed by the analyst. It is *his* rationality, logical trains of thought, and psychological and cognitive states of mind that need to be explained, not those of the observer, despite their eventual self-emasculating consequences. This foundational epistemological position sharply differentiates the constructivism of Nicholas Onuf and Vendulka Kubalkova (a.k.a. the Miami group) from Wendt and from light constructivists, like Kratochwil and his associates. Kubalkova here serves as the representative of this "ideas-all-the-way-down" constructivist ensemble with respect to the Cold War case. Her explanation for its end breaks not only with the paradigms of this volume but also with Wendt and with less rigorous, strict constructionists. Kratochwil, whose linguistic approach to constructivism parallels that of Onuf, is treated more sympathetically but his explanation for the end of the Cold War is still qualified for failing to fully grasp the alleged originality of Soviet New Thinking and its implications for international politics. Most pointedly, it departed radically from its Marxist-Leninist origins. What remained intact, however, was supposedly Gorbachev's insistence that the Communist party would retain its privileged position as the sole vehicle for social theory and knowledge.

Realism and neorealism are summarily dismissed largely on grounds already covered by Wendt and Kratochwil. What is of particular interest to this discussion is the marginalization of Wendt's contributions as little more than a minor amendment to liberal institutionalism theory to explain the Cold War. Kubalkova and the Miami group see little difference between the two positions. They are seen as splitting largely over the weight to be assigned to ideational factors in shaping elite preferences, interests, and policies. Wendt stresses their central importance in informing state behavior, while liberal institutionalists heavily discount them by reducing ideas to facilitating mechanisms in choosing different courses of action.[61] Both are alleged to converge on the view that Soviet reform can be explained simply as a *functional* and instrumental necessity, because the regime was in crisis and "an aggressive posture was too difficult to sustain in material terms."[62]

The upshot of this line of critique is that the differences between Wendt and liberal institutionalists are negligible.[63] Both reduce new thinking to their conceptual frameworks rather than get "inside" the mind of those Soviets who fashioned New Thinking. This is a critical charge. For heavy constructivists, this odd couple of institutionalism and Wendtean constructivism has serious theoretical and policy implications. According to "ideas-all-the-way" constructivists, this misalliance allegedly misrepresents New Thinking. Consequently, it distorts understanding of what is viewed by these critics as the revolutionary thrust of New Thinking in its attempt to reconceptualize international security and thus to create new knowledge of the human condition with associated novel ways of speaking about politics (speech acts) – purportedly key forces for surmounting the conflict and war-making disposition of a decentralized state system. Wendt's constructivism is also viewed as potentially mischievous for security policy-making. As Kubalkova avers "the inability of the Wendtean constructivism to handle 'new thinking' and presenting it as a litmus test of the prowess of soft constructivism becomes serious if this form of constructivism is to be the response that IR scholars in the United States make to the post-Cold War world."[64]

While Kratochwil's delineation of the implications of the Soviet abandonment of the Brezhnev doctrine for international politics is affirmed as a step in the right constructivist direction, heavy constructivists, like the Miami group, contend that this light constructionist position fails to understand the scope and innovative break of New Thinking from prevailing Cold War, realist logic. All fall short of exposing what is contended to be the radical break of New Thinking from Marxist-Leninist *and* Western thought about international relations, precisely because these alternatives to a heavy constructivist position do not fully exploit the conceptual and methodological apparatus of constructivism.[65] Rejected is the notion that

---

[61] Compare Keohane and Goldstein (1993), liberal institutionalists, with Wendt.
[62] Kubalkova (2001: 121).
[63] This critique is developed in detail in Sterling-Folker (2000).
[64] Sterling-Folker (2000: 101).   [65] Kubalkova (2001: 131).

Gorbachev and his fellow reformers were liberal Western democrats in disguise, a portrayal congenial to liberal institutionalism. Cast in this light, Soviet reforms appear to be driven by Western ideas. Rejected, too, is the explanation for social change in Soviet foreign and security policy of liberal institutionalists, *and* many light constructivists – clearly including Wendt and arguably Kratochwil, too – who rely on "the same mechanism of functional, institutional efficiency" to account for these fundamental shifts in Soviet external behavior.[66]

A heavy constructionist interpretation seeks to understand New Thinking on its own terms, however failed and flawed, rather than those of an outside observer.[67] Reared under Marxist-Leninist ideology, Gorbachev's "identity" was purportedly defined by his socialization and commitment to the Communist party as the exclusive source of political truth. For him and many of his reformers Communism was still the "future of mankind."[68] The party then was "vested with a superior way of knowing and could always be paternalistic toward the people, who needed to be led and guided."[69] As leader of the Communist party, "with its *epistemological* roots deep in Marx's ideas," Gorbachev is presented as bound by his formation and personal commitment to strengthen, not risk the dissolution, of the party and the Soviet state on which his power and authority rested. Viewed from this point of view and self-socialization, it was "rational" for him and his New Thinking partisans that, under conditions of extreme internal crisis, they would be prompted to reconstruct world politics on radically different assumptions of actor identities and interests than those animating the superpowers and other states. This transformation led to the reform of domestic and international politics, not vice-versa. If the party was the source of political truth and Gorbachev's identity was structured by this system, then his actions can be understood as an effort to transcend the limits of this system, yet preserve the Communist party and his central role as the sources of political truth.

While reasserting the superior knowledge of Communist dogma and of the party as its historic spokesman – hence remaining within the only structure of knowledge he knew – Gorbachev's New Thinking is interpreted as having gone beyond the Brezhnev doctrine and certainly well beyond Wendt's constrained framework of systemic analysis. For the heavy constructionists of the Miami group, Gorbachev is alleged to have repudiated the more fundamental Marxist-Leninist doctrine of inevitable class warfare. According to this interpretation of a transformation in Communist ideology and, *ipso facto*, of Soviet identity, Gorbachev

---

[66] Sterling-Folker (2000: 97).
[67] Kubalkova (2001a, 2001b) develops this argument at length.
[68] Kubalkova (2001: 131).   [69] Kubalkova (2001: 114).

"argued that in light of global problems threatening humanity's existence, world society had assumed a greater significance than the class struggle, which he put in second place."[70] Communism and the Soviet Communist party would triumph by rejecting the superpower conflict and surmounting the Westphalian interstate system rooted in war. Instead of the balance of terror, Gorbachev and his reformers seriously "proposed a reduction in armaments, changes in their strategic doctrine, and eventually complete disarmament as ways of effectively abolishing the *ultima ratio regnum* of the Westphalian system, with its sovereign states and the legitimacy it gave to the use of violence in IR."[71]

The moral stature of the Communist party would presumably be enhanced through reforms that were designed to bind national populations to local Communist parties. Instead of continued military confrontation and class warfare, Gorbachev is supposed to have shifted to a policy of cultural and ideational attack on Western capitalism and its presumptively vulnerable liberal open societies. The shift in strategy and in efforts to capture the high moral ground resulted in a complete break from a Leninist strategy of incessant, relentless violent class warfare to that of undermining Western capitalistic power by adopting Antonio Gramsci's posture of "counter-hegemony."[72] Superior ideas and moral claims were now allegedly relied upon by Gorbachev to eventually win over superior Western material capabilities. If this particular heavy constructionist interpretation were accepted as the definitive understanding of New Thinking, it would certainly constitute a radical departure from all preceding theories of international relations and security as well as rival constructivist approaches. So sweeping a claim merits evaluation.

Whither constructivism?: a critique

Critiquing constructivism by evaluating its explanation of the end of the Cold War is tricky. As this all-too-brief review of the complex conceptual apparatus of constructivism and of its deep internal splits makes clear, constructivism is not a single, coherent body of thought at this point of its evolution. It is a work in progress whose partisans are as divided among themselves as they are with the established schools of security thought they are contesting. For purposes of comparison it is important to keep in mind that most constructivists challenge prevailing methodological, epistemological, evidentiary, and ontological assumptions underlying leading schools of security and international relations theorizing. Heavy constructivists go further and reject the assumptions of sequential causality

---

[70] Kubalkova (2001: 139).   [71] *Ibid.*   [72] Gramsci (1971).

underlying empirical or rational theory – an epistemological assumption affirmed by this volume.

Recall that constructivism's causal explanation of agent or actor behavior and social change, wherein agent and structure are "instantiated" simultaneously in their mutual construction, cannot be squared with conventional empirical theory, as described in chapter 1. Constructivists portray agents as social constructions, bound by rules, norms, and institutions of their own creation. As Onuf neatly states: "Rules Make Agents, Agents Make Rules."[73] "Rules make agents out of individual human beings by giving them opportunities to act upon the world. These acts have material and social consequences, some of them intended and some not. Through these acts, agents make the material world a social reality for themselves as human beings."[74]

Nor can conventional and widely accepted tests of falsification be readily applied to validate constructivist claims, certainly not those of its most determined "ideas-all-the-way-down" analysts. Falsification itself is contested and problematized; Lakatos need not apply. Most constructivists either reject outright or qualify substantially widely held assumptions and principles of analysis which underpin dominant social inquiry today: that the social and natural worlds are "amenable to the same kinds of analysis";[75] that social facts and values can be separated; that ahistorical regularities and covering rules to explain agent behavior can be discovered; that these patterns exist apart from the methods used to uncover them;[76] and that facts as evidence – empiricism – is the final arbitrator of competing explanations of actor behavior and social change.

Falsification tests resting on these assumptions make little (light) or no ("heavy") sense to constructivists. As Kubalkova puts the case for heavy constructivists,

The falsification of hypotheses and theories ... postulates a correspondence theory of truth between the "world and the word," between the "objective reality" and our representations of it. However, if language is constitutive of the world ... then we cannot really meaningfully compare it with that which it describes ... rule-oriented constructivists hold that intersubjectivity is a process, which makes all facts *social*. As such they are provisional claims, some better founded than others. But always dependent on the subject's (agent's, claimant's) ever-contingent position in an ever-changing stream of deeds."[77]

This posits an infinite regression of claims and counter-claims to political knowledge, including rejection of falsification itself, with no resting place

[73] Onuf (1998: 64).   [74] *Ibid.*   [75] Smith (2001: 42).   [76] *Ibid.*
[77] Kubalkova (2001: 75).

and no stable point of reference to generalize about human or agent-constructed behavior.

In light of this impasse over how to pursue research and theory – and what theory and knowledge even *are* – two lines of analysis will be adopted to critique the constructivist approach in terms of its explanation of the Cold War. First, let's see how constructivists do against each other, using the three orientations from Wendt to "light" to "heavy" constructivist positions to cover the range of viewpoints of this approach. Second, let's apply empiricist criteria to constructivist claims, however much constructivists may object, in order to join key issues and identify splits between rationalist and constructivist approaches within a Lakatosian framework of analysis. Lakatos stipulates, as chapter 1 describes, that bodies of theoretical thought can be viewed as progressive or degenerating research programs. Whether they are going up or down depends on an evaluation of their responses to three questions: does a theory explain what other theories can do; can it explain facts not addressed by other explanations; and can it explain new facts and events that arise within the scope of its claimed explanatory power? Constructivism will be evaluated by these tests, although they are admittedly loaded against constructivism, since these criteria rest on empirical validation.

Constructivists vs. constructivists

Much of the power of analysis of all constructivist positions is their ability to problematize empiricist findings. Constructivists observe that neither realism nor neorealism can convincingly explain the end of the Cold War. The balance of power and terror between the two superpowers would seem to preclude change, yet the Cold War ended abruptly and unexpectedly. Wendt shows (confirmed, too, by liberal and liberal institutionalist research) that the interstate system maps more closely with Lockean than a Hobbesian model. Anarchy is not a given, but is constructed by changes in the identities of states. As their identities change, so also do their interest in supporting, alternatively, a Hobbesian, Lockean, or Kantian system of anarchy.

Neither realism nor Wendt's systemic approach can convincingly explain the break-up of the Warsaw Pact. Here other constructivists have more to say than Wendt about alliance dissolution. Kratochwil's postulation of a domestic political crisis of legitimacy in the Soviet Union and, internationally, within the Warsaw Pact provides a plausible line of analysis for systemic change arising from fundamental changes within the Soviet Union's political regime and its abandonment of the interventionist practices of the Brezhnev doctrine.

The Miami group goes further. It advances the intriguing hypothesis that Gorbachev's reforms aimed simultaneously to restore the privileged position of the Communist party at home and to transform the Westphalian system as a warfare system. Rather than a reversion to the Austrianization of international politics and the warfare system on which it rests, as Kratochwil argues, Kubalkova and her associates pose Gorbachev's reforms within a global strategic framework that makes domestic and foreign policy-making a unified and singular field of action – a distinction without a difference. This enlargement of the scope of constructivism's explanatory power is well beyond Wendt's sharp focus on state systemic change or that of Kratochwil and other light constructivists whose explanation for the end of the Cold War remains within traditional notions of foreign and domestic policy analysis.

Finally, and of no small consequence, all forms of constructivism reintroduce the power of agent-driven change into social analysis. Ideals, values, and agent identity return social theory to human and human-created concerns. These are not easily or comfortably reducible to the material constraints on which other theoretical positions rest. However daunting is the challenge of objectivizing the subjective states of mind of agents as the principal vehicles of meaning and value, as Max Weber recognized over a century ago, constructivists keep open the debate over security by insisting on agents and their self-reflective and reflexive redefinitions of their identities as vehicles of social change. They make the defensible point that social analysis is not supposed to reduce human thinking and action to validate and suit prevailing theories or tailor human thought to their self-imposed procrustean methodological and evidentiary limits. Social analysis is presumptively supposed to explain actor behavior as the latter understands his social conditions, not bolster the findings of researchers' research apparatus. On this score light and heavy constructivists put the individual actor, not just the state, back into social analysis.[78]

Yet the "fact" remains that Gorbachev's reforms of *glasnost, perestroika,* and democratization, designed to save the Communist party and the Soviet state, utterly failed. The alternate light forms of constructivism of Wendt and Kratochwil have no plausible explanation for these events, but merely record them. They cite changes in Soviet behavior and speak of a crisis in legitimacy but offer sparse explanation for how and why these new political facts arose or how and why they sparked specific reform policies and processes and what were the consequences of these evolutionary shifts. They provide no bridge – only the prospect of a link – between rationalism and constructivism.

[78] Compare Evans, Rueschemeyer, and Skocpol (1985).

The Miami group, on the other hand, does seize the nettle and postulates the proposition, consistent with constructivist strictures, that Gorbachev was acting "rationally" within the social context in which he was reared, affording him, as constructivists assert, the opportunity "to act upon the world."[79] Attacking all opponents, constructivists and non-constructivists, Kubalkova states that "it takes a leap of faith to argue with any degree of conviction that any Soviet leader would have agreed on behalf of his country to plunge into the disarray characteristic of the transition in which the former Soviet Union still finds itself."[80]

This line of analysis "saves" Gorbachev as a "rational" actor within the social structure which shaped and informed his identity and which also generated incentives for him to act to save the system and his place within it by transforming both. What is missing is an explanation of why he chose policies that destroyed that system and his own personal authority and power. What is embarrassingly absent from this analysis, much like the dog that didn't bark in Sherlock Holmes' tale of "The Hound of the Baskervilles," is an identification of the compelling social forces, privileged by the other paradigms covered in this volume, that undermined both Gorbachev and his cherished system. The pull of best practices in producing material wealth – the Western open market exchange system and its dependence on global networks of technological innovation and scientific discovery – falls outside of the scope of constructivist thinking of all stripes. As a consequence the reform process is explained by reference to New Thinking as if it were entirely uninformed and insulated from the powerful material lures and allure of these knowledge and productive systems of human enterprise and creativity, no less social constructs than ideas or identities.

A critique of constructivism from conventional wisdom

There is little in constructivist thinking to explain, specifically, why *glasnost, perestroika*, and democratization were chosen as the preferred instruments of reform and why they failed. There is little comfort in a theory or approach, notably among heavy constructivists, that failure was a realistic option and that its pursuit was rational. Particularly puzzling is the resistance of constructivists to highlight what would appear to be an obvious factor consistent with their epistemological orientation. One would have thought that they would have seized on national sentiment, a fundamentally non-material state of mind, as a human construction. This force, whose effects have been felt for over two centuries, helps to explain – certainly to better understand – the break-up of the Soviet

---

[79] Onuf (1998: 64).   [80] Kubalkova (2001: 124).

empire once *glasnost* and democratization were set in motion with all of their unwitting and unintended destructive effects to the Soviet system. These reforms ushered in a renewed expression of nationalism across the Soviet state. More than New Thinking and the rejection of the Brezhnev doctrine, nationalism shattered the bonds between the Communist parties of the empire and between the Soviet state and Russian people. The resurgence of national loyalties over ideological commitments exposed the gap between the political legitimacy of the Soviet state in eliciting public support and the material power it wielded. The election of Boris Yeltsin and Gorbachev's accompanying electoral defeat in the Russian Federation testify to the force of nationalism over the discredited claims of Communist ideology, whether Leninist, Stalinist, or Gorbachev reformist. So the purported insight of heavy constructivists that Gorbachev acted rationally in his own social context is of doubtful value in constructing a theory of international relations and security to understand why the Soviet Union imploded and the Cold War ended.[81]

Ideas, as a light constructivist would concede, "do not float freely."[82] They are embedded in an elaborate set of rules, norms, regimes and institutions, undergirded by tangible and effective political power. Nationalism, as a powerful force in international relations and a source of profound insecurity in world politics, is a necessary, if insufficient, explanation for the end of the Cold War. It fused legitimacy with the monopoly of violence of the state. As President Charles de Gaulle and other classical realists (not neorealists) foresaw,[83] nationalism is an indispensable, if not always totally reliable, predictor of the collapse of the Soviet empire. It destroys empires. Constructivism as an approach to international relations and security theory might well re-examine its resistance to acknowledging nationalism as a force in social construction. As Joseph Schumpeter recognized several decades ago, it is a pre-rational, atavistic force that cannot be reduced to functionalist calculations if it is to be understood and explained.[84]

One can only speculate why constructivists who place so much stress on human creativity and subjective states of mind overlook this force within the scope of their theorizing. In acknowledging national, ethnic, communal, cultural, religious, and linguistic identities and loyalties as compelling social forces, it does not follow that constructivists are necessarily obliged to advocate their adoption and spread. Constructivist theory, however, is so keen to emphasize the possibility of surmounting human conflict and the security dilemma by the sheer exercise of human will and desire that it falsifies the agent whose thinking and behavior it is attempting to explain

---

[81] Carrère d'Encausse (1993) and Kaiser (1994).   [82] Risse-Kappen (1995).
[83] Kolodziej (1974).   [84] Schumpeter (1955).

in real time and circumstance. It risks ignoring or slighting what humans have chosen (or had imposed on them) as their identities, which may well be more oriented toward conflict and the use of force than cooperation and consensus. "What if" wishful thinking trumps "as if" description and explanation.

Similarly, *perestroika* is short-changed in constructivist thinking of all stripes. Much of this oversight can be attributable to the intangible, ideas-driven causal explanations of the constructivist project. Here economic liberal theorists, as chapter 5 suggests, have a point in arguing that the Soviet Union could not compete with the West's solution to the national and global imperative of material welfare sought by the world's populations. Nor, paradoxically, could Soviet elites increase their personal wealth as much as they might have wished by remaining trapped in a command economy that they controlled and within which they enjoyed privileged status, power and authority, but paltry material gains when compared to their Western counterparts. The yawning and widening gaps in economic and technological development between East and West and the daily experience of deprivation of Soviet elites generated incentives, as liberal economic theory expects, for new thinking to adapt to Western best practices – an open economic trading system.

Wendt's narrowly conceived explanation for state behavior as a product of interstate exchanges that instantiate a culture of knowledge or ideas across states cannot reach the construction of an entirely different and competing material system – global markets resting on ceaseless acquisition of new scientific knowledge and its application in innovative technology. One might have expected Wendt and his constructivist fellow travelers at least to insist on the notion that the market system is, arguably, an ideational breakthrough and an ideology in its own right. Friedrich Hayek and his liberal confreres, who are decidedly not constructivists, have no difficulty arguing this case, as chapter 5 delineates.

From radically divergent theoretical vantage points, both Karl Marx and Adam Smith agree that markets and the social interactions and processes associated with them have more to do with making and doing than thinking about these social institutions. The material conditions created by markets and industrialization impact powerfully on human choices. Ideas and values that infuse meaning and significance in human relations and legitimate the exercise of state power are framed in a pre-existing set of material conditions, or what Charles Lindblom calls prior determinants.[85] These shape and shove thinking, choices, and action. This transnational order of exchanges between state and non-state actors

---

[85] Lindblom (2001: 169).

composing the global market system and the enormous material cornu-
copia issuing from this social system structure human interests and incentives as well as the range of choices open to participants in the market
system.

The incentives generated by these material conditions of technological innovation and the globalization of the market system to envelop and
undermine the Soviet Union fall outside Wendt's purview and that of
most constructivists. Incentives for voluntary cooperation of a market
system and for techno-scientific discovery and innovation, material conditions endemic to a Kantian culture of friends, would not appear to be
hostage simply to the idea of the utility of these systems. They derive
from what Marx refers to as the bio-economic composition of humans
or what Smith adds as the inherent tendency of humans, if placed in
a nurturing and supporting social system favoring free exchange and
voluntary economic exchange, to "truck, barter, and exchange." Curi-
ously, too, constructivists who stress freedom of choice and creativity in
the construction of social relations ignore Joseph Schumpeter's widely
acknowledged insight of capitalism's "creative destructive power" and
the reformist impact of entrepreneurs on social structures.

In the way that Montezuma in Mexico and Anatuhalpa in Peru underestimated the material power of the Spanish invaders,[86] Gorbachev made
fatal errors in underestimating the power of Western open economic and
political systems and the attractive pull they exerted on national populations under Communist control. Like Montezuma and Anatuhalpa,
Soviet reformers, in adapting and acceding to Western material power,
utterly failed to foresee the implications of free market reforms on
the Soviet command economy. No less was an ideologically socialized
elite able to understand the power of nationalism as an imploding force
once these political and economic reforms were introduced at the cost of
the Soviet Union and its empire. National, communal, and ethnic antag-
onisms within the Soviet Union proved eventually to be its undoing –
a testimony to one of the decisive lessons of the twentieth century, viz.,
that empires cannot withstand the centrifugal force of competing identities clamoring for their own self-determination within an increasingly
globalizing world of divided populations and states.

Constructivists at this point in the development of their project appear
unable to incorporate the material incentives of a market system, whatever
its explanatory shortcomings, into their approach except to reduce this
revolutionary social system and the creative destruction that it unleashes
to their preferred ideational forms. Light constructivists, like Kratochwil,

---

[86] Diamond (1997), especially chapter 3.

do add the important dimension of domestic and alliance politics and the repercussions of both on the legitimacy of the Soviet state and Communist party. But they, too, like other constructivists, eschew recognition of the telling power of wealth and welfare – an acknowledgment that would undermine their ideational explanation of behavior.

In particular, Wendt's narrow brand of constructivism precludes him from using constructivism to good advantage in examining the impact of domestic politics on the Soviet state and empire. Heavy brands of constructivism, of the kind alluded to by Emmanuel Adler above, can reach some of the wellsprings of opposition to the Soviet system. They can also reach the proposition of the democratic peace.[87] Wendt can't. He has bracketed – that is, excluded – an analysis of domestic politics, whether portrayed in material or ideational form – from his explanation of the emergence of three cultures of anarchy and the identity and interests of states appropriate to these three structural systems. In a sense, in excluding both transnational actor exchanges (economic and market transactions) and domestic politics, Wendt has essentially described the collapse of the Soviet Union and the end of the Cold War through the narrow prism of interstate relations, ignoring these two other levels of actor and social interactions impacting on the Soviet state, as table 1.1 outlines. He has implicitly dismissed these crucial sources of the identity transformation of the Soviet state and its republics. Wendt is aware of these shortcomings, but that acknowledgment does not insulate him from the criticism of one of his detractors, viz., that his constructivist claim "is unsupported by empirical data and confounded by the thinness of norms in the international environment."[88]

Wendt also claims that no big wars between the major powers have arisen because of ideational self-constraints among states, increasingly self-ensnared in a Lockean system of rivals progressively moving toward a Kantian system of friends. While he concedes that material conditions – for example, arms races – can overwhelm state adherence to self-limiting norms, he insists that the latter provide more explanatory power of why the Cold War never became hot.

Wendt's belief that the Cold War did not become a hot war because of the emergence of a Lockean system, which fostered state self-limitation and adherence to international norms, has also been the target of criticism. Neorealists and liberal institutionalists are scarcely convinced that a Lockean system emerged full blown, like the Greek Goddess Athena from the head of Zeus. Two material conditions – one negative, the other positive – offer more explanatory power. On the one hand, the enormous

---

[87] Russett (1993), Russett and Starr (2000), Russett and Oneal (2001), and Lipson (2003).
[88] Krasner (2002: 131).

costs of nuclear war would appear to have more than a marginal effect in discouraging major wars. On the other hand, the incentives for voluntary cooperation of a market system and for techno-scientific discovery and innovation, material conditions endemic to a Kantian culture of friends, would not appear reducible simply to the utility of these systems. Both liberals and Marxists converge on the evolutionary, trial-and-error development of social systems capable of increasing human wealth and welfare. *Ex post facto* rationalizations of this evolutionary process by reversing the causal arrows of ideas driving material conditions is a credible hypothesis, but this characterization of the evolution of the social change still lacks both "empirical data" to make this case stick and logical firepower to contest prevailing counter-positions, notably the paradigms covered in this volume.[89]

The strength of constructivism is its weakness. In problematizing all theories of knowledge, notably international relations and security theories, it implicitly and explicitly brings back human values into the question of a theory of knowledge of human thought and action. That is a defensible move, as even card-carrying liberal economic theorists are now prepared to concede – indeed, insist upon.[90] On the other hand, the conceptual route chosen by constructivists to return human actors and their constructed agents to center stage exposes its principal weakness. Agents as rule-constructed can only act socially if they instantiate themselves in a network of rules, norms, and institutions. These social mechanisms or arrangements, as Onuf insists, provide "opportunities to act on the world."[91] That is tantamount to saying agents or actors act only if they have social power. But no less a fundamental principle of constructivism than the instantiation of the agent–structure relationship is the assertion that all theories of knowledge, as human constructs, are also *ipso facto* problematic, including the constructivist stipulation of this "truth."

There is a fundamental and contradictory tension underlying the optimism of the constructivist project. It is "as if" the problematizing of political truth and power automatically led to a world in which differences were blurred and conflicts were necessarily abated in the act of problematization. This surface property of current constructivist thinking, however estimable, raises doubts about the theoretical import and objectivity of constructivism in explaining actor behavior, not the thinking and action constructivists might prefer. Extreme forms of constructivism are especially prone to the criticism that they rob themselves of any plausible expectation that the legitimate use of power is ever conceivable or possible to achieve the favorable outcomes they largely share – peace,

[89] Compare Waltz (1990, 1964) and John Mueller (1988, 1989).
[90] Kuran (1991, 1995).   [91] Onuf (1998: 64).

prosperity, and justice. Whatever use of power might produce or advance these exalted aims is delegitimated at the very moment of human construction – dead on arrival as a social construction.

There is no theoretical or practical impediment in current constructivist thinking that precludes actors and agents and structures of power to revert to a Hobbesian model and to a regressive and self-destructive endgame. Constructivism does a better job explaining the slowing of violent conflict and, specifically, the passing of the Cold War than explaining why the Cold War started and morphed into a superpower global struggle, tethered precariously and dangerously on a balance of terror whose nuclear detritus still hangs over the fate of the human species.

Do these lines of criticism add up to the charge of one harsh critic that "there are no propositions about state behavior in *Social Theory of International Politics*, not even the 'few and big' propositions that Kenneth Waltz develops ... "[92] That would seem to be too facile and harsh a dismissal of the constructivist project. No closure is warranted at this time in the struggle between paradigms and approaches for hegemony. Constructivism in its many forms is too resourceful an opponent to reject simply because of the particular weaknesses of this light or that heavy constructivist. It would certainly be unfair to dismiss its wide-ranging criticisms of prevailing theories of security and international relations on evidentiary, causal, and methodological grounds appropriate to other perspectives. Building implicitly on the work of Max Weber and Emile Durkheim, as this volume argues, Wendt, Kratochwil and other light constructivists have clearly brought constructivism into the mainstream of international relations theorizing without abandoning in this account central constructivist tenets.

Constructivists are opening new lines of inquiry and attracting growing numbers to their ranks, notably among younger scholars. The bewildering number of agent–structure axes (narratives in constructivist terminology) that can be explored frees it from the constraints of prevailing paradigms. It is not paradigm specific, or bound by any code of conduct to a particular theoretical view. In challenging all other theoretical projects, both as knowledge of empirically accessible social facts and as privileged claims to certain values, interest, power, and legitimacy, constructivism opens the door to exploring a wide range of problems and questions previously off limits to accepted theorizing. It can examine ways closed to realists, neorealists, or Marxists of how the security dilemma might be relaxed and surmounted by human intervention and design.[93] This prompts the need, eschewed by Wendt, of tracing the process *and* the material conditions

---

[92] Keohane (2002: 126).
[93] E.g., Adler and Barnett (1998), Katzenstein (1996), and Frederkind (1998).

necessary to explain how a Hobbesian anarchy can evolve to a Lockean and Kantian mode, much as the evolution of the European state system has moved toward European unity after five centuries of internecine civil war. It is not enough to stipulate a supposed shift in systemic state behavior; an explanation is needed and warranted, too.

While this positive assessment will not sit lightly with "heavy" constructivists, tainted as it is by a commitment to rationalist and empirically driven theory, there is no doubt that fellow constructivists are opening new lines of inquiry, attractive to growing numbers within their ranks. These problematize the state and the state system; erode the artificial conceptual barriers separating domestic and international politics in theorizing about global politics and security; expose the impact of different agent or actor identities on how they define their interests; and challenge both static conceptions of international politics and worn claims to legitimacy and privilege. Ironically, more not less constructivist research and scholarship is needed to establish constructivism's ambitious claims. Constructivism, in any of the forms reviewed here or as a collective enterprise, is not ready to assume the title of hegemon in its battle with the paradigms and approaches covered in this volume. But it is a comer, if not yet a full-fledged contender.

Discussion questions

1. Why is a constructivist explanation of security better characterized as an approach than as a paradigm for international relations and security studies?
2. What are the key elements of the constructivist critique of the behavioral or rationalist approach to security theory and practice?
3. What are the key elements of the constructivist approach to international relations and security theory and practice? Identify the break of constructivists with other social scientists along evidentiary, causal, methodological, ontological, and epistemological dimensions.
4. Distinguish between heavy and light explanations of actor behavior in international relations and in security policy-making. Where would Wendt be situated on a range of constructivists from heavy to light?
5. Evaluate the capacity of the three forms of constructivist critiques in this chapter to explain the rise, evolution, and collapse of the Cold War bipolar system.

Suggestions for further reading

Walter Carlsnaes, Thomas Risse, and Beth A. Simmons (eds.) (2002), *Handbook of International Relations*, London: Sage. This handbook presents the best critical review of international relations theory, divided into the principal sub-fields of the discipline. The essays by Emmanuel Adler on constructivism, and by James Fearon and Alexander Wendt on rationalism and constructivist approaches are particularly pertinent.

Emile Durkheim (1993), *Ethics and the Sociology of Morals*, Buffalo: Prometheus Books. It is helpful to read the greats to grasp the cumulative debt that contemporary theorists and practitioners owe to giants who came before.

Forum (2000), "Forum on Social Theory of International Politics," *Review of International Studies* 26: 123–80. This is the best and most wide-ranging critique of Alexander Wendt's constructivist theory, written by leading international relations scholars, and includes Wendt's rejoinder, which suggests where his thinking is going today.

Peter J. Katzenstein (ed.) (1996), *The Culture of National Security: Norms and Identity in World Politics*, New York: Columbia University Press. This volume, edited by one of the major scholars in international relations and comparative politics, makes the best case for taking light constructivism seriously and of incorporating its insight into mainstream thinking.

Nicholas G. Onuf (1998), "Constructivism: A User's Manual," pp. 58–78 in *International Relations in a Constructed World*, edited by Vendulka Kubalkova, Nicholas Onuf, and Paul Kowert, London: M. E. Sharpe. This is a useful introduction to Onuf's more challenging and comprehensive 1989 work on constructivism: *World of Our Making: Rules and Rule in Social Theory and International Relations*, Columbia: University of South Carolina Press.

John Gerard Ruggie (1998), "What Makes the World Hang Together? Neo-Utilitarianism and the Social Constructivist Challenge," *International Organization* 52: 855–85. If one wishes to begin somewhere to understand constructivism, this is as good a starting point as any. Clearly written, evidencing an enviable grasp of the literature and constructivism's debt to Max Weber and Emile Durkheim.

John R. Searle (1995), *The Construction of Social Reality*, New York: Free Press. This is a foundational volume on constructivism by a leading sociologist.

Alexander Wendt (1999), *Social Theory of International Politics*, Cambridge, UK: Cambridge University Press. This hefty volume summarizes and expands on all of his previous important articles.

Conclusions

8 Whither international security and security studies?

> When someone is honestly 55% right, that's very good and there's no use wrangling. And if someone is 60% right, it's wonderful . . . But what's to be said about 75% right? Wise people say this is suspicious. Well, and what about 100%? Whoever says he's 100% right is a fanatic . . .
>
> – an old Jew of Galicia[1]

After so extensive a review and evaluation of seven contesting schools of thought, are we ready to crown a clear winner – a hegemon in security studies? Hardly. The winning paradigm or approach would have to meet fully the standards for valid theory and reliable practice defined in chapter 1. None do. Yet in varying degrees, and here the reader is the final judge, all meet a minimum test of Imre Lakatos' notion of a progressive research program.

Each would also have to explain the rise and demise of the Cold War – enough to warrant its inclusion in the struggle for hegemony among contesting security perspectives.[2] In greater or lesser measure, each has some value to add to the mix of explanations for this tectonic shift in international relations and global politics. None comes close to offering a definitive explanation for this global struggle and its passing.

Remember this volume nests security studies within the larger and capacious scope of international relations theory. To carve out a special domain for the imperative of security confronting international actors, notably states but extending to other actors, too, I argued that security theory must meet a dual standard. A hegemon should be able to explain why and how actors choose force or choose *not* to use force or coercive threats to get their way – *their* way. Specifically, for states, we want a theory of war *and* peace. In more formal terms, the question to be addressed by a challenger for hegemony is how actors get their preferred outcomes in their interdependent exchanges with other actors for mutually pursued but not necessarily congruent or convergent aims. These outcomes

---

[1] Quoted by Milosz (1954: v).
[2] That this enlarged view of the scope of security studies may be gaining ground is suggested by a widely used reader edited by a prominent realist theorist. See Betts (2005).

307

include not only desired results on aims and means but also on the rules governing future interactions.

It was not enough to meet the standards of this volume to assume, as some realists do, that actors can always be expected to defect and use or threaten force to induce or compel the outcomes they want in their relations with states and other actors. Nor is it sensible, or consistent with experience, to assume for purposes of analysis, as many liberal economists stipulate, that actors will always choose non-violence and consensual, voluntary cooperation to coordinate their preferences with other like-minded actors or compromise their differences peacefully.

None of the schools covered so far fully meets the volume's dual test for defining or resolving security issues. Some do better than others, depending on the historical context to which the paradigm or approach is applied. As chapter 2 delineates, whether state decision-makers and their populations are in a pre-war World War I or II setting makes a big difference in defining what kind of security dilemma they confront. Different state and regime actors with different and divergent interests, aims, and values spell different security scenarios. Each must be evaluated on its own terms, while keeping in mind that the object of security studies as a sub-set of international relations theory is to identify generalizations across actor behavior that apply across time, space, and social circumstances.

As Imre Lakatos cautions, no one test, like the Cold War, can prove or disprove a theory of security or reject an approach to theory building, like behavioral or constructivist research programs. The serious security theorist, practitioner, and interested citizen have then an intellectual, professional, and civic obligation to challenge these schools of thought as reliable guides for public policy, when stubborn countervailing facts and experience undermine the received wisdom of a particular mode of security behavior. The task always is to "disprove" these theories, not to select partial data to support a perspective already asserted as true and valid, while suppressing discrepant observations.[3] What's left after this ceaseless winnowing process is provisionally reliable knowledge about security, pending further testing and perfection in light of new data, changing circumstances, and breakthroughs in theory or methods of study.

For some readers, this may be a disheartening conclusion. For others, including the author, lacking *certain* knowledge invites its pursuit. Knowing what problems and puzzles remain *is* knowledge. Knowing what problems have yet to be tackled and solved is *ipso facto* where the cutting edge of learning is to be found. Richard Collingwood, the influential English

---

[3] Robert Jervis (1976) makes this point in his critique of the misuse of history by social scientists to support their positions.

historian, observed in his attempt to recreate the daily life of Romans in Britain that asking the right questions is more important than getting the right answers.[4] Once the latter have been unearthed, it's time to move on. What's known, while useful, is uninteresting – even dull and boring – from the perspective of science and the social sciences in their search to raise new questions of moment or significance about humans and about their pursuits and purposes. The mantra is "Tell me something I don't know." Recounting tediously, as some theorists are prone to do, that the security dilemma is embedded in the relations of states and in the exchanges of humans and human societies tells me little about how and why this dilemma has been, or can be, relaxed or surmounted – or not.

Where we've been

As a summing up, let's briefly rehearse where we've been and suggest where security studies should be headed. As this volume testifies, there currently exists no one dominant school of thought, a singularly compelling methodology, or exclusive set of policy prescriptions that unerringly predicts the consequences of using or not using force or other forms of hard and soft power to get the results actors seek in their interdependent and mutually contingent transactions. Uncertainty cautions against embracing unconditionally the partisan assertions of those theorists and practitioners associated with these seven security persuasions. By problematizing these schools of thought readers position themselves to make up their own minds about what each paradigm or approach has to offer to explain actor behavior. Readers should now have the makings of a firm opinion about the strengths and weaknesses of each theoretical orientation. They should also have at their disposal a working tool chest of concepts – weapons if you like – useful not only in assessing the worth of each paradigm or approach but also helpful to readers in learning more about international security on their own. If readers now believe they are no longer passive observers or programmed consumers of the opinions of others, however expert they may appear to be, then one of the principal purposes of this volume will have been achieved.

To "disprove" the claims of our seven schools, each was evaluated against its implicit or explicit explanation for the rise, evolution, and demise of the Cold War. The global reach of the Cold War conflict between the United States and the Soviet Union and the unprecedented

---

[4] Collingwood (1939, 1946). See Collingwood's *Autobiography* for his insight about the privileged position of questions, not answers, in human learning. His *Idea of History* elaborates on this challenge.

massing of organized violence to pursue the struggle make a *prima facie* case for using the Cold War as a valid test. If ignited, the enormous military forces, conventional and nuclear, marshaled by both sides in this contest for global hegemony threatened all states and peoples around the world. If a school of thought fails to explain this clash of titans and the titanic proportions of their armed conflict as well as the abrupt end of this fatal duel, almost without a shot fired in anger, then its credibility can reasonably be questioned.

What appears clear is that none of the seven contestants for hegemony is a satisfactory fit for the Cold War. The explanations they advance capture central actors and critical factors, keys to understanding the beginning, middle, and end of the postwar bipolar system. But like the mythical blind men of India, their several and competing depictions of what are security problems, why and how actors address and solve them, and the criteria proposed for decision-makers to guide security policy-making are all flawed. The self-limiting scope of each paradigm or approach, whatever the merit of its claims to rigor, parsimony, or universality may be, exclude key actors and factors impacting on international and global security. Incomplete and problematic claims to knowledge about what factors and actors drive security decisions, actions, and outcomes diminish the utility of a paradigm or approach. Supplementing a research program by ad hoc adjustments and refinements to fill gaps to fend off critics, much like those adduced by partisans of the contesting positions covered in this volume, blurs the coherence of a security model, erodes its explanatory power, and undermines its status as a challenger for hegemony in security studies. We may well have better and more accurate descriptions of how and why specific historical security issues were resolved (or not), but not a theory of security.

Realists, neorealists, and liberal institutionalists have a lot to say about the rise and evolution of the Cold War until its end with the implosion of the Soviet Union. Hobbes, Clausewitz, and Thucydides reach across centuries of time and space and reappear in the modern dress of contemporary realist theorists and practitioners to explain the drive of the United States and the Soviet Union, victor powers from World War II, to impose their clashing ideologies, economic interests, and conceptions of global order and legitimacy on their rivals and on other peoples and states around the world. The superpower Doomsday Machines, the massive conventional and tactical nuclear arms arrayed by the two warring alliances in the center of Europe, and the crazy-quilt patterns of treaties and security alliances and alignments they stitched together, however haphazardly and incoherently, testify to the self-destructive logic of pure war, whether viewed from a state (Clausewitz), societal (Thucydides), or individual (Hobbes) perspective. Conversely, as optimistic realists and liberal institutionalists were able to provisionally show, even seemingly implacable foes – capable of eliminating each other in a single nuclear blow or mindless spasm – could cooperate to control their competition to prevent unintended and unwanted war and to end such a conflict, if it were to erupt, to prevent their mutual annihilation. Calculations of cost, benefit, and risk and, most critically, political and moral aims check the slide inherent in social exchanges – marked by the real or imminent threat of coercion by interdependent actors to get their way – to move to a Hobbesian endgame of war of all against all.

While these perspectives do well to explain why states use or are constrained in appealing to force, they offer inadequate and incomplete understanding about how actors can – and have – relaxed or surmounted their security threats and the dilemmas of choice they raise. Why does no one expect Germany to attack France today? Before September 1, 1939, the date of Germany's invasion of Poland and the start of World War II, everyone expected an attack at some time – and soon. An expectation of voluntary cooperation or appeals to international law, norms, institutions, or non-aggression pacts to resolve these conflicts did not serve decision-makers confronting the imminent prospect of war by a determined, expansionist foe, much as E. H. Carr warned in his depiction of the crisis posed by Nazi Germany.[5] How and why did political and moral aims and interests change so fundamentally between France and Germany, deemed irreconcilable and enduring rivals before World War II, that peace now seems natural and assured between them? What can be learned from this transformation that may apply to other enduring rivalries in the Middle East, Africa, or Asia? What prevents Europe, the Balkans excluded, from slipping back to the habits learned over four centuries of civil war – to competitive threats, incipient war, and armed hostilities in resolving security issues?

The conceptual framework offered by liberal neoclassical thought of an inescapable welfare imperative, quite apart from conflicts over other actor preferences, provides more purchase for an explanation of the end (if not the evolution) of the Cold War than the theorists of chapter 4 or those offered by Marxist or, currently, by power transition theorists. Economic liberal theory rests on the premise that consensual agreements between and among rational egoist actors advance, efficiently and effectively, their strivings to meet their subsistence needs and, more generally, to maximize their material wealth and welfare. The notion of a pure market rests on such voluntary arrangements between otherwise selfish actors. Following

[5] Carr (1946).

the thinking of Adam Smith and his partisans about how to increase the wealth of nations, world markets – as a social system – purportedly generate incentives for consensual cooperation among participating actors. As Joseph Schumpeter (one of the more prominent neoclassical economists of the first half of the twentieth century) argued, ceaseless scientific discoveries and technological innovations, engines of economic prosperity, are viewed as no less dependent on the free flow of ideas and voluntary cooperation between often rival states and diverse peoples across national borders.

Contrary to Marxist-Leninist expectations, the Western, liberal market states outpaced the Soviet command system in producing and distributing wealth and welfare to its citizens. Their best practices were gradually adopted by an increasing number of developing states, Communist China, and, finally, the Soviet Union. Economic liberals can mount a formidable case to show that the end of the Cold War and the seismic shifts in global power that it engendered can be more persuasively explained by the decision of Kremlin leaders to adapt the Soviet economic system to the West's model rather than to continue to pursue a countervailing security strategy that balanced against the West's military might. Market forces under the West's hegemonic control ultimately proved more compelling than its military capabilities in moving the Soviet Union to the Western position and finally to its undoing as a state.

Behavioral approaches and constructivism also provide mixed results. The methodological constraints of current behavioral and rationalist research designs discourage the posing of what is admittedly a broad but still central question for international relations theory and security studies, viz., how and why did the Cold War come to pass and then just pass away overnight? However seemingly relevant this question may be or however significant the impact of the Cold War on billions of people, rigorous scientific protocols and prevailing research methods are neither equipped nor designed to address such problems of vital importance to populations everywhere. For some, the Cold War is just "a mere data point" that could not be used to test or develop theory.[6] That may well be true by methodological stipulation, given the current status of much of behavioral research programs, whether in a structural or strategic mode. Human thought and values, not to mention security interests, do not agreeably lend themselves to be so readily dispatched or defined away by methodological legerdemain.

---

[6] See the quoted observation of a prominent international relations theorist at a symposium on the Cold War in Lebow (1995: ix).

Pending the expansion and perfection of behavioral research programs to address critical security problems that are not reducible to behavioral methods and rules of evidence, it does not seem particularly prudent to dismiss insights about security behavior and practices (anecdotes to behaviorists) – say the triumph of the subjective force of nationalism over the Soviet empire[7]– simply because those insights do not work "in theory." Excluding or minimizing the impact of this and other ideologically and emotively driven forces in the security behavior of peoples and states because we presently lack the methodological tools to measure their causal effects bans them from serious and sober observation. Why neglect or reject the investigation of these forces simply because they cannot be reached by the exclusionary rules of a particular research program? Conversely, just because a research finding, such as the depiction of Africa as a zone of peace, works "in theory," as one finding of PT theory contends, that is no reason to ignore raging conflicts obvious to causal observations that have resulted in millions of deaths just because they await confirmation by the development of conceptual and methodological tools that can explain these dismal facts on scientific grounds. The security analyst should be able to acknowledge what everyday experience readily reveals. The victims of Rwandan and Sudanese genocides and ethnic cleansing in the Balkans pose real, clear, and present dangers for international security that oblige students of security to reach these issues even at the risk of violating or ignoring strict scientific protocols.

Rational or behavioral research necessarily reduces complex processes of human interactions across different and convergent domains of human concern to discrete and putatively replicable data points or observations and relates them to like events drawn from other times and historical circumstances. To view the Cold War as a "data point" makes statistical (if scarcely substantive political and moral) sense, when viewed through the constraining prism of the methodological constraints imposed by behavioral research on the questions it poses and pursues. The scientifically motivated aim is to generalize across these observation points. In this form a data set is created that can be submitted to mathematical and statistical manipulation and validation by widely used, standard techniques and measures. Held constant and in abeyance are the specific socio-economic, political, and moral contexts from which these data points are drawn and the complex processes of actor thought, decisions, and exchanges from which observations are extracted and isolated. The deconstruction of actor behavior, whatever gains in explanatory power may be achieved, inevitably falsifies the wide and deep processes of action

---

[7] Carrère d'Encausse (1993) and Kaiser (1994).

and reaction of multiple international actors coping with violence or coercive threats in their daily pursuit of their preferred vision or model of a global or regional political and moral order that satisfies their interests, aims, and values.

To be fair, let's acknowledge that a behavioral approach can – and does – yield intriguing and valuable insights. PT theory advances a plausible line of analysis to explain why the Cold War never became hot. Western military power and preponderant techno-economic resources proved too formidable to rational Soviet decision-makers to contest by all-out war. This non-trivial concession to PT theory as a research project still begs many questions, like why did the Soviet Union implode and what will be the global repercussions of this seismic event? Narrowly focused proposition-testing exercises, like PT, laudable for their rigor, parsimony, and putative replication and testing properties, are self-constrained from posing such urgent, timely, and relevant questions. Nor are they positioned to explain why the United States – the central power in what is a unipolar system for the first time in the history of the nation-state system – insists on its right to unilaterally declare war on weaker, smaller states, to democratize these states in its own regime image, and to transform the deeply embedded religious and cultural values of their populations, who are dead set against the imposition on them of Western notions of rule dictated by overweening military force. Answers to these and other global impact questions are left to journalistic and media speculation in the absence of a fundamental reformulation of security studies itself.

Constructivists potentially have something worthwhile to say about why the Cold War ended and why an American hegemon expands its sway to make over the identities and interests of other regimes and their peoples. One influential volume of "light" constructivist thought concludes that "the historical evidence compels us to relinquish the notion of states with unproblematic identities. The identities of states emerge from their interactions with different social environments, both domestic and international."[8] In this light, constructivists have something to add to explain the implosion of the Soviet Union into its component republics and then, in turn, their falling out into interstate conflicts (Armenia and Azerbaijan). They might also attempt to explain the civil wars and chronic social strife plaguing the former republics of the Soviet Union, as hitherto suppressed national, ethnic, and religious minorities re-emerged in the Russian Federation, Georgia, and throughout the central Asian republics to insist on their autonomy or independence. Constructivists have yet to

---

[8] Katzenstein (1996: 25–6). See especially Katzenstein's informed commentary in chapters 1: 1–32 and 13: 498–537.

exploit their critique of the state as a problem to be explained or to fully contest the notion of the state as a static Hobbesian or Weberian entity insulated from change or undiluted or uninflected by its social composition. The constructivist insight that challenges the distinction between domestic and international politics is a good start, but only the first step along a long road to a fully developed theory of international politics.

As for the United States, its security interests are apparently not narrowly defined by the real or potential military capabilities of actual or imagined enemies, as realists contend. They are equally cast in the subjective but no less compelling terms of reforming adversaries and even allies to adopt widely held American interests and values. For constructivists these values and their global political and social expression *are* the interests of the United States. This state-centric analysis scarcely scratches the surface of divining what it means to be an American or the core values of American civic culture that oblige those fixed on this ideological loadstar to impress these values on unwilling and recalcitrant peoples around the globe.

An evident drawback in the constructivist project, as it is currently formulated, is the marked tendency of its adherents to assume that problematizing the state or any actor or social movement (say nationalism) which possesses power will necessarily lead to greater cooperation and peace in social exchanges between reconstructed actors. Once the power-seeking proclivities of actors, especially state policy-makers, and their propensity to use force are exposed by constructivist instruction, they presumably will be more disposed to cooperate with rivals and check their previous inclination to coerce others to get their way. Stripped of their claims to legitimacy and the power it conveys, their impotence would supposedly make them more prone to compromise and responsive to popular rule.

The post-Cold War experience suggests that the trend line is not inevitably from Hobbes to Locke to Kant, either regionally or globally. The reverse is just as probable, and arguably more so, both as a matter of empirical observation and as a provisionally plausible conclusion to be drawn from the theories of security examined in this volume, however partial and flawed they may presently be. If all social behavior is reduced to power, then power corrupts and absolute power corrupts absolutely, as Lord Acton presciently observed long before the rise of constructivism as an approach to understand actor behavior. Some constructivists concede these points. They urge their partisans to confront both ends of the security spectrum from Hobbes to Kant; that is, how identities and interests impact on the decision of actors to use coercion or to opt for cooperation and consent in exchanges with others. Such a concerted move would place constructivism squarely within the scope of security studies favored by this volume: as the study of that set of interdependent human exchanges that raises incentives to use or not use force to ensure preferred outcomes from these transactions.[9]

The spiral of violence in Africa, Asia, the Middle East, and the Balkans in the post-Cold War era suggests that Alexander Wendt does have a point when he argues, "Anarchy Is What States Make Out of It."[10] His optimism that the global system has moved to a Lockean mode and is at the cusp of going Kantian would appear to be premature.[11] His vision of the likelihood of world government is simply out of joint at this juncture in the evolution of the international system.[12] As regional conflicts evidence, actors appear quite prepared to opt for Hobbesian anarchy – even chaos – and make a hash of it.

If identities and interests can assume a dark as easily as a light side, then constructivism may also have something to add to our understanding of the post-Cold War behavior of ethnic groups and that of the United States. The stress that constructivists put on culture as a fundamental source of actor behavior cuts two ways: toward cooperation if harmony can be constructed by mutual consent from disparate and contesting identities or toward enhanced reliance on force to compel the submission of rivals. If anarchy is what states – and peoples – "make of it," then it is no less true to assert that culture is what actors make of it, whether conceived as the inherited and powerfully socialized values of the mindsets of individuals and groups or as infinitely manipulable conceptual mediums by which to define actor identities and their interests.

A slate on which are deeply chiseled the intertwined and profoundly clashing values of the world's peoples is not swept clean simply, and never solely, by rhetorical flourishes or "speech acts." The slate's composition is also a product of actor decisions and constructions. It cannot become a *tabula rasa* by the fiat of the security theorist, however well meaning. The "shadow of the past" hangs heavy over the "shadow of the future" and what it might become; it can undo rapidly and unexpectedly any progress that may have been made in resolving security conflicts peacefully and non-violently. Witness at this time of writing the complexities of the peace process in the Middle East, the Hobbesian endgame in the Congo and Sudan, and the proliferation of weapons of mass destruction and the rise of terrorisms around the globe – all threats to regional and international security under the "shadow of the past."

---

[9] Checkel (1996, 1998a, b).
[10] Wendt (1992). For a recent example of this optimistic tendency in current constructivist thinking, see Frederking (2003).
[11] Wendt (1999) here foresees a Kantian endpoint of evolving state identity construction.
[12] Wendt (2003).

The affirmation of infinite human freedom and social malleability may well have explanatory purchase, if the assertion of Jean-Jacques Rousseau that humans are born free but are everywhere in chains is posited as socially true as a normative ideal capable of transforming social conditions to reflect human will and desire. It does not work in practice, however, when that supposed clean slate is examined seriously and systematically in all of its complexity today and when the heavy and resistant historical residue scoring this social slate is accurately noted and assessed. And in the particular case of the United States, the world's reigning hegemon, what explains its insistence not only on its right to eliminate threats to its security from weapons of mass destruction and terrorism but also its determination to modernize and reform the regimes of targeted states to suit its preferred image of legitimate rule? Constructivists are missing a beat in failing to address this seemingly deviant and aberrant behavior when compared to the expectations of realist, neorealist, and PT theorists. Ideology, arguably more than material power, is driving American hegemonic expansion.

Conversely, the structures of military and techno-economic power and the global systems these material power sources imply have, as classical realists, Marxists, and liberal economists persuasively argue, profoundly limited the range of choices available to humans in ensuring favorable outcomes in their interdependent exchanges with other actors. These material conditions frame the question of free choice and define the options of whether force will or will not work and whether non-violent means are likely to work better for actors in getting their way.

Where should security studies be heading?

So where do we go from here? This volume contends that the very shortcomings of the contending paradigms and approaches to security studies invite greater efforts to improve what we know about security. Progress in security studies, theoretical and practical, depends on knowing what problems remain if gaps are to be closed or if contradictions are to be reconciled in research findings. This extended critique of security schools of thought is dedicated to this ground-clearing imperative. This volume also argues against closure in unconditionally affirming or rejecting one or the other of the schools of security as a degenerate research program in the Lakatosian sense outlined in chapter 1. If the strengths and weaknesses of these contenders for hegemony are listed on a balance sheet, three priority research initiatives are suggested to perfect each on its own terms and, more importantly, to draw currently rival partisans into a constructive dialogue to cooperatively address the mounting security challenges of this century.

These priorities can be succinctly stated: (1) each school of thought should seek to perfect *its* model of security to explain the actors and factors bearing on international and global security within the scope of its limited explanatory power; (2) going beyond these self-imposed strictures, security analysts should work together to determine how and why actors move either from using more *or* less violence or coercion to get their way, that is, to identify the conditions, incentives, and causes that move actors along the Hobbesian, Lockean, Kantian continuum from coercion to consent or back again; and (3) rival schools should attempt to integrate the best of prevailing thought and practices to produce better models of security than presently exist to respond to the security needs of the world's diverse and divided peoples.

Movement along this latter line would require abandonment of the struggle for disciplinary hegemony and the collective adoption by the partisans of this volume's paradigms and approaches of a surmounting strategy to explain and resolve the challenges to security confronting the actors who are the objects of security studies. It is too often forgotten or slighted by those in the heat of disciplinary battles that the survival of their paradigms and approaches is, ultimately, not the principal aim of their competitive pursuits. These schools of thought are obliged to explain the actors and factors driving security in international relations. Defense of these paradigms and approaches is secondary to this imperative.

This volume contends that prevailing security schools must engage with each other, if they are to keep pace with the actors they are studying; if they are to adequately explain the decisions of international actors who choose or eschew appeals to violence and threats to get their way; if they are to provide relevant advice to solve security issues, locally and globally; and if they are to enlarge our understanding of the full human dimensions of security on a par with our classical triumvirate. What was for them local challenges is now a global imperative of ending humanity's civil wars, which commenced with the ascendancy of the species on this planet.

There is obviously a lot of work to be done to improve our knowledge about security and how to use this knowledge to construct social rules, norms, principles, institutions and organizations that provisionally relax, if not resolve, the security dilemmas that lie deep within the human condition, and that are now magnified in number and complexity – and in real time – by the emergence of a world society for the first time in the evolution of the species armed with the knowledge and means for the first time, too, to destroy itself.

References

Acheson, Dean. 1969. *Present at the Creation*. New York: Norton.

Adler, Emmanuel. 1997. "Seizing the Middle Ground: Constructivism in World Politics." *European Journal of International Relations* 3: 319–63.

—.2002. "Constructivism and International Relations." Pp. 95–118 in *Handbook of International Relations*, edited by Walter Carlsnaes, Thomas Risse, and Beth E. Simmons. London: Sage.

Adler, Emmanuel and Michael Barnett. 1998. *Security Communities*. Cambridge, UK: Cambridge University Press.

Albertini, Luigi. 1952. *The Origins of the War of 1914*. Westport: Greenwood Press.

Alchian, Armen A. and William R. Allen. 1969. *Exchange and Production Theory in Use*. Belmont: Wadsworth.

Alker, Hayward R. 2002. "On Learning from Wendt." *Review of International Studies* 26: 141–50.

Allison, Graham and Andrew Zelikow. 1999. *Essence of Decision*. Boston: Longman.

Anderson, O. 1967. *A Liberal State at War, English Politics and Economics during the Crimean War*. New York: St. Martin's Press.

Angell, Norman. 1909. *The Great Illusion*. London: Heinemann.

Aristotle. 1947. *Introduction to Aristotle*. New York: Random House Modern Library.

Ashley, Richard K. 1986. "The Poverty of Neorealism." Pp. 255–300 in *Neorealism and Its Critics*, edited by Robert O. Keohane. New York: Columbia University Press.

Aslund, Anders. 1991. *Gorbachev's Struggle for Economic Reform*. Ithaca: Cornell University Press.

—.1995. *How Russia Became a Market Economy*. Washington, DC: Brookings Institution.

Auguste, Byron G. 1998. "What's So New about Globalization?" *New Perspectives Quarterly* 15, 1: 16–20.

Axelrod, Robert. 1984. *The Evolution of Cooperation*. New York: Basic Books.

—.1986. "An Evolutionary Approach to Norms." *American Political Science Review* 80: 1,095–110.

Axelrod, Robert and Robert O. Keohane. 1993. "Achieving Cooperation under Anarchy: Strategies and Institutions." Pp. 85–115 in *Neorealism and Neoliberalism*, edited by David A. Baldwin. New York: Columbia University Press.

Baldwin, David A. (ed.). 1993. *Neorealism and Neoliberalism: The Contemporary Debate*. New York: Columbia University Press.

—.1995. "Security Studies and the End of the Cold War." *World Politics* 48: 117–41.

—.1997. "The Concept of Security." *Review of International Studies* 23: 5–26.

Ball, Desmond. 1980. *Politics and Force Levels*. Berkeley: University of California Press.

Baran, Paul. 1958. "On the Political Economy of Backwardness." Pp. 75–92 in *The Economics of Underdevelopment*, edited by A. N. Agarwala and S. P. Singh. New York: Oxford University Press.

Barber, Benjamin R. 1995. *Jihad vs. McWorld*. New York: Ballantine.

Baylis, John *et al.* (eds.). 2002. *Strategy in the Contemporary World*. Oxford: Oxford University Press.

Becker, Gary S. 1981. *A Treatise on the Family*. Cambridge, MA: Harvard University Press.

Becker, Gary S. and George Stigler. 1977. "De Gustibus Non Est Disputandum." *American Economic Review* 67: 76–90.

Bendix, Reinhard. 1964a. *Nation-Building and Citizenship*. Berkeley: University of California Press.

—.1964b. *State and Society*. Boston: Little, Brown.

—.1978. *Kings or People: Power and the Mandate to Rule*. Berkeley: University of California Press.

Berger, Peter L. and Thomas Luckmann. 1966. *The Social Construction of Reality*. New York: Anchor.

Bergesen, A. J. and M. Bata. 2002. "Global and National Inequality: Are They Connected?" *Journal of World-Systems Research* 8: 130–44.

Berliner, Joseph S. 1988. *Soviet Industry*. Ithaca: Cornell University Press.

Betts, Richard K. (ed.). 2005. *Conflict after the Cold War: Arguments on Causes of War and Peace*. New York: Pearson/Longman.

Bhagwati, Jagdish. 2001. *The Wind of the Hundred Days: How Washington Mismanaged Globalization*. Cambridge, MA: MIT Press.

Blainey, Geoffrey. 1976. *Triumph of the Nomads: A History of Aboriginal Australia*. Woodstock: Overlook Press.

—.1988. *The Causes of War*. London: Macmillan.

Boulding, Kenneth. 1962. *Conflict and Defense*. New York: Harper and Brothers.

Bozeman, Adda. 1960. *Politics and Culture in International Politics*. Princeton: Princeton University Press.

—.1984. "The International Order in a Multicultural World." Pp. 387–406 in *The Expansion of International Society*, edited by Hedley Bull and Adam Watson. New York: Oxford University Press.

Brams, Steven J. and D. Marc Kilgour. 1988. *Game Theory and National Security*. New York: Basil Blackwell.

Braudel, Fernand. 1980. "History and the Social Sciences: The Longue Durée." Pp. 25–54 in *On History*. Chicago: University of Chicago Press.

Breecher, Michael and Frank P. Harvey (eds.). 2002. *Millennial Reflections on International Studies*. Ann Arbor: University of Michigan Press.

Brewer, Anthony. 1990. *Marxist Theories of Imperialism*. London: Routledge.

Bridge, F. R. 2003. "Transformation of the European States System, 1856–1915." Pp. 255–72 in *The Transformation of European Politics, 1763–1848: Episode or Model in Modern History?*, edited by Peter Krüger and Paul W. Schröder. Hamburg: LIT.

Bridge, F. R. and Roger Bullen. 1980. *The Great Powers and the European States System: 1815–1915*. New York: Longman.

Brodie, Bernard (eds.). 1946. *The Absolute Weapon: Atomic Power and World Order*. New York: Harcourt, Brace.

—.1973. *War and Politics*. New York: Macmillan.

Brooks, Stephen G. 1997. "Dueling Realisms." *International Organization* 51: 445–7.

Brooks, Stephen G. and William C. Wohlforth. 2000/2001. "Power, Globalization, and the End of the Cold War." *International Security* 25: 5–53.

Brown, Archie. 1996. *The Gorbachev Factor*. Oxford: Oxford University Press.

Brown, Michael *et al.* (eds.). 1995. *Debating the Democratic Peace*. Cambridge, MA: MIT Press.

Brzezinski, Zbigniew. 1993. *Out of Control: Global Turmoil on the Eve of the Twenty-First Century*. New York: Scribner's.

—.2004. *The Choice: Global Domination or Global Leadership*. New York: Basic Books.

Buchanan, Allen. 1985. *Ethics, Efficiency, and the Market*. Totowa: Rowman and Allanheld.

Buchanan, James M. 1959. "Positive Economics, Welfare Economics, and Political Economy." *Journal of Law and Economics* 2: 124–38.

—.1988. *The Political Economy of the Welfare State*. Stockholm: The Industrial Institute for Economic and Social Research.

Buchanan, James M. and Gordon Tullock. 1965. *The Calculus of Consent*. Ann Arbor: University of Michigan Press.

Bueno de Mesquita, Bruce. 1981. *The War Trap*. New Haven: Yale University Press.

—.1990. "Pride of Place: The Origins of German Hegemony." *World Politics* 43: 22–52.

Bueno de Mesquita, Bruce, and David Lalman. 1992. *War and Reason: Domestic and International Imperatives*. New Haven: Yale University Press.

Bukovansky, Mlada. 1997. "American Identity and Neutral Rights from Independence to the War of 1812." *International Organization* 51: 207–43.

Bull, Hedley. 1969. "International Theory: The Case for a Classical Approach." Pp. 20–38 in *Contending Approaches to International Politics*, edited by Klaus Knorr and James N. Rosenau. Princeton: Princeton University Press.

—.1977. *The Anarchical Society: A Study of Order in World Politics*. London: Macmillan.

Buzan, Barry. 1991. *People, States and Fear: An Agenda for International Security Studies in the Post-Cold War Era*. Boulder: Lynne Rienner Publishers.

—.2004. *From International to World Society?: English School Theory and the Social Structure of Globalisation*. Cambridge: Cambridge University Press.

Buzan, Barry and Richard Little. 1994. "The Idea of International System: Theory Meets History." *International Political Science Review* 15: 231–55.

Buzan, Barry, Richard Little, and Charles Jones. 1993. *The Logic of Anarchy: Neorealism and Structural Realism*. New York: Columbia University Press.

Buzan, Barry, Ole Waever, and Jaap de Wilde. 1998. *Security: A New Framework of Analysis*. Boulder: Lynne Rienner.

Cain, Peter J. 1978. "J. A. Hobson, Cobdenism and the Development of the Theory of Economic Imperialism." *Economic History Review* 31: 565–84.

—. 1979. "Capitalism, War and Internationalism in the Thought of Richard Cobden." *British Journal of International Studies* 5: 229–47.

Callari, Antonio *et al.* (eds.). 1995. *Marxism in the Postmodern Age: Confronting the New World Order*. New York: Guilford Press.

Campbell, David. 1992. *Writing Security: United States Foreign Policy and the Politics of Identity*. Minneapolis: University of Minnesota Press.

—. 2001. "International Engagements: The Politics of North American International Relations Theory." *Political Theory* 29: 432–48.

Carlsnaes, Walter. 1992. "The Agency–Structure Problem in Foreign Policy Analysis." *International Studies Quarterly* 36: 245–70.

Carlsnaes, Walter, Thomas Risse, and Beth E. Simmons (eds.). 2002. *Handbook of International Relations*. London: Sage.

Carr, E. H. 1946. *The Twenty Years' Crisis, 1919–1939*. New York: Harper & Row.

Carrère d'Encausse, Hélène. 1993. *The End of the Soviet Empire: The Triumph of the Nations*. New York: Basic Books.

Chafetz, Glenn R. 1993. *Gorbachev, Reform, and the Brezhnev Doctrine: Soviet Policy toward Eastern Europe: 1985–1990*. Westport: Praeger.

Checkel, Jeffrey T. 1996. *Ideas and International Change: Soviet/Russian Behavior and the End of the Cold War*. New Haven: Yale University Press.

—. 1998a. "The Constructivist Turn in International Relations Theory." *World Politics* 50: 324–48.

—. 1998b. "International Norms and Domestic Politics: Bridging the Rationalist–Constructivist Divide." *European Journal of International Relations* 3: 473–95.

Christensen, Thomas J. and Jack L. Snyder. 1990. "Chain Gangs and Passed Bucks: Predicting Alliance Patterns in Multipolarity." *International Organization* 44: 137–68.

Chua, Amy. 2003. *World on Fire: How Exporting Free Market Democracy Breeds Ethnic Hatred and Global Instability*. New York: Doubleday.

Clausewitz, Carl von. 1976. *On War*. Princeton: Princeton University Press.

Coase, Ronald H. 1937. "The Nature of the Firm." *Economica* 4: 386–405.

—. 1960. "The Problem of Social Cost." *Journal of Law and Economics* 3: 1–44.

Cobden, Richard. 1878. *The Political Writings of Richard Cobden*. London: W. Ridgway.

Cohen, G. A. 2000. *Karl Marx's Theory of History*. Oxford: Oxford University Press.

Collingwood, Richard G. 1939. *An Autobiography*. Oxford: Oxford University Press.

—. 1946. *The Idea of History*. New York: Oxford University Press.

Conquest, Robert (ed.). 1986. *The Last Empire: Nationality and the Soviet Future*. Stanford: Hoover Institute Press.

Conrad, Joseph (ed.). 1962. *Conrad's Secret Sharer and the Critics*. Belmont: Wadsworth.

Cooper, Richard. 1968. *The Economics of Interdependence: Economic Policy in the Atlantic Community*. New York: McGraw-Hill.

Copeland, Dale C. 2000. "Trade Expectations and the Outbreak of Peace: Detente 1970–74 and the End of the Cold War 1985–91." *Security Studies* 9: 15–58.

Corwin, Edward S. 1916. *French Policy and the American Alliance of 1778*. Princeton: Princeton University Press.

Craig, Paul P. and John A. Jungerman. 1986. *Nuclear Arms Race: Technology and Society*. New York: McGraw-Hill.

Croft, Stuart and Terry Terriff (eds.). 2000. *Critical Reflections on Security and Change*. London: Frank Cass.

Daalder, Ivo H. 1991. *The Nature and Practice of Flexible Response: NATO Strategy and Theater Nuclear Forces Since 1967*. New York: Columbia University Press.

Dahl, Robert. 1957. "The Concept of Power." *Behavioral Scientist* 2: 201–15.

Dallin, Alexander. 1992. "Causes of the Collapse of the USSR." *Post-Soviet Affairs* 8, 4: 279–302.

DePorte, Anton W. 1986. *Europe between the Superpowers: The Enduring Balance*. New Haven: Yale University Press.

Dessler, David. 1989. "What's at Stake in the Agent–Structure Debate?" *International Organization* 43: 441–73.

Deudney, Daniel, and G. John Ikenberry. 1991–2. "The International Sources of Soviet Change." *International Security* 16: 74–118.

—.1992. "Who Won the Cold War?" *Foreign Policy* 87: 123–38.

Deutsch, Karl W. 1957. *Political Community and the North Atlantic Area*. Princeton: Princeton University Press.

Deutsch, Karl W. and J. David Singer. 1964. "Multipolar Power Systems and International Stability." *World Politics* 16: 390–406.

Diamond, Jared. 1992. *The Third Chimpanzee: The Evolution and Future of the Human Animal*. New York: HarperPerennial.

—.1997. *Guns, Germs, and Steel: The Fates of Human Societies*. New York: W. W. Norton.

DiCicco, Jonathan M. and Jack S. Levy. 1999. "Power Shifts and Problem Shifts: The Evolution of the Power Transition Research Program." *Journal of Conflict Resolution* 43: 675–704.

Doty, Roxanne Lynn. 2000. "Desire All the Way Down." *Review of International Studies* 26: 137–39.

Doyle, Michael W. 1983. "Kant, Liberal Legacies, and Foreign Affairs." *Philosophy & Public Affairs* 12: 205–35.

—.1986. "Liberalism and World Politics." *American Political Science Review* 80: 1,151–69.

Dunlop, John B. 1993. *The Rise of Russia and the Fall of the Soviet Empire*. Princeton: Princeton University Press.

Durkheim, Emile. 1984. *The Division of Labor in Society*. New York: Free Press.

—.1993. *Ethics and the Sociology of Morals*. Buffalo: Prometheus Books.

Edelheit, Abraham J., and Hershel Edelheit (eds.). 1992. *The Rise and Fall of the Soviet Union: A Selected Bibliography of Sources in English*. Westport: Greenwood Press.

Elliott, John E. (ed.). 1981. *Marx and Engels on Economics, Politics, and Society*. Santa Monica: Goodyear.

Elman, Colin and Miriam Fendius Elman. 1997. "Diplomatic History and International Relations Theory: Respecting Differences and Crossing Boundaries." *International Security* 22: 5–21.

Elster, Jon. 1979. *Ulysses and the Sirens. Studies in the Limitations of Rationality.* Cambridge, UK: Cambridge University Press.

—.1983. *Sour Grapes: Studies in the Subversion of Rationality.* Cambridge, UK: Cambridge University Press.

—.1985. *Making Sense of Marx.* Cambridge, UK: Cambridge University Press.

—.1986a. *An Introduction to Marx.* Cambridge, UK: Cambridge University Press.

—.1986b. "The Market and the Forum." Pp. 103–33 in *Foundations of Social Choice Theory*, edited by Jon Elster and Aanund Hylland. New York: Cambridge University Press.

—.1989. *Solomonic Judgments: Studies in the Limitations of Rationality.* Cambridge, UK: Cambridge University Press.

Elster, Jon and Karl Ove Moene. 1989. "Introduction." Pp. 1–35 in *Alternatives to Capitalism.* Cambridge, UK: Cambridge University Press.

Enthoven, Alain and K. Wayne Smith. 1971. *How Much Is Enough? Shaping the Defense Program, 1961–1969.* New York: Harper & Row.

Ericson, Richard E. 1987. "The Soviet Economic Predicament." Pp. 95–120 in *The Future of the Soviet Empire*, edited by Henry S. Rowen and Charles Wolf. New York: St Martin's Press.

Evans, Peter B., Dietrich Rueschemeyer, and Theda Skocpol (eds.). 1985. *Bringing the State Back In.* Cambridge, UK: Cambridge University Press.

Eyck, Erich. 1968. *Bismarck and the German Empire.* New York: W. W. Norton.

Fearon, James and Alexander Wendt. 2002. "Rationalism v. Constructivism: A Skeptical View." Pp. 52–72 in *Handbook of International Relations*, edited by Walter Carlsnaes, Thomas Risse, and Beth E. Simmons. London: Sage.

Feaver, Peter D. *et al.* 2000. "Brother, Can You Spare a Paradigm? (Or Was Anybody Ever a Realist)." *International Security* 25: 5–55.

Federalist. n. d. *The Federalist (Modern Library Edition).* New York: Random House.

Felice, William F. 2003. *The Global New Deal: Economic and Social Human Rights in World Politics.* Lanham: Rowman & Littlefield.

Fieldhouse, D. K. 1973. *Economics and Empire: 1830–1914.* Ithaca: Cornell University Press.

—.1981. *Colonialism: 1870–1945.* London: Weidenfeld and Nicolson.

Fierke, Karin M. 1998. *Changing Games, Changing Strategies: Critical Investigations in Security.* Manchester: Manchester University Press.

Fierke, Karin M. and Knud Erik Jorgensen (eds.). 2001. *Constructing International Relations: The Next Generation.* London: M. E. Sharpe.

Finnemore, Martha. 1996. *National Interests and International Society.* Ithaca: Cornell University Press.

Firebaugh, G. 1999. "Empirics of World Income Inequality." *American Journal of Sociology* 104: 1,597–630.

Firth, Noel E. and James H. Noren. 1998. *Soviet Defense Spending: A History of CIA Estimates, 1950–1990.* College Station: Texas A&M University Press.

Fitzgerald, Frances. 1972. *Fire in the Lake: The Vietnamese and the Americans in Vietnam.* Boston: Little, Brown.

—.2000. *Way Out There in the Blue.* New York: Simon & Schuster.

Fliess, Peter J. 1966. *Thucydides and the Politics of Bipolarity.* Baton Rouge: Louisiana State University Press.

Flournoy, F. R. 1945. "British Liberal Theories of International Relations (1848–1998)." *Journal of the History of Ideas* 7: 195–217.

Fogel, Robert. 1989. *Without Consent or Contract.* New York: W. W. Norton.

Forde, Steven. 1995. "International Realism and the Science of Politics: Thucydides, Machiavelli, and Neorealism." *International Studies Quarterly* 39: 141–60.

Forum. 1997. "Forum on Realism." *American Political Science Review* 91: 899–935.

—.2000. "Forum on Social Theory of International Politics." *Review of International Studies* 26: 123–80.

Foucault, Michel. 1980. *Power/Knowledge.* New York: Pantheon.

—.1982. "The Subject and Power." *Critical Inquiry* 22: 381–404.

Frank, Andre Gunder. 1969. *Capitalism and Underdevelopment in Latin America.* New York: Monthly Review Press.

Frank, Robert H. 1988. *Passions within Reason.* New York: W. W. Norton.

Frederking, Brian. 1998. "Resolving Security Dilemmas: A Constructivist Explanation of the Cold War." *International Politics* 35: 207–32.

—.2003. "Constructing Post-Cold War Collective Security." *American Political Science Review* 97: 363–78.

Freedman, Lawrence. 1989. *The Evolution of Nuclear Strategy.* London: Macmillan.

Friedman, Jeffrey. 1996a. "Economic Approaches to Politics." Pp. 1–24 in *The Rational Choice Controversy: Economic Models of Politics Reconsidered,* edited by Jeffrey Friedman. New Haven: Yale University Press.

—. (ed.). 1996b. *The Rational Choice Controversy: Economic Models of Politics Reconsidered.* New Haven: Yale University Press.

Friedman, Milton. 1962. *Capitalism and Freedom.* Chicago: University of Chicago Press.

Friedman, Milton, and Rose Friedman. 1980. *Free to Choose.* New York: Harcourt Brace Jovanovich.

Friedman, Thomas. 2000. *Lexus and the Olive Tree.* New York: Farrar Straus, Giroux.

Fukuyama, Francis. 1992. *The End of History and the Last Man.* New York: Free Press.

Gaddis, John Lewis. 1982. *Strategies of Containment.* New York: Oxford University Press.

—.1989. "Hanging Tough Paid Off." *Bulletin of Atomic Scientists* 45: 11–14.

—.1991. "Great Illusions, the Long Peace, and the Future of the International System." Pp. 25–55 in *The Long Postwar Peace,* edited by Charles W. Kegley Jr. New York: Harper Collins.

—.1992–3. "International Relations Theory and the End of the Cold War." *International Security* 17: 5–58.

Gansler, Jacques. 1989. *Affording Defense.* Cambridge, MA: MIT Press.

Garst, Daniel. 1989. "Thucydides and Neorealism." *International Studies Quarterly* 33: 3–27.

Garthoff, Raymond L. 1966. *Soviet Military Policy.* New York: Praeger.

—.1990. *Deterrence and the Revolution in Soviet Military Doctrine.* Washington, DC: Brookings Institution.

—.1995. *Détente and Confrontation.* Washington, DC: Brookings Institution.

Geller, Daniel S. 1992. "Capability Concentration, Power Transition, and War." *International Interactions* 17: 269–84.

Geller, Daniel S. and J. David Singer. 1998. *Nations at War: A Scientific Study of International Conflict.* Cambridge: Cambridge University Press.

Gellner, Ernest. 1983. *Nations and Nationalism.* Ithaca: Cornell.

George, Alexander L. and Richard Smoke. 1974. *Deterrence in American Foreign Policy: Theory and Practice.* New York: Columbia University Press.

Giddens, Anthony. 1971. *Capitalism and Modern Social Theory.* New York: Cambridge University Press.

—.1981. *A Contemporary Critique of Historical Materialism.* Berkeley: University of California Press.

—.1984. *The Constitution of Society.* Berkeley: University of California Press.

—.1993. *New Rules of Sociological Method: A Positive Critique of Interpretative Sociologies.* Stanford: Stanford University Press.

Gill, Stephen. 1997. *Globalization, Democratization and Multilateralism.* New York: St Martin's Press.

Gilpin, Robert. 1981. *War and Change in World Politics.* Cambridge: Cambridge University Press.

—.1987. *The Political Economy of International Relations.* Princeton: Princeton University Press.

—.2000. *The Challenge of Global Capitalism.* Princeton: Princeton University Press.

—.2001. *Global Political Economy: Understanding the International Economic Order.* Princeton: Princeton University Press.

Gils, Barry K. (ed.). 2001. *Globalization and the Politics of Resistance.* New York: Palgrave.

Glaser, Charles L. 1996. "Realists as Optimists." Pp. 122–63 in *Realism: Restatements and Renewal,* edited by Benjamin Frankel. London: Frank Cass.

—.1997. "The Security Dilemma Revisited." *World Politics* 50: 171–201.

Gleditsch, Nils Petter. 1993. "The End of the Cold War: Evaluating Theories of International Relations." *Journal of Peace Research* 30: 357.

Goertz, Gary. 1994. *Contexts of International Politics.* New York: Cambridge University Press.

Goertz, Gary and Paul F. Diehl. 1993. "Enduring Rivalries: Theoretical Constructs and Empirical Patterns." *International Studies Quarterly* 37: 147–71.

Goldman, Marshall I. 1983. *U.S.S.R. in Crisis.* New York: W. W. Norton.

—.1991. *What Went Wrong with Perestroika.* New York: W. W. Norton.

Goldstein, Judith and Robert O. Keohane (eds.). 1993. *Ideas and Foreign Policy: Beliefs, Institutions and Political Change.* Ithaca: Cornell University Press.

Gorbachev, Mikhail. 1987. *Perestroika: New Thinking for Our Country and the World.* New York: Harper & Row.

Gorenburg, Dmitry P. 2003. *Minority Ethnic Mobilization in the Russian Federation.* New York: Cambridge University Press.

Graebner, Norman A. (ed.). 1964. *Ideas and Diplomacy.* New York: Oxford University Press.

Grampp, W. D. 1960. *The Manchester School of Economics.* Stanford: Stanford University Press.

Gramsci, Antonio. 1971. *Selections from the Prison Notebooks of Antonio Gramsci.* London: Lawrence and Wishart.

Gray, Colin. 1984. "Nuclear Strategy: A Case for a Theory of Victory." Pp. 23–56 in *Strategy and Nuclear Deterrence,* edited by Steven E. Miller. Princeton: Princeton University Press.

—.1999. *Modern Strategy.* Oxford: Oxford University Press.

Green, Donald P. and Ian Shapiro. 1994. *Pathologies of Rational Choice Theory.* New Haven: Yale University Press.

Grieco, Joseph M. 1990. *Cooperation among Nations: Europe, America, and Non-Tariff Barriers to Trade.* Ithaca: Cornell University Press.

Gulick, Edward Vose. 1955. *Europe's Classical Balance of Power.* Ithaca: Cornell University Press.

Gurr, Ted Robert. 1993. *Minorities at Risk: A Global View of Ethnopolitical Conflicts.* Washington, DC: United States Institute of Peace Press.

Halberstam, David. 1972. *The Best and the Brightest.* New York: Random House.

Hall, Peter A. and Rosemary C. R. Taylor. 1996. "Political Science and the Three New Institutionalisms." *Political Studies* 44: 936–57.

Hall, Rodney Bruce. 1997. "Moral Authority as a Power Resource." *International Organization* 51: 591–622.

Hardt, Michael and Antonio Negri. 2000. *Empire.* Cambridge, MA: Harvard University Press.

—.2004. *War and Democracy in the Age of Empire.* New York: Penguin Press.

Harnetty, P. 1972. *Imperialism and Free Trade: Lancashire and India in the Mid-Nineteenth Century.* Vancouver: University of British Colombia Press.

Hartz, Louis. 1955. *The Liberal Tradition in America.* New York: Harcourt, Brace.

Harvey, David. 2001. *Spaces of Capital.* New York: Routledge.

—.2003. *The New Imperialism.* Oxford: Oxford University Press.

Hassner, Pierre. 1997. "Rousseau and the Theory and Practice of International Relations." Pp. 200–19 in *The Legacy of Rousseau,* edited by Clifford Orwin and Nathan Tarvoc. Chicago: University of Chicago Press.

Hayek, Friedrich von. 1944. *The Road to Serfdom.* Chicago: University of Chicago Press.

—.1948. *Individual Freedom and Economic Order.* Chicago: University of Chicago Press.

—.1960. *The Constitution of Liberty.* Chicago: The University of Chicago Press.

—.1988. *The Fatal Conceit: The Errors of Socialism.* London: Routledge.

Hayes, Carlton J. H. 1926. *Essays on Nationalism.* New York: Macmillan.

Herken, Gregg. 1985. *Counsels of War.* New York: Alfred A. Knopf.

Hewett, Edward A. 1988. *Reforming the Soviet Economy.* Washington, DC: Brookings Institution.

Hilton, A. J. B. 1988. *The Age of Atonement: The Influence of Evangelicalism on Social and Economic Thought, 1785–1865.* Oxford: Oxford University Press.

Hinsley, F. H. 1963. *Power and the Pursuit of Peace*. Cambridge, UK: Cambridge University Press.

Hirst, Paul and Grahame Thompson. 1999. *Globalization in Question*. Cambridge, UK: Polity.

Hitch, Charles Johnston. 1960. *The Economics of Defense in the Nuclear Age*. Cambridge, MA: Harvard University Press.

Hobbes, Thomas. 1997. *Leviathan*. New York: W. W. Norton.

Hobsbawm, Eric J. 1969. *Industry and Empire*. New York: Pantheon Books.

—.1975. *The Age of Capital, 1848–1875*. New York: Scribner.

Hobson, John A. 1902. *Imperialism*. London: Nisbet & Company.

—.1919. *Richard Cobden: The International Man*. London: H. Holt and Company.

Hochschild, Adam. 1999. *King Leopold's Ghost*. Boston: Houghton Mifflin.

Hogan, Michael J. (ed.). 1992. *The End of the Cold War: Its Meaning and Implications*. New York: Cambridge University Press.

Hollis, Margin. 1994. *The Philosophy of the Social Sciences*. Cambridge, UK: Cambridge University Press.

Holloway, David. 1984. *The Soviet Union and the Arms Race*. New Haven: Yale University Press.

Hopf, Ted. 1998. "The Promise of Constructivism in International Relations Theory." *International Security* 23: 171–200.

—.2002. *Social Construction of International Politics: Identities and Foreign Policies, Moscow, 1955 and 1999*. Ithaca: Cornell University Press.

Hough, Jerry F. 1997. *Democratization and Revolution in the USSR, 1985–1991*. Washington, DC: Brookings Institution.

Houweling, Henk W. and Jan G. Siccama. 1988. "Power Transitions as a Cause of War." *Journal of Conflict Resolution* 32: 87–102.

Howe, Anthony. 1997. *Free Trade and Liberal England: 1846–1946*. Oxford: Clarendon Press.

Huntington, Samuel P., Jr. 1957. *The Soldier and the State*. Cambridge, MA: Belknap.

—.1960. *The Common Defense*. New York: Columbia University Press.

—.1991. *The Third Wave: Democratization in the Late Twentieth Century*. Norman: Oklahoma University Press.

—.1996. *The Clash of Civilizations*. New York: Simon and Schuster.

Hurrell, Andrew and Ngaire Woods. 1995. "Globalization and Inequality." *Millennium* 24: 447–70.

Hutchinson, John and Anthony D. Smith (eds.). 1994. *Nationalism*. Oxford: Oxford University Press.

Ignatieff, Michael. 2001. *Human Rights as Politics and Idolatry*. Princeton: Princeton University Press.

Ikenberry, John G. and Charles A. Kupchan. 1990. "Socialization and Hegemonic Power." *International Organization* 44: 283–315.

Iliasu, A. A. 1971. "The Cobden–Chevalier Commercial Treaty of 1860." *Historical Journal* 14: 67–98.

International Institute for Strategic Studies. 1960–. "The Military Balance: 1960–Present." London.

—.2002. *The Military Balance: 2002–2003*. London: Oxford University Press.

Irwin, Douglas A. 1996. *Against the Tide: An Intellectual History of Free Trade*. Princeton: Princeton University Press.

Jackson, Robert H. 1993. "Continuity and Change in the States System." Pp. 346–67 in *States in a Changing World*, edited by Robert H. Jackson and Alan James. London: Pinter.

Jansen, Marius B. 2000. *The Making of Modern Japan*. Cambridge, MA: Harvard University Press.

Jepperson, Ronald L., Alexander Wendt, and Peter J. Katzenstein. 1996. "Norms, Identity, and Culture in National Security." Pp. 33–75 in *The Culture of National Security: Norms and Identity in World Politics*, edited by Peter J. Katzenstein. New York: Columbia University Press.

Jervis, Robert. 1976. *Perception and Misperception in World Politics*. Princeton: Princeton University Press.

—.1998. "Realism in the Study of World Politics." *International Organization* 52: 971–91.

Jervis, Robert, Richard Ned Lebow, and Janice Gross Stein (eds.). 1985. *Psychology and Deterrence*. Baltimore: Johns Hopkins University Press.

Joll, James. 1984. *The Origins of the First World War*. New York: Longman.

Jones, Anthony, Walter D. Connor, and David E. Powell (eds.). 1991. *Soviet Social Problems*. Boulder: Westview Press.

Jones, Eric Lionel. 1987. *The European Miracle: Environments, Economies, and Geopolitics in the History of Europe and Asia*. New York: Cambridge University Press.

—.1988. *Recurring Growth*. Oxford: Oxford University Press.

Jordan, H. D. 1971. "The Case of Richard Cobden." Pp. 34–45 in *Proceedings of the Massachusetts Historical Society*.

Kadera, Kelly. 1996. "The Conditions and Consequences of Dyadic Power Transitions: Deductions from a Dynamic Model." Pp. 287–312 in *Parity and War: Evaluations and Extensions of the War Ledger*, edited by Jacek Kugler and Douglas Lemke. Ann Arbor: University of Michigan Press.

Kagan, Donald. 2003. *The Peloponnesian War*. New York: Viking.

Kagan, Robert. 2002. *Of Paradise and Power: America and Europe in the New World Order*. New York: Knopf.

Kahn, Herman. 1960. *On Thermonuclear War*. Princeton: Princeton University Press.

Kaiser, Robert J. 1994. *The Geography of Nationalism in Russia and the USSR*. Princeton: Princeton University Press.

Kanet, Roger E. 1989. "Mikhail Gorbachev and the End of the Cold War." *Soviet Union* 16: 193–9.

Kanet, Roger E. and Edward A. Kolodziej (eds.). 1989. *The Limits of Soviet Power in the Developing World: Thermidor in the Revolutionary Struggle*. Baltimore: Johns Hopkins University Press.

Kant, Immanuel. 1970. "Perpetual Peace: A Philosophical Essay." Pp. 200–44 in *The Theory of International Relations*, edited by M. G. Forsyth *et al.* New York: Atherton.

—.1991. *Kant: Political Writings*. Cambridge, UK: Cambridge University Press.

Kaplan, Fred. 1983. *The Wizards of Armageddon*. New York: Simon and Schuster.

Kaplan, Lawrence S. 1999. *The Long Entanglement*. Westport: Praeger.

Kaplan, Robert D. 2000. *The Coming Anarchy: Shattering the Dreams of the Post Cold War*. New York: Random House.

Kapstein, Ethan B. 1995. "Is Realism Dead? The Domestic Sources of International Politics." *International Organization* 49: 751–74.

Katzenstein, Peter J. (ed.) 1996. *The Culture of National Security: Norms and Identity in World Politics*. New York: Columbia University Press.

Kaufman, William W. 1964. *The McNamara Strategy*. New York: Harper and Row.

Keegan, John. 1978. *The Face of Battle*. Harmondsworth: Penguin.

Kegley, Charles W., Jr. 1994. "How Did the Cold War Die: Principles for an Autopsy." *Mershon International Studies* 38: 11–42.

—.(ed.). 1995. *Controversies in International Relations Theory, Realism and the Neoliberal Challenge*. New York: St Martin's Press.

Kelleher, Catherine M. 1975. *Germany and the Politics of Nuclear Weapons*. New York: Columbia University Press.

Kennan, George F. ('X') 1947. "The Sources of Soviet Conduct." *Foreign Affairs* 25: 466–82.

—.1961. *Russia and the West under Lenin and Stalin*. Boston: Little, Brown.

—.1984a. *American Diplomacy: 1900–1950*. Chicago: University of Chicago Press.

—.1984b. *Soviet–American Relations, 1917–1920*. New York: W. W. Norton.

Kennedy, Paul M. (ed.). 1979. *The War Plans of the Great Powers, 1880–1914*. London: Allen & Unwin.

—.1987. *The Rise and Fall of the Great Powers: Economic Change and Military Conflict from 1500 to 2000*. New York: Random House.

Keohane, Robert O. 1984. *After Hegemony: Cooperation and Discord in the World Economy*. Princeton: Princeton University Press.

—.(ed.). 1986. *Neorealism and Its Critics*. New York: Columbia University Press.

—.1988. "International Institutions: Two Approaches." *International Studies Quarterly* 32: 379–96.

—.1993. "Institutional Theory and the Realist Challenge after the Cold War." Pp. 269–300 in *Neorealism and Neoliberalism: The Contemporary Debate*, edited by David A. Baldwin. New York: Columbia University Press.

—.2002. "Ideas Part-Way Down." *Review of International Studies* 26: 125–30.

Keohane, Robert O. and Lisa L. Martin. 1995. "The Promise of Institutionalist Theory." *International Security* 20: 39–51.

Keohane, Robert O. and Helen V. Milner (eds.). 1996. *Internationalization and Domestic Politics*. Cambridge, UK: Cambridge University Press.

Keohane, Robert O. and Joseph S. Nye. 1989. *Power and Interdependence*. Glenview: Scott, Foresman.

—.2001. *Power and Interdependence*. New York: Longman.

Keylor, William R. 2001. *The Twentieth-Century World: An International History*. New York: Oxford University Press.

—.2003. *A World of Nations: The International Order Since 1945*. New York: Oxford University Press.

Keynes, John Maynard. 1936. *General Theory of Employment, Money and Interest*. London: Macmillan.

Kim, Woosang. 1991. "Alliance Transitions and Great Power War." *American Journal of Political Science* 35: 833–50.

—.1996. "Power Parity, Alliance, and War from 1648 to 1975." Pp. 93–106 in *Parity and War: Evaluations and Extensions of the War Ledger*, edited by Jacek Kugler and Douglas Lemke. Ann Arbor: University of Michigan Press.

Kim, Woosang and James Morrow. 1992. "When Do Power Shifts Lead to War?" *American Journal of Political Science* 36: 896–922.

King, Gary, Robert O. Keohane, and Sidney Verba. 1994. *Designing Social Inquiry*. Princeton: Princeton University Press.

Kissinger, Henry. 1957. *A World Restored*. Boston: Houghton Mifflin.

Klotz, Audie. 1995. *Norms in International Relations: The Struggle against Apartheid*. Ithaca: Cornell University Press.

Knorr, Klaus and James N. Rosenau (eds.). 1969. *Contending Approaches to International Politics*. Princeton: Princeton University Press.

Koch, H. W. 1972. "Social Darwinism in the 'New Imperialism'." Pp. 329–54 in *The Origins of the First World War*, edited by H. W. Koch. New York: Taplinger.

Kochanek, Stanley A. 2003. "South Asia." Pp. 144–62 in *A Force Profonde: The Power, Politics, and Promise of Human Rights*, edited by Edward A. Kolodziej. Philadelphia: University of Pennsylvania Press.

Kohl, Wilfrid. 1971. *French Nuclear Diplomacy*. Baltimore: Johns Hopkins University Press.

Kokoshin, Andrei A. 1995. *Soviet Strategic Thought, 1917–91*. Cambridge, MA: MIT Press.

Kolko, Gabriel. 1988. *Confronting the Third World: United States Foreign Policy, 1945–80*. New York: Pantheon.

Kolodziej, Edward A. 1966. *The Uncommon Defense and Congress: 1945–1963*. Columbus: Ohio State University Press.

—.1974. *French International Policy under De Gaulle and Pompidou*. Ithaca: Cornell University Press.

—.1987. *Making and Marketing Arms: The French Experience and Its Implications for the International System*. Princeton: Princeton University Press.

—.1992a. "Renaissance in Security Studies? Caveat Lector." *International Studies Quarterly* 36: 421–38.

—.1992b. "What is Security and Security Studies?" *Arms Control* 13: 1–31.

—.1992c. "What is Security and Security Studies? A Rejoinder." *Arms Control* 13: 531–44.

—.1997. "Order, Welfare, and Legitimacy: A Systemic Explanation for the Soviet Collapse and the End of the Cold War." *International Politics* 1: 1–41.

—.2000a. "The Great Powers and Genocide: Lessons from Rwanda." *Pacific Review* 12: 121–45.

—.2000b. "Security Studies for the Next Millennium: Quo Vadis?" Pp. 18–38 in *Critical Reflections on Security and Change*, edited by Stuart Croft and Terry Terriff. London: Frank Cass.

—.2002a. "NATO and the Longue Durée." Pp. 1–20 in *Almost NATO: Partners and Players in Central and Eastern European Security*, edited by Charles Krupnick. Boston: Rowman & Littlefield.

—.2002b. "Security Theory: Six Paradigms Searching for Security." Pp. 113–40 in *Millennial Reflections on International Studies: Conflict Security, Foreign Policy and International Political Economy*, edited by Michael Breecher and Frank P. Harvey. Ann Arbor: University of Michigan Press.

—.(ed.). 2003. *A Force Profonde: The Power, Politics, and Promise of Human Rights*. Philadelphia: University of Pennsylvania Press.

Kolodziej, Edward A. and Robert Harkavy (eds.). 1982. *Security Policies of Developing Countries*. Lexington: Lexington Books.

Kolodziej, Edward A. and Roger E. Kanet (eds.). 1989. *The Limits of Soviet Power in the Developing World*. Baltimore: Johns Hopkins University Press.

—.1991. *The Cold War as Cooperation*. Baltimore: Johns Hopkins University Press.

—.1996. *Coping with Conflict after the Cold War*. Baltimore: Johns Hopkins University Press.

Korbonski, Andrzej and Francis Fukuyama (eds.). 1987. *The Soviet Union and the Third World: The Last Three Decades*. Ithaca: Cornell University Press.

Kornai, János. 1992. *The Socialist System: The Political Economy of Communism*. Princeton: Princeton University Press.

Kort, Michael. 1993. *The Soviet Colossus: The Rise and Fall of the USSR*. Armonk: M. E. Sharpe.

Koslowski, Rey and Friedrich V. Kratochwil. 1994. "Understanding Change in International Politics: The Soviet Empire's Demise and the International System." *International Security* 48: 215–48.

Krasner, Stephen D. 1999. *Sovereignty: Organized Hypocrisy*. Princeton: Princeton University Press.

—.2002. "Wars, Hotel Fires, and Plane Crashes." *Review of International Studies* 26: 131–36.

Kratochwil, Friedrich V. 2001. "Constructivism as an Approach to Interdisciplinary Study." Pp. 13–35 in *Constructing International Relations: The Next Generation*, edited by Karin M. Fierke and Knud Erik Jorgensen. London: M. E. Sharpe.

Krugman, Paul. 1990. *Rethinking International Trade*. Cambridge, MA: MIT Press.

Kubalkova, Vendulka. 2001a. "Soviet 'New Thinking' and the End of the Cold War: Five Explanations." Pp. 99–145 in *Foreign Policy in a Constructed World*, edited by Vendulka Kubalkova. London: M. E. Sharpe.

—.(ed.). 2001b. *Foreign Policy in a Constructed World*. London: M. E. Sharpe.

Kubalkova, Vendulka, Nicholas Onuf, and Paul Kowert (eds.). 1998. *International Relations in a Constructed World*. London: M. E. Sharpe.

Kugler, Jacek. 1990. "The War Phenomenon: A Working Distinction." *International Interactions* 16: 201–13.

Kugler, Jacek and Douglas Lemke. 2000. "The Power Transition Research Program." Pp. 129–63 in *Handbook of War Studies II*, edited by Manus I. Midlarsky. Ann Arbor: University of Michigan Press.

Kugler, Jacek and A. F. K. Organski. 1989. "The Power Transition: A Retrospective and Prospective Evaluation." Pp. 143–70. in *Handbook of War Studies*, edited by Manus I. Midlarsky. Boston: Unwin Hyman.

Kugler, Richard. 1993. *Commitment to Purpose: How Alliance Partnership Won the Cold War*. Santa Monica: Rand.

Kull, Steven. 1992. *Burying Lenin: The Revolution in Soviet Ideology and Foreign Policy*. Boulder: Westview.

Kuran, Timur. 1991. "Now Out of Never: The Element of Surprise in the East European Revolution of 1989." *World Politics* 44: 7–48.

—.1995. *Private Truths, Public Lies: The Social Consequences of Preference Falsification*. Cambridge: Harvard University Press.

Kux, Ernst. 1993. "The Change in Central and Eastern Europe and the End of the Soviet Union." *Aussen Politik* 44, 2: 135–43.

Laird, Robbin F. and Dale R. Herspring. 1984. *The Soviet Union and Strategic Arms*. Boulder: Westview.

Lakatos, Imre. 1970. "Falsification and the Methodology of Scientific Research Programmes." Pp. 91–195 in *Criticism and the Growth of Knowledge*, edited by Imre Lakatos and Alan Musgrave. Cambridge, UK: Cambridge University Press.

—.1978. *The Methodology of Scientific Research Programmes: Philosophical Papers*. Cambridge, UK: Cambridge University Press.

Lakatos, Imre and Alan Musgrave (eds.). 1970. *Criticism and the Growth of Knowledge*. Cambridge, UK: Cambridge University Press.

Lapid, Yosef. 1989. "The Third Debate: On the Prospects of International Theory in a Post-Positivist Era." *International Studies Quarterly* 33: 235–55.

Lapidus, Gail, Victor Zaslavsky, and Philip Goldman (eds.). 1992. *From Union to Commonwealth: Nationalism and Separatism in the Soviet Republics*. New York: Cambridge University Press.

Layne, Christopher. 1993. "The Unipolar Illusion: Why New Great Powers Will Arise." *International Security* 17: 5–51.

—.1994. "Kant or Cant?: The Myth of the Democratic Peace." *International Security* 19: 5–49.

Lebow, Richard Ned. 1981. *Between Peace and War*. Baltimore: Johns Hopkins University Press.

—.2003. *The Tragic Vision of Politics; Ethics, Interests, and Orders*. Cambridge, UK: Cambridge University Press.

Lebow, Richard Ned and Thomas Risse-Kappen (eds.). 1995. *International Relations Theory and the End of the Cold War*. New York: Columbia University Press.

Lebow, Richard Ned and Janice Gross Stein. 1994. *We All Lost the Cold War*. Princeton: Princeton University Press. Ottawa: Canadian Institute for International Peace Security.

Legro, Jeffrey W. and Andrew Moravcsik. 1999. "Is Anybody Still a Realist?" *International Security* 24: 5–55.

Lemke, Douglas. 1996. "Small States and War: An Expansion of Power Transition Theory." Pp. 77–92 in *War and Parity: Evaluations and Extensions of the War Ledger*, edited by Jacek Kugler and Douglas Lemke. Ann Arbor: University of Michigan Press.

—.2002. *Regions of War and Peace*. Cambridge, UK: Cambridge University Press.

Lemke, Douglas and Jacek Kugler. 1996. "The Evolution of the Power Transition Perspective." Pp. 3–34 in *Parity and War: Evaluations and Extensions of the War Ledger*, edited by Jacek Kugler and Douglas Lemke. Ann Arbor: University of Michigan Press.

Lemke, Douglas and William Reed. 1996. "Regime Types and Status Quo Evaluations." *International Interactions* 22: 143–64.

—.1998. "Power Is Not Satisfaction." *Journal of Conflict Resolution* 42: 511–16.

Lemke, Douglas and Suzanne Werner. 1996. "Power Parity, Commitment to Change, and War." *International Studies Quarterly* 40: 235–60.

Lenin, V. I. 1977. *Imperialism*. New York: International Publishers.

Levin, N. Gordon, Jr. 1968. *Woodrow Wilson and World Politics*. New York: Oxford University Press.

Levy, Jack S. 1992a. "An Introduction to Prospect Theory." *Political Psychology* 13: 171–86.

—.1992b. "Prospect Theory and International Relations: Theoretical Applications and Analytical Problems." *Political Psychology* 13: 283–310.

—.1994. "The Democratic Peace Hypothesis: From Description to Explanation." *Mershon International Studies Review* 38 (Supplement 2): 352–4.

—.2002. "War and Peace." Pp. 350–67 in *Handbook of International Relations*, edited by Walter Carlsnaes, Thomas Risse, and Beth E. Simmons. London: Sage.

Levy-Livermore, Amnon. 1998. *Handbook on the Globalization of the World Economy*. Cheltenham: E. Elgar.

Lewis, Kevin N. 1979. "The Prompt and Delayed Effects of Nuclear War." *Scientific American* 241: 35–45.

Lindblom, Charles E. 2001. *The Market System: What It Is, How It Works, and What to Make of It*. New Haven: Yale University Press.

Lippmann, Walter. 1947. *The Cold War*. New York: Harpers.

Lipson, Charles. 2003. *Reliable Partners: How Democracies Have Made a Separate Peace*. Princeton: Princeton University Press.

Lockwood, David. 2000. *The Destruction of the Soviet Union*. London: Macmillan.

Maine, Sir Henry. 1886. *Popular Government*. New York: Henry Holt.

—.1909. *Ancient Law*. London: J. Murray.

Mallet, Sir Louis. 1878. *The Political Writings of Richard Cobden*. London: Ridgway.

—.1891. *Free Exchange*. London: K. Paul, Trench, Trubner.

Mandelbaum, Michael. 1992. "Coup de Grace: The End of the Soviet Union." *Foreign Affairs* 71, 1: 164–83.

—.2002. *The Ideas That Conquered the World*. New York: Public Affairs.

Mansbridge, Jane. 1996. "Using Power/Fighting Power: The Polity." Pp. 46–66 in *Democracy and Difference*, edited by Seyla Benhabib. Princeton: Princeton University Press.

Martinelli, Alberto. 1994. "Entrepreneurship and Management." Pp. 476–503 in *The Handbook of Economic Sociology*, edited by Neil J. Smelser and Richard Swedberg. Princeton: Princeton University Press.

Marx, Karl. 1970. *A Contribution to the Critique of Political Economy*. Moscow: Progress.

Marx, Karl and Frederick Engels. 1948. *Manifesto of the Communist Party: 1848*. New York: International Publishers.

Mason, David S. 1992. *Revolution in East-Central Europe: The Rise and Fall of Communism and the Cold War*. Boulder: Westview.

Mayall, James. 1992. "Nationalism and International Security after the Cold War." *Survival* 34: 19–35.

McBride, Stephen and John Wiseman (eds.). 2001. *Globalization and Its Discontents*. New York: St Martin's Press.

McCallister, James. 2002. *No Exit: America and the German Problem*. Ithaca: Cornell University Press.

McCord, M. 1967. "Cobden and Bright in Politics 1846–47." Pp. 87–114 in *Ideas and Institutions of Victorian Britain*, edited by R. Robson. London: Barnes and Noble.

McDonagh, O. 1961–2. "The Anti-Imperialism of Free Trade." *Econmic History Review* 14: 489–501.

McKeown, T. J. 1989. "The Politics of Corn Law Repeal and Theories of Commercial Policy." *British Journal of Political Science* 19: 333–380.

McNeill, J. R. and William H. McNeill. 2003. *The Human Web: A Bird's Eye View of Human History*. New York: W. W. Norton.

McNeill, William H. 1963. *The Rise of the West: A History of the Human Community*. New York: Mentor.

—.1983. *The Pursuit of Power: Technology, Armed Force, and Society Since A.D. 1000*. Chicago: University of Chicago Press.

—.1986. *Polyethnicity and National Unity in World History*. Toronto: University of Toronto Press.

—.1992. *The Global Condition*. Princeton: Princeton University Press.

Mearsheimer, John J. 1990. "Back to the Future: Instability in Europe after the Cold War." *International Security* 15: 5–57.

—.1994. "The False Promise of International Institutions." *International Security* 19: 5–49.

Midlarsky, Manus I. (ed.). 1989. *The Handbook of War Studies*. Boston: Unwin Hyman.

—.(ed.). 2000. *Handbook of War Studies II*. Ann Arbor: University of Michigan Press.

Mill, John Stuart. 1848a. *Essays on Some Unsettled Questions of Political Economy*. London: London School of Economics and Political Science.

—.1848b. *Principles of Political Economy*. London: J. W. Parker.

Miller, John. 1993. *Mikhail Gorbachev and the End of Soviet Power*. New York: St Martin's Press.

Miller, K. E. 1961. "John Stuart Mill's Theory of International Relations." *Journal of the History of Ideas* 22: 493–514.

Miller, Steven E. (ed.). 1986. *Conventional Forces and American Defense Policy*. Princeton: Princeton University Press.

Milner, Helen. 1992. "International Theories of Cooperation among Nations." *World Politics* 44: 466–96.

—.1993. "The Assumption of Anarchy in International Relations Theory: A Critique." Pp. 143–69 in *Neorealism and Neoliberalism*, edited by David A. Baldwin. New York: Columbia University Press.

Milosz, Czeslaw. 1951. *The Captive Mind*. Trans. Jane Zielonko. New York: Knopf.

—. 1953. *The Captive Mind*. New York: Knopf.

Mises, Ludwig von. 1922. *Socialism: An Economic and Sociological Analysis*. New York: Macmillan.

—.1949. *Human Action: A Treatise on Economics*. New Haven: Yale University Press.

—.1956. *The Anti-Capitalistic Mentality*. New York: Van Nostrand Reinhold.

Mittleman, James H. 2000. *The Globalization Syndrome: Transformation and Resistance*. Princeton: Princeton University Press.

Mommsen, Wolfgang J. 1992. *The Political and Social Theory of Max Weber.* Chicago: University of Chicago Press.

Monoson, S. Sara and Michael Loriaux. 1998. "The Illusion of Power and the Disruption of Moral Norms: Thucydides' Critique of Periclean Policy." *American Political Science Review* 92: 285–97.

Moravscik, Andrew. 1997. "Taking Preferences Seriously: A Liberal Theory of International Politics." *International Organization* 51: 513–53.

Morgan, Patrick M. 1983. *Deterrence: A Conceptual Analysis.* Beverly Hills: Sage.

—.2000. "Liberalist and Realist Security Studies at 2000: Two Decades of Progress?" Pp. 39–71 in *Critical Reflections on Security and Change*, edited by Stuart Croft and Terry Terriff. London: Cass.

—.2003. *Deterrence Now.* Cambridge, UK: Cambridge University Press.

Morgan, Patrick M. and Keith L. Nelson (eds.). 2000. *Re-Viewing the Cold War: Domestic Factors and Foreign Policy in the East–West Confrontation.* Westport: Praeger.

Morgenthau, Hans. 1951a. *In Defense of the National Interest.* New York: Knopf.

—.1951b. *Scientific Man and Power Politics.* Chicago: University of Chicago Press.

—.1985. *Politics among Nations: The Struggle for Power and Peace.* New York: Alfred A. Knopf.

Morley, J. 1881. *The Life of Richard Cobden.* London.

Morrow, James D. 1996. "The Logic of Overtaking." Pp. 313–30 in *Parity and War: Evaluations and Extensions of the War Ledger*, edited by Jacek Kugler and Douglas Lemke. Ann Arbor: University of Michigan Press.

Mueller, John. 1988. "The Essential Irrelevance of Nuclear Weapons." *International Security* 13: 55–79.

—.1989. *Retreat from Doomsday.* New York: Basic Books.

—.1995. *Quiet Cataclysm.* New York: HarperCollins.

Nau, Henry. 1990. *The Myth of American Decline.* New York: Oxford University Press.

Neff, S. C. 1990. *Friends But Not Allies: Economic Liberalism and the Law of Nations.* New York.

Nogee, Joseph L. and Robert H. Donaldson. 1992. *Soviet Foreign Policy Since World War II.* New York: Macmillan.

Nolan, Janne E. 1989. *Guardians of the Arsenal.* New York: Basic Books.

North, Douglass C. 1986. "Is It Worth Making Sense of Marx?" *Inquiry* 29: 57–64.

—.1990. *Institutions, Institutional Change, and Economic Performance.* Cambridge, UK: Cambridge University Press.

North, Douglass C. and Robert P. Thomas. 1973. *The Rise of the Western World: A New Economic History.* Cambridge, UK: Cambridge University Press.

North, Douglass C. and Barry R. Weingast. 1989. "Constitutions and Commitment: The Evolution of Institutions Governing Public Choice in Seventeenth-Century England." *Journal of Economic History* 49, 4: 803–32.

Nye, Joseph S., Jr. 1988. "Neorealism and Neoliberalism." *World Politics* 15: 235–51.

—.1990. *Bound to Lead.* New York: Basic Books.

—.2002. *The Paradox of American Power: Why the World's Only Superpower Can't Go It Alone.* New York: Oxford University Press.

O'Brien, P. K. 1988. "The Costs and Benefits of British Imperialism." *Past and Present* 120: 163–200.

O'Brien, Patrick and Geofrey Allen Pigman. 1992. "Free Trade, British Hegemony and the International Economic Order in the Nineteenth Century." *Review of International Studies* 18: 89–113.

Odom, William E. 1992. "Who Really Won the Cold War?" P. 29 in *The Washington Post National Weekly Edition*.

—.1998. *The Collapse of the Soviet Military*. New Haven: Yale University Press.

Olson, Mancur. 1965. *The Logic of Collective Action*. Cambridge, MA: Harvard University Press.

—.1982. *The Rise and Decline of Nations: Economic Growth, Stagflation, and Social Rigidities*. New Haven: Yale University Press.

Olson, Mancur, and Hans H. Landsberg (eds.). 1975. *The No-Growth Society*. London: The Woburn Press.

Oneal, John R., Indra de Soysa, and Yong-Hee Park. 1998. "But Power and Wealth Are Satisfying." *Journal of Conflict Resolution* 42: 517–20.

Onuf, Nicholas G. 1989. *World of Our Making: Rules and Rule in Social Theory and International Relations*. Columbia: University of South Carolina Press.

—.1998. "Constructivism: A User's Manual." Pp. 58–78 in *International Relations in a Constructed World*, edited by Vendulka Lubalkova, Nicholas Onuf, and Paul Kowert. London: M. E. Sharpe.

Organski, A. F. K. 1958. *World Politics*. New York: Alfred Knopf.

Organski, A. F. K. and Jacek Kugler. 1980. *The War Ledger*. Chicago: University of Chicago Press.

Orwell, George. 1954. "Shooting an Elephant." Pp. 154–62 in *A Collection of Essays*. Garden City: Doubleday.

Osgood, Robert E. 1953. *Ideals and Self-Interest in America's Foreign Relations*. Chicago: University of Chicago Press.

—.1956. *Limited War*. Chicago: University of Chicago Press.

—.1962. *NATO: The Entangling Alliance*. Chicago: University of Chicago Press.

Papayoanou, Paul A. 1999. *Power Ties: Economic Interdependence, Balancing and War*. Ann Arbor: University of Michigan Press.

Patchen, Martin. 1990. "Conflict and Cooperation in American–Soviet Relations: What Have We Learned from Quantitative Research?" in *Annual Meetings of the International Studies Association*. Washington, DC.

Pearson, Harry W. (ed.). 1977. *The Livelihood of Man: Karl Polanyi*. New York: Academic Press.

Perle, Richard. 1991. "Military Power and the Passing Cold War." Pp. 33–8 in *After the Cold War: Questioning the Morality of Nuclear Deterrence*, edited by Kenneth L. Schwab and Charles W. Kegley. Boulder: Westview.

—.1992. *Hard Line*. New York: Random House.

Pettman, Ralph. 2000. *Commonsense Constructivism or the Remaking of World Affairs*. London: M. E. Sharpe.

Pierre, Andrew. 1972. *Nuclear Politics: The British Experience with an Independent Strategic Force, 1939–1970*. New York: Columbia University Press.

Pinker, Steven. 2002. *The Blank Slate*. New York: Viking.

Polanyi, Karl. 1944. *The Great Transformation*. Boston: Beacon Press.

—.1968. *Primitive, Archaic and Modern Economies*. Garden City, New York: Doubleday.

Polanyi, Karl, Conrad M. Arensberg, and Harry W. Pearson (eds.). 1957. *Trade and Market in the Early Empires*. Glencoe: Free Press.

Polanyi, Michael. 1959. *The Study of Man*. Chicago: University of Chicago Press.

Popper, Karl R. 1963. *Conjectures and Refutations: The Growth of Scientific Knowledge*. New York: Harper & Row.

Posen, Barry. 1993. "The Security Dilemma and Ethnic Conflict." *Survival* 35: 27–47.

Powell, Robert. 1991. "The Problem of Absolute and Relative Gains in International Relations Theory." *American Political Science Review* 85: 1303–20.

—.1993. "Absolute and Relative Gains in International Relations Theory." Pp. 209–33 in *Neorealism and Neoliberalism: The Contemporary Debate*, edited by David A. Baldwin. New York: Columbia University Press.

Pringle, Peter and William Arkin. 1983. *S.I.O.P: The Secret U.S. Plan for Nuclear War*. New York: W. W. Norton.

Rahe, Paul A. 1984. "The Primacy of Politics in Classical Greece." *American Historical Review* 89: 265–93.

—.1992. *Republics: Ancient and Modern*. Chapel Hill: University of North Carolina.

Read, Donald. 1967. *Cobden and Bright: A Victorian Political Partnership*. New York: St Martin's Press.

Rees, Martin. 2003. *Our Final Hour*. New York: Basic Books.

Remnick, David. 1993. *Lenin's Tomb: The Last Days of the Soviet Union*. New York: Random House.

Reus-Smit, Christian. 1997. "The Constitutional Structure of International Society and the Nature of Fundamental Institutions." *International Organization* 51: 555–89.

Richardson, Lewis F. 1939. "Generalized Foreign Politics." *British Journal of Psychology*.

—.1960a. *Arms and Insecurity*. Pacific Grove: Boxwood Publishers.

—.1960b. *Statistics of Deadly Quarrels*. Pittsburgh: Quadrangle Press.

Rischard, J. F. 2002. *High Noon: Twenty Global Problems, Twenty Years to Solve Them*. New York: Basic Books.

Risse-Kappen, Thomas. 1971. "Did 'Peace Through Strength' End the Cold War?" *International Security* 16: 162–88.

—.1995. "Ideas Do Not Float Freely: Transnational Coalitions, Domestic Structures, and the End of the Cold War." Pp. 187–222 in *International Relations Theory and the End of the Cold War*, edited by Richard Ned Lebow and Thomas Risse-Kappen. New York: Columbia University Press.

Ritter, Gerhard. 1969. *The Sword and the Scepter: The Problem of Militarism in Germany*. Coral Gables: University of Miami Press.

—.1979. *The Schlieffen Plan*. Westport: Greenwood.

Robbins, Richard H. 2002. *Global Problems and the Culture of Capitalism*. Boston: Allyn and Bacon.

Robinson, R. and J. Gallagher. 1953–4. "The Imperialism of Free Trade." *Economic History Review* 4: 1–15.

Rodrik, Dani. 1997. *Has Globalization Gone Too Far?* Washington, DC: Institute for International Economics.

ogowski, Ronald R. 1978. "Rationalist Theories of Politics: A Midterm Report." *World Politics* 30: 296–323.

—.1989. *Commerce and Coalitions*. Princeton: Princeton University Press.

osecrance, Richard. 1986. *The Rise of the Trading State: Commerce and Conquest in the Modern World*. New York: Basic Books.

osenberg, David Alan. 1983. "The Origins of Overkill." *International Security* 7: 3–71.

osser, M. V. 1993. "Internal Contradictions Versus External Pressures in the Transformation of the Former Soviet Economy." *International Journal of Social Economics* 20, 9: 43–53.

ostow, Walt Whitman. 1971. *Politics and the Stages of Growth*. Cambridge, UK: Cambridge University Press.

ousseau, Jean-Jacques. 1950. *The Social Contract*. New York: E. P. Dutton.

owen, Henry S. and Charles Wolf, Jr. (eds.). 1987. *The Future of the Soviet Empire*. New York: St Martin's Press.

ubenstein, Alvin Z. 1988. *Moscow's Third World Strategy*. Princeton: Princeton University Press.

uggie, John Gerard. 1982. "International Regimes, Transactions, and Change: Embedded Liberalism in the Postwar Economic Order." *International Organization* 36: 379–415.

—.1998. "What Makes the World Hang Together? Neo-Utilitarianism and the Social Constructivist Challenge." *International Organization* 52: 855–85.

ussett, Bruce. 1993. *Grasping the Democratic Peace: Principles for a Post-Cold War World*. Princeton: Princeton University Press.

ussett, Bruce and John R. Oneal. 2001. *Triangulating Peace*. New York: W. W. Norton.

ussett, Bruce and Harvey Starr. 2000. "From Democratic Peace to Kantian Peace: Democracy and Conflict in International Relations." Pp. 93–128 in *Handbook of War Studies II*, edited by Manus I. Midlarsky. Ann Arbor: University of Michigan Press.

utland, Peter. 1985. *The Myth of the Plan*. London: Hutchinson.

assen, Saskia. 1998. *Globalization and Its Discontents*. New York: New Press.

aul, John Ralston. 2004. "The Collapse of Globalism and the Rebirth of Nationalism." *Harper's* 308: 33–44.

chelling, Thomas. 1960. *The Strategy of Conflict*. New York: Oxford University Press.

—.1966. *Arms and Influence*. New Haven: Yale University Press.

chelling, Thomas and Morton Halperin. 1958. *Strategy and Arms Control*. Washington, DC: Pergamon-Brassey's.

—.1985. *Strategy and Arms Control*. Washington, DC: Pergamon-Brassey's.

chilling, Warner R., Paul Y. Hammond, and Glenn H. Snyder (eds.). 1966. *Strategy, Politics, and Defense Budgets*. New York: Columbia University Press.

chlesinger, Arthur M., Jr. 1992a. "Some Lessons from the Cold War." *Diplomatic History* 16: 47–53.

—.1992b. "Who Really Won the Cold War." P. A10 in *The Wall Street Journal*, September 14.

chroeder, Paul W. 1989. "The Nineteenth Century System: Balance of Power or Political Equilibrium?" *Review of International Studies* 15: 135–53.

—.1992. "Did the Vienna System Rest upon a Balance of Power?" *American Historical Review* 97: 683–706.

—.1994a. "Historical Reality vs. Neo-Realist Theory." *International Security* 19: 108–48.

—.1994b. *The Transformation of European Politics: 1763–1848*. Oxford: Oxford University Press.

—.1997. "History and International Relations Theory." *International Security* 22: 64–74.

—.2003. "Why Realism Does Not Work Well for International History (Whether or Not It Represents a Degenerate IR Research Strategy)." Pp. 114–27 in *Realism and the Balance of Power: A New Debate*, edited by John A. Vasquez and Colin Elman. Upper Saddle River: Prentice Hall.

—.2004. *Systems, Stability, and Statecraft: Essays on the International History of Modern Europe*, edited by David Wetzel, Robert Jervis, and Jack S. Levy. New York; Palgrave.

Schumpeter, Joseph A. 1950. *Capitalism, Socialism and Democracy*. New York: Harper.

—.1954. *History of Economic Analysis*. New York: Oxford University Press.

—.1955. *Imperialism*. New York: Meridian.

Schwartz, David N. 1983. *NATO's Nuclear Dilemmas*. Washington, DC: Brookings Institution.

Schweller, Randall L. 1994. "Bandwagoning for Profit: Bringing the Revisionist States Back In." *International Security* 19: 90–121.

—.1998. *Deadly Imbalances: Tripolarity and Hitler's Strategy of World Conquest*. New York: Columbia University Press.

Searle, John R. 1995. *The Construction of Social Reality*. New York: Free Press.

Semmel, Bernard. 1970. *The Rise of Free Trade Imperialism: Classical Political Economy, The Empire of Free Trade and Imperialism, 1750–1850*. Cambridge, UK: Cambridge University Press.

Silberner, E. 1946. *The Problem of War in Nineteenth-Century Economic Thought*. Princeton: Princeton University Press.

Simon, Herbert. 1975. *Administrative Behavior*. New York: Free Press.

—.1986. "Rationality in Psychology and Economics." *Journal of Business (Supplement)* 59: S209–S224.

Singer, J. David. 1961. "The Level-of-Analysis Problem in International Relations." Pp. 77–92 in *The International System*, edited by Klaus Knorr and Sidney Verba. Princeton: Princeton University Press.

—.1969. "The Incomplete Theorist's Insight without Evidence." Pp. 62–8 in *Contending Approaches to International Politics*, edited by Klaus Knorr and James N. Rosenau. Princeton: Princeton University Press.

Singer, J. David and Paul F. Diehl (eds.). 1990. *Measuring the Correlates of War*. Ann Arbor: University of Michigan Press.

Singer, J. David, S. Bremer, and J. Stuckey. 1972. *Capability, Distribution, Uncertainty, and Major Power War, 1820–1965*. Beverly Hills: Sage.

Singer, Peter. 2000. *Marx: A Very Short Introduction*. Oxford: Oxford University Press.

—.2002. *One World: The Ethics of Globalization*. New Haven: Yale University Press.

nith, Adam. 1937. *An Inquiry into the Nature and Causes of the Wealth of Nations.* New York: Modern Library.

.1976. *The Wealth of Nations.* Oxford: Clarendon Press.

nith, Anthony. 1981. *Ethnic Revival.* New York: Cambridge University Press.

.1986. *The Ethnic Origins of Nations.* New York: Blackwell.

nith, Steve. 2000. "Wendt's World." *Review of International Studies* 26: 151–63.

.2001. "Foreign Policy Is What States Make of It: Social Construction and International Relations Theory." Pp. 38–55 in *Foreign Policy in a Constructed World,* edited by Vendulka Kubalkova. London: M. E. Sharpe.

idal, Duncan. 1993. "Relative Gains and the Pattern of International Cooperation." Pp. 170–208 in *Neorealism and Neoliberalism,* edited by David A. Baldwin. New York: Columbia University Press.

yder, Jack. 1991. *Myths of Empire: Domestic Politics and International Ambition.* Ithaca: Cornell University Press.

ros, George. 2000. *Open Society: Reforming Global Capitalism.* New York: Public Affairs.

ruyt, Hendrik. 1994. *The Sovereign States and Its Competitors.* Princeton: Princeton University Press.

ein, Arthur. 1984. "The Hegemon's Dilemma: Britain, the United States, and the International Economic Order." *International Organization* 38: 355–86.

ein, Janice Gross. 2002. "Psychological Explanations of International Conflict." Pp. 292–308 in *Handbook of International Relations,* edited by Walter Carlsnaes, Thomas Risse, and Beth A. Simmons. London: Sage.

erling-Folker, Jennifer. 2000. "Competing Paradigms or Birds of a Feather? Constructivism and Neoliberal Institutionalism Compared." *International Studies Quarterly* 44: 97–119.

iglitz, Joseph E. 2002. *Globalization and Its Discontents.* New York: W. W. Norton.

range, Susan. 1986. *Casino Capitalism.* New York: Basil Blackwell.

.1988. *States and Markets.* London: Pinter.

romseth, Jane E. 1988. *The Origins of Flexible Response.* London: Macmillan.

vedberg, Richard. 1998. *Max Weber and the Idea of Economic Sociology.* Princeton: Princeton University Press.

mposium. 2001. "A Social Theory for International Relations: An Appraisal of Alexander Wendt's Theoretical and Disciplinary Synthesis." *Journal of International Relations and Development (Ljubljana)* 4: 316–423.

mposium, Security Studies. 1999. "On the Origins of National Interests." *Security Studies* 8.

lbott, Strobe. 1979. *Endgame: The Inside Story of SALT II.* New York: Harper.

.1984. *Deadly Gambits.* New York: Vintage.

mmen, Ronald L. *et al.* 2000. *Power Transitions: Strategies for the 21st Century.* New York: Chatham House.

ylor, A. J. P. 1954. *The Struggle for Mastery of Europe: 1848–1918.* Oxford: Oxford University Press.

.1967. *Bismarck: The Man and the Statesman.* New York: Vintage.

ucydides. 1951. *The Peloponnesian War.* New York: New American Library.

.1998. *The Peloponnesian War.* Trans. Walter Blanco. New York: W. W. Norton.

urow, Lester. 1996. *The Future of Capitalism.* New York: Morrow.

Tilly, Charles (ed.). 1975a. *The Formation of National States in Western Europe.* Princeton: Princeton University Press.

—.1975b. "Reflections on the History of European State-Making." Pp. 3–83 in *The Formation of National States in Western Europe*, edited by Charles Tilly. Princeton: Princeton University Press.

—.1985. "War Making and State Making as Organized Crime." Pp. 169–91 in *Bringing the State Back In*, edited by Dietrich Rueschemeyer, Peter B. Evans, and Theda Skocpol. New York: Cambridge University Press.

—.1990. *Coercion, Capital, and European States, AD 990–1990.* Cambridge, MA: Basil Blackwell.

—.1993. *European Revolutions, 1492–1992.* Cambridge, MA: Blackwell.

—.1995. "To Explain Political Processes." *American Journal of Sociology* 100: 1,594–610.

Tönnies, Ferdinand. 1957. *Community and Society.* Trans. Charles P. Loomis. New York: Harper.

Tuchman, Barbara W. 1962. *The Guns of August.* New York: Ballantine.

Tucker, Josiah. 1764. *The Case for Going to War for the Sake of Trade.*

Tucker, Samuel A. (ed.). 1966. *A Modern Design for Defense Decision: A McNamara-Hitch-Enthoven Anthology.* Washington, DC: Industrial College of the Armed Forces.

US Arms Control and Disarmament Agency. 1973–. "World Military Expenditures and Arms Transfers." Washington, DC.

United States. September 2002. "The National Security Strategy of the United States of America." Washington, DC: White House.

Valkenier, Elizabeth Kridl. 1983. *The Soviet Union and the Third World: An Economic Bind.* New York: Praeger.

Van Evera, Stephen. 1984. "The Cult of the Offensive and the Origins of the First World War." *International Security* 9: 58–107.

—.1994. "Hypotheses on Nationalism and War." *International Security* 18: 5–39.

—.1999. *Causes of War: Power and the Roots of Conflict.* Ithaca: Cornell University Press.

Vasquez, John A. 1993. *The War Puzzle.* Cambridge, UK: Cambridge University Press.

—.1996. "When Are Power Transitions Dangerous? An Appraisal and Reformulation of Power Transition Theory." Pp. 35–73 in *Parity and War: Evaluations and Extensions of the War Ledger*, edited by Jacek Kugler and Douglas Lemke. Ann Arbor: University of Michigan Press.

—.1997. "The Realist Paradigm and Degenerative versus Progressive Research Programs: An Appraisal of Neotraditional Research on Waltz' Balancing Proposition." *American Political Science Review* 91: 899–912.

Vasquez, John A. and Colin Elman (eds.). 2003. *Realism and the Balance of Power: A New Debate.* Upper Saddle River: Prentice Hall.

Viner, Jacob. 1991. *Essays on the Intellectual History of Economics.* Princeton: Princeton University Press.

Volgy, Thomas and Lawrence E. Imwalle. 1997. "Hegemonic and Bipolar Perspectives in the New World Order." *American Journal of Political Science* 39: 819–34.

Walker, R. B. J. 1989. "History and Structure in the Theory of International Relations." *Millennium* 18: 163–83.

—.1993. *Inside/Outside: International Relations As Political Theory*. Cambridge, UK: Cambridge University Press.

—.1995. "International Politics as International Relations." Pp. 306–27 in *International Relations Theory Today*, edited by Ken Booth and Steve Smith. University Park: Pennsylvania State University Press.

Waller, David V. 1992. "Ethnic Mobilization and Geopolitics in the Soviet Union: Towards a Theoretical Understanding." *Journal of Political and Military Sociology* 20, 1: 37–62.

Wallersteen, Peter. 1981. "Incompatibility, Confrontation, and War: Four Models and Three Historical Systems, 1816–1976." *Journal of Peace Research* 18: 57–90.

Wallerstein, Immanuel (ed.). 1974. *The Modern World-System: Capitalist Agriculture and the Origins of the European World-Economy in the Sixteenth Century*. New York: Academic Press.

—.1995. *World Inequality: Origins and Perspectives on the World System*. Montreal: Black Rose Books.

Walt, Stephen M. 1987. *The Origins of Alliances*. Ithaca: Cornell University Press.

—.1991. "The Renaissance of Security Studies." *International Studies Quarterly* 35: 211–39.

—.1998. "International Relations: One World, Many Theories." *Foreign Policy* 110: 29–32.

Waltz, Kenneth N. 1959. *Man, the State and War*. New York: Columbia University Press.

—.1964. "The Stability of the Bipolar World." *Daedalus* 93: 881–909.

—.1979. *Theory of International Politics*. Reading: Addison-Wesley.

—.1981. *The Spread of Nuclear Weapons: More May Be Better*. London: International Institute for Strategic Studies.

—.1986. "Reflections on Theory of International Politics: A Response to My Critics." in *Neorealism and Its Critics*, edited by Robert O. Keohane. New York: Columbia University Press.

—.1990. "Nuclear Myths and Political Realities." *American Political Science Review* 84: 731–46.

—.1993. "The Emerging Structure of International Politics." *International Security* 18: 44–79.

—.1997. "Evaluating Theories." *American Political Science Review* 91: 913–17.

—.2000. "NATO Expansion: A Realist's View." *Contemporary Security Policy* 21: 23–38.

Walzer, Michael M. 1974. *Just and Unjust War*. New York: Basic Books.

Waters, Malcolm. 1995. *Globalization*. London: Routledge.

Watson, Adam. 1984. "European International Society and Its Expansion." Pp. 13–32 in *The Expansion of International Society*, edited by Adam Watson and Hedley Bull. Oxford: Oxford University Press.

—.1992. *The Evolution of International Society: A Comparative Historical Analysis*. London: Routledge.

Wayman, Frank W. and Paul F. Diehl (eds.). 1994. *Reconstructing Realpolitik*. Ann Arbor: University of Michigan Press.

Weber, Max. 1958. *The Protestant Ethic and the Spirit of Capitalism*. New York: Charles Scribner's Sons.

—.1968. *Economy and Society*. Berkeley: University of California Press.

Wendt, Alexander E. 1987. "The Agent–Structure Problem in International Relations Theory." *International Organization* 41: 335–70.

—.1992. "Anarchy Is What States Make Out of It: The Social Construction of Power Politics." *International Organization* 46: 391–425.

—.1994. "Collective Identity Formation and the International State." *American Political Science Review* 88: 384–396.

—.1995. "Constructing International Politics." *International Security* 95: 71–81.

—.1999. *Social Theory of International Politics.* Cambridge, UK: Cambridge University Press.

—.2000. "On the Via Media: A Response to the Critics." *Review of International Studies* 26: 165–80.

—.2003. "Why a World State Is Inevitable." *European Journal of International Relations* 9: 291–542.

Werner, Suzanne and Jacek Kugler. 1996. "Power Transitions and Military Buildups." in *Parity and War: Evaluations and Extensions of the War Ledger,* edited by Jacek Kugler and Douglas Lemke. Ann Arbor: University of Michigan Press.

Werner, Suzanne and Douglas Lemke. 1997. "Opposites Do Not Attract: The Impact of Domestic Institutions, Power, and Prior Commitments on Alignment Choices." *International Studies Quarterly* 41: 529–46.

Wight, Martin. 1966a. "Western Values in International Relations." Pp. 89–131 in *Diplomatic Investigations,* edited by Herbert Butterfield and Martin Wight. London: Allen and Unwin.

—.1966b. "Why There Is No International Theory." Pp. 17–34 in *Diplomatic Investigations,* edited by Herbert Butterfield and Martin Wight. Cambridge, MA: Harvard University Press.

—.1977. *Systems of States.* Leicester: Leicester University Press.

—.(ed.). 1978. *Power Politics.* Leicester: Leicester University Press.

Williams, William Appleman. 1972. *The Tragedy of American Foreign Policy.* New York: Dell Books.

—.1973. *The Contours of American History.* New York: New Viewpoints.

—.1978. *America Confronts a Revolutionary World.* New York: Morrow.

—.1980. *Empire as a Way of Life.* New York: Oxford University Press.

Williamson, Oliver E. 1975. *Markets and Hierarchies.* New York: The Free Press.

Winiecki, Jan. 1988. *The Distorted World of Soviet-Type Economies.* Pittsburgh: University of Pittsburgh Press.

Wohlforth, William C. 1994. "Realism and the End of the Cold War." *International Security* 19: 91–129.

—.1993. *The Elusive Balance.* Ithaca: Cornell University Press.

—.1998. "Reality Check: Revision Theories of International Politics in Response to the End of the Cold War." *World Politics* 50: 650–80.

Wohlstetter, Albert. 1959. "The Delicate Balance of Terror." *Foreign Affairs* 37: 211–34.

Wolfers, Arnold. 1952. "'National Security' as an Ambiguous Symbol." *Political Science Quarterly* 67: 481–502.

Wright, Quincy. 1942. *A Study of War.* Chicago: University of Chicago Press.

—.1956. *The Study of International Relations.* New York: Appleton-Century Crofts.

.1965. *A Study of War*. Chicago: University of Chicago Press.

right, Robert. 2000. *Nonzero: The Logic of Human Destiny*. New York: Vintage.

rong, Dennis H. 1994. *The Problem of Order: What Unites and Divides Society*. Cambridge, MA: Harvard University Press.

st, David S. 1998. *NATO Transformed*. Washington, DC: US Institute of Peace Press.

hfuss, Maja. 2001. "Constructivisms in International Relations: Wendt, Onuf, and Kratochwil." Pp. 54–75 in *Constructing International Relations: The Next Generation*, edited by Karim M. Fierke and Knud Erik Jorgensen. London: M. E. Sharpe.

.2002. *Constructivism in International Relations: The Politics of Reality*. New York: Cambridge University Press.

nnes, Dina. 1976. "The Problem of Cumulation." Pp. 161–6 in *In Search of Global Patterns*, edited by James N. Rosenau. New York: Free Press.

Index